ADVENTURES FOR GROWING FAMILIES

ADVENTURES FOR GROWING FAMILIES

WES & SHERYL HAYSTEAD

VICTOR BOOKS

A DIVISION OF SCRIPTURE PRESS PUBLICATIONS INC.
USA CANADA ENGLAND

Copyediting: Mary Sytsma and Barbara Williams
Cover Design: Joe DeLeon
Cover Illustration: Steve Bjorkman
Interior Illustrations: Al Ochsner

Library of Congress Cataloging-in-Publication Data

Haystead, Wesley.
    Adventures for growing families / by Wes and Sheryl Haystead.
        p.   cm.
    ISBN 1-56476-120-7
    1. Family—Prayer-books and devotions—English. 2. Christian life—1960- 3. Devotional calendars. I. Haystead, Sheryl.
    II. Title
    BV255.H39   1993
    249—dc20   93-4287
                                                                                                      CIP

CONTENTS

INTRODUCTION

Everybody loves a story, and reading stories together is one of the all-time favorite family experiences. *Adventures for Growing Families* provides a full year's worth of read-aloud-stories the whole family will enjoy. Plus, each story is accompanied by thought-provoking questions guaranteed to stimulate interesting conversations in which everyone in the family can participate. And that's not all. Coordinated with the stories and questions *Adventures for Growing Families* also contains a wide variety of creative family activities which help children and parents enjoy exploring the major themes of the Christian faith.

Every week that you and your children read stories in *Adventures for Growing Families,* you will discover:

* A brief introduction to a major theme of the Christian faith, such as:
Joy
The One True God
Knowing God
We Can Be Saved
The Bible Is True
Coping with Hard Times
God Is Father, Son, Holy Spirit
We Have Sinned

* Five brief read-aloud stories, plus questions and Bible verses which stimulate family discussion about the current topic.

* Enjoyable and worthwhile family activities which help build positive values while improving family communication

The Stories in this book depict contemporary families in typical, sometimes humorous, and sometimes exciting situations. The stories can be read aloud to children (ages 4–12) at breakfast, at the dinner table, at bedtime, or any other brief time of quiet family interaction.

The stories are organized by months of the year so that a family can begin using the book at any time. Each day's story is short enough (under five minutes reading time) that if a day is missed, it is easy to include it the next day. Each week's stories are self-contained, so that missing a week will not cause any problem in starting again.

The Questions which accompany each story are placed in two groups: those for younger children and those for older children. Since children differ widely in their abilities and interest in answering questions, use the questions you think will be of most interest to your child.

The Bible Verse which also accompanies each story has been selected as a clear statement of the truth which that story illustrates. Usually, at least one of the questions helps the child relate the verse to the story. For example, you may read a verse to your child and then ask, "How did someone in the story do what this verse says we should do?" Or, "What does this verse help us understand about the story we just read?" Since the questions in this book are designed to encourage you and your child to think about an important topic, the Bible verses are of vital importance to ensure that all family members clearly understand the Bible's message about the topic being considered.

The Family Times are ideas you can use with your child once or twice during each week. These ideas require little preparation and minimal supplies or materials. The following Basic Supplies will enable you to easily try the great majority of the ideas suggested.

Family Times Basic Supplies
Large Bible
Felt-tip pens/Crayons/Pencils
Tape recorder w/blank tape
Scissors
Glue
Index cards

So, gather around the kitchen table or snuggle up on the living room couch and get ready for a year of great adventure and marvelous discovery!

J A N U A R Y

The Joy of the Lord

"A cheerful look brings joy to the heart,
and good news gives health to the bones."
Proverbs 15:30

"A cheerful heart is good medicine.
But a crushed spirit dries up the bones."
Proverbs 17:22

Doctors know that people who laugh often are healthier than people who do not. A sick person who keeps a happy attitude tends to get better faster than a grouch. Many doctors advise their patients to have a big laugh every day.

But sometimes people just do not feel like laughing. Everyone has times when he or she feels sad or angry or afraid or just plain upset. It is hard to be happy and full of joy when things go wrong. How can a person have a cheerful heart when unhappy feelings are so strong?

The Bible does not pretend that happiness is automatic. The Bible tells about people who felt downright miserable at times. The Bible never tries to get by with a silly suggestion to "Stop feeling the way you feel." It never tells us, "Don't worry; be happy!" What the Bible does do is tell us some very good things that help us have a cheerful heart.

As you start this new year reading this week's stories, you and your family will enjoy thinking about the joy God provides for us.

Key Verse
"Rejoice in the Lord always. I will say it again: Rejoice!"
Philippians 4:4

Key Thought
God wants us to enjoy the people and the world He has made.

WEEK 1

DAY 1

Everyone agreed it was just plain silly. It all started when Angela and her brother Hector were practicing the piano together. They were working on a song they had been asked to play in Sunday School the next week. Angela was playing the high notes and working the pedals. Hector was playing the low notes and counting out loud, "One, two, three, four," to help them stay together.

Then it happened. Right in the middle of a song that started out sounding very good, Angela skipped a line of her music — or Hector repeated a line of his. However it happened, it happened.

Suddenly the very nice piano music started to sound awful. The notes Angela was playing sounded like they were shouting at the notes Hector was playing. And the notes Hector was playing sounded like they were fighting back. It really was awful.

But what was that other sound? It sounded like giggles. It was giggles. Angela and Hector started laughing at the same time because the notes they were playing sounded so funny to them.

But those fighting piano notes did not sound that funny to Angela and Hector's mom.

"Hector!" Mom shouted from the kitchen.

"See, I always get blamed, two, three, four," Hector muttered between giggles, as he tried to keep counting.

Angela thought that was even funnier, and she began to laugh and play even harder.

"Hector!" Mom shouted again, this time from right behind the two laughing musicians. And this time she added, "Angela! What are you two doing?" But this time she sounded like she was laughing too.

Angela stopped playing and tried to stop laughing. "We got all mixed up," she said.

Hector stopped playing too. "It sounded so awful it was funny!" he said.

"It sure did sound awful," Mom agreed. "You'd better not sound like that when you play in Sunday School." Suddenly all three of them were laughing so hard they had tears running down their cheeks. The idea of playing that awful noise in Sunday School seemed ridiculous.

Hector wiped his eyes. "I'm sure it would be OK, Mom. God likes to laugh too doesn't He?"

● *"You will find your joy in the Lord." Isaiah 58:14*

● **For Younger Children**
What are some things that make you laugh?

Is it more fun for you to laugh by yourself or with a friend?

How would you answer Hector's question: "God likes to laugh too doesn't He?"

● **For Older Children**
Hector and Angela were laughing so hard together that their mom started

laughing too. Has anything like that ever happened to you when someone else's laughter made you laugh, also?

Do you think Isaiah 58:14 is talking about laughing at silliness or being happy? Why?

What are some ways God brings joy into our lives?

● ●

WEEK 1

DAY 2

"Let's go to the park!"

"Let's go to the library!"

"Why don't we rent a video?"

"I think we should work together and clean the apartment."

"Why don't we vote on it?"

There were times when the De La Rosa family all wanted to do the same thing together on Saturday afternoon. A few times. Maybe once or twice. Most of the time everybody wanted to do something different.

"Why vote?" Angela asked. "Everyone will vote for something different, and we'll be right back where we started."

"In that case," Mom said, "let's clean the apartment."

"Oh," Hector groaned. "I'll change my vote. I'll vote with Robbie. Let's go to the library. That's two votes for the library."

But Robbie, the youngest of the three children, also decided to change his vote. "I want to go ride the subway."

During the next ten minutes at least a dozen new ideas were suggested. Each person who made a suggestion hoped that the other four family members would instantly agree, "Great idea! Let's do it!"

Instead, each new idea was greeted with comments like, "We did that last week," or "You've got to be kidding!"

Just when it looked like the De La Rosa family was going to spend all of Saturday afternoon trying to decide what to do on Saturday afternoon, Dad asked, "Where's my hat?"

Everyone stopped talking and looked at him, thinking Dad was tired of all the talking and was going to go somewhere by himself.

"Your hat?" Hector asked with a worried look on his face.

"That's what I said. Let's write each idea on a different slip of paper, then put them all in my hat. We'll pull one slip out and whatever it says, that's what we'll do."

And that's what they did.

They ended up going to the park. They all had fun running in the grass.

The children had fun climbing in the playground. Then, on the way home, they stopped for ice cream cones. The whole family had a wonderful time.

But the most fun had really been when they were planning together what they were going to do together for the rest of Saturday afternoon.

● *"The joy of the Lord is your strength." Nehemiah 8:10*

● **For Younger Children**

If you were to choose a place for our family to go together, where would it be?

What are some things you like to do with our family?

Let's thank God for some of the good times our family enjoys together.

● **For Older Children**

Why was Hector worried when Dad asked for his hat?

If you were the dad in this story, what would you have suggested the family do?

How does our family decide when each family member wants to do a different thing?

Why do you think it's good for families to do fun things together?

WEEK 1

DAY 3

● ●

"Dyslexia? Hector's got dyslexia?" Robbie was puzzled about the news his mother had just given him about his older brother.

"That's right, Robbie," Mom said. "Dyslexia."

"What's dyslexia?" Robbie asked.

Hector decided if they were going to talk about him, he might as well talk too. "The doctor said dyslexia is a problem in how the brain and the eyes work together for reading."

"Brain?" Robbie felt his own head. "You've got a problem in your brain? Are you mental?"

"Robbie!" Mom asked sternly. "What kind of a question is that?"

"Well, I just wanted to know," Robbie said.

"It's OK to ask," Hector said. "Before they found out what I had, I thought I was stupid. Reading was real hard for me." The boys did not notice that Mom was snuffling and wiping her eyes with a tissue.

"We've been praying that we'd find out what Hector's problem was," she said between sniffs.

"It's kind of cool, Robbie," Hector said. "They found out that when I'm trying to read, some of the letters look backward to me."

"Hey, they all look backward to me. I can't read anything. Except my name," Robbie said. "Do I have dyslexia?"

"You're only four years old," Hector said. "You're not supposed to read yet."

"I'm four-and-a-half and . . . and I want to know where you're going to sleep tonight!" Robbie asked.

"I'm going to sleep in my bed," Hector answered quickly. "Where I always sleep."

"Not in my room," Robbie demanded. "I don't want to catch dyslexia!"

"Robbie," Mom interrupted. "You can't catch dyslexia. It's not like a cold or the flu!"

"Then how did Hector get it?" Robbie wanted to know.

"I probably got it from Dad," Hector said.

"Really?" Robbie asked.

"Well, probably not," Hector said. "But if I can make Dad feel guilty about it, maybe he'll give me a bigger allowance."

Mom laughed. "I'm glad nothing's wrong with your sense of humor, Hector. But I'm also really glad the doctor told us about the exercises you can do to help you become a good reader."

● *"Is any one of you in trouble? He should pray. Is anyone happy? Let him sing songs of praise." James 5:13*

● **For Younger Children**

What do you remember about going to a doctor when something was wrong with you?

Why did Hector's mom say she was glad?

What is a good way to show that you are glad?

● **For Older Children**

What do you know about dyslexia?

What did Hector's mom say she did when she was worried about Hector's reading problem?

Why was it a good thing that she prayed for Hector?

DAY
4

"Tacos!" Hector shouted.

"My favorite!" Robbie yelled.

"Let's eat!" Hector shouted again.

"In a minute!" Dad laughed. "First, we're going to pray!"

"Oh, beans!" Hector muttered.

"You want to pray for the beans?" Angela whispered to her brother.

"No!" Hector whispered back. "I just want to eat without wasting time praying." Hector's whispers were getting a little louder. "God knows what we're eating. Why tell Him about it?"

Suddenly, Hector realized the whole family was staring at him. Quickly he bowed his head.

"Would you like to give thanks tonight, Hector?" Dad asked.

"OK," Hector said. "Thanks God for the food amen pass the tortillas."

"Hector," Dad said, as he picked up the platter with the golden brown tortillas. "Why do I feel that prayer was a little rushed?"

"I said 'Thanks,' " Hector answered.

"But did you mean 'Thanks'?" Dad asked.

It was a little hard for Hector to concentrate on getting everything he wanted inside his tortilla while Dad was asking him hard questions. "Well," Hector said, as some lettuce and cheese spilled onto his plate. "Why pray every time we eat? It gets boring. Especially when I'm hungry." Hector took several big bites out of his huge taco.

"How's the taco, Hector?" Dad asked between bites of his own.

"M-m-ff! Goo-o-d!" Hector said, forgetting the family rule against talking with a mouth full of food.

"I agree," Dad said after swallowing his next bite. "But let's not tell anybody."

"How come?" Hector asked. Dad's comment surprised him.

"Well," Dad put his taco down on his plate. "When something good happens, do you think it's more fun to keep it quiet or to to talk about it with someone you like?"

One more big bite would finish Hector's taco, but he held it in his hand while he thought about Dad's question. "I get it," he said. "Praying to God is like telling a friend about something good."

"You do get it!" Dad said. "Congratulations! Telling God thanks for good things makes those good things seem even better. Even when we're hungry."

● *"May the righteous be glad and rejoice before God; may they be happy and joyful." Psalm 68:3*

● **For Younger Children**

What is your favorite food at dinner?

Who are some of your good friends?

What good thing happened to you today?

Let's tell God thanks for these good things.

● **For Older Children**

What did Hector learn about talking to God?

When are some times you like to talk to God?

Do you think God only wants to hear about the good things that happen to us? Why or why not?

● ●

WEEK 1

DAY
5

"Mom, why did you have two boys after you had me?"

Angela was not happy with her little brothers.

"Mom, how come Angela gets her own room and I have to share one?"

Hector was not happy with his sister.

"Mom, how come I always get picked on?"

Robbie was not happy with anyone.

Some of the unhappiness may have been because they were squeezed together in a hot, crowded subway car. None of the three De La Rosa children was tall enough to hold onto the overhead handrail, and only Angela was close enough to a pole to get a firm grip. Hector was holding on to Angela and Robbie held onto Mom. Mrs. De La Rosa and her three children were all trying not to lose their balance everytime the train slowed down or sped up or went around a curve.

"Must be one of those days," said a very tall man holding onto a briefcase. At least he looked tall to Robbie.

"You can say that again," said Mrs. De La Rosa.

"Why do you want him to say that again?" Robbie asked in a very loud voice.

The very tall man laughed. "That's a good one," he said.

Several other people laughed, too. Even Mom was laughing a little.

"What's funny?" Robbie asked, even louder this time. Now more people on the subway started laughing.

"Yeah, what's funny?" Hector asked, even louder than Robbie.

"Robbie's funny," Angela said.

"I am NOT funny!" Robbie announced.

"Robbie, I'm laughing because I'm so glad you kids are in my family," Mom said. "You three do so many things that make me happy, even when I'm hot and tired and my feet hurt."

Then the tall man spoke. "And I'm laughing because I really have had one of those days and you kids just made it better."

"One of what days?" Robbie asked.

Now EVERYONE on the train began laughing. Even Robbie and Hector and Angela. The tall man said, "It's been one of those days when I just can't wait for this hot, crowded train to take me back to my home and my own family."

Just then the train slowed down and Angela and Hector and Robbie all grabbed on tight to keep from falling. "And I'm REALLY thankful," Mom said, "that this is our stop and we can finally get off."

● *"A cheerful look brings joy to the heart, and good news gives health to the bones." Proverbs 15:30*

● **For Younger Children**
How did the De La Rosa family feel while they were riding on the subway?
   What two things was Mom thankful for?
   What are some things you are thankful for?

● **For Older Children**
Why do you think the people on the subway train began laughing?
   When did something funny happen in our family?
   What are some things about our family that make you glad and thankful?

● ●

FAMILY TIMES Schedule time this week to be together as a family. Select one of these suggested activities to expand your family's understanding of the joy and gladness God gives.

Family Fun
Ask each member of your family (or even Grandma and Grandpa) to tell about something funny that has happened in your family. Write the stories

in a notebook or computer, video tape, or tape record them. Make it a family tradition to add stories the first week of each year.

Tip for Younger Children: The younger the child, the less likely it is that he or she will be able to remember and tell a story. Children will enjoy hearing their parents' stories.

Picture Verses

Read several of these verses: Proverbs 10:1; 15:13, 30; 17:22; 24:17; 28:14. As each verse is read, talk about your answer to this question: "What do we learn about gladness?" Then each person chooses a verse and writes it on a large sheet of paper, drawing pictures for as many words as possible. Display the papers on a bulletin board or wall.

Tip for Younger Children: Draw the outline of a picture for your child to color in.

For Parents Only

Write a short letter to each child telling several things about the child that make you feel glad and thankful.

• •

There Is One True God

Key Verse
"Do you not know? Have you not heard? The Lord is the everlasting God, the Creator of the ends of the earth."
Isaiah 40:28

Key Thought
There is one true God who lives forever.

What is God like? Can I see Him? How old is He? How can I be sure that what I learn about God is really true? These are just a few of the many questions people of all ages have always asked about God.

There are no simple answers to these questions. If we could easily answer all the questions about God, we would be as smart as God is. Either that, or God would not be very great at all.

How do we respond when we realize that there is much about God that no human has ever understood? Do we give up trying to learn about God, feeling there is no way to take in knowledge about a being so great? Do we assume that anyone's ideas about God are as good as anyone else's? Or do we seek to discover those things about God which He has clearly shown to people?

This week's stories will help your family explore some of the most important things we can know about God: there is just one true God, and He is the maker of all that exists in heaven and earth.

• •

WEEK 2

DAY 1

The mall was crowded. Half the people were returning Christmas gifts that were the wrong size or color. The other half wanted to save money at after-Christmas sales. Both halves made the parking lot full, the aisles crowded, and the lines long.

Waiting in long lines with Mother made AJ bored. She was so bored she didn't even notice how restless DJ, her twin brother, had become. While DJ squirmed and hopped and twisted and turned, AJ just stood and stared at the people getting off the nearby escalator.

Suddenly, AJ wasn't bored anymore. Her shining brown eyes focused on a family coming down the escalator. Their hair and skin was almost as dark as AJ's. But AJ had never seen people dressed like that man and woman and two children.

"DJ!" she whispered.

DJ was used to Mom trying to get him to stop squirming, hopping, twisting, and turning. He paid no attention to AJ.

So she whispered louder: "DJ! Look!"

18

DJ untangled himself and looked up.

"Over there!" she whispered even louder, pointing to the escalator. "Look at those people in their pajamas!"

DJ was not the only person who heard AJ's whispers. Everyone in line turned to see whom AJ was pointing at. Even Mom looked. DJ shouted, "Weird! Why are they dressed like that?" Now Mom was embarrassed.

"AJ! DJ!" she started whispering. "It's not polite to point at people or talk about their clothes. Besides, they're not wearing pajamas."

DJ blurted out, "But they look like pajamas! And the woman's got a big dot on her forehead!"

By now the family in the unusual clothes had gotten off the escalator and were headed toward the exit. Mother tried to answer DJ's comments. "I think they're dressed like that because they're from India. I think they are Hindus."

"From India?" DJ asked. "But they aren't wearing feathers!"

"Hindu? What's that?" AJ asked.

"People do not wear feathers in India, DJ. And many people in India are Hindus," Mom answered. "Hindus believe in many gods — or in many forms of god."

"Many gods?" DJ asked. "How many gods are there, Mom?"

"Why don't they believe what we do about God?" asked AJ. Just then the clerk at the cash register said, "Excuse me, Ma'am. It's your turn."

Mom handed her package to the clerk and said to the twins, "We'll have to finish this when we get home."

● *"Hear, O Israel: The Lord our God, the Lord is one." Deuteronomy 6:4*

● **For Younger Children**
When was a time you were bored?
When have you seen people who looked very different from your family?
What would you like to know about God?

● **For Older Children**
What are some ways we can find out what God is really like?
What are some things you have learned about what God is like?
Why do you think people have different ideas about what God is like?

DAY
2

"Hey, Dad!" AJ and DJ yelled. "We're home!"

The door slammed behind them as the twins and their mother carried in the packages from their shopping trip.

"Guess what we saw?" AJ shouted.

"We saw a Hindo family!" DJ yelled.

"DJ, that's Hin-DOO," Mom corrected.

"Guess what Hindus believe?" AJ asked.

"They believe in lots of gods," DJ said.

"DJ!" AJ protested. "I wanted Dad to answer. Not you!"

Dad laughed. "It is a little hard to sneak an answer in around here," he said. "How did you two learn so much about Hindus?"

"They heard it from me," Mom said. "But I really didn't teach them very much. They just told you everything I had time to tell them."

"And she never got to my other question," DJ added.

"What question was that?" Dad asked.

"Aren't many gods better than just one God?" DJ wanted to know.

"Yeah!" AJ chimed in. "A whole bunch of gods could do more stuff than just one could."

"You think so?" Dad asked.

"Why not?" AJ asked back. Dad turned to Mom. "Help me out here, Sandy. You're the one who got this all started."

"Don't blame me," Mom said. "AJ was the one who spotted the family from India."

"So quit stalling," DJ insisted. "Answer the question."

"OK," Dad answered. "I'll try. You two want to know if many gods are better than one God."

"Right!" said AJ.

"The answer," Dad said, "is no."

"How come?" the twins said together.

"Two reasons," Dad said. "First, if this one God were the same as those many gods, the many gods would have an advantage. But the one true God is so great, so powerful, the other gods don't stand a chance." Dad folded his arms and waited while the twins thought about what he had said.

"There really is only one God. Anything else that people worship as gods are not really gods at all, Mom said."

"I've got it!" AJ said. But DJ interrupted: "One true God is better," he said, "than a whole bunch of gods that aren't even real."

"DJ! I wanted to say that!"

"Sorry," DJ said. And Mom and Dad both laughed.

● *"Know that the Lord is God. It is He who made us, and we are His; we are His people, the sheep of His pasture." Psalm 100:3*

● **For Younger Children**

What has God made in our world that shows His greatness and power?

What are some words people use to describe God?

Who has helped you learn about the one true God?

● **For Older Children**

What are some things people might worship instead of the one true God? Why?

What would you say about God to someone who has never heard of Him?

What do you learn about God in Psalm 100:3?

What does it mean when the Bible says that God is our shepherd?

● ●

WEEK 2

DAY 3

"Mom!" AJ yelled. "DJ has my dalmatian!"

"No I don't!" her brother, DJ, yelled louder. "Brutus is MY dalmatian!"

Mrs. Gorman stood in the doorway of DJ's room. "Are you two arguing over those stuffed animals again? Next time Grandma gives you twins identical toys, I will make a permanent mark on each one so we can tell them apart."

"That's what I did with Fluffy," AJ protested. "I drew a red heart on her label!"

"And I cut the label off Brutus!" DJ insisted. "See!" he said, holding up the little stuffed puppy. "No label!"

"That's because you took Fluffy and cut off her label," accused AJ.

"No way!" DJ declared. "This is Brutus!"

"All this bickering isn't helping," Mom said. "Are there any other ways we could tell which one is Fluffy and which is Brutus?"

AJ answered right away. "Fluffy has spots . . ." AJ stopped in the middle of her sentence.

"What about spots?" Mom asked.

AJ answered very softly, "On her tail, but Brutus doesn't." Mom and DJ looked closely at the puppy's tail. No spots.

"I'm sorry," AJ said. "I was wrong."

That night, DJ and AJ were ready for bed, both holding their cuddly, stuffed puppies. AJ had found Fluffy under the dirty clothes in her room. After Mom prayed with them, AJ asked, "Mom?"

"Yes?" Mom answered.

"Remember this afternoon when we couldn't tell if that puppy was mine or DJ's?"

"I remember," Mom said.

"Well," AJ continued. "If we had such a hard time figuring out a stuffed animal, how can we know if God is the one true God? I mean, really know?"

"Yeah!" DJ chimed in. "People who worship other gods say they're right, and we say we're right. Who's really right?"

"I can't prove there's one true God the way we proved which puppy was which," Mom said. "But there are many, many good reasons to believe in the God of the Bible."

"Tell us one," AJ yawned.

"OK. One reason I believe there is one God is because the Bible says so. And I've always found the Bible to be true. I know I can trust what it says."

Now DJ yawned too. "You two had better get to sleep," Mom said. "And remember, one thing the Bible tells about God is that He is always with you. Even when you sleep."

● *"The Lord is the true God; He is the living God, the eternal King." Jeremiah 10:10*

● **For Younger Children**

Have you ever had an argument like AJ and DJ? What happened?
> What makes the Bible different from any other book in the world?
> What does the Bible tell about God?

● **For Older Children**

What does it mean to trust something or someone?
> Why do you think some people don't believe that God exists?
> What are some things you can't see but still believe are real?

● ●

"If I crashed my bike at the bottom of the hill and I was bleeding and unconscious and a big truck ran over me, what would you do?" DJ pointed down the hill, showing his twin sister, AJ, the location of his imagined accident.

"I'd faint," AJ said.

"You're a big help!" DJ snorted. "You'd let me lie there and die?"

"What else could I do?" AJ asked. "I'm no doctor."

"You could check to see if I'm breathing," DJ insisted. "You could give me CPR. You could press on the spots that are bleeding. You could warn that truck to stop."

"I couldn't do those things," AJ said. "I'm only nine. I don't know how to do that stuff."

"You couldn't even call 911?" DJ asked.

AJ thought for a moment. "I guess I could do that. If my bike had a phone."

"I'm dead," DJ moaned. "I'm dying in the street because my sister doesn't have a phone on her bike. Remind me to have my accident when someone's around who knows what to do."

"Maybe that's why Mom and Dad pray so much," AJ said.

"What does that have to do with me crashing my bike?"

"Nothing, I guess," AJ said. "I just thought maybe Mom and Dad talk to God about stuff because He knows what to do. He knows what's best."

"Of course He does!" DJ said. "He's God, isn't He? But what does that have to do with crashing my bike?"

"I just thought," AJ said, "that maybe if you paid more attention to God, you'd learn what's best and not spend your time planning stupid things like crashing your bike."

"Girls!" DJ hollered and started off down the hill.

"Be careful!" AJ shouted as she started right down behind him.

● *"I am the Lord your God, who teaches you what is best for you, who directs you in the way you should go." Isaiah 48:17*

● **For Younger Children**
What silly thing did DJ ask AJ?

Why did AJ say her mom and dad talk to God?

What's something you'll be doing this week? Let's ask God's help.

● **For Older Children**

What important decisions do kids your age have to make?

What does God promise in Isaiah 48:17?

What can you do to pay attention to God and learn what He wants you to do?

● ●

WEEK 2

DAY
5

AJ and her twin brother were exhausted. They had been racing their bikes up and down the street all morning, and now they were sprawled flat on their backs on the front lawn. AJ spoke first. "I thought my tire might pop when I hit the Sullivan's curb."

"Wouldn't it be great?" DJ asked, changing the subject, something he did often. "Wouldn't it be great if we could reach up and touch those clouds up there?"

"We'd have to be as tall as God," AJ answered.

"Do you think God is tall?" DJ asked.

"I guess," AJ said after a moment. "Tall and big and strong. With a long white robe and a beard and a moustache. Like that long cloud over there."

"I dunno," DJ replied. "How could God be tall and have a beard if He doesn't have a body?"

"Who said He doesn't have a body?" AJ asked, sounding insulted.

"Mrs. Lincoln said so in Sunday School," DJ answered.

AJ jumped up and put her hands on her hips. "Well, what if she did? How could God not have a body? Everybody has a body!"

"Not God! He's a Spirit!" DJ insisted. "That's how He can be every-where at once."

Suddenly a large shadow fell across AJ's upturned face.

"Everywhere at once!" said a big, booming voice. "That's me!"

"Uncle Cedric!" AJ shouted. "You surprised me! And you are not every-where at once."

"True," Uncle Cedric laughed. "I'm just so big it seems like I'm everywhere."

"DJ says that God doesn't have a body," AJ told Uncle Cedric.

"That IS what the Bible tells us," Cedric answered. "I've always felt that was one of the hardest things to understand about God."

"Yeah!" AJ responded. "How can I think about God, or talk to God, or love God, if He doesn't have a body? It seems like He isn't really there! Like He doesn't really exist!"

"AJ," Uncle Cedric said, "maybe that's why God sent Jesus, to help us see God in a body."

"Do you think so?" AJ asked.

"Makes sense to me," Uncle Cedric said.

"Me too," DJ added.

"Then let's go inside and see if we can find a snack in the kitchen," Cedric suggested. The twins did not need to be asked twice.

● *"Now this is eternal life: that they may know You, the only true God, and Jesus Christ, whom You have sent." John 17:3*

● **For Younger Children**
What did AJ think God was like?
   Why was it hard for AJ to know what God is really like?
   What have you learned about God?

● **For Older Children**
When you think of God, what picture do you see in your mind? Why did Uncle Cedric say God sent Jesus?
   What do you know about Jesus' actions and the way He treated people? How does that help you learn about God?

● ●

Schedule time this week to be together as a family. Select one of these suggested activities to expand your family's understanding of the one true God.

FAMILY TIMES

Word Fun
Work with your family to list as many words as you can that describe God. Then one person letters one word in the center of a large piece of paper. Each person takes a turn to add another word, connecting it to the first word as shown on next page. Can you connect all the words on your list?

Picture Collage
Cut out pictures that show things God created. Glue the pictures on a large sheet of paper to make a collage. Then play an "I Spy" game. For example, "I spy something brown and furry." Players take turns guessing things they see in the collage until someone guesses the correct item (a bear).

p
loving
w
e
r
faithful
u
l

Sentence Starters

Letter each of these sentence starters on a separate piece of paper. Put the papers in a hat or bowl. Each person takes a turn to choose a paper and complete the sentence.

The Bible tells that God is. . . .

I know God loves me because. . . .

One thing I don't understand about God is. . . .

I'm glad that God. . . .

I wish that God would. . . .

God shows His power when. . . .

We Can Know God

Almost everybody knows something about God. However, what many people know ends up doing them no good at all because they have never discovered that they can go beyond just knowing about God. They can actually know God personally.

Once a person truly begins to know God, all the facts about God become much more than just interesting bits of trivia. While it is good to know that God is love, it is much better to receive God's love and to love Him back. It is comforting to think of God hearing and answering prayer, but it is much better to spend time talking with Him.

Sadly, many people never experience this. They believe that God exists. They accept many truths of what God is like. But they never take the step to get to know God. Perhaps they feel God is too great and powerful to pay attention to them. Or they may feel guilty over things they have done which they know are wrong, and they fear that God will reject them.

This week your family will begin to explore exciting truths about getting to know God in a special, personal way.

Key Verse
"Now this is eternal life: that they may know you, the only true God, and Jesus Christ, whom You have sent."
John 17:3

Key Thought
We can know God and talk to Him about everything.

WEEK 3

DAY 1

Aliki dropped a few bits of fish food into the bowl for her pet goldfish. The fish gulped at each little flake as it hit the water. Aliki watched the little fish swim in rapid circles around the bowl. "Do you get lonely in there, Gergie?" Aliki asked. The goldfish just kept on swimming.

"Sometimes I feel lonely, even when there are people around. What do you think of that, Gergie?" Gergie just kept on swimming, but Aliki liked talking to her fish.

Gergie's bowl was on one side of a small shelf. The shelf divided Aliki's half of her room from her younger sister Midori's half. Midori was next door with a friend. Aliki liked her little sister, but she also liked the peace and quiet when Midori was gone.

"Do you have any sisters or brothers, Gergie?" Aliki asked. Gergie swooped to the top of the water to gulp a flake that had been missed before. "Sometimes I wish I had a big sister instead of a little sister," Aliki told her fish. "I could play with her toys and try on her her clothes."

The goldfish dove for the bottom of the bowl, splashing a few drops of water onto the shelf. "Gergie!" Aliki scolded. "Are you even listening?" Aliki sighed. "No, you're not paying any attention. You just want to swim."

Aliki rolled over on her bed and saw the Bible she had earned in Sunday School. She could read some of its words, but she thought she would never be able to read all of it. "Why did You make Your book so big, God?" She asked. "A short book would have been easier for You and for me."

"Are you talking to your fish again?" Aliki looked up. Her little sister was back.

"No, Midori," Aliki answered. "I was talking to God."

"Oh," Midori said. "What did He say to you?"

"Well, nothing, I guess," said Aliki.

"Just like your goldfish," Midori said. "He never answers either."

"But God understands me," Aliki said.

"How do you know?" Midori asked.

"Well," Aliki thought for a moment. "He HAS to understand. He's God!"

"But what if He's not listening?" Midori persisted. "I bet He's too busy."

"Do you think so?" Aliki asked.

"If He doesn't talk back, He's not listening," Midori said as if she knew all about it. "Just like talking to your goldfish."

"Do you really think so?" Aliki asked again with a worried look on her face.

● *"I will make them want to know Me, that I am the Lord. They will be My people, and I will be their God." Jeremiah 24:7,* EB

● **For Younger Children**

What kind of pet would you like to have?

What did Aliki wish her goldfish could do?

One way God talks to us is in the Bible. What is something you remember God has said in the Bible?

● **For Older Children**

When is a time you might feel lonely?

Whom do you like to talk to?

What are some things Aliki and Midori need to know about God?

What do you think is the difference between knowing things about God and really knowing God?

DAY 2

Aliki was walking toward the grocery store. Her head was down as she kicked at scraps of paper on the sidewalk. She kicked a candy wrapper, then a paper cup, and a flattened aluminum can. But she was not thinking about what she was kicking.

All around her on the busy city sidewalk, people were walking, in a hurry to get to the corner before the light turned red. Aliki was usually nervous about being alone with so many strangers around. But Aliki was not thinking about all the busy people.

It was a very cold day, and Aliki's breath made puffs of steam around her head. On cold days Aliki usually liked to wave her hands in front of her mouth, blowing warm steam in every direction. But Aliki's hands were tightly clenched in front of her. Aliki was not paying any attention to the things she usually noticed.

Aliki was thinking. Her little sister, Midori, had made her wonder if God really did hear her prayers. Midori had said that talking to God was like talking to a goldfish. Aliki was worried that maybe Midori was right.

Aliki stopped at a busy corner. She stopped because a very large woman had stopped right in front of her. If Aliki had taken one more step she would have bumped right into her. Aliki looked up to see why the woman had stopped. She saw that the light was red, and the busy street was filled with noisy cars and trucks in a hurry to get somewhere. For a moment Aliki forgot her questions about God and looked around to see where she was.

None of the buildings looked familiar. She expected to see the bright green sign for the grocery store. Quickly looking in every direction, she saw that the green sign was nowhere in sight. How far had she walked? Had she turned at the wrong corner? Had she gone past the store? Was she lost?

"Please, dear God," Aliki whispered. "Help me find my way home." Suddenly she had a terrible thought. "What if God was just too busy to pay attention to a little girl's prayers? Even a little girl who is lost and afraid?"

Slowly, one small tear slid quickly down the side of Aliki's nose, and she felt very, very cold.

● *"We know and rely on the love God has for us. God is love."*
1 John 4:16

● **For Younger Children**

Have you ever been lost? How did you feel?

If you were Aliki, what would you say to God?

● **For Older Children**

What was Aliki's problem?

Besides being lost, what else was Aliki worried about?

How would it have helped Aliki if she had remembered 1 John 4:16?

What's a problem you need to talk to God about? Let's talk to Him now.

● ●

WEEK 3

DAY

3

Seven-year-old Aliki knew the way from her apartment to the bus stop. She knew the way to the grocery store, the little park, and the building where her friend Natalie lived. But Aliki did not know the way home from the corner where she was standing. Aliki was lost.

Aliki had never been lost before. Should she start walking back the way she had come and hope she would see a familiar building or sign?

But which way had she come? The shadows were getting longer, and soon it would be dark. Could she stop one of the strangers walking by on the sidewalk and ask for help? What if no one cared? What if they were too busy? What if the person she spoke to was dangerous?

Aliki decided to pray. She really wasn't sure if God was listening. She wondered way down deep if God really cared about the trouble she was in. "Please, dear God," she said, "I'm lost." Aliki felt a little better after she said that. She decided to pray some more.

"And God," she continued, "I don't know what to do. Please help me think of what to do now." Aliki let out a big breath of air, making a long puff of steam in the cold evening air. Just then Aliki had an idea. She walked quickly up the sidewalk, looking in the windows of the buildings she passed. She stopped in front of a drug store where she could see several people shopping. Aliki opened the door, went inside, and walked up to the counter.

"Can I help you?" the clerk asked.

"My name is Aliki Yasuda. I'm lost. May I use your telephone?"

The clerk looked at Aliki for a moment. Then she asked, "Do you know your phone number? Will somebody be there?"

"Yes," Aliki said, and then the words started to gush out, "I was going to the store and I must have made a wrong turn and I've never seen this block before and. . . ."

The clerk interrupted her. "Sure, you can use the phone. I'll show you where it is."

Aliki called home and the clerk helped her tell where she was. Then Aliki stood by the front door of the drug store and waited for her father to come.

"Thank You, God," Aliki whispered. "Thank You for helping me think of what to do."

● *"Search me, O God, and know my heart; test me and know my anxious thoughts." Psalm 139:23*

● **For Younger Children**
What did Aliki ask God to help her do?
    How did God help Aliki?
    When is a time God has helped you or our family know what to do?

● **For Older Children**
Why was talking to the clerk such a good idea?
    When was a time you were worried and needed God's help?
    Why is it good to tell God when you are worried about something?
    How do you know God will help you?

●●

WEEK 3

DAY
4

Aliki was embarrassed about having gotten lost just three blocks from home. She felt foolish when she realized that all her trouble came because she had turned the wrong way at the very first corner.

"You were really lost?" her little sister Midori asked. "Boy, are you in big trouble!"

Aliki had already heard a big lecture from her father. And then another one from her mother. She was not going to be allowed to go outside the apartment by herself for three weeks.

But being embarrassed and being in trouble did not really bother Aliki very much. She was just glad to be back home.

"Weren't you scared?" Midori asked. "Did you cry?"

"I was scared," Aliki answered. "And I started to cry. But then I prayed."

"You prayed?" asked Midori. "What good would that do?"

"I wasn't sure," Aliki said. "But it sure helped."

"How could it help?" Midori wanted to know. "Did God tell you where you were?"

"No," Aliki said. "I just felt like I wasn't alone. I think God helped me not be so afraid."

Aliki didn't tell Midori that she had not really stopped being afraid as soon as she prayed. She had felt better when the friendly clerk had helped her. But it was not until Father walked into the drugstore that she really knew for sure that she was safe. Seeing someone who knew and loved her really made a big difference.

Aliki thought about that at bedtime when she opened her Bible and saw a picture of Jesus. She felt sure that Jesus knew her and really loved her. Aliki thought about Jesus helping her and everyone else to know what God is like. That night Aliki did not dream about being lost or afraid. She went to sleep thinking about how glad she was that she could talk to God, anytime, anyplace.

And she knew for sure that the next time she went to the store by herself, she would make the right turn at that first corner.

● *"We know also that the Son of God has come and has given us understanding, so that we may know Him who is true." 1 John 5:20*

● **For Younger Children**
Have you ever been lost?
What did Aliki learn about God?
Let's tell God thank You for hearing our prayers wherever we are.

● **For Older Children**
What made Aliki glad?
What did Aliki learn about God?
What are some things you want to remember about God when you talk to Him?

● ●

WEEK 3

DAY 5

Aliki really did not mind not being able to go outside by herself. She knew that her parents were being fair in "grounding" her for the next three weeks. She was sure that the next time she was sent to the store she would pay very close attention to where she was going.

Aliki also did not mind being kept inside because she had a stack of library books to read. Three of the books were really a little too hard for her, but whenever she came to a strange word, she just skipped it and kept reading. Usually she could still tell what the sentence was about, but sometimes she had to skip whole sentences. Then the books got a little confusing.

The one thing Aliki did mind was that her little sister Midori kept talking about how Aliki was in "BIG TROUBLE!" Every chance she got, Midori would say, "You really did something bad, Aliki." Or she would say, "I can't believe you turned the wrong way and got lost. Even I know the way to the store."

Or Midori would say, "Mother won't even let you go over to Natalie's apartment by yourself. I'm only five, and I can go to Kelley's whenever I want."

Aliki really wished that Midori would forget all about Aliki getting lost. And she wished that Midori would forget all about Mother and Father not letting her go out by herself for three weeks. But mostly, Aliki wished that Midori would just be quiet so that Aliki could keep reading her books. Just then, Midori said something that Aliki was really surprised to hear. Aliki was even glad to hear it.

Midori said, "I'm just glad that you didn't stay lost."

Aliki was so surprised, she said, "You are?"

"Sure," Midori answered. "I'm glad you came back safe."

"I'm glad too," Aliki answered. "I'm really glad."

Aliki and Midori were quiet for a few minutes. Then Midori said one more thing. She said, "I'm glad you knew how to talk to God. I need to learn how to do that too."

● *"Be joyful always; pray continually; give thanks in all circumstances."*
1 Thessalonians 5:16-18

● **For Younger Children**
What did you like the best about this story?

God loves all people and wants them to talk to Him. What are some things we can tell God about right now?

● **For Older Children**
What did Midori learn from her older sister?
What are some things people do to get to know God?
What are some things our family does to get to know God?
What are some things we can thank God for?

●●

FAMILY TIMES

Schedule time this week to be together as a family. Select one of these suggested activities to expand your family's understanding of ways they can know God.

Favorite Book

Ask a child to find a favorite book. Read the book (or a chapter) together. Then ask, "In this book, what could (main character) have thanked God for? When might he or she have needed God's help? If (character) had talked to God, what might he or she have said?

Tip for Younger Child: Look at a picture book with your younger child. Talk with your child about the pictures using questions such as, "What do you see on this page that you are thankful to God for? What could the girl on this page tell God about?"

Personalized Calendar

Talk with your family about ways you can get to know God. List your ideas (read the Bible, pray, go to Sunday School, read books about God, etc.). Design a symbol or stick-figure drawing to represent each action. Draw the symbol or drawing on a calendar to mark the days in the next few weeks when your family will do each action together.

●●●

God's Wonderful Plan

Two weeks ago we thought about some ways we can know that there is one true God. Last week we learned that prayer is one way we can get to know God personally. This week we will discover that not only can we know God, we can become part of His family — forever!

If a child is growing in a secure, loving family, it is easy for him or her to accept the truth of God's love. Becoming part of God's family is very appealing. A child who has not known consistent parental love finds it harder to believe that God loves him or her. Such a child may be afraid of the idea of being God's child.

It is never enough that we talk about God's love. Words alone do not make us feel loved. That is why God did not just give us a book that told us about His love. God also gave us His Son, Jesus, who showed how great God's love really is.

At times it is very difficult to put into words truths about God that we want to explain to a child. While a child may be too young to understand many things, no child is ever too young to receive and give love. The words that are spoken this week may or may not be remembered next week. But when we show God's love, the memory of our caring actions goes on and on.

Key Verse
"For God so loved the world that He gave His one and only Son, that whoever believes in Him shall not perish but have eternal life."
John 3:16

Key Thought
God has a wonderful plan to bring people into His own loving family forever.

●●

WEEK 4

DAY 1

After school, a bully chased Arthur, knocked him down, and gave him a bloody nose. All the way home, Arthur's nose kept bleeding, people passing on the sidewalk kept staring at him, but no one offered to help. By the time Arthur climbed the stairs to his apartment, sniffing and sobbing all the way, his face, hands, and shirt were a mess of blood and dirt streaked with tears.

Arthur unlocked the apartment door, leaving red smudges around the doorknob. He went into the bathroom, looked at himself in the mirror, and started to cry again.

When his mother got home from work later that afternoon, she saw the smudges on the door right away. "Arthur?" she called. "What on earth happened?" There was no answer.

On her way down the hall to Arthur's room, she looked inside the bathroom. She saw a very messy sink and a washcloth, towel, and shirt wadded into a disgusting heap on the counter. "Arthur!" she yelled, and hurried back to his bedroom.

Arthur was sitting on his bed. His eyes were red from crying. Even though Arthur had tried to wash up, there were still dark red smudges on his chin and his hands.

"Arthur!" his mother said for the third time. "What happened?"

"I got beat up," he said, his voice shaking.

"Why were you fighting?" Mother asked.

"I wasn't fighting!" Arthur insisted. "A bully chased me after school, and. . . ." Arthur was having a hard time telling this story.

"And what?"

"And he knocked me down and punched me."

Arthur's mom sat down on the edge of the bed and held Arthur's face in her hands. Arthur was crying, and his mom was crying, and neither of them spoke for a long, long time.

"Mom?" Arthur asked finally. "Why are some people so mean? Why do bullies and bad people hurt other people?"

Arthur's mom took a deep breath and said, "Those are hard questions to answer, Arthur. Probably, that bully was mean to you because someone else has been mean to him. He's let himself get full of hurt and anger. We've all done things that are selfish, that hurt someone else. And then the person who gets hurt wants to hurt someone else, and the problem spreads. It's what the Bible calls 'sin.' "

Arthur wiped his eyes. "Wow! That sounds worse than a bloody nose."

"It is, Arthur," his mom said. "Sin is much worse."

● *"For all have sinned and fall short of the glory of God." Romans 3:23*

● **For Younger Children**
How did Arthur and his mom feel?
> What are some bad things you have seen people do?
> According to Romans 3:23, who has sinned?
> What is something selfish or unkind that you've done?

● **For Older Children**
Why is sin so bad?
> What are some results of sin in our world?
> How do you think God feels when you and others sin?

DAY 2

Arthur felt almost like new as he crawled into bed. He had taken a shower and washed off the last of the dark red, sticky smudges from his bloody nose. All the dried, salty tears that he had cried were gone. Arthur felt good enough that he had almost forgotten about the bully who beat him up after school. Almost.

"Mom," Arthur said. "You said that bully was mean to me because someone else was mean to him."

"That's probably what happened," said his mother.

"Then someone else was probably mean to that person," Arthur said. "And another someone else was mean before then, and . . . how did it all start?"

Arthur's mom wasn't sure if Arthur really wanted to learn something or if he just wanted to stay up later. Arthur was known for doing almost anything to keep from going to bed on time. But since Arthur had been very upset about his bloody nose, she decided he was not just trying to avoid bed time. "Where did all the meanness and unhappiness start?" she asked. Arthur's mom often repeated his questions to get more time to think of an answer.

"That's what I asked," Arthur said. He knew all his mom's tricks and wanted her to answer his question.

"Well," she said. "The Bible says that it all began when the very first people disobeyed God. They wanted to do things their own way instead of God's way. That's pretty much what still causes people to be selfish and unkind."

"So," Arthur asked, "Why doesn't God do something about it?"

"Oh, He has, Arthur. He already has." Arthur's mom started to get up and leave Arthur's room.

"Are you going to tell me what He did?" Arthur asked.

"What God did?" his mother asked, realizing that he wanted to learn more. She sat back down again. "Arthur, God did the most wonderful thing to solve the problem of people being selfish and disobedient. He sent His very special Son to live on earth. His Son's name was Jesus, and He came to tell us and show us all about God's love."

There was more Arthur's mom wanted to tell him. But she noticed that Arthur had fallen asleep. "I guess he had a hard day," she thought as she turned out the light.

● *"And we have seen and testify that the Father has sent His Son to be the Savior of the world." 1 John 4:14*

● **For Younger Children**

What did God do to solve the problem of sin?

What do you know about Jesus?

Let's tell God thank You for sending Jesus.

● **For Older Children**

How would you define the word "sin"?

How did the problem of sin start?

Why did God send Jesus?

● ●

WEEK 4

DAY
3

Breakfast was Arthur's favorite meal of the day. Until lunch, that is. Come to think of it, right after school he really enjoyed an afternoon snack. And he could never wait until Mom had dinner ready. Then there was a bedtime snack every night.

But first thing in the morning, when Arthur hadn't eaten since the night before, breakfast ranked right at the top of his list. That was why his mother was surprised that Arthur had not come into the kitchen to pour his usual bowl of cereal. "Arthur!" she yelled up the hall. "You'd better come and eat, or you'll be late for school."

"I'm not hungry, Mom," Arthur called back down the hall. Now Arthur's mother was more than surprised. She was worried. Arthur? Not hungry?

"Arthur," she said. "Are you OK?" Maybe Arthur was afraid to go back to school where that bully might beat him up again.

Arthur came into the kitchen. "I'm OK, Mom," he said. "I was just wishing God would change bullies. Like stop them from being mean and make them nice."

"God has done that with a lot of bullies," Mom answered. "Did you know I used to be kind of a bully myself?"

"You?" Now Arthur was surprised.

"That's right." Mom said. "When I was in school, I used to do some unkind things."

"Did you give anyone a bloody nose?" Arthur asked.

"No," Mom answered. "But I gave one girl a black eye."

"Wow!" Arthur had never thought his kind, gentle mother might have once been a bully. "How come you're not a bully now?"

"I didn't really want to be a mean person," Mom explained. "But I didn't know how to change. So I asked God to help me."

"Did He?" Arthur asked.

"Yes, He did. I learned that Jesus died on the cross to take the punishment for the bad things I had done. I learned that if I admitted to God that I had done wrong, and that if I asked God to forgive me, He would."

"And that stopped you from being a bully?"

"Yes, Arthur. God's love can change anyone who asks."

"Wow!" Arthur said. "Can I have my breakfast now?"

● *"Yet to all who received Him, to those who believed in His name, He gave the right to become children of God." John 1:12*

● **For Younger Children**
What did Arthur's mom ask God to do?
    What did she learn about Jesus?
    How does God's love and forgiveness make you feel?

● **For Older Children**
What was God's plan for Jesus?
    What does it mean to forgive someone?
    How can knowing about God's love and forgiveness help you?

● ●

WEEK 4

DAY

Arthur was finishing his second bowl of cereal. His mom was packing their lunches. In between bites, Arthur kept asking questions.

"But Mom," Arthur said. "Why doesn't God just get rid of all the bullies and bad people?"

Mom was squeezing a very big sandwich into a very small sandwich bag. "Well, Arthur," she said. "If God got rid of all the people who've done something bad, He'd have to get rid of everyone. Remember, the Bible says, 'All have sinned.' The bully who beat you up, and me, and you, and everyone."

But Arthur really thought God should do something to punish bullies and other bad people. He was thinking so much that he almost missed what his mother said next.

"Besides, Arthur, the Bible says God did not send Jesus to earth to point out the bad things people have done."

"What?" Arthur said. "I thought God wanted to stop bad things."

"Oh, He does," Mom said as she opened a package of cookies. She put three of them in each lunch bag. "But He's more interested in saving people. You see, Arthur, God sent Jesus to show love to everyone. And the ones who have done the worst things are the ones who need God's love the most."

"God loves bullies?" Arthur sounded insulted. He picked up his cereal bowl and brought it to the sink.

"Yes, God loves bullies," Mom said. "He doesn't love the mean things they do, but He loves them just the same."

"God really loves bullies?" Arthur did not sound convinced that this was a good idea.

"Just think, Arthur," Mom said as she closed up their lunch bags. "That means you don't ever have to worry that you've done something so bad that God cannot forgive you. That's a wonderful thing to think about while you rush off to school so that you won't be late."

"I'm going! I'm going!" Arthur said as he grabbed his lunch and ran out the door. His mom was just locking the apartment door on her way to work when she heard Arthur talking to himself on the way down the stairs. "God loves bullies? Wow!"

● *"For God did not send His Son into the world to condemn the world, but to save the world through Him." John 3:17*

● **For Younger Children**

How did Arthur feel when he heard that God loves bullies?

Why does God forgive us when we sin?

Let's thank God for His love.

● **For Older Children**

What were the new things Arthur learned about God?

What would happen if God got rid of everyone who sinned?

When have you or someone you know done something so bad you thought God would never forgive you?

● ●

WEEK 4

DAY
5

Arthur was sitting quietly on his bed, staring at his toes, thinking.

When his mom came into the room to put him to bed, she noticed right away how quiet Arthur was.

"What'cha thinking about, Honey?" she asked.

Usually, Arthur hated being called "honey." But tonight, he just said, "I'm thinking about whether God would really forgive me for stuff."

"Have you asked Him to forgive you?" Mom asked.

"Not yet," Arthur answered.

"Do you want to do it now?" Mom sat down on the edge of the bed.

"What if He won't?" Arthur asked.

Mom thought for a moment. "Well, Arthur," she said. "Do you think God would ever break a promise, especially a promise that He put in writing for everyone to read?"

"No," Arthur answered.

"Well, listen to this promise in the Bible." Mom reached over to the shelf and picked up a Bible. She turned a few pages, then put her finger under some words. "Right here, Arthur. Read what God promised."

Arthur read out loud, "If we confess our sins, He is faithful and just and will forgive us our sins and purify us from all unrighteousness."

"What that means, Arthur," Mom said, "is that if we admit to God that we have done wrong things, He will forgive us. Not only that, He will also make us clean, taking away those sins. All we have to do is ask."

Arthur was silent. His mom could tell he was thinking.

"Would you like to do that tonight?" she asked.

Arthur looked up. "Yeah," he said. Arthur's mom led him in a simple prayer. First, she prayed a sentence, then Arthur repeated it. They thanked God for sending Jesus to take away sin. They admitted that they had done wrong and asked to be forgiven. They asked that God would help them follow Jesus.

"Is there anything else you want to tell God?" Mom asked.

"Yeah," Arthur said. "Thanks, God, for keeping Your promise to forgive me."

● *"If we confess our sins, He is faithful and just and will forgive us our sins and purify us from all unrighteousness." 1 John 1:9*

● **For Younger Children**

What does 1 John 1:9 say we should do about our sins?

When we confess our sins, it means we tell God what we've done wrong and ask Him to forgive us. Would you like to pray to God like Arthur did?

● **For Older Children**

What did Arthur ask God to do?

What did Arthur thank God for?

Why can you believe God's promise to forgive you?

Let's ask God to forgive us and help us do what is right.

● ●

FAMILY TIMES   Schedule time this week to be together as a family. Select one of these suggested activities to expand your family's understanding of God's love and forgiveness.

Heart of Love

Draw an outline of a heart on a large piece of paper. Write sentences or phrases in the heart telling ways God shows His love to you. Thank God in prayer.

Tip for Younger Children: A younger child may dictate his or her ideas to you.

Clues

Tell your family that you are going to give clues to help them guess the name of a person in Bible times who learned about God's love and forgiveness. Clue #1: The person is a man. Clue #2: He lived in Jerusalem. Clue #3: He was a Pharisee. Clue #4: He put Christians in jail. Clue #5: He had two names. Clue #6: One of his names started with the letter P. Clue #7: He wrote many letters we can read in the New Testament.

After family members guess the name Paul, briefly talk about how he came to believe Jesus was God's Son, or read Acts 9:1-16.

Tip for Younger Children: Read a children's book about Paul to your child. Bible story books are available from your church library or from your local Christian bookstore.

Playdough Shapes

As a family, follow the recipe on page 43 to make playdough.

Mix 2 cups flour, 1 cup salt, 1 teaspoon cream of tartar, 2 tablespoons oil, 2 cups cold water, and 1 teaspoon food coloring in a heavy pan. Cook over low to medium heat until dough pulls cleanly away from the sides of the pan. Knead the dough 8–10 times; then let it cool in an airtight container.

After the playdough is cool, use it to make shapes which remind you of God's love: heart, cross, Bible, happy face, etc.

Tip for Younger Children: Younger children will enjoy making shapes of their own choosing. You may make and talk about the suggested shapes.

God Gave Us the Bible

The Bible can be an intimidating book for grownups as well as children. Its size and scope and diversity all contribute to making many people feel like the Bible is beyond them.

Still, there are those who agree with Mark Twain's comment: "Most people are bothered by those passages in Scripture which they cannot understand; but as for me, I always noticed that the passages in Scripture which trouble me most are those which I do understand." Many of the clearest, simplest statements in the Bible are the ones we resist the most:

"Be kind and compassionate to one another, forgiving each other" (Eph. 4:32).

"And do not forget to do good and to share with others" (Heb. 13:16).

"Command them to do good, to be rich in good deeds" (1 Tim. 6:18).

"Pray continually" (1 Thes. 5:17).

"For whoever keeps the whole law and yet stumbles at just one point is guilty of breaking all of it" (James 2:10). This list of things we know the Bible tells us, but our personal desires often wish it didn't goes on. As you introduce your child to the Bible and its truths, remember that your example of reading and obeying God's Word is far more influential than any instructions or explanations you may give.

Key Verse
"All Scripture is given by God and is useful for . . . teaching how to live right."
2 Timothy 3:16, EB

Key Thought
God gave us the Bible to teach us about Himself and to guide us in how we should live.

WEEK 1

DAY 1

Laura was sitting in church next to her three brothers. At least, she was trying to sit in church. She was very warm, and her green sweater made her itch. It was hard to sit on chairs built for grownups. And the sermon seemed longer than usual this week.

Laura reached down and picked up the Bible her Sunday School teacher had given her. She opened it very quietly.

"Sh-h-h!" said her oldest brother, Ryan.

"I'm trying!" Laura whispered as quietly as she could.

"You can't read that anyway," Ryan whispered back.

"I can so!" Laura insisted. "I'm in second grade."

Ryan leaned closer to her. "The Bible is too hard. It's for grownups."

Laura thought, then she asked, "So why did my teacher give it to me?"

People sitting nearby were starting to turn and look at Laura and Ryan. Even Mrs. Finch who was hard of hearing turned all the way around in her seat and gave Laura a long, hard stare.

Dad put his finger to his lips and tried to look stern. Ryan tried to look as though he had been listening to the sermon all along. Laura just stared down at the open Bible in her lap and felt hotter, itchier, and more uncomfortable than ever.

Finally, Laura could stand it no longer. She looked up at her Dad, and in a LOUD whisper, she said, "But we were talking about the BIBLE!"

Even Mrs. Finch almost giggled.

On the way home after church, Dad asked what Laura and Ryan had been whispering about. Laura explained and then asked, "Why DID my teacher give me a Bible if it's too hard for kids to read?"

Dad answered. "There are many parts of the Bible you probably can't understand yet. There are even parts I don't understand, and I've been reading the Bible for years."

"Really?" Laura asked.

"Really," her dad answered. "But, Laura, the Bible also has many parts you can understand. As you're learning to read, it will get easier and easier. And I'll be glad to help you find some places where you can understand what God wants you to know. Deal?"

"Deal!" Laura answered with a big smile.

● *"Your word is a lamp to my feet and a light for my path." Psalm 119:105*

● **For Younger Children**

Have you ever felt like Laura did in church?

What does Psalm 119:105 say the Bible is like?

What does a lamp help you do?

How does the Bible help you?

● **For Older Children**

Do you agree or disagree with Ryan's comment that the Bible is for grown-ups? Why?

What's something you've read in the Bible that's hard to understand?

Let's ask God to help us understand His words.

DAY
2

It was bedtime for Josh, Laura, and Chris. Ryan was older and got to stay up a little later, but he liked listening to his mom or dad read to the younger kids.

"Read the Berenstain Bears!" Chris asked as he looked through a stack of well-worn books at the foot of his bed.

"Not them again!" Dad groaned. "Besides, I've got a great Bible story all picked out."

"No!" Josh demanded. "We want Berenstain Bears!"

"Yeah, Dad!" Ryan chimed in. "Lighten up!"

Dad tried to sound gruff. "Listen, you guys! You know I don't like those books. They always make the father look like a doofus!"

"That's why we like them!" Laura shouted.

Dad gave Laura a bear hug and roared, "What? You like books where the father is a doofus?"

"YES!" all four kids shouted together.

Just then Grandma Norris stuck her head in the doorway.

"What's all the ruckus in here?" she asked. "I thought you were supposed to be putting them to bed, Marvin, not starting a riot!"

"You're right, Mom," Dad answered. "Only a doofus would get this wild bunch wound up at bedtime. And we ALL know—dads aren't doofuses!"

"So what are you going to read, Dad?" Ryan asked.

"I'll make a deal with you," Dad said. "First, I'll read one of those AWFUL Bear books. Then I'll read the Bible story I picked out, so that you can go to sleep thinking about something worthwhile."

"Sounds wise to me," Grandma said to the four children. "Maybe your dad is pretty smart, after all."

"Grandma," Ryan said to her. "Dad does this every night. He thinks it's funny to make jokes about the books we choose."

"But I always choose a good Bible story, don't I?" Dad chimed in.

"Yeah, Dad. You do," Laura said. "Sometimes they're even better than Berenstain Bears."

"Just sometimes?" Dad asked.

"Don't push your luck, Marvin," Grandma said. "Besides, you'd better start reading pretty soon, or Chris will sleep through it all."

Sure enough, Chris was having a hard time keeping his eyes open. But he seemed to wake up a little when Dad opened the first book.

● *"I have hidden Your word in my heart that I might not sin against You."*
Psalm 119:11

● **For Younger Children**
What's your favorite book to read?
   What's a favorite Bible story you've heard?
   The stories in the Bible help us learn the best way to live.
Let's tell God thank You for the Bible.

● **For Older Children**
What kind of books do you like to read?
   Why is it important to read the Bible?
   What would you be like if you never read God's Word?

●●●●●●●●●●●●●●●●●●●●●●●●●●●●●●●●●●●●●●

WEEK 1

DAY
3

Josh sat on the front edge of his chair. Mr. Baldwin was telling the most exciting Bible story Josh had ever heard in Sunday School. The story was about Moses leading a big crowd of people through a hot, dry desert.

Josh could almost feel the hot sun burning down on Moses. He could almost feel his tongue getting dry and his lips starting to crack.

Just then, Mr. Baldwin raised both arms high over his head as if holding a big stick. Mr. Baldwin said, "Moses lifted his rod and then. . . ." Mr. Baldwin paused to be sure everyone was paying attention. Everyone was.

"Then," Mr. Baldwin said, as he swung his arms down hard. "Then, Moses hit a big rock with his rod! And a great stream of water gushed out, enough for everyone to have water to drink."

Josh leaned back in his chair. He folded his arms and looked straight at Mr. Baldwin. Then Josh said, "Yeah, right!" Mr. Baldwin looked straight at Josh. "What do you mean?" he asked.

"Water can't come out of a rock," Josh insisted.

Mr. Baldwin smiled. "Oh, but it DID, Josh!"

Josh's friend, Alan, asked, "How do we KNOW it really happened?"

Mr. Baldwin kept smiling. "You boys are really thinking this morning. I'll tell you three reasons why I believe this story and all the stories in the Bible really happened. OK?"

Josh and Alan both said, "OK."

"First, since God made water and rocks, it's easy to believe God could make water come out anywhere He wants to. Right?"

Josh and Alan both said, "Right."

"Second, we can find out about many Bible stories in other ways. People have read other ancient writings and discovered many of the places where Bible stories happened, and the Bible has never been wrong. That tells me the Bible is a book I can trust. Right?"

Josh and Alan both said, "Right."

"Third," Mr. Baldwin said, "I've always found that doing what the Bible says is the best way to live. That also tells me I can trust the Bible. So if the Bible says Moses hit the rock and God made water come out, I believe it happened just that way."

Josh and Alan were both silent. They were both thinking.

● *"For the Word of the Lord is right and true; He is faithful in all He does."*
Psalms 33:4

● **For Younger Children**

What are some exciting stories you've heard?

What was exciting about the Bible story Mr. Baldwin told?

Who has helped you learn about the stories in the Bible?

● **For Older Children**

Have you ever felt like Josh and Alan and wondered if the Bible was true?

This Bible story about Moses tells of a miracle—something only God can do. What are some other miracles the Bible tells about?

How would you explain to someone what it means to trust the Bible?

● ●

WEEK 1

DAY
4

When Ryan got off the school bus late each afternoon, he usually hurried up the road and then down the driveway into his family's farm. But today Ryan wanted to take as long as he could before he got home. He was carrying a note from his principal, a note he didn't want anyone in his family to see any sooner than necessary.

Ryan had been sent to the office for fighting. David Beecham had pushed Ryan's friend, Kyle, and before Ryan knew what was going on, David and Kyle were swinging at each other. Ryan had stepped in and tried to stop them. Then Ryan had gotten in trouble along with David and Kyle.

As Ryan headed toward the barn, he dreaded what his family would say. He was sure it would be even worse than the session with the principal.

"Hey, Ryan! You're a little late." It was Dad coming out of the barn. "What happened?"

"Uh . . . nothin'," Ryan mumbled.

"Are you sure? You don't sound too thrilled with life."

"Uh . . . I'm not," Ryan mumbled some more.

"Do you want to tell me about it, Ryan?" Dad asked. So Ryan told the whole story about David Beecham and Kyle.

"Ryan," Dad said slowly. "You know the Bible tells us that Jesus said, 'Blessed are the peacemakers.' "

"Some blessing I got," Ryan protested. "I should've let David and Kyle have it out."

"So why do you think the Bible tells us what Jesus said?" Dad asked.

"I dunno. But it doesn't sound like it fits at my school," Ryan said. "Maybe the Bible is too old-fashioned."

"Is it old-fashioned to want a world where people try to keep friends from hurting each other?" Dad asked.

"No, but I wish I hadn't gotten involved!" Ryan insisted.

"I understand that feeling," Dad said. "But God knows that if we stand aside when there's trouble, there'll just be more trouble and anger and hurt. Sometimes the Bible says things that are hard for us to do, but, all my life I've found the Bible's way is always best. Now let's go inside and explain this note to your mother."

● *"But those who do what Christ tells them to will learn to love God more and more." 1 John 2:5,* TLB

● **For Younger Children**

Have you ever been in an argument or fight? What happened?

What Bible command did Ryan forget to obey?

What does the Bible tell you to do instead of fighting or arguing?

● **For Older Children**

What did Jesus mean when He said, "Blessed are the peacemakers"?

What could Ryan have done besides fighting?

What are some Bible commands you try to obey?

DAY
5

Five-year-old Chris picked up Grandma Norris' Bible. He turned it over and looked at it carefully. Then he opened it and gently touched the worn and shabby edges.

"Grandma," Chris said. "Why don't you buy a nice new Bible?"

"Why do I keep this old Bible?" she asked. "Because your grandfather gave me this Bible many years ago, and it was the best present I ever received."

Chris snuggled in close to Grandma's side, and she slipped one arm around him.

"But wouldn't a new one be better?" Chris asked. "Or a video game?"

Grandma poked Chris in the tummy. "You know I wouldn't play a video game. But I've used this old Bible so long that it just seems to open right up to the places where I want to read."

"Let me try," Chris said.

"OK," Grandma said. "The 119th Psalm is a beautiful poem about how wonderful God's Word is. Open the Bible right near the middle, and I think you'll be very close to Psalm 119."

Chris stuck out his tongue and tried very hard to measure the middle of the Bible. Then he opened the old book.

"What's that?" he asked.

"You did it, Chris," Grandma said. "Look, up at the top of the page. It says P-S-A-L-M-S. That's Psalms. And we're just a few pages away from chapter 119."

Gently Chris turned the well-worn pages. Then he pointed his finger at some underlined words. "What's that say?" he asked.

Grandma said. "You've found one of my favorite verses. I marked it so I could read it again and again. It says, 'Thy testimonies are also my delight and my counselors.' Do you know what that means?"

"No," Chris answered.

"It's telling God," Grandma explained, "that His teachings, or His rules, give me pleasure—they make me happy. They give me good advice."

"The Bible makes you happy?" Chris asked.

"It sure does, Chris," Grandma said. "It's full of good news from God, and when you learn to read, you can have a Bible of your own."

"Grandma," Chris asked, "Can I have a nice old Bible like yours?"

Grandma gave Chris a hug. "When you get a Bible and start reading it every day, I'm sure it will end up looking very much like mine."

● *"Your rules give me pleasure; they give me good advice." Psalm 119:24,* EB

● For Younger Children

Why did Chris' Grandma like her old Bible?
> How did she say reading the Bible made her feel?
> Use a Bible to find the Psalms the way Chris did.

● For Older Children

What makes God's teachings so special?
> What good advice have you learned from the Bible?
> Let's ask God's help in obeying His teachings.

● ●

Schedule time this week to be together as a family. Select one of these suggested activities to expand your family's understanding of the benefits of reading the Bible.

FAMILY TIMES

Before and After Game

As a family, choose one of the Bible verses from this week. Letter each word of the verse on a separate index card or piece of paper. Mix up the cards and try to put them in order, saying the verse aloud several times. Then put all the cards in a bowl or hat. Each person takes a turn to choose a card. He or she tries to tell the word before and/or after the word on the card.

Hidden Treasure

Letter each of the Bible verses on page 44 on a separate index card. Tape a dime or quarter to each card. One at a time hide each card in your house. Each person takes a turn to search for the hidden treasure. Guide the person by saying "hot" (close) or "cold" (far away). When the treasure is found, read the Bible verse aloud.

Bookmark

Cut two 2x9-inch strips of clear Con-Tact paper for each person. Collect some small leaves or flower petals. Each person writes a Bible verse on a 1x6-inch strip of colorful paper. Place the paper and small leaves or flower petals on one of the strips of Con-Tact paper. Firmly press the other strip on top. Punch a hole at the top, and tie a yarn or ribbon bow through it.
> Tip for Younger Children: Write the verse your younger child chooses.

●●

When Hard Times Come

Key Verse
"[God] comforts us in all our troubles, so that we can comfort those in any trouble with the comfort we ourselves have received from God."
2 Corinthians 1:4

Key Thought
God always helps His children in times of trouble.

Many people expect that faith in God should give them immunity from the troubles which life brings. "Foxhole Christians" is a label applied to those who make promises to serve God if He will insulate them from whatever disaster looms over them.

While the Bible is full of promises of God's protection for His people (i.e., Psalm 91; Proverbs 1:33; 2:7-8; 12:21), it is also filled with accounts of godly people (i.e., Job, Joseph, Naomi, Hannah, Elisha, Jeremiah, Paul) who endured a wide variety of painful, even traumatic situations. While there were times when God miraculously delivered people from trouble, there were also times when He did not. In all cases, however, one thing was always true: God was always with His people, ready to comfort and strengthen them in hard times:

"When you pass through the waters, I will be with you; and when you pass through the rivers, they will not sweep over you." Isaiah 43:2

WEEK 2

DAY
1

●●

AJ had always called her grandmother "Mama." AJ remembered how much she used to love going to Mama's house. She remembered the delicious smell of the cookies Mama baked. AJ thought about the times Mama had braided her black, shiny hair and tied bows on her pigtails. She remembered how Mama's beautiful, dark brown eyes sparkled and how every part of Mama would shake when Mama laughed.

But now AJ was afraid to go to Mama's house.

Mama was sick. She was very, very sick. AJ's mom and dad had talked to AJ and her twin brother, DJ, and told them that Mama was so sick she probably could not live much longer. AJ's mom had said, "We're all going to drive over to Mama's tomorrow. She wants to see us, and it might help her feel better."

AJ did not want to go to Mama's house.

When she told DJ, he asked, "You don't want to see Mama? You always love to go to Mama's."

"Not anymore," AJ said. "I'm scared."

"Scared?" DJ asked, sounding like he had never been afraid of anything.

"Why are you scared to go to Mama's?"

" 'Cause Mama's dyin', " AJ said. "And 'cause . . . 'cause I don't want to see her almost dead." Then AJ said, "And 'cause I don't want to catch what made her sick."

DJ had to think about that for a moment. "Could we catch something really bad from Mama?"

"I don't know," AJ said. "But what if Mom and Dad catch something from Mama? What'll we do if they die too?"

"What if who dies?" Mom asked as she walked into the room.

"AJ's afraid we'll all catch something bad from Mama," DJ said.

"I see," Mom said, and she sat down next to AJ. "And maybe you're so sad that Mama is dying that you don't want to think about it at all."

A tear slid down AJ's cheek.

Mom put one arm around each of the twins and said, "We're all very sad that Mama is so sick, but it's good that we can help her and show we love her. And it's good to know that God loves her very much, and He loves us, and He's promised to always be with us, especially in hard times like this."

● *"I will say of the Lord, 'He is my refuge and my fortress, my God in whom I trust.' " Psalm 91:2*

● **For Younger Children**

How would you feel if you were AJ?

What makes you feel sad?

What can you remember about God when you feel sad?

● **For Older Children**

What are some hard times kids your age might have?

When has our family had a hard time?

How did God help us? Let's tell Him thank You.

● ●

WEEK 2

DAY
2

DJ heard a knock on the front door. He thought it might be his friend, Cory, wanting to get to school early to shoot baskets. So DJ took two quick bites of cereal and hurried to the door.

It wasn't Cory. It was the tall man with the moustache who worked at the paint store on the next street over. DJ's dog, Skippy, liked to bark at the men from that store when they played catch with old paint can lids on their lunch hour. The tall man started to say something, then he turned away from the door. DJ did not know what to do, so he went back inside and closed the door.

"Who was at the door, DJ?" his mom called from the bedroom.

"A man from the paint store," DJ answered.

"What did he want?" Mom asked.

"I don't know," DJ said. "He never said."

"That's odd," Mom said, coming down the hall. She looked out the window and saw the tall man still standing outside. DJ went back to his cereal while Mom stepped out to talk with the tall man.

A few minutes later, Mom came back inside. She called for DJ's sister, AJ, to come to the kitchen. The twins looked at Mom, waiting for her to say something.

"The man from the paint store had to tell me some very sad news," Mom said. "He was driving to work this morning and a dog ran in front of his car. He tried to stop, but couldn't. It was Skippy. He must've gotten out of the backyard."

The twins were silent. Finally AJ asked, "Is Skippy hurt?" Mom wiped her eyes and said, "Skippy's dead."

DJ didn't remember much more about that awful day, except that he felt a big, heavy lump in the back of his throat.

And he remembered that Mom put her arms around him and said, "I know how sad you are, DJ. And God knows how sad you are too. I'm so glad He loves us, especially in sad times like this."

● *"Blessed are those who mourn, for they will be comforted." Matthew 5:4*

● **For Younger Children**
Have you ever felt as sad as DJ? Why? What happened?
   Who comforted and helped DJ?
   Who comforts and helps you when you feel sad?

● **For Older Children**
Have your mom or dad ever told you sad news? What happened?
   What does Matthew 5:4 say about sad people?
   How can God comfort you when you are sad?

DAY
3

DJ hated having asthma attacks. They always seemed to happen when he was having fun, and they made it very hard to breathe. He hated having to take medicine. He really hated having to breathe through an inhaler. But he mostly hated feeling that other kids thought he was weird.

The only good thing DJ could see about his latest asthma attack was that he got to miss school. Staying home while his twin sister, AJ, had to go to school seemed like an adventure at first. But since he had to keep quiet and not do anything very active, it did not take DJ long to get bored. Especially since the only other person in the house was Mrs. Lucas, the world's crabbiest neighbor.

It seemed that every time DJ even moved, Mrs. Lucas told him he was supposed to stay still. And every time DJ took a deep breath, Mrs. Lucas was after him to breathe through that inhaler that he hated. Worst of all, she thought TV was bad for kids and wouldn't let him watch anything.

Finally, Dad came home from work. Mrs. Lucas gave him a long, crabby list of all the "problems" she had had with DJ. Dad listened to it all and thanked her for all her help. After she was gone, DJ breathed a sigh of relief. "I'm so glad you're home, Dad. Mrs. Lucas is a nag."

Dad sat down next to DJ. "Well, she did us one big favor by staying with you while Mom and I were at work. And we asked her to keep a close eye on you until your breathing gets back to normal. You know, DJ, Mrs. Lucas really likes you."

"I guess," DJ muttered.

Then Dad asked, "How about if we worked together to make a thank-you card to let her know we appreciate her help and concern?"

"Well, it's better than being bored," DJ answered. "Besides, she does make good brownies."

"She gave you brownies?" Dad laughed. "Then that deserves a card and flowers!"

"Let's not get carried away," DJ said. And he laughed too.

● *"Praise be to the God . . . of compassion and the God of all comfort."*
2 Corinthians 1:3

● **For Younger Children**
What was DJ's problem?
  Who helped him?

God helps us by giving us people who care for us. Who has cared for you when you've had a problem?

● For Older Children

Do you know someone like Mrs. Lucas? Who?

Why was it hard for DJ to be thankful for Mrs. Lucas' help?

Who are the people God gives to care for you—even when you aren't too thankful for their help?

● ●

WEEK 2

DAY
4

Being sick and missing school one day was a little bit of an adventure. Being sick and missing two days was just plain boring. DJ was staring out the window, wishing he did not have asthma and feeling as if everyone had forgotten him. Mom and Dad were at work. His twin sister, AJ, was at school. Even Mrs. Lucas, who was taking care of DJ, seemed to be less interested in how DJ was doing than she had been yesterday.

When DJ sat still, he felt fine, but as soon as he got up and walked across the room, it was hard to get a full breath of air. DJ would have to stop and take a few deep breaths. Occasionally, he had to use his inhaler to help clear his breathing passages.

At least, that was what happened yesterday and this morning. This afternoon he felt better, but he didn't want to take chances. So he sat. And stared out the window. And felt bored. And when DJ was bored, he was miserable.

Just then there was a knock at the front door. It reminded DJ of the morning a knock on the door announced that his dog had gotten run over. Now DJ felt even more miserable. He heard Mrs. Lucas talking to someone at the front door, and her high, scratchy voice just added to DJ's miseries. Suddenly, DJ's best friend, Cory, came into the room.

"Hi, Deej," Cory said. "Do you want to play?"

"I can't play yet," DJ said. "My asthma is still here."

"You can't even trade baseball cards?" Cory asked.

"I guess I could do that," DJ said. "Did you bring any good ones?"

For the next hour and twelve minutes, DJ was not bored. He and Cory looked at hundreds of cards and traded some of their best ones.

When it was time for Cory to go home, DJ said, "Thanks for coming Cory. I prayed this morning that I wouldn't have to spend the whole day here by myself."

● *"I sought the Lord and He answered me; He delivered me from all my fears."*
Psalm 34:4

● **For Younger Children**
What did DJ pray?
   How did God answer DJ's prayer?
   What's something you'd like to ask God? Let's pray right now.

● **For Older Children**
If you were really bored, what would you like to do?
   Why does God want to know about ALL our feelings?
   What promise does God make in Psalm 34:4?

● ●

WEEK 2

DAY
5

DJ's mom sat on the edge of his bed, while DJ ate one of the brownies she had baked for him. "Is it as good as the ones Mrs. Lucas made for you?"

"Mm-m," DJ said, licking his fingers. "Better."

"We've had some pretty tough times lately, haven't we?" Mom said.

"Mm-m," DJ said, licking several other fingers.

Mom kept on talking. "First, Mama died. Then a few weeks later Skippy got run over. Now you're having asthma trouble."

"Mm-mph," DJ said, taking another huge bite of brownie.

"You look like you've come through it all pretty well, Deej," Mom said.

DJ swallowed, then said, "I guess so." DJ was starting to think about something besides brownies. He was thinking about how much he still missed his grandmother and his dog. And how much he wanted to be healthy so he could go to school and play with his friends.

Mom reached over and picked up DJ's Bible from the shelf. "DJ," she said. "I'd like you to read a verse from the Bible that has helped a lot of people when life gets tough." She handed the Bible to DJ.

"OK," DJ said. "Where is it?"

"Can you find the Psalms?" she asked him.

"Sure," DJ said. "It's right in the middle. Where in Psalms?"

"Chapter 23," Mom said.

"Let me find it," DJ said.

"I want you to read verse 4," Mom said.

DJ found the right chapter and the right verse, and then he read out loud:
" 'Even though I walk through the valley of the shadow of death, I will fear

no evil, for You are with me; Your rod and Your staff, they comfort me.' That's all, Mom?"

"That's the verse, DJ," Mom said. "It tells us that even in the middle of the worst trouble that could possibly happen, 'the valley of the shadow of death,' we don't have to be afraid. And do you know why we don't have to be afraid?"

"Why?" DJ asked.

"Because," Mom said, "God will always be with us."

● *"Even though I walk through the valley of the shadow of death, I will fear no evil, for You are with me; Your rod and Your staff, they comfort me."*
Psalm 23:4

● **For Younger Children**

Why did DJ's mom want him to read Psalm 23:4?

What hard time does Psalm 23:4 talk about?

Let's thank God for always being with us and caring for us.

● **For Older Children**

Who are some people you know who have been through hard times? What's something scary you worry about happening?

What can you do when you're afraid of a hard time?

● ●

FAMILY TIMES   Schedule time this week to be together as a family. Select one of these suggested activities to expand your family's understanding of God's love and comfort in hard times.

Picture a Psalm

Read Psalm 23 together. Talk about your answers to the questions, "What is God like? How does God promise to care for us?" Then each person draws a picture of a scene described in one of the verses. (Stick figures are OK!)

Prayer Partners

Think of someone in your church, neighborhood, or community who is having a hard time. As a family, pray for that person. Ask God to give your family an opportunity to show God's love and comfort to the person.

For Parents Only

You may want help in talking with your child about hard times he or she may be facing. Your local Christian bookstore should have (or be able to order) helpful children's books about death, serious illness, divorce, child abuse, etc. Reading a book with your child will not only give helpful information but will provide an opportunity to talk about your child's feelings.

• •

God's Special Names

Most people in Western cultures are named either in honor of someone important to their parents or because of how the first name went with the family's last name. While people are often interested to discover the meaning of a particular name, rarely is a given name used to describe a person. Bill and Susie and Carlos and Daisy make us think of the people we know who are called by those names, not of any particular attributes the names suggest.

Nicknames are often another matter. If someone is called "Red," "Lefty," "Moose," or "Freckles," there's usually some obvious, expected characteristic which motivated people to attach that label.

Even though people do not often think of the original meaning behind their names, everyone views his or her name as more than just a label. Everyone winces a little when his or her name is misspelled or mispronounced, or worst of all, forgotten.

Is it any surprise, then, to discover that God's name is to be treated with great respect? Isn't it to be expected that God would use a variety of descriptive names which help people understand important truths about Him? A study of some of the names of God is an intriguing way to discover more about what God is really like.

Key Verse
"Let the name of the Lord be praised, both now and forevermore."
Psalm 113:2

Key Thought
The Bible uses special names for God which show us what He is like.

WEEK 3

DAY 1

• •

Robbie De La Rosa had been four years old for a long time. But it was still going to be a long time before he was five years old. He was getting tired of telling people he was "four-and-a-half years old" whenever they asked how old he was. That was part of the problem the morning that Robbie's mom stopped outside their apartment to talk with Mrs. Hernandez. Robbie got a frustrated look on his face when Mrs. Hernandez asked that question all grownups seem to ask children whenever they can't think of anything else to say.

"My you're getting big, Robbie!" Mrs. Hernandez said. "How old are you now?"

Being tired of being four-and-a-half was only part of the problem. The other part was that Robbie had just spent most of the morning over at his friend Gabriel's house. And Robbie had heard Gabriel say some very interesting words. Without really thinking about it, Robbie answered Mrs. Hernandez's question with a big sigh, and then he said, "O God, I'm four-and-a-half!"

Mrs. Hernandez thought Robbie's answer was funny. Robbie's mom didn't say anything right away, but when they got inside their apartment, she put her hand on Robbie's shoulder and said, "*Niño,* we must talk."

Robbie knew that whenever his mother used Spanish words (*Niño* means boy), she had something important to say.

"*Niño,*" she said again. "Have you heard someone say God's name when he was mad or upset?"

Somehow, Robbie knew he should be careful in how he answered Mom's question. Cautiously he said, "*Sí.*" Sometimes speaking Spanish made Mom a little less serious.

"Some people don't know that God's name is very special," Mom said. "Because as God is very special, the Bible tells us to be very careful about how we use His name."

"Can I use God's name when I pray?" Robbie asked.

"Of course," Mom laughed. "Or when we are talking about God. Those are good ways to use His name. But not when we're being silly or smart or trying to show that we're angry. And besides," she went on. "Next month is your birthday and you won't have to say you're four-and-a-half anymore."

It still seemed like a long, long time to Robbie De La Rosa.

● *"You shall not misuse the name of the Lord your God." Exodus 20:7*

● **For Younger Children**
What did Robbie do that his mom didn't like?

What do you need to remember about God's name?

What's a good thing to say or do when you're mad or frustrated like Robbie was?

● **For Older Children**
What was wrong about what Robbie said?

Have you ever accidentally (or even on purpose) used God's name in a wrong way?

Using God's name in a wrong way is called swearing. What can you do if you're around someone who swears a lot?

DAY
2

Hector was very excited as he burst in the front door. "Mom! Dad!" he yelled. "Someone robbed Mrs. Hernandez!"

Sometimes Hector De La Rosa exaggerated. That means he sometimes made things sound bigger or worse or more interesting than they really were. But this time, Hector was telling exactly what happened. The night before, while Mrs. Hernandez was sleeping, someone had broken a window in her apartment and had stolen some money and some jewelry and her new camera.

At first the news got everyone in the De La Rosa family as excited as Hector. "Did she see who did it?" "Did she call the police?" "Did the robber have a gun?" "Was it someone from a gang?" No one knew the answers to the questions they were all asking each other.

Later that night, the excitement of the news had gone away. In its place was a new feeling: *worry*. As Mrs. De La Rosa was tucking little Robbie in bed, he asked, "Will the robber come to our apartment tonight?"

"He better not!" Hector bragged. "I'll beat him up!"

"Oh, sure," said his big sister, Angela. Then she turned to her mother. "What if a robber comes to our place?"

"It sounds like everyone's a little bit nervous tonight," Mom answered. All three of her children were absolutely quiet. "It's OK to be afraid when you think of something that could be dangerous. That's why Dad and I have done everything we can think of to protect our apartment. But do you know the main reason we don't really have to be frightened?"

Angela and Hector and Robbie tried to think of an answer. They looked at each other. They looked at Mom. None of them said a thing. Finally, Mom spoke. "I'll tell you the main reason we don't have to be afraid. It's because the Bible says, 'The name of the Lord is a strong tower; the righteous run to it and are safe.' "

Angela and Hector and Robbie were all thinking about what Mom said. Still, none of them said a thing.

"When we pray tonight," Mom said, "let's think about one of God's names being 'a strong tower.' That will help us remember that He will take care of us, even when a robber is around."

Finally, Hector spoke. "A strong tower? God's name is a strong tower?"

Now Angela spoke. "I like that name. Strong tower is a good name."

Finally, Robbie spoke. "Can we pray now? I'm sleepy."

So they did.

"The name of the Lord is a strong tower; the righteous run to it and are safe."
Proverbs 18:10

● **For Younger Children**

Why did the children like the name "strong tower?"
   When might you or someone your age be afraid?
   Let's ask God to help us when we're afraid.

● **For Older Children**

What are some other objects, besides towers, that are big and strong?
   Why is God like a "strong tower"?
   When do you need to remember this special name for God?

● ●

WEEK 3

DAY
3

It was the middle of the night, and Robbie had a bad dream. He woke up yelling, and his big brother, Hector, sat straight up in his bed.

"Robbie!" Hector squealed. "What's wrong?"

Robbie was still half asleep and did not remember most of his dream. But he did remember one thing. "Robbers!" Robbie said. "There were robbers!"

"Robbers, Robbie?" Hector tried to ask. But Hector was still sleepy and the two words sounded so much alike that they came out sounding more like "Rubbers, Rubbie?" So he tried again. And it sounded worse: "Robbles, Robber?" Suddenly, both Robbie and Hector were wide awake. And they were laughing at each other, trying to think of the silliest sounds they could make out of the words, robber and Robbie.

Suddenly, Robbie stopped laughing. He turned on the light in their room. Squinting in the bright light, he announced, "I had a bad dream. About robbers."

"Oh," Hector said. "So, let's go back to sleep." He flicked off the light.

"But I was scared," Robbie protested in the dark.

"You didn't sound scared with all that laughing," Hector answered.

"That's 'cause I'm macho!" Robbie announced.

"Macho? You?" Hector asked.

"Señor Macho! That's me!" Robbie bragged, flexing his muscles.

"Oh, brother," Hector said. "That name really doesn't fit you."

Then the light went back on. It was Angela, their older sister. "I can hear every word you two say," she said. "What name doesn't fit Robbie?"

"Señor Macho," said Hector. "Robbie's trying to pretend he's not afraid when he has a bad dream about robbers."

Angela thought for a minute. "I've got an idea," she said.

"Instead of pretending you're brave, why not do what Mom said last night?"

"What's that?" Hector asked.

"Think about one of God's names that remind us of His help for us when we're afraid," Angela said.

"Like strong tower?" asked Robbie.

"Yeah. Or like 'Almighty,' " Angela suggested. "I've read that name in the Bible lots of times."

" 'Almighty,' " Hector repeated. "That's pretty strong."

"Better than 'macho,' " Angela said. "Now go back to sleep," and she flipped off the light one last time.

● *"God . . . is called by the Name, the name of the Lord Almighty." 2 Samuel 6:2*

● **For Younger Children**

Who helped Robbie when he had a bad dream?

"Almighty" means that God is more powerful than anything or anyone. How does knowing about God's power make you feel?

● **For Older Children**

What's a bad dream you've had? How did you feel? What did you do?

What has God done to show that He is mighty?

Robbie had bad dreams that made him afraid. When do you need to remember that God is almighty?

WEEK 3

DAY 4

"What do you want to be when you grow up, Robbie?" Robbie's older brother, Hector, wanted to be a hockey player. Robbie's big sister, Angela, wanted to be a plumber, like their dad. But Robbie, the youngest of the three De La Rosa children, did not want to think about growing up.

Growing up meant going to kindergarten. And high school. And college.

Growing up meant going in the army. And going to work. Robbie De La Rosa did not want to have to do any of those things. He really wanted to stay at home the rest of his life. And have his mom and dad take care of him. He wanted everything in his family to stay the same.

So Robbie answered Hector's question this way: "I just want to be ME!"

"You're always going to be you, silly," Angela said. "But you're still going to grow up and get to do a lot of other things."

"I don't want to grow up!" Robbie argued. "What if . . . What if . . ."

Hector interrupted. "What if what? What are you worried about?"

"Nothing!" Robbie snapped. "I'm not worried!" And Robbie stomped out of the room.

"Pretty noisy nothing," Hector muttered.

"Yeah," Angela said. "I remember when I was little. I worried about what might happen in the future. Like if something bad ever happened to Mom or Dad, who'd take care of me?"

"Don't tell anybody," Hector said as he got up to leave the room. "I still worry about that sometimes."

"Me too," Angela admitted. "It's a good thing God knows what's going to happen to us."

"He does?" Hector asked. "How does God know stuff that hasn't happened yet?"

"I don't know," Angela answered. "But I know that one of God's names is 'the Eternal God.' That means He's God of the future, and the present, and the past."

"Are you sure?" Hector asked.

"Maybe we should ask Mom or Dad," Angela suggested.

"Good idea," Hector said. So they did just that.

"The Lord is the true God; He is the living God, the eternal King." Jeremiah 10:10

- **For Younger Children**

  "Eternal God" means that God has always been alive and that He always will be alive. God also knows everything that has happened or will happen to us.

  What's something that happened to you last week?

  What's something you're planning to do tomorrow?

  Let's tell God thank You for always taking care of us.

- **For Older Children**

  What do you think the parents said to explain the name, "Eternal God"?

  Why do you think it's a good thing that God is eternal?

  Why is it it good that God knows what will happen to us in the future?

WEEK 3

DAY
5

● ●

"How many names does God have?" asked Robbie De La Rosa.

"Lots," said his sister Angela.

"I only know two," said their brother Hector.

"Which ones?" Angela asked.

"I know God," Hector said. "And Lord."

"Is one of those His middle name?" Robbie asked.

"I don't think so," Angela said. "I know more than two of God's names."

"I betcha don't," said Hector.

"Betcha I do," said Angela. "Remember, one of His names is 'strong tower.' "

"Oh, yeah," said Hector. "I knew that one."

"And," said Angela, " 'Almighty.' The Bible calls Him 'God Almighty.' "

"I knew that one too," Hector said.

"And, 'Eternal God,' " said Angela.

"Oh, yeah," said Hector.

"And there's lots more in the Bible," Angela said.

"But I don't know them all," Robbie said, sounding worried.

"I don't think that matters," Angela said.

"So which name should we use?" Robbie asked.

"You mean when we pray?" Hector asked back.

"Yeah," Robbie answered.

"You can use whichever name you want, Robbie," Angela explained. "God won't get confused."

Robbie looked relieved. "Oh, good," he said. "Sometimes I forget stuff."

"I bet God understands," Hector assured his little brother. " 'Cause even I forget things sometimes."

"More than sometimes," Angela laughed.

"Yeah," Hector laughed too. "More than sometimes."

"Maybe I'll just call Him 'Father,' like Jesus did," Robbie said.

"See," said Angela. "There's a name Hector and I both forgot."

"Way to go, Robbie! You're better at remembering than you thought," Hector added.

"I guess so," Robbie said. Then he jumped up and started up the hall, "Hey, Mom!" he yelled. "Guess which one of God's names I remembered?"

Mom couldn't guess.

● *"O Lord, our Lord, how majestic is Your name in all the earth!" Psalm 8:1*

● **For Younger Children**

How many of God's names can you say?

Which of God's names is your favorite to think about? Why?

Which of God's names do you use when you pray?

● **For Older Children**

Which of God's names tells the most about Him?

What does Psalm 8:1 mean when it says that God's name is majestic?

Think of one characteristic of God. What name would you call God to show that characteristic?

● ●

Schedule time this week to be together as a family. Select one of these suggested activities to expand your family's understanding of God.

FAMILY TIMES

Like a Rock

One of God's names is "the Rock" (Psalm 18:2). From your backyard, the beach, or a park, collect a fist-sized rock for each person. Wash and dry the rock. Then use paints or felt-tip pens to write one of God's special names on the rock.

Tip for Younger Children: Write the name your younger child chooses. He or she will enjoy using paints or felt pens to decorate the rock.

Charades

Letter each of these names for God on a separate piece of paper: Shepherd, Father, Guide, Comforter, Rock, Almighty, Savior, King. Put the papers in a bowl or hat. Each person takes a turn to choose a paper. He or she panto-mimes (acts out without words) the name on the paper. Others try to guess the name — and tell why God is called by that name.

Tip for Younger Children: Whisper the name to the child and suggest appropriate actions as needed.

Candlelight Talk

Sit with your family in a darkened room. Talk about the disadvantages and problems of living in the dark. As a grownup lights a candle, explain that another name for God is Light. Ask, "What difference does the light of this candle make in our room?" Then talk about the difference knowing God makes in our lives. Thank God for being our "light."

God the Father, Son, and Holy Spirit

The doctrine of the Trinity is one of the most difficult biblical ideas to understand, let alone to explain to a child. When introduced to the idea of God the Father, God the Son, and God the Holy Spirit, it is not at all uncommon for a child to assume there must be three separate Gods.

Most simple explanations of the Trinity have ended up being judged to be heresy, for they tend to ignore some essential factor that Scripture states about the nature of God.

It is also common for young children to confuse the persons of God the Father and God the Son. When asked a question which should be answered "Jesus," a young child is as likely to say "God," as to give the correct answer.

Similarly, a question which should be answered "God" is likely to be answered "Jesus." Adding the third person of the Godhead makes matters even more complicated.

Rather than trying to define for children the differences between each person of the Trinity, it is generally best to emphasize what is equally true of each. Simple affirmations of what is clearly taught in Scripture are essential, even when we seemingly must scratch our heads and wonder at how such a thing can be.

Key Verse
"I will ask the Father, and He will give you another Counselor to be with you forever."
John 14:16

Key Thought
The Bible teaches that there is one God who is Father, Son, and Holy Spirit.

WEEK 4

DAY 1

Jessie's best friend Monica had spent the night at Jessie's house. They had a wonderful time on Saturday night, eating pizza and popcorn and doing everything they could think of to annoy Jessie's big brother, Eric. They wanted to stay awake all night, but Jessie's mom finally made them go to bed. Jessie tried to stay awake even then, but it's hard not to fall asleep when you're snuggled up in a warm bed.

The next morning, Monica had gone with Jessie and her family to Sunday School and church. It was Monica's first time at church, and she was full of questions on the way home:

"Why do you try to memorize those verse things?" Monica asked.

"What does B-I-B-L-E spell?" Monica asked.

"Did you really know the words to all those songs?" Monica asked.

"Why did that man talk so long?" Monica asked.

"Who was that man with the sheep in that big picture?" Monica asked.

Jessie hardly had time to try to answer one question before Monica was asking another one. And then Monica asked a question that Jessie could not answer. The question was, "Is there just one God, or are there three gods?"

"Three gods?" Jessie asked. "Who said there could be three gods?"

Monica answered, "I heard someone talk about God the Father, God the Son and . . . and . . . and, God the something else."

"The Holy Spirit?" Jessie asked.

"Yeah!" Monica said. "That's the one! God the Holy Spirit. That makes three gods, doesn't it?"

"Oh," Jessie said, sounding worried. "I don't think so. It couldn't mean that."

"Well," Monica said firmly, "That's what it sounds like to me."

"I guess it does sort of sound like that," Jessie agreed. "But I know it's not right."

"Sounds right to me," Monica insisted.

"I wonder whom I could ask to find out the real answer," Jessie wondered.

"Would your brother know?" Monica asked.

"Eric?" Jessie didn't think Eric knew anything. "No way! Anybody but Eric!"

● *"And the Holy Spirit descended on Him in bodily form like a dove. And a voice came from heaven: 'You are My Son, whom I love; with You I am well pleased.' " Luke 3:22*

● **For Younger Children**

What do you like to do when you have a friend over?

Why did Monica ask so many questions?

What should you do when you have a question about God?

● **For Older Children**

In Luke 3:22 what did God the Father say about God the Son?

What have you heard about God the Holy Spirit?

Whom can you ask to find out more about the Holy Spirit?

WEEK 4

DAY
2

Jessie and her friend Monica were fixing an afternoon snack. Jessie was spreading soft cheese on crackers and Monica was trying to peel a banana so she could slice it in half.

"My mom says somebody should put zippers on banana peels," Monica grunted as she struggled with a very tough banana. "I'm pushing so hard on the end of this banana, I'm going to turn it to mush."

"Why don't you just slice it with the peeling on?" Jessie asked.

"That's a good idea," Monica said with relief. "How come I never thought of that?"

"I never thought about there maybe being three gods," Jessie said.

"Are you still wondering about how many gods there are?" Monica asked as she sliced open the banana.

"Sort of," Jessie answered. "I know there's really only one God, but I just don't understand about God the Father, God the Son, and God the Holy Spirit."

"What's to understand?" Monica responded as she peeled the sections of the banana. "There's just gotta be three gods."

"No," Jessie insisted. "I know I've heard something in the Bible about only one God. And I know at Christmas I've heard about God the Father coming to earth as a Baby."

Monica finished putting the banana slices on napkins as Jessie handed her several crackers with cheese. "Yeah," Monica said. "I've heard that Father and Son part somewhere before too. But that Spirit part sounds spooky to me."

"I still think we should find someone to ask about it," Jessie said. "Someone besides my brother! We could ask my dad, but he'd want to talk about it forever. Let's go ask my mom!"

Monica waved her hand and pointed to her mouth. She was trying to swallow a large mouthful of crackers and cheese. Finally, she could talk. "Good idea. But could I have a glass of milk first? I can't eat crackers and talk at the same time."

● *"Go and make followers of all people in the world. Baptize them in the name of the Father, and the Son, and the Holy Spirit." Matthew 28:19,* EB

● **For Younger Children**
What do you like to eat for snack?

What were Jessie and Monica confused about?

What ideas about God have ever confused you?

● **For Older Children**

Why was Jessie sure there is just one God?

Why was Monica sure there is more than one God?

How many gods do you think there are? Why?

●●

"Mom!" Jessie called. "Mom! Hey, Eric! Where's Mom?" Jessie's older brother, Eric, looked up from his magazine.

"She went to the store," he answered. "What do you need?"

"Monica and I wanted to ask her a question," Jessie said. "When will she be back?"

"Depends," Eric said. "If she checks out that sweater sale, she could be awhile. What's your question?"

Jessie was just getting ready to say "Never mind," when Monica answered instead. Monica said, "We're trying to find out if there are three gods or just one God."

"Wow!" Eric said. "Heavy duty stuff!"

"Yeah," Monica said, smiling at Eric.

Eric put down his magazine. "So how come three gods? Why not two gods or four gods? Why three?"

This time Jessie answered first. "Because of Father, Son, and Holy Spirit, brother. Any ninny knows that."

"Well, I'm not any ninny," Eric said. "I'm a special ninny. And the Father, Son, and Holy Spirit aren't three different gods. They're all one God."

Now Monica jumped in. "That doesn't make sense, Eric. How can one God be the Father and the Son and the Holy Spirit?"

"Hey, if I knew the answer to that, I'd be as smart as God," Eric said.

"And we all know," Jessie said quickly, "that there's no chance of you ever being that smart!"

"Thank you, Little Sister," Eric said with exaggerated politeness. "But do you want an answer to your question?"

"Sure!" Monica answered.

"Well then," Eric said. "Someone explained it to me once that there is just one, true God who shows Himself to people in three ways. Like, when

He takes on human form, He's God the Son."

"Like disguises?" Jessie asked, starting to think that perhaps her brother might know something after all.

"No," Eric said. "It's not like God pretends to be the Son for a while and then switches back to being the Father. He really IS the Father. And He really IS the Son. Both at the same time."

"But what about the Spirit?" Jessie asked.

"I don't know," Eric admitted. "God must be a whole lot greater and more complicated than we can understand."

"At least more than YOU can understand," Jessie laughed.

"That's the thanks I get for trying to help out?" Eric laughed with her. Monica decided she might as well laugh too.

● *"Jesus said, 'I and the Father are One.' " John 10:30*

● **For Younger Children**
What are some things you know about Jesus, God's Son, that are also true about God the Father?

Because Jesus was kind and loving, does that mean God the Father is kind and loving also? Why?

● **For Older Children**
Eric had heard that the one true God shows Himself to people in three ways. Have you heard any other ways of explaining the Father, Son, and Holy Spirit?

The idea of one God who is so great He exists in three Persons is called the doctrine of the Trinity. Why is it OK that people can't understand everything about the Trinity?

Why is it important for us to know that Jesus and God the Father are really the same?

WEEK 4

DAY 4

It was dinnertime and Jessie was playing in front of Monica's house. "Eric!" Mom said. "Please run to Monica's and tell Jessie it's time for dinner."

"Why don't we eat without her?" Eric joked. "Think of how quiet dinner would be."

"Eric!" Mom said. "Please, just go get your sister!"

"OK, Mom," Eric said as he started out the door. "Just kidding!" Eric walked down the street to find Jessie. Jessie and Monica were busy trying to coax a squirrel into trying some peanuts they had set on a tree branch.

"Dinner, Jessie!" Eric shouted when he saw her.

"Sh-h-h!" Jessie snapped. "You'll scare our squirrel."

"He'll come back when you're inside eating!" Eric said.

"I don't want to come in yet," Jessie argued. "It's too early for dinner."

"It's time," Eric replied. "Mom told me to get you."

"I don't believe you," Jessie said. "I'm going to stay."

"OK," Eric said as he started home. "You're going to be in trouble."

"Do you think you should go with him?" Monica asked Jessie.

"No," Jessie answered. "He was trying to fool me."

But Jessie was wrong. It really was time for dinner. And when Eric told Mom that Jessie hadn't come home, Mom had to go after her. That did not make Mom happy!

"Jessie," Mom said as they hurried home together. "When Dad or I send Eric to give you a message, it's just as if we came ourselves."

"I'm sorry, Mom," Jessie said. "I thought Eric was teasing me."

"People in a family have to trust each other," Mom said.

"Well," Jessie said, "it's easier to trust you and Dad than Eric."

Finally, the family was all together at the dinner table.

After Dad thanked God for the food, Jessie announced, "I'm sure glad we can count on whatever Jesus says about God. I'm glad we don't have to wonder if He might be teasing us."

"I never thought about that before," Mom said. "But you're right. Since God and Jesus are really One, we can always be certain that what Jesus says about God is true."

"Now if I could just be certain about Eric," Jessie muttered.

● *"Jesus answered, 'I am the way and the truth and the life. No one comes to the Father except through Me.' " John 14:6*

● **For Younger Children**

How did Jessie think Eric was tricking her?

Why can we be certain that what Jesus says about God is true?

What's something we learn about God from Jesus' words?

● **For Older Children**

What difference do you think it makes to know that Jesus is truly God, not just someone who talked about God?

What do you think Jesus meant when He said that He is the only way for anyone to reach God the Father? (John 14:6) Why is this important for us to understand?

● ●

WEEK 4

DAY
5

"I've got it all figured out," Eric told his sister, Jessie.

"Figured what out?" Jessie asked.

"Don't you remember?" Eric snorted. "You and Monica were asking all those questions about how many Gods there are?"

"Oh, yeah," Jessie said. "Monica thought there were three Gods."

"Well, Dad showed me some verses where the Father, Son, and Holy Spirit are all mentioned together," Eric explained.

"So, what did you figure out?" Jessie asked again.

"Well," Eric answered, "I didn't figure it ALL out. But one verse Dad showed me talks about God—that's God the Father, you know."

"I know," Jessie said.

"Well, the verse says that God has sent the Spirit of His Son to be within us." Eric talked as though he didn't think Jessie would understand him. "That's God the Spirit and God the Son, right there together in one verse with God the Father."

"I know," Jessie said again. "So, what did you figure out?"

"Well, to be honest," Eric scratched his head. "I'm still not sure I really understand about one God and three persons. But when I think of God as three Persons, it helps me realize how great God is. See, God the Father, the Son, and the Holy Spirit each do different things to help us."

"Different?" Jessie asked. "Different how?"

"Well, just think about God as Father. We can think about all the good things our parents do for us, and that helps us know that God does even better stuff."

Jessie interrupted. "Like He takes care of us?"

"Yeah," Eric said. "Like that. And we know that God the Son is our example, and He died to show us how much God really loves us."

"That makes sense," Jessie agreed.

"And God the Spirit is right here in us," Eric added. "Helping us every day to live the way God wants us to.

"Sounds good to me," Jessie said.

"I told you I had it all figured out," Eric added.

● *"Since you are God's children, God sent the Spirit of His Son into your hearts." Galatians 4:6,* EB

● **For Younger Children**

What are some things a good father does for his child?

God the Father is even better than the most perfect father on earth. What are some things God does for you?

● **For Older Children**

Eric told Jessie that Jesus is our example. What are some things we can do to be more like Jesus?

How does it make you feel to think about being one of God's children?

How does the Holy Spirit help members of God's family?

● ●

Schedule time this week to be together as a family. Select one of these suggested activities to expand your family's understanding that God is Father, Son, and Holy Spirit.

FAMILY TIMES

Family Worship

Lead your family in a brief time of worship before or after a meal or before bedtime. Include a prayer of thanks for God the Father, God the Son, and God the Holy Spirit. Sing one or more familiar choruses or hymns which praise God as Father, Son, or Holy Spirit. Read aloud the following poem, with other family members repeating each line after you:

> "God the Father loves each one,
> So He gave His only Son.
> Jesus died so we could live,
> All our sins He will forgive.
> God the Spirit helps us know,
> All we need to learn and grow.
> Thank You God for loving me,
> I'm glad I'm in Your family."

The Apostles' Creed

The Apostles' Creed is one of the oldest statements of Christian belief. While there are words and concepts in the creed which are difficult for children to understand, children still enjoy learning and reciting at least part of this declaration which has been spoken by Jesus' followers around the world. Select as much of the creed to use with your children as you feel will be meaningful to them. Consider their ages, interest, and whether or not they have already been introduced to this creed at church.

Bible Verse Banner

Make a banner or poster illustrating one of this week's Bible verses. Family members may work independently on their own banners, or they may work with a partner, or the whole family may work together on one group project. Select a key word or idea in the verse and draw a simple picture or symbol to illustrate it. Then letter the words of the verse around that symbol. Hang the banner in a place where all family members will see it at least several times each day.

God Loves Us As a Father or Mother

For vast numbers of people, the image of God as loving Father is very meaningful and comforting. Rather than being shown to us as an impersonal force or a disinterested deity, He is revealed as having the deepest concern for our well-being.

Sadly, there are large numbers of people whose experience with a human father has made this picture of God difficult to accept. The term "father" conjures up images of abuse or absence for these people. Still, there remains within all of us the ability to conceive of an ideal father or mother.

This week, as you and your child consider the idea of God as loving father, give attention to the many ways your life is a living illustration to your child of God's great love.

Key Verse
"Yet to all who received Him, to those who believed in His name, He gave the right to become children of God."
John 1:12

Key Thought
The Bible teaches that God is a loving Father of those who are His children.

WEEK 1

DAY
1

The Gorman twins were wrestling with Dad. DJ had a bear hug around one of Dad's legs. AJ was behind Dad with her arms wrapped tightly around his neck. Dad was huffing and puffing and grunting—and laughing. The twins were squealing and laughing.

Suddenly, Dad reached up over his head and grabbed AJ's waist. Quickly he pulled her across his shoulder and set her down on top of DJ. "I'm the champion!" Dad shouted.

"Not yet!" DJ and AJ shouted back. "We've got your legs!"

And they did. Each twin hung on to a different leg.

"OK! I surrender!" Dad agreed.

"Not yet!" DJ and AJ shouted again. "We're going to get you down!"

"Oh, no, you're not!" Dad laughed, and he began tickling the twins in their ribs.

"No fair! No fair!" they yelled, as they squirmed away, laughing. Then all three of them sat as each of them tried to catch his breath.

"I think *(puff-puff)* that you two *(huff-huff)* are getting too big *(gasp)* for me," Dad wheezed.

Just then Mom came into the room, looked at the furniture that had been pushed back to the walls, and said, "I declare this match . . . a draw! Now it's time to put this room back together, then you two can read QUIETLY for fifteen minutes before bed."

"Aw, Mom," AJ moaned.

"We're too tired," DJ groaned.

"Let's see how strong you two really are," Dad laughed.

"Grab onto that end of the couch. Now, all together, PULL!"

After the furniture was back in place, the twins each grabbed a book. After a minute or two, DJ asked, "Do you think Dad was really trying his hardest?"

" 'Course not," AJ said. "He just pretended to be worn out."

Another minute or two passed. Then DJ asked, "Do you think God is anything like Dad?"

"Say what?" AJ asked.

"Is God anything like Dad?" DJ repeated. "Doesn't the Bible say God is like a father?"

"Yeah," AJ answered. "But I don't think God wrestles and acts silly."

"Or snores," DJ said. Both twins burst out laughing.

Mom's voice came from down the hall, "That doesn't sound like reading!"

The twins stopped giggling and opened their books again. DJ whispered, "I still wonder if God is anything like Dad."

AJ whispered back, "I sure hope so."

● *"How great is the love the Father has lavished on us, that we should be called children of God." 1 John 3:1*

● **For Younger Children**

Why were AJ and DJ having so much fun?

How would you describe a good mom or dad?

What do you think God is like?

● **For Older Children**

What are some things good parents do for their children?

Why did AJ and DJ hope that God is like their dad?

What do you learn about God from 1 John 3:1?

DAY
2

• •

"So you two want to know if God is like your dad," Mrs. Gorman said to AJ and DJ, her nine-year-old twins. Mrs. Gorman and the twins were running water into the kitchen sink. They were trying to find a leak in a flat tire from AJ's bike.

"We sorta wondered," AJ said.

"How will we know where this inner tube leaks?" her brother DJ asked.

Mom had shown the twins how to take the tire off the wheel. DJ had pumped up the flat tube, but he didn't see a leak anywhere.

"Turn off the water, AJ," Mom said. "Did either of you think of any ways that God might be a little bit like Dad?"

"Well, Dad's real kind, like God's supposed to be," DJ offered. "But I still don't see any leak in this tube."

"Put the tube in the sink," Mom said, "and watch."

"Dad's pretty smart," AJ said, "but I'll bet God's smarter."

DJ put the bottom part of the inner tube in the water. "God better be smarter than Dad," he said. "I had to show Dad how to use the VCR. And what's with this tube? Nothing's happening."

"Try turning the tube," Mom suggested. "Put the dry part under water."

DJ turned the tube. AJ looked up from the sink and said to her mom, "And sometimes Dad blames me for things DJ did!"

"Bubbles!" DJ yelled. "Look at the bubbles." A thin stream of bubbles gushed out of the inner tube.

"That's the leak we have to patch," Mom said. "And you're right, AJ. Dad's not perfect and he's not as smart as God. But if you think about some of the things you love best about him, it might help you understand some things about what God is like."

"What do we do with the tube, now?" DJ asked.

"First dry it off," Mom answered.

"I hope God's a little bit like you too, Mom," AJ said. Mrs. Gorman looked down at her daughter. "And, AJ," Mom said, "I hope that the more you learn about God, the more you'll know you can always trust Him and love Him."

"The tube's dry," DJ said.

"Good work, DJ," Mom said. "You found the leak, so let's have AJ put on the patch."

• *"Dear friends, let us love one another, for love comes from God." 1 John 4:7*

● **For Younger Children**

What did AJ and DJ want to know about God?

What did they find out?

What did AJ and DJ like about their dad?

Let's tell God thank You for people who show God's love to us.

● **For Older Children**

How did AJ and DJ say their dad was like God? How was their dad different from God?

What are some things you love best about your mom or dad?

What have you learned about God's love from your mom or dad?

● ●

WEEK 1

DAY 3

"Hey, Cory!" DJ yelled across the street to his friend. "Can you play?"

"I guess," Cory said, not sounding very interested.

DJ looked both ways, then scooted across the street. "I thought your dad was gonna take you to the hockey game today," DJ said to Cory.

"Yeah," Cory grunted, kicking his foot at some loose grass.

"But he had to work today, so we can't go."

"Bummer!" DJ said.

"Yeah," Cory grunted again, this time kicking his other foot. "But Dad's always tellin' me we're gonna do something, and then he has to work or go to a meeting or something."

"Bummer!" DJ said again. He walked over to the curb and sat down. Cory followed behind him. He picked up a stick and began poking at some leaves in the gutter.

"Does your dad break promises like that?" Cory asked.

"Not usually," DJ said. Now he picked up a stick and began poking at Cory's stick. "One time he got the flu, and we couldn't go out for pizza. But I don't think that was his fault."

"You're lucky," Cory said, waving his stick in the air like a sword.

"My dad's OK," DJ said, getting up and hitting his stick against Cory's. "But he's not perfect. That's what I told my mom when she told me God's kind of like a dad." Now both boys were vigorously swinging their sticks, lunging and ducking and poking.

"Do you think God is anything like your dad?" Cory asked, suddenly stopping the sword fight.

"Well, I know God's smarter," DJ said. "But Dad's kind and tries to do what's right and does his best to take care of me and AJ. I think those are things like God does."

Cory thought for a few moments. Then he looked at DJ.

"Maybe," Cory said, "God is the way I wish my dad was."

● *"God is not a human being, and He will not lie. . . . What He says He will do, He does. What He promises, He makes come true." Numbers 23:19,* EB

● **For Younger Children**

Why was Cory disappointed?

Why did DJ say his dad was like God?

The Bible tells us God always keeps His promises. What's one promise God has made to us?

● **For Older Children**

What were the good things DJ said about his dad?

What has God done for you or our family to show that He is like a loving father or mother?

How do you feel about God's love for you?

● ●

WEEK 1

DAY
4

DJ and his twin sister, AJ, were climbing the tree in their backyard. "It's weird climbing this tree when there aren't any leaves on it," AJ said.

"It's neat," DJ said. "I can climb higher and see a lot farther this way."

"Look!" AJ pointed. "I can see our school over there!"

"And over there is the mall!" DJ said.

"I wonder," AJ asked, "if we could see all the way to heaven from up here?"

DJ was concentrating on trying to climb to a higher branch, so he didn't answer. So AJ answered her own question.

"Probably not," she said. "We're high, but not that high."

"I am so up high," DJ insisted, not having really paid attention to what AJ was saying.

But now AJ was moving to another branch and not listening to what DJ said. Besides, thinking about seeing all the way to heaven reminded her of something.

"Hey, DJ," she said after she got to the perch she wanted to reach.

"Yeah?" DJ asked.

"We were talking about God being kind of like Dad, remember?"

"I remember," DJ said.

"Well," AJ went on, "Is there anyone we know who's really like God? Even more than Dad is?"

"How about Pastor Lewis?" DJ asked.

"Or our Sunday School teacher?" AJ asked. "I really like Mrs. Lincoln."

"What about Mom?" DJ suggested. "She's really neat!"

"I'd vote for her!" AJ said.

Suddenly the twins became silent. DJ held tightly to a tree branch and looked up into the sky. AJ hung onto her branch and also looked up.

"You know what?" AJ asked after a few moments.

"What?" DJ asked.

"I bet God is better than all those together," his sister said.

● *The Lord said, "As a mother comforts her child, so will I comfort you."*
Isaiah 66:13

● **For Younger Children**

What made AJ think about heaven and God?

Who were some of the other people the twins thought were like God?

What does Isaiah 66:13 say about God?

When might you need God to comfort you?

● **For Older Children**

What are some characteristics of people you know that remind you of what God is like?

Why did AJ say that God is better than all the good people the twins had named?

Why do you think it's important for people to know what God is really like?

● ●

WEEK 1

DAY

5

"Is dinner ready?" Mr. Gorman asked as he came in the door. "I'm hungry as a bear!"

"What do bears eat, Dad?" asked AJ.

"They sure don't eat casserole," said DJ.

"You two knuckleheads," Dad laughed. "You know I don't want to eat what bears eat. I was making a comparison."

"What's a comparison?" AJ asked.

Just then Mom came into the living room.

"AJ, you know what a comparison is," Mom said.

"I do?" AJ asked.

"Sure," Mom said. "We've been talking all day about how the Bible uses comparisons to help us understand what God is like."

AJ looked puzzled, but DJ thought he knew what Mom was talking about. "You mean when the Bible says God is like Dad, that's a comparison?"

"God is like me?" Dad asked, looking first at his wife, then at the twins.

"You know, Dad," DJ said. "Heavenly Father and all that."

"Yeah, Dad," AJ said. "It's a comparison. Isn't it?"

"I guess you're right, AJ," Dad said. "The Bible lets us compare God to some people or things we know about. That helps us understand God better."

"But God's more than just a regular dad," DJ said. "He's . . . well, He's God!"

"This is all very interesting," Dad said. "But I definitely smell something from the kitchen."

"The casserole!" Mom yelled. "C'mon, everyone! Let's eat!"

The family was quickly seated around the dinner table. After DJ prayed and Dad dished out some casserole for everyone, Mom said she wanted to make an announcement.

"Can we eat while you announce?" DJ wanted to know.

"Of course," Mom said. "I just wanted to make sure you understand one thing about the Bible comparing God to a father or mother. Even when a parent makes a mistake or does something wrong . . ."

"Like almost burning the casserole?" AJ asked.

"Or even worse," Mom said. "It doesn't mean God makes mistakes. God is much greater and more perfect than anything or anybody we can compare Him to."

● *"Though my father and mother leave me, the Lord will receive me."*
Psalm 27:10

● **For Younger Children**

Who is a loving person you could compare God to?

What did the twins learn about how God is different from anyone else?

What have you learned from these stories about what God is like?

83

● **For Older Children**

What mistakes might a parent make?

How do we know that God doesn't make mistakes?

Let's tell God thank You for His greatness and perfection.

● ●

FAMILY TIMES

Schedule time this week to be together as a family. Select one of these suggested activities to expand your family's understanding of God as a loving parent.

Tell a Friend

Together think of one or more people who have shown God's love to you. Write a family letter (or write individual letters) thanking the person for his or her caring actions.

Tip for Younger Children: Your child may dictate his or her letter to you.

Pass It On Game

Explain to your family that this game will help remind them to pass on God's love to other people. Work together to list four or five ways God's love can be shown to others—kindness, forgiveness, helpfulness, patience, sharing, etc. Write each word or phrase on a separate index card. Put the cards in a bowl or hat. At breakfast the next day, each person chooses one card. During the day each person shows God's love in the specific way listed on the card. At dinner, each person shares how they were able to "pass it on" during the day.

Tip for Younger Children: A parent should act as a partner with a younger child, choosing one card as a pair and planning together how to demonstrate the word on the card.

Backward Verse

Secretly choose one of the Bible verses from this week. Write the verse backward on a large sheet of paper. Family members try to read the verse and then tell what they learn about God from the verse.

Everyone Has Sinned

It has always been easier to recognize the other person's sin than to admit our own. It seems only natural to explain our "failures" as being much less serious than the "crimes" committed by others. Yet Scripture gives us no room to let ourselves escape the blame for our acts of disobedience. Among the things we share in common with all other people are two ears, two eyes, one mouth, and a sinful nature which leads us to seek our own advantage at the expense of other people.

As you and your child consider the question of sin this week, the purpose is not to accuse or create guilt. Instead, you can help your child begin to understand the root cause of life's injustices and tragedies. And the blame is not assessed against "them," for we are each responsible for our own acts of sinful selfishness. As a child comes to accept responsibility, he has a strong foundation for healthy growth.

Key Verse
"For all have sinned and fall short of the glory of God."
Romans 3:23

Key Thought
All people have disobeyed God and done things they knew were wrong.

WEEK 2

DAY
1

The trouble happened at Mr. Amadi's grocery store. Christopher's mom was working late, so he had gone with Arthur and his mom to buy a few things for dinner.

While Arthur's mom was paying Mr. Amadi, Christopher and Arthur admired the display of candy bars near the cash register. "Want a candy bar?" Christopher whispered.

"Sure," Arthur whispered back. "But Mom won't buy me one before dinner."

"We don't have to pay for it," Christopher said. "Mr. Amadi lets me take candy whenever I want. He likes me. What kind do you want?"

"Wow! Free candy! Anytime you want! 'Snickers,' " Arthur said, without stopping to think. Christopher slipped a candy bar from the rack and tucked it in Arthur's pocket. "Thanks," Arthur said.

That evening, after Arthur and his mom finished dinner, Arthur brought out his candy bar. He had just taken one bite when his mom asked, "Where'd you get that candy, Arthur?"

Arthur answered, "Christopher said Mr. Amadi lets him take candy whenever he wants." Suddenly, what Christopher had said did not sound quite so true. A few minutes later, Arthur and his mom were on their way back to Mr. Amadi's store.

Mr. Amadi greeted them as they walked in, "Forget something for dinner?"

Arthur's mom just said, "Arthur has something to tell you, Mr. Amadi."

Mr. Amadi looked at Arthur and waited.

Arthur was so embarrassed. He wanted to disappear into a crack in the floor. But he knew what he had to say. "I took a Snickers bar without paying for it." Arthur reached in his pocket and took out some coins that were from the bank on his bedroom shelf. "Here's the money."

Mr. Amadi took the coins and counted them. He looked sternly at Arthur. "I'm disappointed that you took the candy bar. That was wrong, Arthur. But I'm glad you came back to make it right."

Arthur knew he had to say something else. So he did. "I'm sorry, Mr. Amadi. I won't do it again."

"That's for sure," his mom said, as she and Arthur headed home.

● *"There is not a righteous man on earth who does what is right and never sins." Ecclesiastes 7:20*

● **For Younger Children**
What did Arthur do that was wrong?
   What kinds of wrong things do kids your age sometimes do?
   What wrong thing have you done?

● **For Older Children**
Has anything like this ever happened to you?
   How would you have felt if you were Arthur?
   What kinds of wrong things are you tempted to do?

● ●

WEEK 2

DAY 2

Arthur was not very happy with his neighbor Christopher.

"Boy, you sure got me in trouble last night," Arthur said.

"Trouble?" Christopher asked innocently. "What kind of trouble?"

"That candy you took from the store," Arthur said. "That kind of trouble." Arthur was still embarrassed about having to admit to Mr. Amadi that he had taken a candy bar. He was even more embarrassed that his mom had caught him eating the candy he and Christopher had taken. But he was most embarrassed that he had believed Christopher that it was OK to take candy from Mr. Amadi's store.

Since Christopher was a full year older than Arthur, Christopher often tried to act as though he knew everything there was to know. This time, he tried to act as though getting in trouble over stealing a candy bar was hardly worth mentioning.

"Is that all?" Christopher asked. "Taking a candy bar is no big deal."

"Haven't you ever gotten into trouble?" Arthur asked.

"Sure," Christopher said, acting like he was much too grown up to bother with little problems like getting in trouble.

"What did you do?" Arthur asked.

"Oh," Christopher said slowly. "Lots of stuff. You know, the usual. Stuff that everyone does. No big deal."

"Stuff that everyone does?" Arthur was beginning to wonder if Christopher really knew what he was talking about.

"Sure," Christopher said. "Everyone does stuff to get in trouble. All my friends do it all the time."

"Well that sure sounds dumb!" Arthur said. It was the first time he had ever said that something Christopher said was dumb. Arthur was surprised he had said it. But he was sure he was right. "Why would anyone be dumb enough to go around doing stuff they know will get them in trouble?"

And for the first time, Christopher couldn't think of anything to say.

● *"But the Scripture declares that the whole world is a prisoner of sin." Galatians 3:22*

● **For Younger Children**

Why was Arthur mad at Christopher?

Have you ever gotten in trouble for doing something wrong?

How do you feel when you get in trouble?

● **For Older Children**

Why did Christopher act like stealing was "no big deal"?

Why does the Bible say that stealing and other wrong actions really are a big deal?

What can you say to someone who tells you to do something wrong?

DAY
3

Arthur's friend, Christopher, was mad. He was really mad! He was partly mad at his mother for making him wear his new sweatshirt to the park on a sunny day. He was partly mad at himself for having left his new sweatshirt on the park bench while he and Arthur were playing tag. But he was mostly mad at whoever had stolen his new sweatshirt.

"Mom is really gonna give it to me," Christopher said, looking toward the basketball courts to see if anyone had his sweatshirt. "If I ever see anyone wearing my sweatshirt, I'll . . . I'll. . . ." Christopher was so mad, he couldn't think of what he would do.

"How would you know it was your sweatshirt?" Arthur asked, trying to be helpful. "Those things are so popular, lots of kids have 'em."

"I'd know!" Christopher grunted, now looking toward the playground "And I'd get that guy, and I'd . . . I'd. . . ."

"Getting ripped off is really pretty crummy," Arthur said, still trying to be helpful.

"Worse than crummy," Christopher said, looking both ways along the main walkway in the park "It's rotten!"

"I wonder if that's how Mr. Amadi feels when kids steal candy from his store?" Arthur wondered to himself.

As Christopher and Arthur walked home together, all Christopher could think about was that sweatshirt. All Arthur could think about was that stealing was really bad for everybody. But neither of them said anything to the other. They climbed the stairs and stood outside the doors to their apartments. Arthur felt like he ought to say something to Christopher. "I'm sorry you got ripped off," he said.

"Yeah," said Christopher. "Me too." He started to unlock his door.

"I wonder," Arthur added, as he took out the key to his apartment. "I wonder if God feels crummy like this every time someone steals or lies or hurts someone else."

"Huh?" Christopher grunted. Sometimes Christopher had a hard time following the way Arthur thought about things.

"It was just an idea I had," Arthur said. "I'll think about it some more. Good luck telling your mom about the sweatshirt." They both opened their doors and went inside.

● *"We have done many wrong things against our God; our sins show we are wrong." Isaiah 59:12,* EB

● **For Younger Children**

What happened to Christopher?

How did he feel? Have you ever felt like that?

How does God feel when people do wrong things?

● **For Older Children**

Why did Christopher feel so upset?

Do you agree with Arthur's idea that God is sad when we do wrong? Why or why not?

●●●

WEEK 2

DAY
4

Arthur had promised his mom. She had gone over the instructions that morning. "You can count on me, Mom. I promise! I'll come straight home from school, and I'll put the lasagna in the oven."

Arthur was certain he would remember what to do without needing the notes his mother placed around the apartment. Unfortunately, on the way home from school, Arthur's neighbor, Christopher, invited him to stop by for frozen yogurt. "My mom bought a big carton of chocolate last night, and she said we could have some after school."

Unfortunately, chocolate frozen yogurt sounded too good to resist.

Even more unfortunately, once inside Christopher's apartment, the two boys started playing video games, and Arthur never once thought about his promise. Not until Christopher zapped a video monster and yelled, "You're frozen solid!"

"Frozen!" Arthur croaked. "Frozen lasagna!" Quickly, he rushed to his own apartment and shoved the baking dish in the oven. It needed to bake for an hour and a half. But he was a full hour late! There was only one thing to do! He set the timer for 30 minutes and turned the oven as hot as it would go. He was sure his mother would never notice.

Unfortunately, the first thing his mother noticed when she came home was the smell of something burning. Rushing to the oven, she squealed, "Five hundred degrees?! Arthur, you've burned the lasagna to a crisp!" Sure enough, the lasagna was black, smoking, and hard as a rock.

It took awhile for the full story to come out, but finally Arthur told his mom everything. "Arthur Mack," she said, as sternly as possible, "I'm upset about the lasagna. I'm upset because you broke your promise. And then you tried to fool me by turning the oven up too high! Are you surprised that I am REALLY upset?!"

"No," was all Arthur could say.

Later that evening, after eating bologna sandwiches for dinner, Arthur thought of two other things he wanted to say. First, he said, "Mom, I'm really sorry I messed up." Then he asked, "How come I can't do the right thing sometimes, even when I want to?"

His mom put her arm around him and said, "That's a problem we all have, Arthur. Unfortunately."

● *"I do not do the good things I want to do, but I do the bad things I do not want to do." Romans 7:19,* EB

● **For Younger Children**

How did Arthur feel when he finally remembered the lasagna?

Why was Arthur's mom REALLY upset?

What did Arthur learn about himself?

● **For Older Children**

Have you ever done something wrong and then tried to cover it up? What happened?

What question did Arthur ask his mom?

The Bible tells us that no one is ALWAYS able to do right things, no matter how he or she tries. What is something right you try hard to do?

● ●

WEEK 2

DAY 5

"Hey, Mom," Arthur asked, trying to stretch out bedtime, so he wouldn't have to go to sleep yet.

"Yes, dear," his mom answered. She was standing at the door, ready to switch off the light. "What now?"

"Remember when I took that candy bar from Mr. Amadi's store?" Arthur asked.

"Yes, dear," his mom answered. "I remember."

"And remember when Christopher's sweatshirt got stolen?"

"Yes, dear. I remember."

"And remember when I didn't come straight home and put the lasagna in the oven, and then I tried to cook it fast so you wouldn't find out about it?"

"Arthur," his mom said, "that just happened today. Of course I remember!"

"Well, why do people do things that are wrong? Don't they know any better?"

Mom decided those were questions that needed a little time to answer. She came over next to Arthur's bed and sat on the edge. "Why do you save the hardest questions for bedtime, Arthur?"

Arthur raised up onto his elbow. "Well, it's hard to go to sleep when my brain keeps thinking."

"OK," Mom agreed. "Let me try to answer these questions, the last ones for tonight." Mom paused for a moment and thought. "I guess we keep doing wrong things because we want our own way instead of God's way."

Arthur didn't say anything now, which was highly unusual for Arthur. His mom waited a few moments, then she went on.

"Arthur, you know that the wrong things people do are called sins."

Arthur still didn't say anything. He just nodded his head. So Mom kept explaining. "And you know that the Bible tells us sin spoils things. Whenever we disobey God, we end up hurting ourselves and other people, and we push God's love away."

Arthur looked up at his mom and said, "Sounds pretty bad."

"It is, Arthur," Mom said. "Sin is worse than the air pollution or the litter that spoils the beauty in the world. Sin spoils the goodness in the world and ends up bringing unhappiness and fighting and even death."

"I wish everyone would stop doing things that are bad," Arthur said before he rolled over and went to sleep.

● *"For the wages of sin is death, but the gift of God is eternal life in Christ Jesus our Lord." Romans 6:23*

● **For Younger Children**
What bad things happen because people sin?
Why do people sin?
What was Arthur's wish?

● **For Older Children**
What did Arthur's mom say is worse than air pollution or litter? Why?
When have you asked God to help you keep from sinning?
What does Romans 6:23 say is the result of sin?
How do you feel about the sin in our world?

● ●

FAMILY TIMES

Schedule time this week to be together as a family. Select one of these suggested activities to expand your family's understanding of the cause and effect of sin.

Newspaper Hunt

With your family look at newspapers and/or news magazines to find articles about the results of sin in our world. Cut out the articles and glue them to a large piece of paper. Then with a red felt-tip pen write Romans 6:23 in large letters across the articles. Thank God for loving us in spite of our sin.

Tip for Younger Children: Suggest younger children look for pictures. Or younger children may use tape to attach articles to large piece of paper.

Bible Story Time

Introduce this activity by saying, "Sometimes we think that the people who lived in Bible times were perfect and always did what God wanted them to do. But the Bible tells us that EVERYONE has sinned and done what was wrong." Ask family members to name people in the Bible who sinned. Or read these Scripture passages together: Genesis 3:1-8; 12:10-20; Matthew 27:1-5. Consider these questions: "What sin was committed? What was the result?"

● ●

God Will Judge Sin

The idea of a secret has great appeal to a child. There is magic in being the only person—or one of a select group—to know about something that happened. But it is very hard to keep a secret. Protecting private information is sometimes more than a youngster can bear.

The one type of secret that every child wants to keep private is any knowledge of his or her misbehavior. What child has not at sometime said, "I hope Mom and Dad don't ever find out that I. . . ." There seems to be safety in keeping such incidents hidden.

Sadly, this desire to hide knowledge of certain actions is cynically used by child molesters who pledge the child to "keep our little secret." Often abuse is able to continue only because of the cloak of secrecy which the child thinks is a protection but instead leaves him or her at the mercy of far worse danger.

Most people tend to shy away from the recognition that God knows all we have done or thought and will hold us accountable for even that which we have wanted to hide. But as we get to know God and His pure love and justice, we begin to gain great comfort from knowing that we can openly admit our sins to Him. We need not pretend to be what we are not, for He knows us better than we know ourselves. And to all who confess and claim Jesus Christ as Savior, the Judge is also the one who pardons freely.

Key Verse
"For God will bring every deed into judgment, including every hidden thing, whether it is good or evil." Ecclesiastes 12:14

Key Thought
The Bible teaches that God is fair and will judge each person.

● ●

The sun had gone down over the Norris family farm. The horses and cows were in the barn. The chickens were in the coop. The engine on the tractor had cooled down. Outside the big farmhouse, the only sounds were the breeze moving the branches of the trees and a family of tree frogs trying to make more noise than the crickets in the tall grass.

Inside the big farmhouse, the Norris family was in the living room, mostly watching the news on TV. Mr. Norris was waiting for the weather report, so he could learn whether thunderstorms were likely to arrive that night. Mrs. Norris was sewing a patch on her husband's overalls, not really paying attention to the newscaster.

Ten-year-old Ryan and eight-year-old Josh were hoping the sports report

WEEK 3

DAY
1

would come soon. They wanted to know whether their favorite basketball team had won. Laura, who was seven, sat under the floor lamp, making a list of all the things she wanted for her birthday. Chris, the youngest, was sprawled in the center of the floor, playing with two cars and a truck.

Suddenly, everyone in the room was listening carefully to the television news report. Perhaps it was the words, "violent attack," which caught everyone's notice. Even Chris put down his cars as the reporter told of a feared criminal being sentenced to a very long term in prison.

"Wow!" Ryan said. "Thirty years in jail!"

"That's longer," Laura said, "than I've been alive."

"I bet," said Chris, "it's longer than DAD'S been alive."

"Not quite," Mom said. "But thirty years is a long, long time."

"Especially if you have to spend it all in jail," Dad added. "That man must have done something very, very bad."

"Who decides how long he has to go to jail?" Josh asked.

"There's a judge," Ryan answered, wanting to show he knew more than Josh. "The judge decides what the punishment should be. Kind of like God judging us."

Josh gulped. "God is like a judge?" he asked.

"A very good and fair judge," Dad said. "And everyone will be judged some day."

Josh gulped again. "I never thought of that before."

● *"I will judge you, each one according to his ways, declares the Sovereign Lord." Ezekiel 18:30*

● **For Younger Children**

What do you know about being a judge?

What kind of judge did Mr. Norris say God is like?

Whom do you know that makes fair decisions?

● **For Older Children**

Do you think it's hard or easy to be a good judge? Why?

Why did Mr. Norris say God is like a good and fair judge?

When you think of God judging you, how does it make you feel?

● ●

DAY
2

Mrs. Poindexter could hear the noise as she returned to her classroom. She had been called to the office for a moment and had told her third- and fourth-graders to take out their library books and read quietly. Obviously, something else was going on.

As she approached the door, Mrs. Poindexter heard a voice inside the class yell, "Here she comes!" Suddenly, all was quiet inside, and every student appeared to be fully absorbed in reading.

Mrs. Poindexter walked slowly to the front of the class. She spoke softly. "Please close your books and put them away," she said.

Twenty-three books had never been put away so quietly in the history of the school. Mrs. Poindexter looked into the eyes of twenty-three students before she spoke again. "Since you chose not to read while I went to the office, you will all continue with your reading—during recess."

Emily Potter, a fourth-grader who sat in front of Josh Norris, raised her hand. "Yes, Emily?" Mrs. Poindexter asked.

"But, Mrs. Poindexter!" Emily protested. "I WAS reading. I wasn't making noise!"

Almost two dozen hands shot into the air, their owners ready to plead innocence also. But Mrs. Poindexter said, "Unless those who were making the noise want to tell me what they were doing, I have no way of knowing who was reading and who wasn't." And the whole class did spend their recess reading—and listening to the rest of the school having fun on the playground.

"It wasn't fair!" Josh lamented to his brother Ryan as they got on the school bus after school. "Why should all of us miss recess just 'cause a few kids messed around?"

Ryan liked explaining things to his younger brother. He said, "Lots of people get hurt by things that aren't their fault. Like pollution. And litter."

Emily Potter, who was very interested in this conversation, leaned across the aisle of the bus. "And like sin," Emily said. "My dad says sin doesn't just hurt the person who does it. It usually hurts innocent people too."

"Your dad's probably right," Ryan said.

"I sure hope," Josh said, "that when God judges everyone, He can tell who really did what. Not like Mrs. Poindexter."

● *"He causes His sun to rise on the evil and the good, and sends rain on the righteous and the unrighteous." Matthew 5:45*

● **For Younger Children**

What was the problem in the classroom?

Why did Mrs. Poindexter make everyone stay inside during recess?

Was her decision fair? Why or why not?

● **For Older Children**

What would you have done if you were Mrs. Poindexter?

What are some other times one person's sin hurts others?

How do we know that God is able to decide who really sinned?

● ●

WEEK 3

DAY
3

Ryan spotted the cigarettes. They were in a bright red package. The package was under a chair. The chair was in the community center where Ryan's scout troop met every Thursday.

Ryan and his friends had been running around outside, waiting for Mr. Potter to unlock the building. When the front door was finally opened, Ryan was the first to run inside—and the first to see the cigarettes.

"Hey, Alex," he called to his best friend, picking up the pack that was more than half full. "Want a smoke?"

Now Ryan Norris had never smoked anything in all ten years of his life. And he had no intention of smoking any of these cigarettes. But it seemed like a funny thing to say.

"All right!" Alex said, grabbing the pack. "Let's sneak out back and try these."

"Are you nuts?" Ryan asked. "Those things can kill you! Besides, we'll get in trouble."

"One cigarette," Alex insisted, "won't kill anybody. And Mr. Potter's not ready to start yet. No one will ever know."

Maybe no one would ever have known, except Alex had to ask almost every boy in the troop for matches. By the time he found a boy who had some, every other boy in the troop followed Alex and Ryan out back. Unfortunately, or fortunately, Alex had just gotten the first match lit when Mr. Potter came out back to see where everyone had gone.

Not only did Mr. Potter collect the cigarettes and the matches, but Ryan and Alex both knew that once Mr. Potter knew, their parents would also soon know. It was not a happy walk home that night for Ryan and Alex.

"No one will ever know," Ryan snorted. "Right! Everyone in the whole county knows!"

"Yeah," Alex mumbled.

"And," Ryan continued. "even if no one else DID know, I'd know, and you'd know—and God would know."

"God?" Alex asked.

"Hey, man," Ryan kept on. "Don't you know that God knows exactly what we do even when no one else knows? And He's gonna judge us on what we really did, not just on what other people found out about?"

All Alex could say was, "Oh, wow!"

● *"For God will bring every deed in judgment, including every hidden thing, whether it is good or evil." Ecclesiastes 12:14*

● **For Younger Children**

What did Alex and Ryan do that got them into trouble?

Who always knows when you do something wrong?

Why is it important to remember that God knows everything we do?

● **For Older Children**

What would you have done with the cigarettes?

What does Ecclesiastes 12:14 say God will do?

Think about your answer to these questions: What wrong thing have you done that only you and God know about? What good things have you done that only you and God know about?

● ●

WEEK 3

DAY
4

Laura Norris was scandalized. It had been bad enough yesterday when her brother, Josh, along with all the other third- and fourth-graders, had been kept in during recess. It seemed to Laura that the whole school would think her brother was a troublemaker.

Then last night, her oldest brother, Ryan, had been caught with cigarettes outside his scout meeting. That sounded to Laura as if her brother must have been launching a life of drugs and crime.

What fiendish punishment must await? Laura was torn between her feelings of love for Ryan and the excitement of getting to witness the worst punishment ever!

"So what are you and Dad going to do to Ryan?" she asked her mom. "Are you going to lock him in his room? Or whip him? Or banish him from watching TV for a year?"

Mom just laughed.

"What's funny?" Laura wanted to know.

"I was just imagining," Mom said, "what terrible thing Ryan might have to do for us to lock him in his room."

"But he did," Laura exclaimed. "He . . . he . . ."

"Laura, honey," Mom said. "Ryan did something he knows he shouldn't have done. But Dad and I are not about to do any terrible things to him."

"But . . ." Laura tried to think.

"We're not being wishy-washy," Mom explained. "We love Ryan, so we're trying to be fair and do what is best for him."

Laura did not know whether to be relieved or disappointed. After a moment she asked, "Does that mean God won't ever really punish anyone?"

Laura's mom was not sure where Laura got that idea. So she asked, "Where did you get that idea?"

Laura answered, "Well, if God loves us and wants to be fair and do what's best, how can He punish people?"

Mom thought, then she asked, "Have I ever punished you or the boys?"

Laura remembered a few times of misbehavior in the Norris family.

"Yeah," she said.

"And would you say Dad and I are cruel and vicious, or kind and loving?" Mom asked.

"Kind and loving," Laura said.

"Sometimes it's necessary to judge or punish," Mom explained. "Just remember that. God is fair and always does what is right, even when He has to judge people."

● *"Abraham asked, 'Will not the Judge of all the earth do right?' " Genesis 18:25*

● **For Younger Children**
What did Laura think her parents might do to punish Ryan?
What did Laura learn about God?
Let's tell God thank You for always being fair and loving.

● **For Older Children**
Would you have punished Ryan? Why or why not?
How can someone show love and act as a judge at the same time?
What should you remember about God, the Judge?

DAY
5

The front door of the Norris farmhouse slammed shut. Heavy footsteps stomped up the stairs and into Josh's room. Then that door slammed shut. Josh had come home, and the sounds he was making did not sound like he was in a good mood.

"Josh!" his sister, Laura, yelled from her room. "Do you want to play?"

There was no answer from inside Josh's room unless you count a dresser drawer slamming shut. Josh was definitely in a mood for slamming.

But Laura never gave up easily. "Hey, Josh!" she yelled again. "Let's play a game!"

Suddenly Josh's door flew open. "I've had enough games!" he growled.

"Sounds bad," Laura sympathized. "What happened?"

"We were playing basketball in Alex and Henry's driveway," Josh began. "But everybody was fouling, and no one would admit it."

"You need a ref," Laura suggested.

"Yeah," Josh agreed. "The game's no fun if no one follows the rules."

"That's what Mom says," Laura added.

"Huh?" Josh asked. He didn't know his mom knew much about basketball.

"Mom said life isn't good if people don't follow God's rules," Laura went on. "That's why it's good to know God will judge us. He's sort of the referee of life."

"The referee of life," Josh repeated. "That's good, Laura. Really good."

● *"And so we know and rely on the love God has for us. God is love. Whoever lives in love lives in God, and God in him. In this way love is made complete among us so that we will have confidence on the day of judgment."*
1 John 4:16-17

● **For Younger Children**
Why is knowing and obeying the rules of a game important?

Why does it help to have a referee at a game?

What does 1 John 4:16-17 say we should remember about God when He judges us?

● **For Older Children**
What are some of God's rules?

Why isn't life good if people don't follow God's rules?

Why does 1 John 4:16-17 say not to be afraid when God judges us?

• •

FAMILY TIMES

Schedule time this week to be together as a family. Select one of these suggested activities to expand your family's understanding of God as the fair and loving judge of all people.

Game Night

Play a game (pick out a family favorite or choose one that's new) with your family. As you play, talk about what would happen if no one followed the rules. Then, just for fun, use the playing pieces of the game and try to invent a new game. Write your own rules! Finish off the game night with a bowl of popcorn or ice cream.

Bible Verse Pass

Read 1 John 4:16-17 together several times. Then "pass" the verse to each other. Sit in a circle. One person says the first word of the verse. Pass the verse around the circle with each person saying the next word until the verse is completed. When you repeat the verse, begin with a different person.

You Be the Judge

Purchase or make plain sugar cookies. Provide white frosting and a variety of decorations (sprinkles, raisins, coconut, cinnamon candies, etc.). Each person decorates a cookie. Designate one person in the family (or a friendly neighbor) as the judge. Give awards in a variety of categories: Most Creative, Most Colorful, Best Design, etc.

God Planned Our Salvation

Key Verse
"God had . . . decided to make us His own children through Jesus Christ. That was what He wanted and what pleased Him."
Ephesians 1:5, EB

Jesus told two stories about people who did not plan ahead (Luke 14:28-32). He told about a builder who started to construct a tower without planning whether he had enough money to complete the job. Then He told of a king who went to war without planning whether his army was strong enough to win. Good planning has always been part of the very nature of God.

From the opening chapters of Scripture, we see God's plan taking shape. Over the centuries which followed, in spite of human rebellion, God continued to work out His plan. At the center of His plan for the world has always been the intention to love, forgive, and purify a family of people.

While the full scope of God's plan may be overwhelming to children, even the youngest child can respond to the good news that "God loves you and has planned a way for you to be His child."

Key Thought
God has always planned to show His love to all those who trust His Son Jesus.

WEEK 4

DAY
1

Looking at pictures in the family photo albums was a good thing to do on a cold, rainy day. The windows of Midori's living room were streaked with rain and steam. But the inside of the apartment was warm and cozy. And the books of family pictures were very entertaining.

Midori's favorites were the ones when she was little. She liked seeing her baby pictures and trying hard to remember what it might have been like to be that small.

Her next favorite pictures were those of her big sister, Aliki. It was fun to see pictures of Aliki when she was younger than Midori was now. "Aliki thinks she's so big sometimes," Midori thought to herself, "but she used to be littler than me." Since Aliki was still at school today, Midori was enjoying having all of the photo albums to herself.

Suddenly, Midori saw a picture that made her think. Her Father was painting a wall—in her bedroom! And right below was a picture of her Mother, hanging curtains in the same room.

"I don't remember you and Father working in my room," Midori said to her mother. Mother walked over and looked at the photographs, then she smiled brightly.

"Where was I?" Midori asked.

"You weren't born yet," Mother said. "You were still growing inside me."

"Did you know who I was?" Midori asked thoughtfully.

"We knew you were going to be our child and that you would be very special," Mother said. "We planned what your name would be and where we would put your crib. And we knew we were going to love you very much."

"Even before I was born?" Midori asked.

"I know someone who planned even more than that," Mother said. "Someone who knew all about you long before you were born. God has always wanted you to be His child, and He planned to help you grow and learn so you can become more and more like Jesus." Then Mother gave Midori a huge hug.

● *"From the very beginning God decided that those who came to Him . . . should become like His Son [Jesus]." Romans 8:29,* TLB

● **For Younger Children**

What would you like to know about the way we planned for you to be born?

What do you think God has planned for you?

Let's ask God's help as you grow as His child.

● **For Older Children**

How did Midori's mom and dad plan for her birth?

How would you describe God's plan for you?

What has God done to help you follow His plan and become more like Jesus?

● ●

WEEK 4

DAY

2

When Midori got home from kindergarten, the first thing she usually asked was, "What's for lunch?"

When her older sister, Aliki, got home from school later in the afternoon, her first question was usually, "What's for snack?"

Since Midori had already checked the refrigerator and cupboard, she usually answered Aliki's question. This made Aliki feel like her little sister was deciding what snack Aliki could have. Perhaps that is why Aliki was so surprised today when she asked her usual question about snack, and Midori gave a very unusual answer.

Midori's answer was, "I don't know about snack, but Mother says God made special plans for me."

Aliki set down her backpack, looked at her little sister, and asked, "What special plans?"

Midori had wanted to impress her big sister. She had not expected Aliki to ask her a hard question. Midori's forehead wrinkled, and she turned to Mother. "What did God plan for me?" Midori asked.

Mother closed the refrigerator door and brought two peach yogurt cups to the table. She smiled at Midori and said, "God made wonderful plans for both you and Aliki, and for Father and me—long before any of us were born."

This sounded very interesting to Aliki, who had been listening while she got spoons and napkins for herself and her sister.

"What plans?" Aliki asked.

Mother said, "God planned to love you. And He planned a way for you to be His child, even though He knew you would disobey Him sometimes."

Midori was licking the lid of her yogurt cup. She wasn't sure she was pleased that other people had been included in God's special plans. She had thought God's plans were special because they were only for her. But Mother was still talking.

"God loves each of you so much that He planned for Jesus to come to earth and show God's love to everyone."

What Mother said sounded pretty good to Midori. It even sounded good enough that she decided it was all right that Aliki was included in God's good plans.

● *"And you also are among those who are called to belong to Jesus Christ." Romans 1:6*

● **For Younger Children**

What word would you use to tell what God's love is like?
  Whom did God send to earth to show His love for you?
  How does God's special love make you feel?

● **For Older Children**

When have you wanted something special to be just for you?
  Whom has God included in His wonderful plans?
  How might you feel if you never heard of God's wonderful plans?

WEEK 4

DAY 3

Something did not sound the way it should. Aliki was still half asleep, but she was aware of something missing. She opened one eye and saw the early morning sunshine peeking past the edges of the window shade. She saw her lamp and her stuffed panda and her goldfish and her hamster cage. Her hamster cage!

Suddenly Aliki sat straight up in bed.

Her hamster cage was silent. She hadn't heard any of the usual sounds of little Honda running in his wheel or scuffling through the sawdust. Aliki leaned over to look at the cage. She saw something that made her heart jump. The door to Honda's cage was wide open!

Soon the whole family was looking everywhere for the little hamster. Aliki and her sister and their mother and father were all looking behind furniture, in closets, under beds. Aliki was looking at the back of her bookshelves when suddenly Mother said, "Look what I found."

Aliki turned around and let out a squeal. Mother was holding little Honda. "He had crawled under the pile of laundry in the hallway," Mother said. "I guess he thought it was a great nest."

Aliki was so glad when Honda was safely back inside his cage. She and her mother watched Honda burrow into a dark corner where he could sleep through the day. Mother patted Aliki's hand and said, "I knew that Honda was going to escape."

Aliki was surprised. "How'd you know?" she asked. Mother said, "I know you sometimes forget things, so I expected that someday you would forget to close the cage tightly. And I know that if the cage door is left unlocked, sooner or later, the hamster will get out."

Aliki thought about what Mother had just said. "Wow," Aliki exclaimed. "You know the future, just like God."

Mother laughed. "Mothers know a lot," she said. "But we're a long way from knowing all that God knows. It makes me feel safe that God really knows the future, because He's planned all the good things He wants to happen to those who love Him."

"Did He know that we'd find Honda?" Midori asked.

"What do you think?" Mother asked in return.

● *"But God demonstrates His own love for us in this: While we were still sinners, Christ died for us." Romans 5:8*

● **For Younger Children**

What are some good things that have happened to you?

The best thing God has planned for you is to become part of His family. Would you like to know more about becoming God's child?

● **For Older Children**

Why did Aliki's mom say she felt safe?

What are some choices you'll probably make in the future?

Let's ask God to help you follow His plan now and in the future.

● ●

WEEK 4

DAY
4

Aliki's father had been working at the kitchen table for a very long time. Aliki wanted him to read a new library book with her. She had asked him several times how much longer he would be. Each time he had said, "Quite awhile, Aliki. I still have a lot of bills to pay."

Besides being bored waiting for Father to finish, Aliki was a little worried at the big stack of bills on the table. Finally she asked, "Will we have any money left after you pay all those?"

Father laughed. "Not much, Aliki," he said. "Just enough." Then Father got serious again. Aliki could always tell when Father was serious because he would push his glasses up on his nose and press his lips together. "Besides," he said in his serious voice, "they're not all bills. Let me show you something." Father reached into the stack of envelopes and papers and pulled out two sheets that had rows of very tiny numbers on them.

"These are statements of savings accounts for you and Midori," he said. Aliki looked closely at the tiny numbers, trying to discover what they meant. "Ever since you were born, Mother and I have been putting money in these accounts to help pay for you and Midori to go to college."

"Oh," Aliki said. She did not sound impressed. She had been hoping the money could be spent right away on something fun. Father kept on pointing to the rows of tiny numbers, explaining how much money was in each savings account. Aliki did not really understand most of what he said. But then she heard him say, "Mother and I really want you and Midori to learn all you can. That's why we planned to save this money for you."

Aliki answered, "Just like God planned ahead?"

Father was puzzled by that. All he could say was, "Huh?"

Aliki decided to explain, "Sure! God planned a long time ago to save us as His children."

Father pushed his glasses up on his nose and pressed his lips together. "How did you know that?" he asked.

Aliki shrugged. "I'm a kid, but I'm not dumb!" she said. "Besides, Mother told me that yesterday."

● *"The Lord loves you. God chose you from the beginning to be saved."*
2 Thessalonians 2:12, EB

● **For Younger Children**

Where do you save your money?

God's plan to save us means that He planned to save or rescue us from the punishment of sin. According to 2 Thessalonians 2:12, why has God planned to save you?

● **For Older Children**

What's something our family has planned ahead to do?

What did Aliki say about God's plan for all people?

When we become God's children, it means we accept God's love and His plan to save us—to keep us safe from the punishment of sin. Have you accepted God's love? Would you like to right now?

WEEK 4

DAY
5

Aliki and her father had just finished reading a chapter of a new library book. In the book, two friends had gotten very, very mad at each other. Father rested the book in his lap and pushed his glasses up on his nose. "I remember when I was a boy," he said. "I got very mad at my best friend. I stomped into our house and shouted, 'He makes me so mad!' "

Aliki's eyes grew wide as she looked up at her father. "You stomped?" she asked.

"As loud as I could," Father said, "But, thankfully, your grandfather was not home then. Only my brother, your uncle, Tomoko. He asked me, 'Are you through being his friend?' "

"What did you say?" Aliki asked.

"I said," said Father, " 'Oh, no. We're still best friends.'"

"What did Uncle Tomoko say?" Aliki asked.

"He asked," said Father. " 'Are you going to do something terrible to get even?' "

"And what did you say then?" Aliki asked.

"I said, 'Of course not. I don't want to ruin our friendship.' "

"So did you and your friend stay mad?" Aliki asked.

"Of course not," Father said. "He came over to my house and apologized for whatever it was he had done. I forgave him. Everything was OK."

"What had your friend done to make you mad in the first place?" asked Aliki.

"I don't remember now," Father said. "Maybe I thought he wasn't playing fair. I do remember, though, that it was easy to forgive him because I wanted to keep on being friends more than I wanted to win a game."

Aliki smiled, "Way to go, Father!" she said, giving her father a pat on the shoulder.

"Thank you," Father said, bowing his head toward his daughter. "Did you know God's even better at forgiving us? He always forgives when we admit we have done wrong. He has always wanted us to be His children, so He has planned to always forgive those who ask."

"I like your story better than the library book," Aliki said.

Father just laughed and let his glasses slip forward on his nose.

● *"Therefore, there is now no condemnation for those who are in Christ Jesus."* Romans 8:1

● **For Younger Children**

What did Aliki's father do when he was mad at his friend? Aliki's father and his friend forgave each other and stayed friends. When God forgives us, He forgets all about our sin. In order to receive God's forgiveness, what do we need to do when we sin?

● **For Older Children**

When have you argued with a friend? Did you stay friends? Why?

Why do you think God forgives us when we do wrong?

Let's ask God's forgiveness and thank Him for always loving us.

● ●

Schedule time this week to be together as a family. Select one of these suggested activities to expand your family's understanding of God's plan to show love and forgiveness to us.

FAMILY TIMES

Family Photo Night

Look at some old family pictures together. Talk about the plans your family made before each child was born. (Nearby grandparents will enjoy telling stories about the plans they made for their children.) If you have more than one child in your family, put out several unlabeled baby pictures of each child. See if your children can identify each picture.

Interviews

Write these questions on separate index cards: Who first told you about God? How did you learn about God's plan of salvation? What happened when you decided to become a Christian? What's the best part about being a child of God? Put the cards in a bowl or hat. Let the children take turns choosing cards and reading the questions aloud to interview Mom or Dad. Continue until both parents have answered all questions.

Tip for Younger Children: Even though they may not be able to read the questions, younger children will still enjoy choosing cards and hearing Mom or Dad's answers.

God's Plan for the World

Help your family think about the variety of people included in God's plan of love and forgiveness. Look through magazines to find and cut out pictures of as many different kinds of people as possible—age, nationality, physical characteristics, etc. See how many pictures your family can find. Glue the pictures to a large piece of paper. Letter a title, "God's Love Is Worldwide."

Tip for Younger Children: Younger children may need help with cutting out pictures, or you may suggest they rip out entire pages.

Jesus Died for Our Sins

Key Verse
"He took our suffering on Him and felt our pain for us. . . . But He was wounded for the wrong we did; He was crushed for the evil we did. The punishment which made us well, was given to Him, and we are healed because of His wounds."
Isaiah 53:4-5, EB.

The concept that Jesus died to take the punishment we deserve is a difficult one for children to grasp. Children do not readily see a connection between their acts of disobedience, anger, or deceit and the story of Jesus' crucifixion. How can something that happened 2,000 years ago have anything to do with them?

This week you and your child will read a story of a thirteen-year-old boy (Eric Lacey) who did a foolish, spiteful thing to his sister and caused far greater problems than he intended. Eric recognized that he deserved to be punished, but then he is astounded when his grandfather offers to pay to repair the damage Eric caused. As you and your child follow Eric's story, you will have opportunities to compare Eric's offense with the wrong things you and your child have done. You can then liken Grandpa Ed's offer to pay Eric's penalty with Jesus' willingness to die as our substitute, taking the punishment we deserve.

Key Thought
Jesus died on the cross to pay the penalty for all our sins.

WEEK 1

DAY

1

It didn't take much for Eric to get mad at his younger sister. Nor did it take much for Jessie to get mad at her older brother. That's why no one in the Lacey family could remember why Eric was mad at Jessie that day. But no one in the Lacey family will ever forget what happened when Eric got mad at Jessie on that cold, windy day in April.

Everyone in the family remembers that the trouble started when Eric decided he would do something to scare Jessie. He thought it would be a good way to get back at her for something, something no one can remember.

While Jessie was reading in the living room, Eric slipped quietly into Jessie's bedroom. He already knew exactly what he was going to do that would frighten Jessie and make her scream. He reached down into the doll bed by the window and picked up Jessie's favorite doll. This was the doll

Jessie had loved since she was in kindergarten. Most of her other dolls looked pretty ragged and shabby, but Jessie had kept this one special doll looking beautiful and new. Eric placed the doll under his arm and crept down the hall into the living room. Jessie had not noticed him. He waited a few moments, and then he struck.

"Hi-yah!" Eric shouted, jumping into the middle of the room holding the doll above his head. "I'm gonna get even with you! I'm gonna rip off your doll's head!!" Grabbing the doll's head with one hand, he pretended to pull and twist with all his might. Suddenly, to Eric's horror, the doll's head actually broke off.

Jessie, who had not even looked up to see Eric's performance, did not notice the awful damage Eric had done. She just said, "Eric, leave me and my doll alone! I'm busy!"

Usually Eric would have had answered with a smart remark and kept on bothering his sister. But this time, he just turned and left the living room, keeping both arms wrapped tightly around the broken doll. Once in the hallway, he looked down at the doll, hoping he had just imagined that the head had come off. But there was no doubt. The doll's neck had ripped all the way through. Eric was sure he had just done the most terrible thing ever.

● *"God demonstrates His own love for us in this: While we were still sinners, Christ died for us." Romans 5:8*

● **For Younger Children**
How would you feel if you were Eric?
   Have you ever broken something that belonged to someone else? What happened?

● **For Older Children**
Has anything like this ever happened in our family?
   What punishment does Eric deserve?
   When we sin against God by disobeying one of His rules, what punishment do we deserve?

DAY 2

Eric's heart was beating rapidly, and his palms were damp with sweat. He had just ripped the head off his sister's favorite doll. He hadn't meant to do it. He had just been trying to scare Jessie.

What could he do now? Maybe he could tie a scarf around the doll's neck, and it would keep the head attached. Quickly, Eric looked around Jessie's room and spotted a blue scarf hanging from a hook. Holding the doll's head in position, he wrapped the scarf around the neck, pulling it as tight as possible.

"Maybe this just might work," Eric thought to himself. Then he held the doll upright and let go of its head. It wobbled for a moment and then fell to the floor.

"Rats!" Eric muttered. "Now what can I do?"

His next idea was to bury the doll in the backyard where no one would ever find it. Or he could put it at the bottom of a trash bag and let it get taken away with the rest of the family garbage. Either of those ideas might work if Jessie wouldn't ever notice the doll was missing. She was eight years old now and didn't play with dolls much anymore.

"Nah!" Eric said out loud. He knew Jessie would notice if the doll wasn't there.

Once again Eric slipped into his sister's room. Very carefully, he arranged the broken doll in the doll crib by the window. He was certain that if Jessie didn't look too closely, she wouldn't notice the jagged tear across the doll's neck. Tiptoeing out of Jessie's room, Eric was hoping no one would try to pick up the doll for a long, long time. By then, maybe Jessie would have forgotten that Eric had brought the doll into the living room.

That was what Eric hoped. But it was not to be. Just a short time later Eric, and probably everyone in the neighborhood, heard Jessie scream. "My doll!" she sobbed. "Eric ruined my best doll!"

Eric sat alone in his room and knew he was in very deep trouble.

● *"God made Him who had no sin to be sin for us, so that in Him we might become the righteousness of God." 2 Corinthians 5:21*

● **For Younger Children**

What was Eric trying to do with the broken doll? Did it work?

How do you feel when someone finds out you've done wrong?

What's a good thing to do when you've hurt someone?

● **For Older Children**

How does Eric feel?

What should he do now?

When you've hurt someone, what do you usually try to do?

● ●

WEEK 1

DAY
3

"You're just mean!" Jessie cried. "You did it just to be mean!" Tears were running down Jessie's cheeks as she held the doll her brother Eric had broken.

"It was an accident," Eric insisted. "I didn't mean to break it."

"You said you were gonna rip her head off!" Jessie accused. "And that's just what you did!"

"I'm really sorry," Eric said sadly. "I really am!"

Jessie's tears and Eric's apologies continued for quite a while. Finally, Dad spoke up from where he sat on the edge of Eric's bed. "Jessie has every right to be very upset about this, Eric," he said.

"I know," Eric answered, looking down at the floor.

"And whether you were just trying to tease Jessie, or really planned to do what you told her, the doll is still just as broken."

"I know," Eric answered, still looking at the floor.

"It seems to me we have four pretty big problems here," Dad said.

Eric looked up. "Four?" he asked.

"First," Dad said, "we have a broken doll. Second, we have Jessie's feelings which have been hurt pretty badly. Third, we have you acting in a way that didn't show respect for another person's property and feelings. And fourth, we have you trying to hide what you had done instead of admitting the problem. That's four."

"Right," Eric answered. "Four."

"We were all going to go ice-skating tonight," Dad reminded the family. "But I think Eric should stay home and think about what he should have done. Then we can talk tomorrow about what he can do to make up for breaking the doll."

Ice-skating was one of Eric's favorite things to do. He had been looking forward to going skating for days. Now he was going to miss out, but he knew his dad was being very fair.

Just then Jessie said something that surprised everyone "Oh, Dad," she said. "Let him come! It's not as much fun skating if Eric doesn't come." At first, Dad wanted to stick to his first decision and leave Eric home. But

112

finally he and Mom agreed to go along with Jessie's request. However, everyone knew the decision about Eric's punishment had just been postponed till later.

● *"This is how we know what real love is: Jesus Christ gave His life for us."* *1 John 3:16, EB.*

● **For Younger Children**

What were the problems Eric's actions caused?

Did Eric deserve to go ice-skating?

When has someone been kind to you—even when you didn't deserve it?

● **For Older Children**

Which of the four problems is the worst? Why?

Would you have said what Jessie did? Why or why not?

Jessie showed love to Eric. What does 1 John 3:16 say Jesus did to show His love?

●●

WEEK 1

DAY 4

Eric had not really enjoyed ice-skating with his family. He felt too guilty about having broken Jessie's favorite doll and then trying to hide what he had done. He had not really slept well during the night, even though he was tired from having skated hard. Neither had he really enjoyed his breakfast, even though he had gotten to open a new box of Honey Frosted Sugar Puffs, his favorite cereal.

Just as Eric was capturing the last three puffs floating in milk, Dad and Mom sat down at the kitchen table. Eric knew the moment had come to learn what his punishment was to be.

"We've made a decision, Eric," Dad said.

"We talked about this for a long time late last night," Mom added.

Eric didn't say anything. He didn't catch those last three cereal puffs either.

"Our decision," Dad said, "is that you need to pay for fixing the doll or else buy Jessie a new one." Eric gulped. "How much will that cost?" he asked.

"We're not sure, Eric," Mom said. "Jessie really wants this particular doll, so we'll have to find out if it can be fixed and what the cost will be. In the meantime, you had better start thinking of some ways you can earn money to pay for it."

That very afternoon, Eric started trying to line up jobs to earn money. He went to each of the neighbors. He even telephoned Grandfather Lacey to see if he would hire him.

"You need to earn money to pay for Jessie's doll that you broke?" asked Grandpa Ed.

"Yes," Eric said softly. It was embarrassing having to admit why he needed to earn money.

"Sounds fair to me," Grandpa Ed announced. "You broke it; you've got to pay for it."

"Right," Eric said. He just had no idea how long it would take him to earn the money.

"You're hired!" said Grandpa Ed. "When can you start?"

Suddenly Eric felt a little bit better. Maybe he would be able to stop feeling guilty and sad and embarrassed about what he had done. Maybe he could make things right for Jessie again.

● *"Christ Himself died for you. And that one death paid for your sins. He was not guilty, but He died for those who are guilty. He did this to bring you all to God." 1 Peter 3:18,* EB

● **For Younger Children**
What did Grandpa Ed do to help Eric?
    Who has helped you when you've done something wrong?
    According to 1 Peter 3:18, how does Jesus Christ help us?

● **For Older Children**
If you were Eric's parents, what would you have decided his punishment should be?
    Why did Eric start to feel better?
    According to 1 Peter 3:8, how has Jesus made things right for us?

WEEK 1

DAY 5

●●●

For three afternoons in a row, Eric had been working hard in Grandpa Ed's backyard. Eric had pulled weeds and mowed grass, causing raised blisters on his hands. And there was still a lot more work to do in Grandpa Ed's huge backyard. Also, there was still a lot more money Eric needed to earn to pay to fix the doll that he had broken.

"Do you want to quit yet?" Grandpa Ed asked.

"Can't," said Eric. "Still an hour until dinner."

"Keep workin' this hard," Grandpa Ed said, "you may not last 'til dinner."

"I'm OK, Grandpa," Eric said, bending down to grab another clump of tall weeds.

"April showers bring forth May weeds," Grandpa joked. Then Grandpa Ed got serious. "Come and talk to me before you go home."

"OK, Grandpa," Eric grunted and pulled up his handful of weeds, roots and all.

When it was time for Eric to go home, he walked into Grandpa Ed's den. Grandma called it a den because she said Grandpa Ed growled at anyone who bothered him there.

"You wanted to see me, Grandpa?" Eric asked.

Grandpa looked up from his book. "Eric," he said, "you seem to be pretty sorry you broke Jessie's doll and hurt her feelings."

"Yeah," Eric agreed. "It was a really crummy thing to do to her."

"And," Grandpa said, "having to do all this work must make it seem even more crummy."

"Not really," Eric said. "I deserve being punished. Besides, working helps me feel I'm fixing the problem I caused."

"In that case," Grandpa said, "I'm going to pay for the doll. I think you've learned a hard lesson, and I want Jessie to have that doll as good as new."

"Oh! Wow!" Eric had never been more surprised. "You don't have to do that, Grandpa."

"I know, but I want to," Grandpa said.

"OK," Eric said. "But I'm still going to do all the jobs I promised."

"You don't have to pay me back," Grandpa said. "I'm fixing the doll as a gift. You don't have to earn it."

Eric scratched his head. "I'm not going to keep working to pay you back, Grandpa. I'm going to work because I love you."

Then Eric and Grandpa Ed shook hands and smiled.

● *"We believe that Jesus died and rose again." 1 Thessalonians 4:14*

● **For Younger Children**

How did Grandpa Ed feel about Eric?

What did God do because of His love for us?

Let's tell God thank You for sending Jesus to take the punishment for our sins.

● **For Older Children**

Would you have done what Grandpa Ed did? Why or why not?

What do you think Eric learned from this experience?

What have you learned about the importance of Jesus' death on the cross?

● ●

FAMILY TIMES

Schedule time this week to be together as a family. Select one of these suggested activities to expand your family's understanding of Jesus' death.

What Do You Think Of?

Ask each person to tell the word or phrase he or she thinks of when hearing each of these words: punishment, love, death, sin, Jesus. Then work together as a family to write a sentence using each of the words. Each sentence should tell something about God's love. Thank Jesus for His love and death on the cross.

Family Ties

Introduce this activity by saying, "The family in these stories showed love and helped each other, even when there were problems. Let's talk about some of the ways our family loves and helps each other." Sit in a circle. One person holds the end of a ball of yarn, tells a way a family member has helped him or her, and tosses the yarn ball to that person. Continue until each person has had several turns. Then look at the pattern of family ties you have created.

Tip for Younger Children: Before using the yarn ball, talk together about the ways family members help each other.

Family Poem

Write a non-rhyming poem together about Jesus and His actions to take the penalty for our sins. Follow this pattern:

Jesus

(two words describing Jesus)

(three words telling Jesus' actions)

(four words telling how you feel about Jesus)

(one word that is another name for Jesus)

Tip for Younger Children: In addition to suggesting words, younger children may enjoy drawing pictures or a decorative border around the poem.

Jesus Rose from the Dead

The Apostle Paul made it very clear that the entire fabric of our faith rests on the reality of Jesus' bodily resurrection: "If Christ has not been raised, then our preaching is worth nothing, and your faith is worth nothing" (1 Corinthians 15:14, EB). Therefore, of all the topics you and your child will ever discuss, none are more vital than this one.

The most helpful thing a parent or teacher can do for a child's celebration of Easter is to express joyful gratitude for Christ's return to life. The seasonal trappings of celebration (eggs, rabbits, lilies, etc.) can be pleasant means of showing joy for the life that only Jesus gives. Or they can become ends in themselves, cute and sweet, but ultimately hollow. The difference between the two is found only partly in the explanations we provide. The ultimate difference is our own personal relationship with our risen Lord.

Key Verse
Jesus said, "I am the Living One; I was dead, and behold I am alive forever and ever!" Revelation 1:18

Key Thought
God raised Jesus to life to show His power over sin and death.

WEEK 2

DAY 1

It felt so good to stay in bed in the morning and not have to get up to go to school. Hector stretched his toes. Then he stretched the rest of him. Then he gave a deep, happy sigh. "Spring vacation!" Hector whispered to himself. "Yes!"

Hector's big sister, Angela, poked her head through the bedroom doorway. "Awesome!" she laughed. "The Great Sleepyhead finally wakes up!"

Hector stretched again, looked over to his little brother Robbie's bed, and noticed that it was empty. Angela laughed again. "Robbie's been up for hours. I've been up for hours. You're sleeping your vacation away!"

Hector yawned and then grinned at his sister. "I can't think of a better way to spend a vacation. I think I'll just stay in bed until next Monday."

"Then you'll miss Easter Sunday!" Angela replied.

"Is Easter going to be this week?" Hector asked, snuggling back into his pillow.

"Hector, you're loco!" Angela teased. "Of course Easter is this week! Why do you think the schools give us the week off?"

"We get a vacation because of Easter?" Hector asked.

"Well," Angela answered. "I'm not sure if schools close because of it, but I know Easter is a lot more important than any other reason for a holiday."

"Whatever," Hector said, closing his eyes and pulling his blanket up tight under his chin.

"Whatever?" Angela shrieked. "Easter's not a 'whatever!' It's one of the most important days of the year."

"Well then," Hector yawned and rolled over, "wake me up for Easter. I'll check it out."

Angela squealed, jumped on top of Hector and began tickling him. "I'm waking you up right now, you lazy lunk!" And she did!

● *"By His power God raised the Lord [Jesus] from the dead." 1 Corinthians 6:14*

● **For Younger Children**
Why was Hector happy?
    What do you like about Easter?

● **For Older Children**
What do you like to do on a vacation day?
    What did Angela say about Easter?
    What would you say about Easter to someone who had never heard of it?

● ●

WEEK 2

DAY
2

Angela and Hector were helping their little brother color Easter eggs. They were trying hard to pretend to each other that they were only doing this for Robbie. They were acting like they were too big to get excited about colored eggs. It was actually hard work to keep from showing how much fun they were having.

Robbie did not have that problem. He was four-and-a-half years old, and he was so excited about Easter that he could hardly stand it. "Look at this egg!" he shouted, holding up an egg that was a deep, rich purple on one end and bright yellow on the other.

Hector really liked those colors and wanted to make one of his own just like it. But he did not want Angela and Robbie to think he was a baby. That's why all he said was, "Not bad, short stuff."

"It's better than your ugly eggs!" Robbie retorted.

And Hector knew that Robbie was right. Hector had been experimenting with dipping his eggs in all the different colors. By the time he finished, they were all a dull, murky brown. But all Hector would say was, "I'm into brown this year."

Angela usually thought it was funny when they teased each other. Today she did not want them to get angry with each other and spoil the fun of coloring eggs. She decided to do something. She asked a question, "Robbie, what do you like best about Easter?"

Robbie did not even stop to think. He just blurted out, "The Easter Bunny! And candy. Chocolate candy. And I like finding eggs."

Angela was afraid Robbie would keep going, telling her everything he had ever heard about Easter. She decided to interrupt and ask another question. "But what about Jesus?" she asked. "Easter is important because of Jesus."

"I know that!" Robbie declared. "Easter is when Jesus came out of the grave, and the Easter Bunny hopped after Him."

Angela looked at Hector. "I think there are some things we need to explain to our brother," she said.

"Don't look at me!" Hector responded. "I can't even color eggs right!"

● *"God has indeed been raised from the dead." 1 Corinthians 15:20*

● **For Younger Children**
Have you ever colored Easter eggs?
   What funny thing did Robbie say about the Easter Bunny?
   Acts 2:32 tells us why Easter is so important. What does this verse say?

● **For Older Children**
What does our family do to celebrate Easter?
   If you were Angela, what would you explain to Robbie about Easter?

● ●

WEEK 2

DAY
3

Angela and Hector had taken Robbie to the park for the Giant Neighborhood Easter Egg Hunt. It had sounded like fun until they got there and saw children yelling and screaming and running in every direction. There were a few minutes of partial calm while a lady from the Parks Department shouted instructions through a bullhorn. But once the hunt began, children were once again yelling and running everywhere.

It was all over in a few frantic minutes. Robbie found three eggs and a handful of candy, which he thought were wonderful rewards for all the running he had done.

"Shall we eat the eggs and candy?" Hector asked hopefully. He knew that his little brother was not usually keen on sharing his treats with anyone, especially his big brother.

"OK!" Robbie said, surprising Hector and Angela. So the three of them sat down in a quiet corner of the park. Angela cracked and peeled Robbie's egg, while Hector concentrated on trying to pick off several small pieces of shell that stuck to his egg.

Hector, who had forgotten what it was like to be four-and-a-half years old, muttered, "I've never seen so much running around."

Angela handed Robbie his egg and said to Hector, "All that running reminds me of the very first Easter."

Hector looked at his sister. "They hunted eggs on the first Easter? In the Bible?"

Angela laughed. "No, silly. But the Bible tells about people running back and forth because they were so excited Jesus was alive."

"I'd rather run for eggs and candy," Robbie said, as he started to unwrap something that looked like a chocolate egg.

"That's OK, Robbie," Angela answered. "Little kids are supposed to like eggs and candy and bunnies."

"What's wrong with eggs and candy and bunnies?" Hector asked.

"Nothing," Angela said. "But they're just ways we show we're happy about Jesus. Jesus is what's really important!" Angela took a good look at her two younger brothers. She wasn't at all sure either one of them understood what she had just said.

● *"We believe that Jesus died and rose again." 1 Thessalonians 4:14*

● **For Younger Children**
Have you ever been on an Easter egg hunt? What did you find?

At Easter we do lots of fun things to show we're happy that Jesus is alive. What else do you know about Jesus that makes you glad?

Let's thank God for Jesus.

● **For Older Children**
What do you remember about why Jesus died? What do you remember about Jesus' resurrection?

If Jesus had not died and risen again, how would our lives be different?

DAY

4

Why do big sisters love to torment younger brothers? And why is a big sister's favorite torment to nag a younger brother to do something? Those were the questions Hector De La Rosa was asking as he looked at the stiff new white shirt spread out on his bed. And the stiff black long pants next to them. The reason those new, uncomfortable looking clothes made Hector ask questions about older sisters was because of Angela.

While Hector was having breakfast, she had opened Hector's closet and taken the shirt and pants off their hangers. She had arranged them neatly on his bed. Then she had announced loudly for the whole neighborhood to hear, "I got your new Easter clothes ready for you, Hector. They're on your bed!"

Hector scowled at those stiff new clothes. "I hate long pants!" Hector grumbled to himself. "I hate long-sleeved shirts. And I especially hate long-sleeved shirts with scratchy collars!"

Just then there was a knock on his bedroom door. Angela announced, "Robbie looks terrific in his Easter clothes. How are YOU coming, Hector?"

"Go away!" Hector growled at his sister. "I don't need your help!"

"You need SOMEbody's help, Hermano," Angela giggled, then she ran down the hall to finish getting herself ready.

Hector decided to look through his drawers to see if he could find another shirt that would be acceptable. Probably none of his black T-shirts would go over on Easter. How about the dark green one with gold lightning bolts on the back?

Just then he heard another knock on his door. The door opened. It was Dad. "Trying to find something more comfortable, Hector?" Dad asked.

"Yeah," Hector answered. "Just 'cause it's Easter, why do we have to wear hot, stiff clothes?"

"I know you're not used to long pants and sleeves, Hector," Dad said. "But Easter is a special day. Wearing our best clothes is a way of showing it's important. So, we're all going to some extra trouble. Can you handle that?"

"OK," Hector said, picking up his bright new long-sleeved shirt.

● *"If you confess with your mouth, 'Jesus is Lord,' and believe in your heart that God raised Him from the dead, you will be saved." Romans 10:9*

● **For Younger Children**

Have you ever felt like Hector? When?

The De La Rosa family made colored eggs and bought new clothes to celebrate Jesus' resurrection. What is your favorite way to celebrate Easter?

● **For Older Children**

Easter bunnies, colored eggs, and new clothes all remind us of new life and things that grow. What are some other things you see this time of year that remind you of new life?

What does Romans 10:9 say will happen when you believe that Jesus is alive?

Let's thank God for the new life Jesus gives us and that we can grow as members of God's family.

WEEK 2

DAY 5

It was Easter Sunday, after church. The whole De La Rosa family had gathered at Uncle Manuel and Aunt Carmela's house for a big Easter dinner. The delicious smells filled the house, and Robbie was sure he was hungry enough to eat everything Aunt Carmela had cooked.

"I gotcha!" Uncle Manuel shouted as he grabbed Robbie around the waist and swung him in a circle. "Happy Easter, Robbie!" his big voice boomed. "What did you learn at church today?"

Robbie stared into his uncle's big laughing eyes and announced, "I learned 'bout Jesus in prison."

"Jesus in prison?" Uncle Manuel looked surprised. "On Easter? Do you mean when the soldiers arrested Jesus before He died?"

"No, Tio Manuel," Robbie said. "After Jesus died. THEN he was in prison."

Uncle Manuel put Robbie down and looked over at Robbie's dad. "I never heard the story that way. What do you. . . ?"

Angela interrupted her uncle. "I know, Tio," she said. Then she spoke to Robbie. "You mean, 'Jesus died, then He was RISEN.' "

"That's what I said," Robbie insisted. "Jesus in PRISON!"

"Ah," said Uncle Manuel. "Two words that sound the same. Robbie, you mean 'risen.' Risen means Jesus came back to life after those soldiers killed Him."

Robbie was impressed with his uncle's knowledge. No one at church had realized Robbie's misunderstanding. Perhaps his uncle knew even more. "Tio Manuel," Robbie asked. "Were you there when Jesus rose?" Even though Robbie was very serious, no one else could keep from laughing. Uncle Manuel put his arm on Robbie's shoulder and smiled his big, friendly grin. "Robbie, I wish I'd been there when Jesus rose, but I wasn't."

"So how do you know He rose?" Robbie asked.

"I know Jesus is alive because the Bible says so. And I know Jesus is alive because He's always with me. I can talk to Him anytime, anyplace. And that's why Easter is so special for me."

Just then, Aunt Carmela came into the living room and announced, "Dinner is ready."

And Robbie jumped out of Uncle Manuel's arms and announced, "So am I!"

● *"Through Him you believe in God, who raised Him from the dead and glorified Him, and so your faith and hope are in God." 1 Peter 1:21*

● **For Younger Children**
What two words did Robbie get confused?
  What does the word "risen" mean?
  Why can you believe that Jesus is alive?

● **For Older Children**
What are some words you had trouble understanding when you were younger?
  Why did Uncle Manuel say he believes that Jesus is alive?
  Why is Easter a special time for you?

● ●

Schedule time this week to be together as a family. Select one of these suggested activities to expand your family's understanding of Jesus' resurrection.

FAMILY TIMES

Easter Quiz
Ask each person in the family to write two or three questions about the first Easter. Write each question on a separate index card or piece of paper. Place the cards in an Easter basket. Each person takes a turn to choose a card, read the question aloud, and tell the answer.

Tip for Younger Children: Write each of these words on a separate card—Jesus, alive, Easter, Bible, eggs, bunnies. When a child chooses a card, tell him or her the word on the card. Help your child think of a sentence which uses the word to tell something about the first Easter.

Easter Messages

Several days before Easter, work with your family to write several short sentences expressing your joy that Jesus is alive. For example, you might write "Good news! Jesus is living!" or "Thank You, God, for Jesus!" Then have a parent write each sentence on separate pieces of paper. Choose one of these ways to send the messages on Easter morning: (1) Place each paper in a plastic egg. Put the eggs in Easter baskets. (2) Roll up each paper and tie with brightly colored yarn or ribbon. (3) Place each paper on plates to be read at Easter breakfast or dinner.

Family Video Night

The week before Easter rent or purchase a video which tells the Easter story. Or check your local television guides to see when movies about the life of Jesus may be shown. Prepare a special treat to eat while your family watches the video or movie. Afterward ask questions such as, "What is your favorite part of this story? Which character would you like to be? What parts of the movie are the same as the true Bible story of the first Easter? Which parts are imaginary?"

• •

Glorify and Enjoy God

While very few people still believe the world is flat or that tobacco smoke is harmless, there are seemingly great numbers of people who still hold to the false notion that the Christian faith is a sad, sober, and solemn way of life. While there are many very serious aspects to Christianity, the end result of vital faith in Jesus Christ is a life of abundant joy.

Too many people seek enjoyment in temporary things and find themselves ultimately disappointed. Scripture calls us to focus on God as the source of enjoyment that truly lasts. Paul wrote to Timothy to warn people "not to put their hope in wealth, which is so uncertain, but to put their hope in God, who richly provides us with everything for our enjoyment" (1 Timothy 6:17).

When we glorify God, when we honor and respect Him and His Word, we are living as He intends and are able to enjoy His wonderful goodness. This week, even if your child does not fully understand the meaning of glorifying God, your example of praise, worship, and thanksgiving will impress your child and set a healthy pattern for your child to follow.

Key Verse
"I will praise You, O Lord my God, with all my heart; I will glorify Your name forever."
Psalm 86:12

Key Thought
God is worthy of all honor and glory. He created us to glorify and enjoy Him.

• •

WEEK 3

DAY
1

Chris was surprised when he jumped off the school bus to see his dad waiting for him. Mr. Norris was usually too busy working on the farm to wait for Chris to come home from kindergarten. But today, there he was.

"C'mon Chris!" Dad said with a big smile, as he started back up their long driveway. "We've got some excitement in the barn this morning!"

Chris hurried to keep up with his dad's long steps. "What?" Chris asked. He was always interested in excitement.

"Lulu's about to drop her lamb," Mr. Norris said. "Any minute now. Mom's with her."

Chris knew that Lulu was their big, woolly sheep. Chris had never seen a lamb being born. Had he stopped to think about it right then, he would have remembered that he had never seen any animals being born, other than some chicks hatching. He had seen baby lambs and baby calves and baby kittens when they were a few hours old. But he had never seen one actually being born. Getting to see the birth of a baby lamb sounded like something worth hurrying for. Chris started to run toward the barn. He whizzed past his dad, who started to walk faster and shouted after Chris, "That's a long way to run!"

Mr. Norris was right. Chris kept running all the way to where the driveway curved around the big oak tree. Then he had to slow to a jog and then a fast walk. But he was determined he was going to get to the barn before that lamb was born. Once the barn door was in sight, Chris started to run again and began to shout, "I'm coming, Lulu! Wait for me."

As he entered the barn, Chris slowed to a walk. His heavy breathing was matched by a similar sound from a dark corner off to his left. Lulu was almost ready to give birth. Chris' mom was kneeling next to the big, woolly ewe. "You're just in time, Chris," she said softly as she stroked Lulu's side. "Just in time to see one of God's special wonders, a newborn lamb."

● *"Glory in His holy name; let the hearts of those who seek the Lord rejoice."*
1 Chronicles 16:10

● **For Younger Children**
What are some baby animals you have seen?

Baby sheep are called lambs. What are the names of other baby animals (cat, dog, cow, horse, etc.)?

What are some ways to thank and praise God for the wonderful world He has made?

● **For Older Children**
Why did Chris' mom say the birth of a lamb was "one of God's special wonders"?

What are some other wonderful things God has made?

Let's tell God thank You for these wonderful things.

● ●

WEEK 3

DAY
2

Chris had never seen anything like it. Lulu, his family's big, woolly sheep, had just given birth to a tiny, scraggly baby lamb. Chris knew there would be some blood. He also knew the lamb would not be all cute and woolly at first. But he still could not help saying, "Ew-w! Gross!" as he caught his first glimpse of the baby lamb's head.

Once the lamb's head was out, it was just a few moments until the newborn lamb was snuggled up against its mother. Chris was both excited and worried, wondering whether everything was OK. He looked up at his mom and dad and was relieved to see the big smiles on their faces.

Chris sat near Lulu and the baby lamb for quite a while, watching every movement they made. Now that he had seen the lamb being born, he also wanted to see the lamb stand up for the first time. Dad put his hand on Chris' shoulder and quietly talked to him. "Y'know, son," Dad said. "I've probably seen hundreds of animals being born, but I still get goose bumps every time. There is really something wonderful about a brand new life."

"What shall we name it?" Chris asked.

"Since you were right here when she was born, why don't you choose a name?" Mom asked.

"I wanted to name it Fluffy," Chris said, "but it doesn't look fluffy."

"That's a fine name," Dad answered. "It won't be long 'til she's as fluffy as can be."

"Should we thank God for it, I mean for Fluffy?" Chris asked.

"Good idea," Dad answered.

Chris bowed his head and prayed, "Thank You, God, for Fluffy, our new lamb. And thank You that Lulu is OK. And . . . and . . . Amen."

Dad stood up and smiled down at Chris. "This is the best part about being a farmer," Dad said. "Being up close to so many wonders of God's creation. Some people glorify God by preaching or singing. I enjoy glorifying God for all the wonderful things He made."

Chris looked up at his Dad. "What's glorify?" he asked.

● *"The Lord has done great things for us, and we are filled with joy."*
Psalm 126:3

● **For Younger Children**
What name would you give a baby lamb?

God planned for animals to be born and grow. In God's plan, who is to take care of baby animals?

Whom has God given to take care of you and help you grow?

● **For Older Children**
How would you answer Chris' question, "What's glorify?"

What does Psalm 126:3 say makes people joyful?

What are some things that make you glad and joyful?

WEEK 3

DAY 3

• •

Chris could not wait for Ryan, Josh, and Laura to get home from school. He was bursting with excitement about seeing the baby lamb being born. As the big yellow school bus came closer, Chris bounced from one foot to the other and waved his arms over his head.

Then Chris began shouting, "I saw our new lamb born!" He kept on yelling about the lamb as the bus door opened and his brothers and sister climbed down. They were embarrassed to have their little brother making so much noise in front of their friends on the bus.

Ryan, the oldest in the family, was the first one off. He said, "Put a lid on it, Chris. They can hear you all the way to town."

Chris was too excited to quiet down. He kept right on telling everything about the baby lamb.

Josh, the next one off, tried to act like seeing a lamb being born wasn't worth getting excited. "Big deal, Chris," he said. "Everyone's seen lots of baby lambs."

Suddenly, Chris realized what Ryan and Josh had said. The excitement on his face disappeared. He looked hurt and confused. Laura, the last one off the bus, almost said something like Ryan and Josh. But when she saw Chris' face, she changed her mind and asked, "Did you name it yet?"

Instantly, the unhappy look was gone, and Chris announced, "I named her Fluffy!" Then he asked his sister, "Did you ever see a lamb born, Laura?"

"I saw two," Laura said, as the four Norris children walked together up their long driveway. Then she added, "The first animals I saw born were puppies. They were so tiny!"

Then Josh told about seeing a foal born to one of their horses, and Ryan told about seeing a calf born. As they got closer to the barn, they all walked a little quicker, all anxious to see Fluffy, the baby lamb. They all stopped at the door to the barn and looked in at Lulu and Fluffy. Chris was the only one to say anything. He said, "Wow! God sure makes neat stuff."

● *"Glorify the Lord with me; let us exalt His name together." Psalm 34:3*

● **For Younger Children**
What do you think are some of the good things about living on a farm?

What are some of God's wonders that children might see who live where you do?

Let's thank God for what He has made.

● **For Older Children**

If you had been looking in the barn with Chris, what do you think you might have said about the lamb?

Read Psalm 34:3. What do you think "glorify" means? What do you think "exalt" means?

● ●

WEEK 3

DAY 4

The four Norris children stepped quietly into the barn, not wanting to disturb Lulu or her baby lamb, Fluffy. The mother and baby were snuggled together and appeared to be sleeping. As Ryan moved closer to them, Lulu opened one eye.

"It's OK, Lulu," Ryan whispered. "Are you OK, girl?"

No one expected Lulu to answer Ryan's question, but Chris felt the question deserved a reply. "She's fine," Chris said, also whispering. Then, just in case the other children might doubt that Chris knew what he was talking about, he added, just a little louder, "Mom told me."

"Mom should know," Ryan said.

"The lamb looks good," Josh commented.

Ryan agreed. "It has one head, four legs, two eyes."

Chris added, "And one tail!"

"Fluffy's a good name, Chris," Laura whispered. She was still trying to make up for the way Ryan and Josh had pretended not to be interested in the baby lamb.

"A good name for a girl sheep," Josh whispered a little louder, still trying to act like baby lambs were no big deal.

Lulu opened her other eye.

"Are you sure Fluffy's a girl?" Ryan asked.

"Mom said so," Chris answered.

"Mom should know," Ryan replied.

Lulu lifted her head and looked at the children.

"And Dad said he was glorifying God," Chris added, wanting the other children to know that both parents had been present at the moment of birth. Somehow, Chris seemed to think it was a more important event if both Mom and Dad were involved.

"Dad said what?" Ryan asked.

"He said he was glorifying God," Chris repeated. "What's glorifying?"

● *"Rejoice in the Lord always. I will say it again: Rejoice!" Philippians 4:4*

● **For Younger Children**

The Norris children enjoyed looking at the baby lamb. What special things have you seen with the people in your family?

How do you feel when you see something special God made?

● **For Older Children**

When we glorify God, it means we praise and thank Him and tell others about the wonderful things He has done. How often does Philippians 4:4 say we should be happy and celebrate the wonderful things God does?

What is something you can thank God for?

WEEK 2

DAY 5

The three older Norris children were sure they could explain to Chris what "glorify" meant. They were used to helping their five-year-old brother learn things. Chris had asked them to explain this word because of Dad saying something about glorifying God for the birth of a healthy, baby lamb. The four children were watching Fluffy trying to get up onto her thin, wobbly legs.

Ryan, as the oldest in the family, never liked to admit to his brothers and sister that there might be something he did not know. So he was first to try explaining things to Chris.

"Glorify means . . ." he started. Then there was a pause, as Fluffy lurched to her feet and stood still, trying to get her balance. Ryan thought about just what he would say. "It means to give glory," he said, feeling pleased that he had solved the matter. "That's it. Glorify means to give glory."

"What's glory?" Chris asked.

"Mrs. Poindexter says you can't use the same word to explain itself," Josh answered, trying to sound like he knew more than his older brother. Fluffy took a few careful steps and then stopped.

Not ready to admit defeat, Ryan decided to make another attempt at answering Chris' question. "Uh . . ." he started, "glory is like praise or worship. That's it. Glorify means to praise or worship God."

Chris did not look like he understood this answer any better than the first one.

Seeing the confused look on his little brother's face, Josh decided it was his turn to clear things up. "I think glorify means to honor God. Or something." Fluffy stumbled, but quickly regained her balance.

Laura knew she had heard the word glorify at church. She also thought maybe Grandma Norris had used it in some of her long prayers at supper. So Laura said, "It means to thank God. It means . . . it means . . . to pray."

Chris still was not sure what glorify meant, but he decided he had heard enough explanations. He said, "At least we know it's something good." Meanwhile, Fluffy stood firmly next to her mother, looking like she was ready to try learning to run.

● *"Now, our God, we give You thanks, and praise Your glorious name."*
1 Chronicles 29:13

● **For Younger Children**
Have you ever seen a baby learn to walk?

How did Chris' brothers and sister explain the word glorify?

When we praise and thank God, it shows that we honor God—we think He is special. What are some reasons why you think God is special?

● **For Older Children**
Why did Mr. Norris say he glorified God when he saw the baby lamb?

People glorify God by the words they say and by their actions. How would you describe the kind of actions that glorify God?

● ●

Schedule time this week to be together as a family. Select one of these suggested activities to expand your family's understanding of what it means to glorify God.

FAMILY TIMES

Praise Envelope
Ask each person to think of several reasons to glorify God. To help family members think of reasons, ask, "What is something God made? What is a characteristic of God?" Then each person writes his or her responses on separate small pieces of paper. Put the papers in an envelope labeled, "We Praise God." During the next week before each meal, choose one of the papers and read the response aloud. Thank and praise God together.

Tip for Younger Children: Provide magazines. Children cut out pictures of items for which they wish to thank God.

Psalm 150
Read Psalm 150 together as a family. Then think of ways to add expression to the reading—read certain words softly or loudly, in high or low voices, read certain phrases as solos or duets. Keep notes about what you decide as you practice reading the psalm several times. If possible, tape your family reading the psalm on a tape recorder or video camera.

Penny Walk
Enjoy a springtime walk with your family looking for signs of new life. To make this walk unique, each time you come to a corner, toss a penny. If the penny lands heads up, turn left. If the penny lands heads down, turn right. Remember to thank and praise God for the things you see.

God Is in Control

Key Verse
"And we know that in all things God works for the good of those who love Him, who have been called according to His purpose."
Romans 8:28

One of the essential needs of every young child is a sense of security and safety. This need is exhibited in every setting the child encounters. From infancy, parents must nurture a feeling of trust, letting the child know parents are dependable sources of nourishment, protection, and comfort. When the child goes to church or school or is left with a sitter, the child can experience very real anxiety, until the child discovers if the person in charge truly cares about the child and will provide the child's needs.

In a world beset by unexpected problems and tragedies, there is great comfort in knowing that God is ultimately in control. While human society is temporarily controlled by the evil one (1 John 5:19), it is deeply reassuring to know that nothing happens to us without our Heavenly Father's knowledge (Luke 12:6-7). While we are never promised immunity from the dangers of life in this world, we are assured that, no matter what may befall us, God will turn even the most difficult circumstance imaginable into an opportunity for good. This week, help your child learn to look at life's problems through the eyes of faith and hope and trust.

Key Thought
God is in control of everything and will take even the worst problem and produce a good result for those who belong to Him.

WEEK 4

DAY

1

Aliki was stunned. Her little sister, Midori, was silent. And their mother and father were very nervous and upset. Aliki's father had just told the two sisters that he had been laid off from his job. "My company has been losing money," Father had said. "They cannot pay all their workers. So they had to decide which workers to keep and which workers not to keep."

"They should have kept you," Midori announced. "They should have fired someone else."

"Then someone else would have been out of work," Mother said. "Maybe someone who does not have God to help them."

"It doesn't seem like God's helping us very much," Aliki said. "Couldn't God keep Father from losing his job?"

"What's going to happen to us now?" Midori asked before anyone could answer Aliki's question.

"Are we going to be poor?" Aliki asked before anyone could answer Midori's question.

"Will we be homeless?" asked Midori.

Father laughed. This surprised the girls, for they were both very worried that their family could lose their nice apartment and not be able to buy clothes and food. "What's funny?" Midori wanted to know. "Why are you laughing about not having a job?"

Father pushed his glasses up and explained. "Nothing is funny about losing my job. I am just laughing because you two are asking so many questions so fast. They are very good questions," he said. "I don't know the answers to all of them. I don't know everything that is going to happen. I do know that Mother still has her job, and I'm going to start looking for a new one tomorrow. Until I find a new job, we will have to be more careful than usual about how we spend our money."

The girls thought about that, and then Mother said, "Being careful with our money means there will be some things we may want that we will not be able to afford for a while."

"But . . . but . . ." Aliki stammered. "How can God can let this happen? Can't He take better care of us?"

"Just wait, Aliki," Father said. "You'll see that God is taking very good care of us. Very good care."

● *"For it is God who works in you to will and to act according to His good purpose." Philippians 2:13*

● **For Younger Children**
What did Aliki's father say about God?

How might God help Aliki's family?

How has God shown that He takes good care of you and your family?

● **For Older Children**
What made Aliki worried?

Have you ever wondered if God loved and cared for you? What happened?

What do you learn about God from Philippians 2:13?

DAY

2

Every day for three weeks, Aliki and Midori had waited for their father to come home. Every day they hoped he would have good news to share about finding a job. They were certain there must be many companies that would be eager to hire their father.

At first they expected Father to come in the door laughing and tell them of his wonderful new job. But every day for three weeks, Aliki and Midori had watched their father come in the door and say, "Nothing yet, girls. Nothing yet."

Today, while waiting for Father to come home, Midori had declared, "If I owned a company, I'd give Father a job. A good job."

"Me too," Aliki said. "And I'd pay him lots of money.

But when Father came in the door, the girls knew right away that there was no good news.

Silently, Father hung up his jacket. Next he took off his shoes and put on his slippers. Then he sat down on the couch. Aliki climbed up and sat on one side of him. Midori snuggled up on the other side. Father smiled at his two daughters and put one arm around each of them.

"It's hard not to get discouraged," Father said as he pushed his glasses up. "But let's not be glum. Let's enjoy being together."

Aliki smiled at her father, but Midori looked worried. "What's discouraged, Father?" she asked.

"Discouraged," Father said. "That's a big word that tells how people feel when they have a problem and don't seem to be able to fix it. It's a helpless, sad feeling."

"I don't want you to feel helpless," Midori said as she put both her arms around Father's neck. He could feel a wet tear on her cheek.

"I don't want to feel helpless either," Father said. "That's why I'm sure glad I can keep talking to God about finding a job."

"How do you know," Aliki asked, "that God can do anything to help?"

"Sometimes, Aliki," Father answered, "sometimes I wonder if God only takes care of big things like gravity and weather. Maybe He leaves people to muddle through by themselves. But then I remember all the other times in my life that He's helped me, and I know He'll help this time too."

● *"O Lord, God of our fathers.... Power and might are in Your hand, and no one can withstand You." 2 Chronicles 20:6*

● **For Younger Children**

How did Aliki and Midori feel about their father's problem?

What does 2 Chronicles 20:6 say about God?

How does knowing about God's power make you feel?

● **For Older Children**

Have you ever felt helpless? Why?

What did Aliki's and Midori's Father say he does when he feels helpless?

Why is it good to talk to God about our problems?

● ●

WEEK 4

DAY
3

Aliki felt happy for the first time since Father had lost his job. Part of her happy feeling was because her class was going on a field trip, and Aliki always liked field trips. Another part of her good feeling was because the class was going to the natural history museum, and she loved the museum.

However, most of her excitement was because Father was going to go with Aliki's class as a parent helper. Other children had parents who came to class and helped the teacher. Other parents had gone on field trips before. But Aliki's mother and father had never been able to do that because of their jobs. Now that Father did not have a job, he could help Aliki's class.

At breakfast, Aliki could not stop talking about all the things she wanted to show Father at the museum.

On the way to school, Aliki said to her friend Natalie, "Father's coming on our field trip."

At school, Aliki told all her friends, "That's my father. He's coming on our field trip."

On the bus, Aliki sat next to Father and told him she wanted to go see the dinosaur bones first.

At the museum, Aliki, Natalie, and two other girls were one of the small groups. Father was supposed to be with them.

That night, Aliki spent most of the dinnertime telling Midori and Mother what she and Father had seen at the museum.

"It sounds like you two had a great day together," Mother said.

"We had a good time," Father answered as he pushed his glasses up. "Being able to go with Aliki was a good thing that came from not having a job right now. But I can't afford to be a parent volunteer much longer. I really need to find a job."

Suddenly, Aliki's happy smile faded. In all the fun of going with Father to the museum, she had almost forgotten about their family's problem. Now that she remembered it, she began to worry again—and wonder if God could really do anything to make things better.

● *"I am the Lord your God, who teaches you what is best for you, who directs you in the way you should go." Isaiah 48:17*

● **For Younger Children**

What made Aliki feel happy?

One way God helps us is by making good things happen even when we have big problems. What are some good things that have happened to our family?

Let's tell God thank You for always being with our family and helping us have good times together.

● **For Older Children**

Have you ever gone on a field trip with your class at school? What did you like best about it?

Isaiah 48:17 tells us that God will help us know what is best for us to do. What choices do kids your age have to make?

Ask God to teach you what is best for you and thank Him for His help.

● ●

WEEK 4

DAY
4

Aliki was helping her mother clean up the kitchen after dinner. Father had cooked dinner, and Mother was doing dishes. Aliki's father had been doing more of the cooking than usual. Ever since he had lost his job, he had more time at home.

Aliki liked having Father home more than before, but his dinners did not taste as good as those Mother cooked. Perhaps it was because they were not able to afford some of the things Aliki was used to eating. She was getting very tired of rice. Especially the way Father cooked it. And the soup tonight had tasted like burned grease. Maybe not quite that bad. But almost.

Just as Aliki was remembering Father's soup, she heard their front door buzzer. Her little sister, Midori, ran over to push the button and talk to the person downstairs at the front door. "Who is it?" she shouted into the little speaker box. "Hi, up there!" the box squawked. "It's David Lee from church."

"Let him in, Midori," Mother said. Midori pushed the button to unlock the downstairs door of the apartment building.

"I wonder why David's here?" Father said, as he pushed his glasses up and walked over to open the door to their apartment. A few moments later Aliki heard voices in the hall, and then three people from their church came in the door, each carrying big bags filled with groceries.

"We figured things might be getting tough with no job yet," one of the men said. "So a bunch of us wanted to help out."

Aliki thought that Father and Mother looked embarrassed. This was the first time that Aliki had ever seen them receiving help.

Mother was the first one to say something. "Oh, David," she started to say, when Father interrupted.

"We're really making out OK," he said; then Mother interrupted him.

"But we really appreciate your thinking of us."

Then all five grownups began talking and laughing together, and Mother began unpacking the groceries. Aliki was glad when she noticed some of her favorite things to eat. She just hoped Father knew how to cook them right!

● *"Do you know how God controls the clouds and makes His lightning flash? Do you know how the clouds hang poised, those wonders of Him who is perfect in knowledge?" Job 37:15-16*

● **For Younger Children**
Who came to help Aliki and Midori's family? How did they help?

Who has helped you when you had a problem?

Do you know someone with a problem? How could you help him or her?

● **For Older Children**
How did the family feel when their friends brought groceries to them?

Read Job 37:15-16. Because the Bible tells us that God is powerful enough to control the clouds and lightning, we know that God is powerful enough to help us when we are having problems. Sometimes God uses other people to help us. What else might someone do to help this family?

● ●

DAY
5

Aliki and Midori waited quietly as Father closed the door behind him. They tried to tell from his face whether he had any good news about finding a job.

Father took off his jacket and hung it up. Next he took off his shoes and put on his slippers. Then he sat down on the couch. Aliki climbed up and sat on one side of him. Midori snuggled up on the other side. Father smiled at his two daughters and put one arm around each of them.

"I have a job," he said softly.

Midori jumped off the couch and shouted, "Hooray!"

Aliki squeezed Father's hand and smiled. And smiled.

Mother came into the living room and said, "Tell us about it."

"Well," Father said, "the salary is not as much as my old job."

"Will we still be poor?" Midori asked.

"We're not poor," Father said as he pushed his glasses up. "We'll still have to cut back on some things, but we'll make it."

"I wish you had your old job," Aliki pouted.

"I agree, Aliki," Father replied. "But I can see ways God is doing some good things in all of this."

"What good things?" Aliki asked, still pouting.

"Many good things happened while I didn't have a job. I got to spend more time at home." Aliki nodded. "I got to go with your class on a field trip." Aliki nodded again. "I learned how much our friends at church care about us." Aliki kept nodding. "I became a better cook than I was." Aliki didn't nod this time, but Father didn't notice.

"Is that all?" Midori asked.

"No, God keeps on doing good for us," Father said. "At my new job I think I'll make some new friends. And I'm going to learn some new things I've always wanted to do."

Mother came and sat down on the couch with Father and the girls. "I think we should thank God that He's really in charge of everything. Even when problems come." And that's what they did.

● *"God, the blessed and only Ruler, the King of kings and Lord of lords. . . . To Him be honor and might forever. Amen." 1 Timothy 6:15-16*

● **For Younger Children**

What did the Yasudas learn about God in these stories?

The Bible tells us that God knows everything about us and always cares for us, no matter what happens. If you were Aliki or Midori, what would you say to God?

● **For Older Children**

What things did God give the Yasudas when Mr. Yasuda didn't have a job?

What does it mean to say God is in charge of everything?

● ●

FAMILY TIMES

Schedule time this week to be together as a family. Select one of these suggested activities to expand your family's understanding of God's presence and power in times of trouble.

Family Time Line

To help your family think about the good things God has given you, work together to make a family time line. Draw a line in the center of a long sheet of paper. Choose a starting date to write at the left end of the line. Your time line may cover a one-month period, the summer, or a year. To help family members think of time line events, ask questions such as: "What was something we did that we really enjoyed? How did someone help us in a special way? Who are some new friends our family made?" Display the time line on a wall or door.

Tip for Younger Children: Younger children will enjoy drawing pictures to illustrate the time line.

Bible Verse Quiz

Read Romans 8:28 together. Then ask family members to think of one or two questions to ask someone about what this verse means. Each person writes his or her question on a separate piece of paper. Take turns answering each other's questions.

Tip for Younger Children: Help younger children learn Isaiah 48:17. Repeat the verse several times. Then say it again, leaving out the last word. Children try to supply the missing word. Continue the process, each time leaving out another word.

Maze Walk

Use chairs, cardboard boxes, pillows, etc. to make a maze in one or two rooms of your house. (If possible, build the maze outdoors.) Introduce this activity by saying, "Sometimes things happen to us that don't make much sense. Sometimes it's hard to understand why God allows bad things to happen to us. But because we know God loves us and wants the best for us, we can trust or depend on His directions to help us. This maze walk is a fun way to remind ourselves of the importance of trusting." Blindfold one person and lead him or her to the beginning of the maze. Then another family member gives the blindfolded person directions to find his or her way through the maze. Repeat until each person has had a turn to walk through the maze.

Key Verse
"God raised [Christ] to the highest place. God made His name greater than every other name so that every knee will bow to the name of Jesus — everyone in heaven, on earth, and under the earth. And everyone will confess that Jesus Christ is Lord and bring glory to God the Father." Philippians 2:9-11, EB

Jesus Is King

Young children find it easy to visualize Jesus in the stories from the Gospels. First as a baby, then as a boy, finally as a man, Jesus is a very real, very active figure.

But what about now? It is more difficult for a child to grasp the present reality of Jesus. No longer limited by a human body, Christ has taken His rightful place at the right hand of God the Father. Still, your child can begin to understand that Jesus is not just an attractive, powerful leader in history, but is truly Lord of all. Beyond that, your child can also begin to appreciate his or her standing as a child of the King.

Key Thought
Because Jesus is the King over all kings, everyone who belongs to Him is really a King's child.

WEEK 5

DAY 1

Arthur's kindergarten class was rehearsing a special program. Most of the children were to be circus animals or performers. Arthur was to be the ringmaster who announces all the circus acts. He had been chosen because he could talk louder than anyone.

While Arthur's teacher was showing the clowns what to do, Arthur muttered to the lion tamer, "This is a STUPID program!"

Arthur's loud whisper was heard by everyone in the class. "Arthur," the teacher said, "that is NOT a helpful thing to say."

Without thinking, Arthur blurted out, "Well, it IS stupid!"

The teacher crossed the room and stooped down to talk directly to Arthur. "If you talk like that, we may need someone else to be our ringmaster."

Now Arthur said, "GOOD! Being ringmaster is stupid!"

Arthur's teacher was very patient. She said, "I want you to think about this over the weekend. When you come back to school on Monday, we'll decide the best thing to do."

The rest of Arthur's morning at kindergarten and afternoon at day care was awful. Just plain awful.

When his mother picked him up, she took one look at Arthur and said, "Not a good day, was it?" Arthur just shrugged.

On the way home, Mom tried to find out what had gone wrong. However, Arthur just grunted and shrugged and said everything was stupid.

When they got home, Mom said, "Arthur, I know something's bothering you. But I can't help until you tell me your problem."

Mom noticed one big tear sitting in the corner of Arthur's eye. Suddenly, he started to cry. Between sobs he told about not wanting to be the ringmaster in that "stupid" show because he was afraid he would forget what to say and all the kids and parents would laugh at him. "I can't do it!" he wailed. "I'm no good!"

Mom held Arthur very close until the tears stopped. Then she said, "Mrs. Barrett did give you a hard job, but she knows you can do it. We'll play some games this weekend to help you remember. I've got confidence in you, 'cause you're special. You're one of God's children."

Arthur wiped his eyes, but he was not convinced.

● *"God exalted Him [Jesus] to His own right hand as Prince and Savior." Acts 5:31*

● **For Younger Children**

Why did Arthur feel so awful?

How would you have felt if you had the job of ringmaster?

Why did Arthur's mom say he was special?

● **For Older Children**

When have you felt like Arthur? What happened?

Why did Arthur's mom say she had confidence in Arthur?

What hard job have you been given?

WEEK 5

DAY
2

Arthur was still wiping his eyes when his friend, Christopher, knocked at the door of the apartment. Arthur always knew when it was Christopher knocking because Christopher always did three quick, little knocks and one big, loud knock. Arthur did not want Christopher to see that he had been crying. He did not want Christopher to know that he was afraid to be the ringmaster in his kindergarten class program. He did not want Christopher to know that he had gotten in trouble at kindergarten and at day care. But he knew that if he didn't answer the door, Christopher would just keep knocking, three quick, one loud. Three quick, one loud.

Mom was no help. She just said, "You can play with Christopher while I fix supper." Even Mom recognized Christopher's knock.

Arthur rubbed his face on his sleeves, sniffed twice, then opened the door in the middle of three quick knocks. Christopher took one look at Arthur and asked, "Why are you crying?"

"I'm not crying," Arthur sniffed.

"Well," Christopher asked as he walked into the apartment, "why WERE you crying?"

Arthur closed the door and decided to tell Christopher his problem. " 'Cause I don't wanna be in a stupid program for my class."

After Arthur explained his fear of forgetting what to say, Christopher said, "I don't blame you. Awful things can happen to kids in programs." Since Christopher was a full year older than Arthur, Arthur tended to think Christopher knew what he was talking about.

So Arthur asked, "What awful things?"

This was the kind of opening Christopher loved. He gleefully started to list the most awful catastrophes. "The costume could be too HOT and make you sweat. Your PANTS could fall down. You could WET your pants! You could get SICK and. . . ."

"Christopher!" It was Arthur's mom to the rescue. "Quit telling Arthur those awful things. Arthur's going to do fine in his program."

Suddenly, Arthur wished he could remember what Mom had said about being God's child. Would God let any of those terrible things happen to one of His children? Arthur wished he knew.

● *"Let us look only to Jesus, the One who began our faith and who makes it perfect. . . . And now He is sitting at the right side of God's throne."*
Hebrews 12:2, EB

● **For Younger Children**

What were some of the awful things Christopher said could happen?

What made Arthur feel afraid?

Who helps you when you feel afraid?

● **For Older Children**

Why didn't Arthur want Christopher to know that he had been crying?

What does Hebrews 12:2 tell about Jesus? How does this verse help you have confidence that Jesus can help you?

● ●

WEEK 5

DAY
3

Arthur sat on his bed with his arms wrapped around his knees. He was thinking about what his friend, Christopher, had said. Christopher had warned Arthur about the terrible things that could go wrong if Arthur were the ringmaster in his kindergarten class program. There was a knock on his bedroom door. This was definitely not Christopher coming back with more disaster stories. This was Mom's knock: TWO quick knocks and then a pause. "Come in," Arthur said, not sounding very friendly.

"You look worried," Mom said.

"I can't be ringmaster!" Arthur announced. "I don't remember which kids are clowns or lions or dancers."

"Not now you can't," Mom said. "But the day of the program, they'll all be in costumes. It'll be easy to know who's who."

"Oh, yeah, huh," Arthur said. He hadn't thought about that.

"And as long as you don't spend any more mornings in the principal's office," Mom said, "you'll have lots of chances to practice."

"Oh, yeah, huh," Arthur said. He hadn't thought about that either.

"And!" Mom said, "Don't forget that you're special. You're one of God's children."

This time Arthur did not say, "Oh" or "yeah" or "huh." Instead, he asked, "What good is that? How can being God's child keep my PANTS from falling down, or something WORSE?"

"Good question, Arthur," Mom said, and she sat down on the floor beside his bed. "Let me tell you something. You remember about Jesus dying on the cross for us?"

"Yeah," Arthur said.

"And you remember about Jesus coming back to life and then going up to heaven?" Arthur nodded.

"Well," Mom said. "Jesus did all that for us, so that we can enjoy all that's good for us."

Arthur asked, "Really?"

"Sure," Mom said. "So even if something bad or embarrassing happens to us, we just remind ourselves whose family we're in."

"God's family?" Arthur asked.

"Right!" Mom said.

● *"And since we are His children, we will share His treasures—for all God gives to His Son Jesus is now ours too." Romans 8:17, TLB*

● **For Younger Children**

What did Arthur's mom say he should remember when something bad or embarrassing happens?

What does Romans 8:17 say will happen when we become God's children?

Let's tell God thank You for giving us good things.

● **For Older Children**

What bad or embarrassing thing has happened to you?

According to Romans 8:17, what does it mean to be one of God's children?

What treasure has God given you?

●●

WEEK 5

DAY

4

Arthur had just finished his last piece of French toast when his friend Christopher knocked on the door. Three quick knocks and then one loud one. That was how Christopher always knocked.

"Maybe Christopher would like to help us practice for your class program," Mom suggested. "I'll do the dishes and then we can get started."

When Arthur told Christopher what they were going to do, Christopher acted surprised. "You're gonna go ahead and be in the program?" Christopher asked. "Even if you get all nervous and forget everything and mix everyone up?"

Arthur winced at the thought of such a calamity. But he said, "Mom really wants me to do it. And she's been telling me a bunch of stuff about being God's child."

Christopher scratched his head. "How can that help?" he asked.

"Well," Arthur answered, "Jesus is in heaven, and He's in charge."

"So you can't mess up?" Christopher asked.

"I don't know," Arthur said. "Mom? Will Jesus make sure I don't mess up in the program?"

Mom left the breakfast dishes to soak in the sink and came over to where the boys were talking. "Not if you don't practice," she said. "Jesus is in charge, but He leaves a lot of stuff up to us. Let's get started."

Mom told Arthur to stand in the middle of the room like a circus ringmaster. Then she said she would whisper to Christopher the name of a circus animal or performer. He would start pretending to be whatever Mom had whispered. And Arthur would pretend he was announcing that circus act. The first word she whispered in Christopher's ear was "lions." Christopher tried to look fierce, showed his big sharp claws and growled.

Arthur stood tall in the center of the room and announced in a very loud voice, "Lay-deez and Gentle-men! Intro-du-cing the fierc-est a-ni-mal in the jungle! The my-tee KING of BEASTS!" Mom and Christopher clapped their hands. They were sure Arthur was going to be a terrific ringmaster.

"See," Mom said. "When you know you're one of God's special children, you can just relax and do your best."

● *"Jesus has gone into heaven and is at God's right side ruling over angels, authorities, and powers." 1 Peter 3:22, EB*

● **For Younger Children**

Which circus animal would you like to pretend to be?

Practicing what to say was a good idea for Arthur. What's something you're learning that you need to practice?

Ask God for help in doing your best.

● **For Older Children**

What would you say to introduce the lions? The elephants?

First Peter 3:22 tells us that Jesus is in charge over everything that happens. But what does Jesus expect of us when we have a job to do?

What's one of your jobs? How can you do your best at that job?

WEEK 5

DAY
5

Everyone agreed that it had been a marvelous circus. The clowns had been hilarious. The strong man had lifted heavy weights as though they were made out of paper. The animals had been ferocious. The acrobats had done amazing somersaults. And the ringmaster. Everyone had loved the ringmaster.

As Arthur and his mom started home after his kindergarten class program, other parents and children called to him, "Good job, Arthur!" and "Great ringmastering, Arthur!" and "Arthur! Way to go!"

Arthur just smiled and waved back at them. His voice was a little hoarse after all the loud announcing he had done.

"How about stopping for a donut?" Mom asked.

"All right!" Arthur croaked. "Can I get a big one with chocolate chips?"

"I think you deserve an extra treat," Mom said. "Because you worked so hard learning what to say about all those circus acts."

At the donut shop, Arthur eyed the big chocolate chip donuts and smiled big when the lady asked, "Are you sure you can eat all that?"

"I was ringmaster in our circus!" he announced, certain that would convince the lady he could do just about anything.

Arthur and his mom sat down at one of the little tables near the window. "Let's thank God for our treat and for having such a good time at the circus," Mom said. She bowed her head and said a short prayer.

Before she could say "Amen," Arthur added a quick prayer of his own. "And thank You that Jesus is King and I'm a prince, Amen."

Mom looked up and smiled. "A prince?" she asked.

"Sure!" Arthur said, taking his first big bite of chocolate. "You said I'm one of God's children. So if Jesus is King, I'm a prince!"

Mom laughed. "You sure are, Arthur," she said. "You sure are."

● *"How great is the love the Father has lavished on us, that we should be called children of God!" 1 John 3:1*

● **For Younger Children**
How did Arthur feel after the program?
What did Arthur and his mom thank God for?
What's special about you?

● **For Older Children**
What kind of treat would you have wanted?

What made Arthur say he was a prince?

How could knowing you're one of God's children make a difference in your life?

● ●

Schedule time this week to be together as a family. Select one of these suggested activities to expand your family's understanding of what it means to be a special child of the King.

FAMILY TIMES

Paper Doll Autobiographies

For each family member draw an outline of a person on a separate large piece of paper. (Optional: If you have large enough paper, lie down on it and have someone trace around you to make your drawing life-size.) Each person adds drawings, words, and/or magazine pictures to tell about him- or herself. As family members work, comment, "As a child of God, you are special! The drawings, words, and pictures on your outline show some of the ways God has made you special."

Tip for Younger Children: In addition to drawing pictures, younger children may dictate words and/or phrases to you.

"You Are Special" Dinners

Honor each person in your family at a special dinner. The person being honored chooses the menu, receives cards made by other family members, plans a centerpiece of his or her favorite items, chooses dinnertime music to listen to, etc. At the conclusion of the meal, each family member tells something he or she likes about the honored person.

Tip for Younger Children: Make a construction paper crown decorated with star stickers for a younger child to wear.

Who Am I?

Take turns reading each of these Bible verses aloud. As you read, write a description of yourselves as children of the king, based on the information in the verses. Ephesians 1:3-5, 7; 2:6; 4:7, 24; 5:1.

Tip for Younger Children: A younger child may decorate the description with pictures of your family.

May

Key Verse
"But the fruit of the Spirit is love, joy, peace, patience, kindness, goodness, faithfulness, gentleness and self-control."
Galatians 5:22-23

Key Thought
God has sent His Holy Spirit to be with and to help those who love and follow Jesus.

The Holy Spirit Helps Us (Pentecost)

The Holy Spirit is the least understood and most neglected Person of the Godhead. This is especially true in dealing with children. It is much easier for a child to understand the concept of God as Father and God as Son than to grasp the idea of God as Spirit. Many people prefer to avoid the subject of the Holy Spirit when teaching children, reserving it until children are older and better able to understand abstract and spiritual concepts.

However, many others find talking with children about the Holy Spirit is very exciting and rewarding. Usually, the easiest way to introduce children to the Holy Spirit is to talk about some of the wonderful things the Holy Spirit does. This week's story and verses will help your child begin to understand how God's Spirit helps us in very real, practical ways.

WEEK 1

DAY 1

AJ and her twin brother DJ walked together down the side steps of their school building. All around them were other children on their way home after school. "I wish it was Friday," DJ moaned.

"What's wrong with Thursday?" AJ asked.

"Thursday is the day before our spelling test," DJ explained. They stopped at the curb and waited for the crossing guard to step out with her big red stop sign. "If it was already Friday, I wouldn't have to study tonight for the test. It would be all over."

"The words are easy this week," AJ said. "I got all of them right when we took the pretest on Monday."

"You're better at spelling than I am," DJ said as they crossed the street together. "You're better at spelling, and I'm better at math."

"No, you're not," AJ said. "I'm as good as you."

The twins continued on their way home, arguing over who was better in what. Suddenly, DJ felt a strong grip on his shoulder.

"Hey!" DJ yelled and spun around. He was looking straight at a big, mean-looking boy who hung around the neighborhood. And behind him were four more mean-looking boys, all several years older than the twins. A gang.

"You're on our street, little man," the leader of the gang said.

"We're just walkin' home," DJ answered.

"This is our street," the gang leader said, grabbing hold of DJ's sleeve. "You walk on our street, you pay."

"You leave my brother alone," AJ protested, stepping in between the gang leader and DJ.

"You let your sister take care of you, little man?" one of the gang members teased. The leader tightened his grip on DJ's jacket, pushed his face close to DJ's, and said, "You come walkin' our street again, you'll pay big." Then he shoved DJ hard. DJ stumbled and fell, and the gang members all stood over him. "Girl," one of the gang members said to AJ. "Get your little brother off our street. Fast."

DJ got to his feet, then began to run, with AJ right alongside. They didn't slow down until they were inside their apartment building. "Oh, wow!" DJ puffed. "What are we gonna do?"

● *Jesus said, "The Holy Spirit, whom the Father will send in My name will teach you all things and will remind you of everything I have said to you." John 14:26*

● **For Younger Children**

What would you do if you were one of the twins?

What kind of help do the twins need?

Who does John 14:26 say will remind the twins of Jesus' help?

● **For Older Children**

Has anything like this story ever happened to you? How did you feel? Who helped you?

John 14:26 says the Holy Spirit will remind God's followers of everything Jesus has said. What do you remember about Jesus' words that could help the twins?

How might Jesus' words help you?

WEEK 1

DAY
2

"This gang said what?" DJ's mom asked.

"They said if we walk on their sidewalk, we have to pay," DJ answered.

"And big!" added DJ's twin sister, AJ.

"They can't do that," Mom insisted. "It's not their sidewalk."

"They say they can," AJ said.

"And their leader is big enough that I believe they can," DJ added.

Mom turned to look at her husband, who had not said anything yet. "Jim!" she said, "We can't let a gang terrorize our children!"

"What do you suggest?" Dad asked.

"We should call the police or the school or somebody!" Mom insisted.

"Don't do that!" DJ begged. "That'll just make the gang mad, and they'll really pound me."

"How about if I take a late lunch from work for a few days and walk home with you two?" Dad suggested.

"That's even worse!" DJ wailed. "All the kids will think I'm a sissy. It's bad enough I have to walk home with my sister!"

"I understand, DJ," Dad said. "But there's no way we're going to leave you alone in a dangerous situation. That's what families are for. Mom and I will talk about it and decide what to do."

"OK," DJ muttered. "Just don't do anything to embarrass me."

After the twins had gone to bed, their parents talked about the gang. "What if the twins walk home another way?" Mom suggested.

"What if we talk to other parents and arrange for four or five kids to walk home in a group?" Dad offered.

"What if we find out who these gang members are and talk to their parents?" Mom proposed.

"What if we pray to know what we should do?" Dad advised.

"That's the best idea, yet," Mom answered. "Why didn't we think of that earlier?"

They joined hands and prayed. They told God how fearful they were that this gang might hurt their children. They asked for His help to know the right thing to do. When their prayer ended, they still weren't sure how to solve the problem, but they certainly felt much better about what might happen tomorrow after school.

● *"But when He, the Spirit of Truth, comes, He will guide you into all truth." John 16:13*

● **For Younger Children**

What did the twins' mom say was the best idea?

Why is it so important to tell God how we feel and ask for His help?

John 16:13 tells us that the Holy Spirit will help us know the right things to do. What is something good and right you have done?

● **For Older Children**

Which of the ideas, beside praying, would be the best to do? Why?

When is it hard for you to know what to do?

Ask God for the Holy Spirit's help in knowing the right things to do.

● ●

WEEK 1

DAY
3

AJ and her twin brother DJ walked together down the side steps of their school building. "I wish it was Saturday," DJ moaned.

"What's wrong with Friday?" AJ asked.

"Nothing, except we have to walk past that gang," DJ said.

"You should have let Dad come with us," AJ said, as they waited for the crossing guard to signal them to cross the street.

"Well," DJ said when they were on their way again, "if the gang tries anything, you run home as fast as you can and call Dad or 911 or somebody."

AJ and DJ walked along, discussing what to do if the gang attacked. What they did not know was Dad was walking half a block behind them. He did not want the twins to know he was there, but he was ready to come to their aid if they needed help with the gang.

Suddenly, there they were. The gang stood in the middle of the sidewalk with their feet spread wide and their hands on their hips. DJ and AJ hesitated for a moment, then continued walking until they came up to the gang. They stopped and waited for someone to speak.

From half a block behind, Dad could not hear what anyone said, but the gang members certainly did not look friendly. Dad stopped and waited, trying to tell if the gang was going to grab or hit DJ. For almost five minutes, AJ and DJ stood talking with the gang. Then Dad saw DJ and AJ start walking on toward home. The gang members turned and watched them go.

Dad stood and watched long enough to be sure the twins were safely on their way; then he turned in the other direction and headed back to work.

As he walked along, Dad prayed silently, his worry and fear having disappeared. "Thank You, God," he prayed. "I don't know what happened there on that sidewalk, but I thank You that DJ and AJ are safe." A few moments later he added, "And help me not to forget that Your Spirit is always with us." Then he started whistling a very happy tune.

● *"May the God of hope fill you with all joy and peace as you trust in Him, so that you may overflow with hope by the power of the Holy Spirit."* Romans 15:13

● **For Younger Children**
How do you think AJ and DJ felt when they saw the gang?
What did Mr. Gorman say in his prayer?
When is a time you need to remember that God's Spirit is with you?

● **For Older Children**
What do you think AJ, DJ, and the gang members said to each other? What would you have said?
What do you think it means to trust in God and in the power of the Holy Spirit?

● ●

WEEK 1

DAY

4

The TV was on. AJ and her twin brother DJ were flat on their backs with their feet propped up on cushions from the couch. They were watching a big cartoon animal chase a little cartoon animal. Just as the little animal made a narrow escape, the front door opened, and Dad arrived home from work. AJ jumped up and snapped off the television.

"Dad!" she almost shouted. "Guess what happened with our gang?"

"OUR gang?" Dad asked.

"My carTOONS!" DJ shouted because AJ had turned off the TV.

"Oh, Deej," AJ said. "Our story is a lot more exciting than that dumb cartoon."

"Exciting?" Dad said. "Tell me what happened? Did the gang give you any trouble?"

Without pausing for a breath, AJ began telling every detail of their walk home from school, right up to the moment they walked up to the gang. As AJ talked, Mom came into the living room and listened. She had already heard the twins' story.

"So what did the gang say to you?" Dad asked.

"They didn't get a chance to say anything," AJ answered, " 'cause DJ invited them all to Sunday School."

"You what?" Dad asked DJ.

"I just asked them if they did anything fun on Sunday mornings," DJ said. "When they said no, I invited them to Sunday School."

"So what did they say?" Dad asked.

"The big kid said they'd think about it," DJ answered. "I got the feeling none of them know anything about Sunday School."

"You're probably right," Dad said. "But when did you get the idea to invite them to church?"

"Beats me," DJ said. "It just sorta came out. The weird thing is, I suddenly wasn't scared like I was the day before."

Then Mom spoke: "I know why," she said. "Last night we prayed that God would help with this problem. And He did. His Spirit helped DJ think of the right thing to say."

"Really?" AJ asked. "The Holy Spirit did that?"

"Why not?" Mom asked. "Jesus promised that God's Spirit will always be with us. And one thing He does is help us tell people about Jesus."

"Wow!" AJ said. "That's cool!"

● *"But you will receive power when the Holy Spirit comes on you; and you will be My witnesses." Acts 1:8*

● **For Younger Children**

How were DJ's feelings different when he saw the gang the second time? How did the Holy Spirit help the twins?

It's good to remember Jesus' promise that God's Spirit will always be with us. What is a place you go to often? How might the Holy Spirit help you there?

● **For Older Children**

Do you think the gang members will come to Sunday School? Why or why not?

How did God answer Mr. and Mrs. Gorman's prayer?

How would you say Acts 1:8 in your own words?

WEEK 1

DAY 5

AJ and DJ were both in bed. Mom and Dad were sitting in the living room, talking about whatever it is parents talk about when kids are asleep. On most nights they would have been talking about whose turn it was to go to the grocery store and what to do about the funny noises the vacuum cleaner was making. Exciting stuff like that.

Tonight, however, Dad and Mom were talking about DJ's encounter with the neighborhood gang and his invitation for them to come to Sunday School. "I thought my walking behind the twins without their knowing I was there was a pretty good idea. If they found out I was there, I figured I could make it a good example of how God watches over us."

"Instead," Mom said, "the Holy Spirit gave DJ the idea to invite the whole gang to church."

"So what do we do with this gang now?" Dad asked. "What if they really do come to Sunday School?"

"It sounds," Mom said, "as if they're a bunch of lonely kids who need someone to be kind and loving to them."

"That's not easy with kids like that," Dad said. "It's hard to be loving to people who are always trying to pick a fight."

"It sounds like we need to pray about this problem just like we did about the twins' walking home safely," Mom said. "Since the Holy Spirit helped DJ talk to the gang, we should also expect the Holy Spirit to help us find a way to help them."

"We should probably also pray that the Holy Spirit will help whoever their Sunday School teacher may be," Dad said.

"Oh, my," Mom said. "I hadn't thought about that. Should we call and warn someone that this gang may show up Sunday morning?"

"Maybe," Dad said, "I should volunteer to help out with that class for a few weeks, just in case."

"Good idea, Jim," Mom said. "Good idea. Now let's start praying." And they did.

● *"God has poured out His love into our hearts by the Holy Spirit, whom He has given us." Romans 5:5*

● **For Younger Children**

Why might it be hard to show love to a gang?

Who does Romans 5:5 say shows God's love to us?

Thank God that His Holy Spirit is always with us to help us and show God's love to us.

● For Older Children

Romans 5:5 says that the Holy Spirit shows God's love to us. How did DJ and AJ show God's love to the gang?

What are some other ways the gang members might need help?

What could you do that is like the actions of DJ and AJ?

● ●

Schedule time this week to be together as a family. Select one of these suggested activities to expand your family's understanding of how God's Spirit helps us.

FAMILY TIMES

Author! Author!

With your family make up a story like the one for this week. Use the names of your family in the story. Be sure the story shows how the Holy Spirit is with your family and helps you. Write your story on paper.

Tip for Younger Children: A younger child will enjoy drawing pictures to illustrate the story.

What Did You Say?

Cut several sheets of construction paper into large conversation balloons. Read Galatians 5:22-23 together. Talk about your answer to this question, "To show love, what might a person in our family say or do?" Write sentence ideas on separate conversation balloons. Display conversation balloons on walls or doors in your house.

Tip for Younger Children: Ask a younger child to dictate his or her sentences to you.

Shape Scenes

Ask each family member to think of a time he or she needs the help of God's Spirit. "When do you have a choice to make? When might you feel afraid? When do you need help to show God's love?" Then each person draws a scene about the time using only geometric shapes (squares, rectangles, triangles, half circles, circles).

Tip for Younger Children: Younger children may draw their pictures using stick figures.

God Made Everything

Key Verse
"You are worthy, our Lord and God, to receive glory and honor and power, for You created all things."
Revelation 4:11

Key Thought
God showed His great power and wisdom in the wonders of the universe He created.

Most young children have only an imperfect sense of how anything is made. Every parent discovers this truth when trying to explain to an impatient child why dinner does not automatically appear on the plate the moment a child declares, "I'm hungry! Let's eat!" Most urban and suburban young-sters are unaware of the steps which go into producing either food or clothing.

Recognizing this lack of experience and understanding raises the question of how much a child grasps of the creative efforts of God. It is one thing to say, "God made everything." It is another thing to begin to understand the wondrous complexity of all that God made, and the abilities God gave people in order to make a wide variety of useful things out of that which God created.

This week provides opportunity for you and your child to explore God's creation, both the vast marvels of the universe and the everyday necessities of life.

WEEK 2

DAY 1

"Everybody got a flashlight?" Dad asked.

"How about jackets?" Mom asked.

It was dark and chilly. The Norris family was on their way out into the fields behind their farmhouse to watch an eclipse of the moon. Ryan's fourth-grade class had been assigned to watch some of the eclipse that night. Ryan had explained to his younger brothers and sister that "an eclipse of the moon means the earth gets between the moon and the sun and makes a shadow on the moon."

Going out in the fields at night sounded like an adventure to the Norris children. Dad had suggested that if they got farther away from the lights on the county road, they would see more stars. "Then," he said, "when the moon is in shadow, we may see more stars than ever."

The children were having fun shining their flashlights in every direction. Suddenly, a strange noise from out of the darkness made everyone stop walking. "What was that?" Laura asked. Laura was seven years old, and she sounded frightened.

"Whoo-oo!" the noise went again.

"It's just an owl," Ryan laughed. "You've heard owls before." "Not that loud," said Laura.

"And what's that?" five-year-old Chris asked suddenly. He heard another strange noise.

"It's just cows," Josh assured his little brother. "You're not afraid of cows, are you?"

"If I can't see them, I am," Chris answered.

"Well, shine your flashlight at them," Ryan suggested.

"What if that makes them mad?" Laura asked.

"Yeah!" Chris chimed in. "Nothing looks friendly out here at night. Why did God make dark?"

"To sca-are little boy-ys!" Ryan shouted, holding his flashlight under his chin to make his face look scary.

"Ryan!" Mom said. "Quit scaring Chris." She reached out and took hold of Chris' hand. "I'm glad God made the dark, Chris," she said.

"You are?" Chris asked.

"Sure," Mom said. "The dark is the best time for sleeping, for seeing the moon and stars, for hearing owls. And for snuggling up with someone you really like," she said, giving Chris a huge squeeze. "Besides, when God made the dark, He said it was very good."

Chris felt a little better about the dark.

● *"In the beginning God created the heavens and the earth." Genesis 1:1*

● **For Younger Children**
What do you like to do in the dark?
Where do you go to see a lot of stars?
What did God say about the darkness?

● **For Older Children**
Have you ever seen a lunar eclipse? Where were you?
Why did God say the dark was good? What do you like about the darkness?
What might you see or hear in the darkness that you can't see or hear during the daytime?

WEEK 2

DAY
2

All six members of the Norris family were outside at night to watch an eclipse of the moon. When they got to a spot where no trees blocked their view, they spread several blankets on the ground.

"Time for hot chocolate and brownies by moonlight," Dad said, opening the picnic basket. "Two marshmallows and one giant brownie for everybody."

"Who made the brownies?" Josh asked.

"Don't be so suspicious," Dad laughed. "I made them from Grandpa Norris' Famous Brownie recipe." "Grumpu Nurriff hud u bruhwnuh ruffupee?" Ryan asked with his mouth full. In the dark, no one was sure if his mouth was full of brownies or marshmallows.

"Not bad, Dad," said Chris, who had taken a much smaller bite. "Almost as good as Mom's."

"What do you mean 'Almost'?" Dad asked. "What do you think of my brownies, Laura?"

"I don't know," Laura said softly. "I haven't tried one yet."

"Why not?" Mom asked. "They're actually pretty good."

"Yeah, why not?" Ryan asked. "You're the main chocolate fan around here."

"Well," Laura said. "What if those cows smell the brownies and come over here."

"Can cows smell that well?" Chris asked.

"Do cows like brownies?" Josh asked.

"Who knows?" Ryan answered. "But since I finished mine, I'm not worried. You guys better eat fast or the whole herd might thunder over here."

"Ryan," Mom said, "quit teasing. Besides, we didn't come out here to talk about cows. We came to watch the eclipse."

"How come Ryan's all finished," Josh asked, "and we haven't prayed yet?"

"Do we have to pray over brownies and hot chocolate?" Ryan asked.

"Und murffmuhlluhs?" Chris added. His mouth was now as full as Ryan's had been.

"We don't HAVE to pray," Dad said. "But it's a good idea, Josh. Since you remembered, do you want to thank God?"

"Sure!" Josh said. "Close your eyes, everybody."

"What difference does it make in the dark?" whispered Ryan.

"Shhh!" whispered Mom.

"Thanks God for making the stars and the moon and the world," Josh prayed. "And especially the stuff brownies come from. Amen."

"Amen," said Laura. Then she took her first bite.

● *"God saw all that He had made, and it was very good." Genesis 1:31*

● **For Younger Children**

What snack did the Norris family eat? What snack would you like on a nighttime picnic?

What was the Norris family thankful for?

● **For Older Children**

How many different things did Josh thank God for?

What is something you have made? How did it turn out? Were you happy with it? Why or why not?

What are some of the good things God has made? Let's tell God thank You.

● ●

WEEK 2

DAY
3

"Everyone, turn off your flashlights and lie on your back on a blanket," Mom said. It was night on the Norris farm, and all six family members were waiting for the eclipse of the moon to begin.

"Lie down?" Laura asked. "Out here? In the dark?"

"Sure," Dad said. "If you lie on your back, you can see more of the sky at one time than if you're sitting or standing. Try it."

Everyone did. Chris was the first one to speak.

"The moon sure is bright," he said.

"It's a full moon," Dad said. "We could see more stars on a darker night when the moon wasn't full."

"This is plenty dark," Laura said.

"We can still see a lot more stars than people who live in the city," Mom said.

" 'Cause we have better eyes?" Chris asked.

"No," Mom laughed. "Because there aren't a lot of city lights out here. Remember, when we turned off the flashlights, we could suddenly see more stars."

"Yeah," Ryan exclaimed, pointing toward the sky. "There's the Big Dipper. And over there's the Little Dipper and Orion's Belt."

"Where?" everyone asked at the same time.

Ryan helped the others find those groups of stars.

"I bet I could reach up and touch some of those stars," Chris said.

"They do look really close," Mom agreed.

"But they're millions of miles away. Trillions!" Ryan said. "Light years, even."

"What's a light year?" Laura asked. "A year with no darkness?"

"No, Silly," Ryan said. He liked showing off how much he had learned at school. "A light year is how far light travels in one year. Lots of stars are hundreds or thousands of light years away. That means the light we see tonight left those stars thousands of years ago."

"Wow!" Josh said. "How did God build space so big?"

No one answered Josh's question. They all just stared up at the sky and thought about God and the universe He had made.

● *"Do you not know? Have you not heard? The Lord is the everlasting God, the Creator of the ends of the earth." Isaiah 40:28*

● **For Younger Children**

What do you like about looking at the stars?

What do you learn about God from looking at and thinking about the wonderful stars He made?

Tell God thank You for what you see in the nighttime sky.

● **For Older Children**

What constellation or star names do you know?

How many words can you think of to describe the stars and galaxies?

What would you like to know about how God created our universe?

● ●

WEEK 2

DAY

4

"I see it!" Ryan shouted. "The eclipse is starting!"

Ryan and his family had been waiting in the dark, watching for the first shadow to start moving across the moon. Ryan had explained that the earth was moving between the sun and the moon. Even with all his explaining, his younger brothers and sister still seemed uncertain of what to expect.

Now they could all see a large, curved shadow gradually darkening one edge of the moon.

Ryan pointed down to the ground. "See," he said. "The sun is on the other side of the world now. So the earth is starting to block the sun's light from that corner of the moon." Ryan was definitely excited.

"Cool!" Josh added. "It looks like someone's taking a bite out of the moon."

Chris, however, was getting tired and bored. He yawned and asked, "How long will it take to cover the moon?"

"I've got an idea," Mom said, changing the subject. "Let's play a game while we watch the eclipse."

"What game?" Laura asked. "It's too dark for 'I Spy.' "

"How about an alphabet game?" Mom said. "We've been thinking about the universe God made, so let's think of things God made. Things that start with different letters. The first person names something God made that starts with A, the next person says something that starts with B, and so on."

"I'm first!" said Chris, suddenly wide awake again. "I say Apple. It starts with A."

Laura was next, and she said, "Bear." Then she wished she hadn't, since thinking of bears on a dark night was a little scary.

Next came Cat, then Dog, then Elephant, Fish, Gerbil, Hyena, Iguana, Jack rabbit, Kangaroo, Lizards, Melons, Neptune (the planet), Ostrich, and Pluto (another planet). It was Mom's turn when they got to Q.

"Look!" Mom said, pointing at the moon. "The shadow is growing!"

"Quit changing the subject, Mom," Ryan said. "You've gotta think of something God made that starts with Q.

They ended up skipping Q, and eventually they skipped X. And they went through the alphabet four more times before Chris yawned again.

● *"Ah, Sovereign Lord, You have made the heavens and the earth by Your great power and outstretched arm. Nothing is too hard for You." Jeremiah 32:17*

● **For Younger Children**
What would you have said for the letters A, B, and C? Of all the animals God made, which is your favorite? Why?

● **For Older Children**
Is there anything on the Norris' alphabet list you have never seen? Which ones?

What word does Jeremiah 32:17 use to describe the Lord?

WEEK 2

DAY 5

Half of the moon was in shadow. The earth was slowly blocking more and more of the sun's light from reaching the moon. Out in the fields at the Norris farm, Dad and Mom and Ryan and Josh were having a great time watching the eclipse and telling stories. However, Chris and Laura, the two youngest of the four Norris children, were almost asleep.

"Can we go back inside, now?" Chris whimpered.

"Not yet!" Ryan and Josh yelled in unison. "We're having fun!"

"I'm bored," Laura muttered.

"How about," Dad suggested, "if I take Chris and Laura back inside while you three stay out here for a while?"

Suddenly, Chris was on his feet. "Yeah, Dad," he said. "Take me back in now."

"And put me to bed," Laura added.

"All right," Dad said, getting up. "Grab your flashlights, and let's do it."

"Give me a piggyback ride," Chris asked. "I'm too tired to walk."

"I want a ride too," Laura said.

"There's no way I'm carrying both of you," Dad said.

"I asked first, so carry me," Chris insisted.

"It's not fair if you carry him and don't carry me," Laura argued.

"OK!" Dad said. "I know what I'll do. Chris can ride to the gate, then Laura can ride the rest of the way. Is that fair?"

"OK," Laura agreed.

"OK," Chris said. "Here I come!" And he jumped onto Dad's back.

"Umph!" Dad grunted and started off across the field, holding Laura's hand. When they got to the gate, Chris slid down, and Laura got up. "Umph!" Dad grunted again. Then the three of them continued back toward the house.

At the back door, Laura slid down. Dad said, "Take one more look at the moon, kids." The three of them stood together for a few moments. "Let's say our bedtime prayers out here," Dad suggested, taking each child by the hand.

"I'm first!" said Chris. He then thanked God for all the things God made. It seemed as though he named most of them. Then it was Laura's turn to pray. "Thanks, God, for making dads," she prayed. "And moms."

● *"Worship Him who made the heavens, the earth, the sea and the springs of water." Revelation 14:7*

- ### For Younger Children
If you were Laura or Chris, what would you have thanked God for?

Revelation 14:7 tells us to worship God because of the things He made. Worship means to think about the great things God has done and give Him thanks and honor. When can you worship God?

- ### For Older Children
Why did Mr. Norris want Laura and Chris to say their bedtime prayers while they were still outside?

How many different ways of worshiping God can you think of?

What is your favorite way of worshiping God?

• •

Schedule time this week to be together as a family. Select one of these suggested activities to expand your family's understanding of God's wonderful creation.

FAMILY TIMES

Check It Out!
With your family go to a library or video store to borrow a book or video about stars and or constellations. Some books give nighttime sky diagrams which will help you identify specific stars and/or constellations. (Optional: Visit a planetarium or observatory.) As you learn together about the universe God has made, take time to thank Him.

Word Games
Driving in the car, waiting at a restaurant, or sitting in a doctor's office are all good opportunities to play word games. Play the same game as the Norris family listing things God made, or play this variation of the game. The first player says the name of something God has made. The second player must name something else that begins with the last letter of the first player's word.

Star Fun
Purchase a package of gummed stars. (Or provide yellow crayons.) Give each person a sheet of dark blue or black construction paper. Each person creates his or her own constellation by placing stars on the paper (or drawing with yellow crayon) to form the outline of an object or animal. Each person names his or her constellation.

Key Verse
"Honor your father and your mother, as the Lord your God has commanded you." Deuteronomy 5:16

Key Thought
God's Word teaches that respect for parents is essential for individuals and for society.

Respect for Parents (Mother's/Father's Day)

The Apostle Paul singled out the commandment to honor father and mother, noting that it "is the first commandment with a promise" (Ephesians 6:2). Paul linked this ancient instruction to a long life of satisfaction and well-being. Rebellion and disrespect toward parents strikes at the most crucial of all human relationships.

As you teach your young child about the biblical directives to obey parents, be aware that these verses in no way provide an opportunity for parents to exercise selfish control over children. Instead, the instructions to children actually place a great responsibility on the parent. Because the child's obedience "pleases the Lord" (Colossians 3:20), the parent should give guidance and commands which truly reflect the love and wisdom of the Lord.

WEEK 3

DAY 1

• •

Eric did not know how to help his friend, Jason, make the right decision.

Eric and Jason were on a baseball team which had a good chance to make the playoffs, largely because of Jason's hitting. But Jason's dad, who lived in Arizona, wanted Jason and his sister to spend the next three weeks with him. Jason really wanted his team to get to the playoffs. But he also really wanted to see his dad. It had been a long time since they had been together at Christmas.

"If I stay to play ball, Eric," Jason said, "what can I say to keep from hurting Dad's feelings? I don't know how long it'll be until we get another chance to be together."

"But if you go to Arizona," Eric said, "what will you tell the guys on the team? They'll think you're running out on them."

"Maybe I could tell Dad I'm sick," Jason suggested. "My sis could cover for me. And if we don't make the playoffs, I could tell him I'm better and go to Arizona then."

"But can your sister sound convincing?" Eric asked. "What if your dad starts to ask her questions about how you're doing?"

"Well, how about if I get Mom to tell the guys on the team I was practicing my slide and broke my ankle and I have to be in the hospital with no visitors, and meanwhile I'll be in Arizona having fun with Dad." Jason seemed to think that idea could work.

"You really think your mom would lie for you?" Eric asked.

"No, she's real big on telling the truth," Jason answered.

Then Eric suggested, "What if you got the coach to call your dad and tell him you're the best hitter on the team, and we don't stand a chance without you?"

"Or," Jason proposed, "what if I got Dad to call the coach and say he was dying from a brain tumor and needed to see me before he slipped into his final coma?"

"Oh, right!" Eric laughed.

"It's not funny, Eric!" Jason insisted. "What do I tell my dad I'm going to do?"

"Let me think about it," Eric said. "Maybe I'll come up with something."

● *"Each of you must respect his mother and father." Leviticus 19:3*

● **For Younger Children**
What choice does Jason have to make?
　How does Jason feel about his dad?
　What's something you like about your dad or mom?

● **For Older Children**
What makes Jason's decision so hard?
　Have you ever had to choose between doing two good things?
　What advice would you give Jason?
　What could Jason do to obey the command in Leviticus 19:3?

● ●

WEEK 3

DAY
2

Eric was trying to explain to his own dad and mom about the problem his friend, Jason, had with his dad. "So, all-wise parents of mine," Eric said, "any bright ideas I could give Jason?"

"Well," Dad said slowly, trying to think of something wise to say, "it seems that Jason's biggest problem is he wants to do two things at once. He wants to go to Arizona to see his dad, AND he wants to keep playing baseball."

"That IS a problem," Mom said. "But I think his BIGGEST problem is that he doesn't want to hurt anyone's feelings. He wants to please his dad and his coach and teammates."

"That IS a problem," Dad said. "But I think an even BIGGER problem is that he keeps coming up with excuses that won't work and that just aren't true."

"So," Eric asked again, "do you have any suggestions I could give him?"

"What do you think he should do?" Dad asked.

"I knew you were going to ask that question," Eric said.

"So," Dad asked, "do you have an answer ready?"

"Not really," Eric answered. "I just think that, instead of coming up with all these different excuses, Jason should just pick a story and stick with it."

"Even if it's not true?" Mom asked.

"Well, no," Eric replied. "I guess not. But he's not having any luck thinking up a good solution."

"What if," Mom said, "Jason made a choice between baseball and Arizona and then told the truth about it?"

"Or," Dad said, thoughtfully, "what if Jason just asked his dad if he could come to Arizona after baseball is over?"

"Not bad, Dad," Eric said. "That might solve the whole thing."

"Or maybe not," Mom said. "A later time might not work for Jason's dad."

"It's worth a try though," Eric said as he went off to phone Jason with his dad's idea.

● *"Listen to your father, who gave you life, and do not despise your mother when she is old." Proverbs 23:22*

● **For Younger Children**

What was Jason's biggest problem?

Whom does Proverbs 23:22 say we should listen and pay attention to?

Tell about a time today you paid attention to your mom or dad's instructions.

● **For Older Children**

What might be some other solutions to Jason's problem?

Why did Eric's dad say the biggest problem was Jason thinking up untrue excuses?

Why is telling the truth always a good idea?

DAY
3

● ●

"Nice hit!" Eric shouted to his friend, Jason, as they both watched a long fly ball soar deep into the outfield at the local baseball field. "But my center-fielder's got it. That's two out!"

"OK!" Jason said. "But my runner at third scored after the catch. I'm ahead, 12–10."

"Yeah," Eric said. "But I get last ups."

Eric and Jason were the only two players at the field, but they had invented imaginary teams to catch and throw the balls that they hit. Whoever was pitching announced whether a ball was caught or if the batter had hit safely and reached base. Occasionally there were arguments when the batter thought a ball had gotten safely past the imaginary fielders, but mostly the boys agreed with each other. Besides, if the pitcher called every batter out, he knew the same thing would happen when it was his turn at bat.

When their game was over the two boys walked together toward their homes. "I would have beat you if I hadn't hit so many popups," Eric said.

"Yeah," said Jason. "But you hit some good ones too. My dad calls those hard ones 'zingers.' "

"Did you talk to your dad about going to visit him?" Eric asked.

"Yeah," said Jason. "I used your idea and told him about the playoffs and asked if I could come see him when baseball is over."

"What did he say?" Eric asked.

"He thought it was a great idea," Jason answered. "Dad said he was glad I told him how much I want to finish the baseball season. And he asked Mom if she'd get one of the parents with a video camera to tape one of our games and send him a copy, so he can sort of see me play."

"All right!" Eric shouted. "We're on our way to the playoffs!" Then Eric asked, "Did you tell him it was my parents' idea?" Eric asked.

"Well," Jason said, "it was kind of my mom's idea too. I think my dad knows I had a little help."

● *"A wise son brings joy to his father, but a foolish son grief to his mother."*
Proverbs 10:1

● **For Younger Children**
What imaginary games do you like to play?
  What made Jason's dad glad?
  What is something you do that makes your mom or dad glad?

● **For Older Children**

Does playing with imaginary baseball teams sound hard or easy?

How would you describe a wise son or daughter? What does he or she do or say?

Can you think of a time your foolish actions made your parents sad? When have your actions made them glad?

● ●

WEEK 3

DAY
4

"How come I hit so many popups?" Eric asked his dad. Baseball was not an unusual topic at the Lacey family dinner table. But it WAS unusual for Eric to ask his dad for advice about his batting swing. Eric always tried to act as though he was doing everything correctly. Especially when his sister, Jessie, was around. Everyone in the family knew that Eric must be frustrated with his hitting to ask for advice at the dinner table.

This was too good an opportunity for Jessie to pass up. Before Dad could answer, she jumped in with her own suggestion. "It's just because you're a lousy player."

It was not unusual for Jessie and Eric to tease each other at the dinner table. But it WAS unusual for Eric to ignore Jessie's teasing. He must REALLY have wanted help with his hitting, because all he said was, "Any ideas, Dad?"

"If you're hitting a lot of balls up in the air," Dad said, "you might be holding your hands a little too low. Or you might be taking too long a stride when you swing. Or you might be swinging up instead of level."

"But which one is it?" Eric asked. "I don't know," Dad said. "Maybe we should go down to the batting cages, and I can watch you swing at a lot of pitches."

"But I've got homework tonight," Eric said. "Spelling and math."

"And piano practice," Mom added.

"And it's my night to do the dishes," Eric remembered.

"It sounds," Dad said, "as though you need to talk with your coach at your next practice and follow his suggestions. If you do what he says about hitting as well as what Mom and I tell you to do around here, you'll be fine."

Dad and Mom winked at each other, and Eric looked down at his plate, a little embarrassed by the compliment his dad had just given him.

"Way to go, Eric!" Jessie exclaimed, before she realized she had actually congratulated her older brother.

● *"My son, keep your father's commands and do not forsake your mother's teaching." Proverbs 6:20*

● **For Younger Children**

What did Eric ask his dad?

What are some things you've learned from your parents?

What's something new you'd like to learn?

● **For Older Children**

Why was Eric embarrassed?

Read Proverbs 6:20. Do you think this verse is talking about learning to play baseball or learning how to live like God wants you to?

How have your parents helped you learn to obey God?

● ●

WEEK 3

DAY
5

It was the most exciting game of the season. Eric and Jason's team had won by just one run, and now they were in the playoffs. Jason was the hero for their team because he had gotten two important hits. Eric had gotten one hit and made a fine running catch of a fly ball to end the game. Eric was thrilled that his team had won. But he did feel a little bad about the two times he had hit short pop flies to second base.

"I've really been working on not hitting popups, Dad," Eric said as he and his parents walked home. "And then in the big game, I hit two of them!"

"But, Eric," his mom said, "your team won! You should be celebrating, not criticizing yourself."

"I know, Mom," Eric replied. "But if I'd hit those two balls right, we'd have won by more."

"Good point," Dad said. "I'm glad you believe you can still do better. That's a good way to feel, 'cause it'll help you keep improving."

"Just once," Eric said, swinging an imaginary bat at an invisible ball, "just once, I'd like to hit one over that fence."

"That would be great," Dad agreed. "I'd lead the cheering."

"I think it would be great too," Mom said. "But let me tell both of you baseball nuts something I think is even greater."

"What's that, Mom?" asked Eric.

Mom put her hand on Eric's shoulder. "Even if you NEVER hit the ball, even if you STRUCK OUT every time, and your team lost ALL its games,

I'd still be terrifically proud of you."

"Me too," Dad said. "Mom and I feel much better about the kind of person you are growing to be than we do about how good a ball player you are. You're doing a great job learning the things we want you to know about yourself, and about life, and about God."

Eric stood still and looked down at his feet. Then he looked up and smiled. A very big smile.

"But please," Mom said, "during the playoffs, don't strike out very often."

● *"Children, obey your parents in everything, for this pleases the Lord."* *Colossians 3:20*

● **For Younger Children**
Why were Eric's parents proud of him?

What does Colossians 3:20 tell you to do?

Obeying parents is one way to please God. What are some other ways you're learning to please God?

● **For Older Children**
What did Eric still want to get better at doing?

Eric's parents were proud of him because of the kind of person he was growing to be. When have your parents been proud of you?

What have you learned about God and how He wants you to live?

According to Colossians 3:20, what is one thing that pleases God?

● ●

FAMILY TIMES
Schedule time this week to be together as a family. Select one of these suggested activities to expand your family's understanding of the benefits of living and learning in a family.

Family Fill-Ins
With your family complete as many of these sentences as you can:

We are a family who

likes . . .

learns . . .

cares for . . .

helps . . .

would never . . .
would rather . . .
loves to . . .
would be better off if . . .
has the good habit of . . .
has the bad habit of . . .
will someday . . .

Family Memory Game

Make and play a memory game to help your family remember special family times. Talk about special events your family has enjoyed (vacations, celebrations, awards, etc.). Each person chooses one or two events and draws and/or writes sentences describing the events on separate index cards. Make two of each card. Play the game by mixing up all the cards and placing them face down on the table or floor. Each player takes a turn to turn over two cards. If the cards match, the player gets to keep the cards. If the cards do not match, turn them face down again. The game continues until all cards have been matched.

Tip for Younger Children: You may wish to add a sentence to a younger child's drawing. And when playing the game, limit the number of cards to ten.

Promise Coupons

Write the name of each family member on a separate piece of paper. (Not needed if you're a family of two!) Put the papers in a bowl or basket. Each person chooses a name and makes a promise coupon to give to the person. On each coupon (index card or construction paper square) write "This coupon good for (name an action)." Ideas for action include: playing a game of your choice; walking the dog; setting the table; vacuuming the living room; folding the laundry; taking a walk to the park.

Tip for Younger Children: A younger child may dictate the words for the coupon and then decorate the coupon with felt-tip pens or stickers.

Angels

Key Verse
"For He orders His angels to protect you wherever you go."
Psalm 91:11, TLB

Key Thought
Angels are God's powerful servants who help and protect God's people.

Angels appear frequently in the pages of Scripture. We are told of their actions and given occasional descriptions of how they looked to people on the scene. But we are told very little about their nature and given only sketchy glimpses of their role in our lives. Perhaps because there are so many unanswered questions about angels, many people shy away from giving them serious consideration, let alone teaching children about them. However, just because there is much we do not know, we should not neglect that which Scripture plainly teaches. Therefore, this week's stories provide you and your child with an introduction to some basic teachings about angels, focusing on those things which tend to have interest and meaning to young children.

WEEK 4

DAY 1

From far down the dark tunnel came a rush of wind and the sound of the approaching subway train. Angela held tightly to her younger brothers' hands. When the train stopped and the doors opened, Angela, Hector, and Robbie hurried to find two seats that the three of them could squeeze into.

They had just gotten seated when the train lurched forward. Except, to Angela and her brothers, it felt as though it had lurched backward, since the seats they had found faced that direction.

Eight-year-old Hector liked looking out the windows into the dark tunnel, trying to guess when the train would begin to slow down and the lights of the next station would appear.

Angela was also looking out the windows, carefully reading the names of each station, counting silently the ones they must pass before they reached their own.

Robbie, the youngest of the three, liked looking at the people on the train. There were always interesting faces, and most people would smile when they noticed him. It was Robbie who first noticed the two men walking down the aisle toward them. The men wore identical jackets and small hats. They looked carefully at all the passengers as they made their way through the train.

"Who are those guys?" Robbie asked loudly.

Hector looked up and saw the two men. "Those are Guardian Angels," he said.

Robbie looked surprised and asked, "Really? Angels? In jackets and hats?" Robbie did not seem to notice that the people around them were starting to snicker. Robbie looked closely at the two men as they went past. Then he turned to Angela and said, as loudly as before, "I thought angels had wings."

Angela decided she should explain a few things to Robbie before he said something that would make people start laughing out loud. "Those aren't real angels, Robbie," she said. "It's just a name they use when they kind of help guard the subways and protect people. They try to do good, sort of like angels do."

Robbie seemed disappointed. He was thinking about what it would be like if real angels rode the subway.

● *"For the Angel of the Lord guards and rescues all who reverence Him."*
Psalm 34:7, TLB

● **For Younger Children**
Have you ever ridden on a subway?
　What did Robbie think angels were like?
　Angela told Robbie that angels do good. What good thing does Psalm 34:7 say that angels do?

● **For Older Children**
Why might Robbie have thought that angels have wings?
　What have you heard about angels?
　What do you learn about angels from Psalm 34:7?

● ●

"They sure didn't look like angels," Robbie said.

Robbie and his family were laughing together about Robbie's trip on the subway. Robbie was having great fun describing two men who Angela said were called "Guardian Angels."

"I knew they weren't REAL angels," Robbie said. "I bet they couldn't even fly."

"They couldn't shine either," Hector added. "People always talk about 'shining angels,' but these guys looked dull."

"I liked the little hats the men wore," Angela said. "I thought they were cute."

Then Robbie asked the question all three children had been wondering about. He asked, "But what do REAL angels wear?" Before anyone could answer Robbie's question, he thought of several more to ask. "And what do REAL angels do? And what ARE angels, anyhow?"

Actually, Angela and Hector were glad that Robbie asked those questions. They had both HEARD about angels and felt they should KNOW about angels. Still, neither of them knew the answers to Robbie's questions. But they did not like admitting they really did not know much about angels.

Hector was just about to say, "You're too little to understand angels." But his dad spoke first.

"Good questions, Robbie," Dad said. "Lots of stories in the Bible have angels in them, but there aren't many places I know of where angels are explained. Let's see, what DO angels wear?"

"White robes," Angela said. "When Jesus rose from the dead, the Bible says the angel that moved the stone was all in white. And I think it says the angel looked like lightning."

"Right, Angela," Mom said. "You did a good job remembering."

"And aren't angels supposed to protect us?" Hector asked.

"Right, Hector," Dad said. "The Bible says that's one of the things angels do. And often, in the Bible, angels brought important messages from God to people."

"But what ARE angels?" Robbie asked.

"Well," Dad said, "there's a lot about angels we don't understand. But we know God made them to be very special. They have bodies like people, but they seem to be able to appear and disappear."

Robbie thought a moment. Then he said, "I thought angels were ladies with wings."

● *"Are not all angels ministering spirits sent to serve those who will inherit salvation?" Hebrews 1:14*

● **For Younger Children**

What were some of the questions Robbie asked about angels?

What did Angela and Hector remember about angels?

How are angels different from people?

● **For Older Children**

What Bible stories about angels do you remember?

What is special about angels?

Why do you think God made angels?

●●●

DAY
3

The whole De La Rosa family had gotten very interested in angels. They played a trivia game, with everyone trying to remember a story in the Bible that had an angel in it.

Robbie remembered that an angel told Mary she was going to have a baby who would be God's Son Jesus.

Hector remembered that an angel told shepherds of Jesus' birth in Bethlehem. "And then a huge crowd of angels started praising God," Hector added.

Angela remembered that an angel got Peter out of prison. "The angel and Peter walked out right past the guards."

Dad remembered that angels helped Jesus when He was alone in the desert.

And Mom remembered that an angel warned Joseph to take Mary and Baby Jesus away from Bethlehem because King Herod wanted to kill Him.

"Wow!" said Robbie. "I wish an angel would help me."

"You've got your wish," Mom laughed. "The Bible says that's what angels do. They help people who love God."

"But I'd like to talk to an angel," Hector said. "Especially if some mean dudes are messin' with me. I'd just say, 'Angel! Take care of those guys.' "

"What if we were home alone and a fire started?" Angela asked. "Could I just say, 'Mr. Angel! Put out the fire'?"

Robbie decided to get into the game. "Since angels protect me, can I do anything I want? Can I play in the street? Can I jump out the window?"

"Wait a minute! WAIT A MINUTE!" Dad interrupted. "We can't expect angels to protect us when we don't use the good sense God gave us."

"But," Hector interrupted, sounding worried, "if I do something wrong, am I on my own? I mean, do angels give up on us if we're not perfect?"

"If you do something wrong, Hector," Mom said, "admit it to God and ask His help in doing what's right. And when you turn away from doing wrong, guess what the angels do?"

"What?" Hector asked.

"They have a party," Dad said. "They celebrate for you."

"Really?" Hector asked. "Angels sound neat!"

● *"I tell you, there is rejoicing in the presence of the angels of God over one sinner who repents." Luke 15:10*

● **For Younger Children**

What did Robbie wish an angel would do?

   Who are some people in Bible times who saw angels?

   When might someone your age need an angel's help?

● **For Older Children**

Which of the Bible stories about angels would you have liked to see?

   How did some of the people in Bible times feel when they saw an angel?

   What's something new you've learned about angels?

● ●

WEEK 4

DAY

4

It was a cold, rainy Saturday. Raindrops pelted the windows of the De La Rosa family apartment. Inside, Angela, Hector, and Robbie were bored. Bored, bored, bored!

"There's nothing on TV," Angela complained.

"There's nothing to read," Hector complained.

"No one will play with me," Robbie complained.

Their mom was fed up with all the complaining. She was almost desperate enough to send them outside to play in the rain. Anything for a little peace and quiet.

Hector pressed his nose against the window. His breath fogged the glass. Without thinking, he traced a simple outline on the window pane.

"Hey, look!" he exclaimed. "A rain angel!"

"Hector!" his mom said sharply. "Please do not draw on the window. It smears, and I have to wash it."

"Sorry, Mom," Hector said, watching his angel outline gradually disappear.

"I wonder," Robbie asked, "if angels get bored on rainy days."

"Angels don't have rainy days, silly" Hector said. "They're on top of the clouds, sitting around playing their harps. Maybe they make it rain."

"Where'd you ever hear that nonsense?" Angela asked.

Mom knew that when the De La Rosa children started to call names and make fun of each other's ideas, she needed to step in.

"C'mere, you three," she said. "Time to learn about angels and weather and being bored. Everyone sit!"

All three children sat.

"Three things about angels." Mom was definitely into her teaching mode. "One, I don't know if angels have rainy days. Two, I can't imagine them ever getting bored. The Bible says they praise God, and I doubt they ever run out of things to praise Him for."

"Maybe," said Hector, "angels praising God is what gives people the idea that angels sing and play harps."

"Maybe," Mom agreed. "And three! Angels do whatever God tells them to do. I'm sure He keeps them busy. And that gives me the idea that my three favorite 'angels' need something to do right now. Roll up your sleeves. We're going to make tamales!"

"Beats being bored," Hector said.

● *"Praise the Lord, you His angels, you mighty ones who do His bidding, who obey His word." Psalm 103:20*

● **For Younger Children**

When have you been bored like the De La Rosa children?

Why did Mrs. De La Rosa say she didn't think angels were ever bored?

If you were an angel, what would you praise God for?

● **For Older Children**

What do you like to do on rainy days?

What kinds of things might angels praise God for?

What might God tell His angels to do today to help and protect people?

● ●

WEEK 4

DAY 5

It was Saturday afternoon. The De La Rosa family apartment was filled with the warm, spicy smells of freshly made tamales. It was one of Angela's favorite aromas. She had enjoyed working in the kitchen with her mom and younger brothers.

Just as the last of the bowls and pans were being put away, the sun broke through the clouds that had made everything dark all day long. Angela looked out the window where everything looked fresh and glistened in the sun. "Now THAT," Angela said, "looks like something an angel would paint."

Hector and Robbie looked out the same window to see what Angela was talking about. "Yeah!" Robbie said. "Look how the sun shines off the windows across the street."

179

"And," Hector added, "the trees look really shiny too."

"Even the street sparkles," Angela said. "Definitely angel quality shininess."

"But angels really do better stuff than this," Robbie said.

"Such as?" Hector asked. Hector never thought his little brother knew very much.

"Mom said they praise God and Jesus," Robbie said. "And that's better, because all this shininess goes away. But God and Jesus stay forever."

"You're right," Hector said. Hector hated to admit that Robbie was right about anything.

Just before Robbie and Hector turned away to find something to occupy their afternoon, Angela said one more thing. "By the way," she began. "Have you two noticed that I was named after angels?"

"What do you mean?" Hector asked.

"Which angels?" Robbie asked.

"All angels," Angela said. "My name is Angela."

"So?" Hector asked, sounding as though he thought his sister was not making any sense.

"Do I have to spell it for you?" Angela asked, sounding exasperated that her brother did not seem to understand. "It's A-N-G-E-L-A. That's angel with an A on the end."

Suddenly, Hector understood. But what he said was, "I knew that."

● *"There were thousands and thousand of angels saying in a loud voice: 'The Lamb [Jesus] who was killed is worthy to receive power, wealth, wisdom, and strength, honor, glory, and praise.' " Revelation 5:11-12,* EB

● **For Younger Children**

Why did Angela think her name was special?

According to Revelation 5:11-12, what did the angels say about Jesus?

Let's thank God for angels who help us.

● **For Older Children**

What colors or pictures do angels make you think of?

Why do the angels praise God and Jesus?

Why is praising Jesus so important?

• •

Schedule time this week to be together as a family. Select one of these suggested activities to expand your family's understanding of God's servants — angels.

FAMILY TIMES

Bible Times Interview
Choose one of these Bible stories to read aloud — Judges 6:11-22; Luke 1:26-38; Acts 1:4-11; 12:1-17. Then one person pretends to be a character (Gideon, Mary, a disciple, Peter) in the story. Other family members ask questions about the character's meeting with an angel. Suggested questions: "Where were you when you saw the angel? How did you feel when you first saw the angel? What did the angel say to you? Did the angel have a special message for you? What was it? How did the angel help you? Did you do what the angel told you?" Optional: Record the interview on cassette or video recorder.

Nighttime Reminders
Trace around a cookie cutter or draw a simple angel outline (see sketch) on a piece of light-colored construction paper or white paper plate. Paint the angel with glow-in-the-dark paint (available from craft supply stores). After the paint dries, punch a hole at the top of the angel and tie a yarn or ribbon loop through the hole. Hang the angel in a child's bedroom as a visual reminder of God's angels.

J U N E

Key Verse
"Keep your lives free from the love of money and be content with what you have, because God has said, 'Never will I leave you; never will I forsake you.' "
Hebrews 13:5

Key Thought
God's Word teaches us to be thankful and content rather than to grumble and complain.

Contentment vs. Complaining

The Old Testament is full of stories about people who grumbled, often for no good reason. One continuing example occurred after God delivered Israel from Egypt. The people grumbled when they were thirsty. They grumbled when they were hungry. They grumbled again when they got tired of eating manna. They grumbled when Moses did not return immediately from Mt. Sinai. They grumbled when they found out the land God promised them was inhabited by giants. Their complaining attitude was their destruction, keeping them from recognizing the amazing and good things God was doing for them. In contrast, the Apostle Paul, imprisoned for teaching about Jesus, declared that "I have learned to be content whatever the circumstances" (Philippians 4:11). Paul's attitude enriched his life and set a great example from which every child and parent can benefit.

WEEK 1

DAY 1

"Hey, Mom!" Arthur shouted as he burst in the front door of their apartment. "Guess what Christopher got?" Christopher lived in the apartment next door to Arthur and his mother. Christopher was a year older than Arthur.

"How many guesses do I get?" Arthur's mom asked.

"Three," Arthur said. Usually, if Arthur wanted to play guessing games, he would announce a very high number of guesses. "Leventy twelve" was his second favorite big number. "Infinity" was his most favorite. When he suggested only three guesses, it meant he was bursting to tell the answer.

"I guess that he's got chicken pox," Mom said. Mom knew that was not the answer. She was just joking.

"No!" Arthur said, impatiently.

"Has he got poison oak?" Mom asked.

"No! He's not sick!" Arthur knew his mom was joking. He decided to give her a clue. "He's got something in his room."

"Dirty laundry!" Mom laughed. Arthur did not think his mom's jokes were very funny.

"Aw, Mom," he said. "He's got a TV set. His very own TV set!"

"Does he?" Mom replied. "That's probably more fun than chicken pox."

Arthur decided to ignore his mom's joking. He had something more important on his mind. "When can I get a TV in my room?" he asked. "When I'm six like Christopher?"

"How about when I'm rich, or at least when all our bills are paid?" Mom answered. That was not the answer Arthur wanted to hear.

"Aw, Mom!" Arthur whined. "I really want a TV set. I really, really want one." Arthur believed that if he asked more than once, his mom would be more likely to do what he wanted. It had worked once or twice in the past, and he thought it was worth it to keep trying, just in case it ever worked again.

Somehow, Mom's reasons for not buying a TV did not seem to impress Arthur. They did, however, start him on his next approach: complaining. "I never get any neat stuff like Christopher. It's not fair. All I have is junk. It's not fair."

The conversation ended with Arthur sitting on the floor, arms folded tightly across his chest, and his lower lip sticking out a long, long way. If Arthur was good at complaining, he was great at pouting.

● *"Do everything without complaining or arguing." Philippians 2:14*

● **For Younger Children**

Why did Arthur want a TV in his own room?

When has your mom or dad said you couldn't have something you really wanted?

How did you feel?

● **For Older Children**

What words would you use to describe Arthur's feelings and actions?

When has a friend gotten something you really wanted to have? How did you feel about it? What did you do?

Philippians 2:14 says not to complain. What often happens when a person complains a lot?

WEEK 1

DAY 2

Arthur was pouting, convinced that his mother and the rest of the world were just not fair. He came to this conclusion because his mother had said "No" to letting Arthur have a television in his room. Since Arthur's friend Christopher did have a TV, Arthur was certain it was only right that he should have one.

But Arthur's mother had other ideas on the subject, at least four of them, which she patiently explained to Arthur when he continued to complain about not having a TV. First, Mom said, "We can't afford a TV for your room. We just don't have the money." Second, she said, "I want us to be together as much as possible when we're home. If we watch TV in separate rooms, we keep ourselves apart, and that's not good for us."

Her third reason was, "There are things on TV that are not good for us. If something comes on that teaches wrong things, I need to be with you to talk about it, or to change the channel, or even to turn the TV off."

"But Christopher gets to watch TV in his room," Arthur pleaded. "HIS mother lets him watch whatever he wants."

"And the fourth reason," Mom continued, "is that just because Christopher does something does not make it a good thing."

"Yuh-huh!" Arthur argued. Actually, "Yuh-huh" is not much of an argument, but it was the only thing Arthur could think of at the moment. Then he thought of something else to complain about.

"Christopher has lots more neat things than me. He says I just have baby stuff." Once Arthur got started complaining, he quickly began to think of more. "And Christopher gets to stay up later, and he gets to watch stuff I can't. He gets comic books you don't let me have. He goes to movies that I never get to see."

The more Arthur talked, the more he convinced himself that he was being treated unfairly. The more unfair he thought everything was, the more miserable he became. And his mom was not exactly happy either.

● *"Give thanks in all circumstances." 1 Thessalonians 5:18*

● **For Younger Children**
Why was Arthur feeling so miserable?

Do you think Arthur's mom was fair? Why or why not?

When are some times you feel like complaining? What does 1 Thessalonians 5:18 say you should do instead?

● **For Older Children**

How were Arthur's complaints making his mom feel? Why?

If you were Arthur's mom, what would you have done when Arthur complained so much?

Which reason for not getting a TV do you think is the best? Why?

● ●

DAY
3

Arthur's mom was tired of all Arthur's complaining. Ever since Arthur found out that his friend Christopher had a TV in his room, Arthur had complained without stopping. Almost without breathing. "I know you wish you had your own TV set," Mom said, "but instead of making yourself unhappy by thinking of all the things you DON'T have, try thinking about all the good things you DO have."

"Christopher says I don't have ANY good stuff," Arthur protested.

"What about your collection of action figures?" Mom asked.

"Christopher says they're baby stuff," Arthur answered.

Mom could tell this was not going to be easy, but she was not going to give up. "What about your miniature cars and trucks that you and Christopher play with all the time?"

"They're old," Arthur insisted.

"Those cartoon videos that Grandma bought for your birthday aren't old," Mom said.

"I've seen 'em all," Arthur replied.

This went on for quite a while. Mom would mention something of Arthur's that she KNEW he liked. Then Arthur would inform Mom that he REALLY DIDN'T like it.

After she had mentioned almost everything in Arthur's room except the contents of his underwear drawer, Mom started naming things Arthur had done and places he had been. Arthur could find something wrong with everything Mom talked about.

Finally, Mom looked at Arthur and Arthur looked at Mom. And they both started to laugh. "This is silly, Arthur. You're complaining so much, you can't even enjoy what you do have."

"I know," Arthur answered. "But I just want a TV."

"Is complaining helping?" Mom asked.

"Not yet," Arthur said. He was still hoping that Mom would give in and do what he wanted. He didn't know she could be just as stubborn as he was.

● *"A heart at peace gives life to the body, but envy rots the bones."*
Proverbs 14:30

● For Younger Children

Do you have any of the same toys as Arthur?

What are some of your favorite things to play with?

What are some of your favorite places to go?

Thank God for the good things you have and fun places you've been.

● For Older Children

Why did Arthur and his mom start to laugh?

Read Proverbs 14:30. How does someone show he or she is envious? What are the results of envy?

Ask God's help in being content with what you have.

● ●

WEEK 1

DAY
4

Arthur's friend Christopher was on the floor playing with Arthur's little cars. Both boys were complaining about how mean their moms were. "My mom's not fair," Christopher complained, making it sound like his mother was the meanest mom in town.

"My mom's not fair either," Arthur added, trying to make his mom sound even meaner. "My mom won't let me have a TV in my room."

"MY Mom won't get cable for my TV," Christopher complained. "I can't get any of the really good programs."

Arthur's mom looked up. She was in the middle of paying bills. She looked a little frazzled, but she did not look mean. "Let me get this straight, Christopher," she said. "You mean, you have a TV in your room, and you're not happy?"

"Well," Christopher said, as if everyone should agree that he had a valid problem, "I don't have cable."

"I understand that," Mom said. "But Arthur sounded like he was unhappy because he doesn't have his own TV. You DO have your own TV, but you're not happy either."

Christopher was not sure what to say. He just repeated what he had said before, "I don't have cable."

"Tell me, Christopher," Mom went on. "Would you rather have cable, or would you rather be happy?" Again, Christopher did not know what to say. This time he just said, "What?"

"It seems that getting more stuff does not really make someone happy." She paused for a moment and let the two boys think about what she had said. "You've both been complaining about not having certain things, but having them won't really bring happiness."

She paused again, waiting to see if the boys would have something to say. When neither one said anything, Mom added one more comment. "Perhaps you should spend time finding out what really makes a person happy."

Interestingly, Arthur's mom did not hear any more complaining from either boy the rest of the afternoon.

● *"Better one handful with tranquility than two handfuls with toil and chasing after the wind." Ecclesiastes 4:6*

● **For Younger Children**

Why wasn't Christopher happy?

How would you have answered the question, "Would you rather have cable, or would you rather be happy?"

Do you feel happy? Why or why not?

● **For Older Children**

Would Christopher be happy if he got cable? Would Arthur be happy if he got his own TV?

Do you agree with Arthur's mom's statement that "getting more stuff does not really make someone happy?"

What DOES make a person happy?

● ●

WEEK 1

DAY

5

"What does make a person happy?" Arthur asked his mom. His friend Christopher had gone home, and Arthur was thinking about his mom's words that getting things did not bring real happiness. Deep down, he still thought a TV in his room would be a neat thing, but he had learned that complaining all the time was no fun.

Mom put down her newspaper and smiled at Arthur. "Lots of things can make a person feel happy for a while," Mom said. "I always feel happy when I hug you."

Even though Christopher said hugs were for babies, Arthur still liked it when his mom hugged him. However, he did hope his mom wasn't going to start talking about hugging.

Mom leaned forward and talked a little softer, almost in a whisper. "Let me tell you one secret of happiness the Bible gives us." Arthur loved secrets, so he leaned a little closer toward her. "It's not really a secret," Mom said, "because anyone can read it in the Bible, plain as day." Arthur leaned back a little, feeling disappointed that this secret was not a real secret.

Mom kept talking without noticing Arthur leaning back and forth. "But," she said, "it's kind of a secret."

"Why's that?" Arthur asked, staying where he was.

"It's kind of a secret because there don't seem to be very many people who have learned what the Bible says."

That caught Arthur's interest. He liked the idea of knowing something most other people did not know. Most of the time things seemed to be the other way around, with everyone else knowing things Arthur did not. Mom went on talking.

"One important secret of being happy is to learn to be content with what you do have. Learn to be glad for what God has given you, instead of making yourself unhappy about what you don't have."

As usual, what Mom said made pretty good sense to Arthur. He decided to quit asking for his own TV set. At least for a while.

● *"I have learned to be content whatever the circumstances." Philippians 4:11*

● **For Younger Children**
Why was Arthur interested in what his mom had to say?
    What is something that makes you feel happy for a while?
    What was the secret about being happy that Arthur's mom told him?

● **For Older Children**
What did Arthur learn about happiness?
    What are you glad to have?
    Thank God for the good things He's given you.

● ●

FAMILY TIMES
Schedule time this week to be together as a family. Select one of these suggested activities to expand your family's understanding of thankfulness and contentment.

Correct Me, Please!

Read and discuss Hebrews 13:5 together. What does this verse say is more important than money or possessions? Knowing that God loves us and is always with us is the best possession we could ever have! Then play this game to help your family memorize the verse. The first player says the verse substituting one or two incorrect words. Other players correct the wrong words. Continue until each person has had a turn.

Tip for Younger Children: Play the game using the first half of the verse.

Thankful Chain

Challenge your family to see how long a thankful chain they can make. Cut 2x6 inch strips of construction paper. Write on each strip something for which your family is thankful, an experience you've enjoyed together, or a characteristic of a family member for which you're grateful. Tape or staple the strips together to form loops for a paper chain. Add loops to the chain for the next several days.

Tip for Younger Children: A younger child may draw pictures on the paper strips.

Psalm Search

Read Psalm 103:1-5 together with your family, looking for as many reasons as you can for God's followers to be content and thankful. List the reasons on paper. Then work together to rewrite verses 3-5, substituting specific reasons your family is happy because of what God has given you.

Body, Soul, and Spirit

Key Verse
"May your whole spirit, soul and body be kept blameless."
1 Thessalonians 5:23

Key Thought
God created people with both a body and an inner, more important, part which cannot be seen.

"Body, soul, and spirit." Three words are often used to describe the very complex nature of human beings. The body is the easiest of the three to accept, even though there is much about it that is not fully understood. The soul and spirit are more difficult to understand.

Some people contend that soul and spirit are two words for the same thing. Others believe that there is a difference between the two. For a child, such a debate only creates confusion. It is enough to help the child begin to realize that there is a very real, very important part of every person which is distinct from the physical body.

It is important that we try to take care of our bodies, to be careful about what we eat and what we drink, to exercise properly. But it is far more important to nurture our inner being, to develop healthy and godly attitudes, affections, and ambitions. This week's stories will help your child to think about this inner being and God's great love.

WEEK 2

DAY 1

"Hey! Grandma!" Ryan's shouting and the screen door slamming made enough noise to wake Grandma Norris from her mid-afternoon nap. Ten-year-old Ryan burst onto the porch where Grandma was stretched out on a lounge chair.

"Goodness, Ryan," Grandma said with a yawn. "Home from school already? What's all the excitement?"

"I'm s'posed to interview you," Ryan announced. "It's an assignment for class."

Grandma Norris sat up. She was suddenly wide awake. "Interview me? What for? I don't know anything."

"Sure you do, Grandma" Ryan responded. "I'm supposed to ask you questions about the olden days."

Grandma Norris laughed. "Olden days? You must think I'm a relic!"

"Well," Ryan answered, "you are the oldest person I know. And Mrs. Johnson said that's who we should interview."

"Don't let all these wrinkles fool you," Grandma said with another laugh. "I may be old on the outside, but my heart is still young."

Ryan looked puzzled. "Isn't your heart the same age as the rest of you?" he asked, then he quickly added another question. "Or did you get a transplant?"

Grandma thumped her fist on her chest. "Nope," she said. "This heart has been pumping inside me for eighty-two years!"

"That's not a very young heart, Grandma," Ryan said.

Grandma explained. "When I said I have a young heart, I wasn't talking about the heart that I can feel beating inside my chest."

She reached out and tapped Ryan's chest. "That's just part of our body. I was talking about my feelings, my sense of humor, my soul. You know, the real me."

Ryan still looked puzzled. But he was afraid Grandma was about to start making one of her long speeches, and he wanted to get started with his interview. So instead of asking her to explain some more about the body, and the heart, and the soul, he just said, "What about my interview?"

"I guess I could answer a few questions," Grandma said, "as long as you don't ask me anything too embarrassing."

● *"Love the Lord your God with all your heart and with all your soul and with all your strength." Deuteronomy 6:5*

● **For Younger Children**

Who is the oldest person you know?

What part of Grandma Norris looked old? What part of her did she say was still young?

The part of you that thinks and feels is sometimes called your heart and soul. What does Deuteronomy 6:5 say you should do with your heart and soul?

● **For Older Children**

What did Grandma Norris mean when she said her heart was still young?

What are the parts of people we can't see?

Read Deuteronomy 6:5. What part of you should show love for God?

DAY 2

Ryan Norris had no idea that his grandmother could tell so many stories about her childhood. When he had asked to interview her for a school assignment, he had thought she would simply answer two or three questions, and that would be all. But each question Ryan asked made Grandma Norris think of one story after another.

She told about learning to ride bareback on her family's pony. She told about taking care of chickens and goats and milking cows. She told about the fun it was to jump off a low tree branch into the deep water of the creek that ran behind their property.

With each story she told, her dark eyes would glow brightly as she recalled the fun and adventure of life on her family's farm.

"Did you go to school?" Ryan asked.

"Did I go to school?" Grandma snorted. "Of course I went to school!" Then Grandma began talking about her friends and teachers and the cold winter morning when one of the older boys smeared foul-smelling cheese on the back of the old wood-burning stove. Grandma laughed heartily as she told about the class being sent out for an early recess while the teacher tried to find the source of the bad odor.

"What about church?" Ryan asked.

"We had a wonderful little church," Grandma said. "Sometimes the services seemed to last forever, but I loved it." That started a series of church stories, including a happy one about her Sunday School teacher giving her an apple and a candy cane for Christmas. And a funny one about swallowing a fly while singing a solo in front of the whole church.

"You sang solos?" Ryan asked. Grandma Norris' scratchy voice did not sound very musical to Ryan.

"I still remember," Grandma said, "the song I was singing when that fly attacked." Softly, and not very scratchy at all, Grandma began to sing.

Ryan wanted to ask what Grandma did when the fly flew in her mouth. Instead, he quietly listened as his grandmother, with her eyes closed, sang and remembered.

● *"O God, my heart is ready to praise You! I will sing and rejoice before You."* Psalm 108:1, TLB

● **For Younger Children**
What would you do if a fly flew in your mouth while you were singing?

Did Grandma Norris enjoy singing the song?

Singing that song was a way for Grandma Norris to show that she knew God would always love her. What's a song you have sung that reminds you of God's love for you?

● **For Older Children**

Which story of Grandma Norris' was the most interesting?

What were the words of the song Grandma Norris sang?

When she sang that song, Grandma Norris was showing that she was loved by God. When have you felt loved and cared for by God?

●●

DAY
3

"Is that enough stories for your interview?" Grandma Norris asked Ryan. Ryan had no idea how he was going to remember even half of all that Grandma had told him. Even that much would be far more than he wanted to write for his school assignment.

Ryan thanked Grandma for her help, then headed upstairs to his room so he could write down some things Grandma had told him.

Ryan sat down at his desk. He took a quick look out the window, hardly noticing the familiar fields of his family's farm. Very carefully, Ryan took out a blank sheet of paper and wrote his name and the date at the top. Then he began to write his questions and a few of Grandma's answers.

He had been working for just a few minutes, when his father stuck his head in the door. "I hear you've been interviewing Grandma," Mr. Norris said. "How'd it go?"

"Fine," Ryan said. "Except she told me so much stuff, I don't know how to squeeze it all into my report."

"Grandma does tend to talk a lot once she gets started," Dad agreed. "If I were you, I'd probably just write down what I thought was most interesting."

"It was ALL interesting," Ryan said. "But there IS something I don't understand, Dad."

"What's that?" Dad asked.

"Did Grandma really DO all that stuff she said?" Ryan asked. "Stuff like singing solos in church, and jumping into a creek, and riding a pony?"

"Sure, Ryan," Dad answered. "She wouldn't make it up."

"But how COULD she?" Ryan asked. "She can hardly walk, and WHO would ask her to sing? Her voice is totally scratchy, and her false teeth click!"

"You don't think Grandma looks much like a horse-riding, solo-singing swimmer?" Dad asked.

"No way!" Ryan said. "She looks like . . . like an old lady!"

"Well, her body may be old," Dad said, "but, like the Bible says, our body 'is a temple of the Holy Spirit.' I think that belief is a big part of why she's kept her body healthy so many years."

Once again, Ryan got a very puzzled look on his ten-year-old face.

● *"Do you not know that your body is a temple of the Holy Spirit?"*
1 Corinthians 6:19

● **For Younger Children**

Why did Ryan have a hard time believing that his grandma had done so many different things?

Grandma Norris believed that because God's Spirit lived in her, it was important for her to keep her body healthy. What are some healthy foods you eat? What are some exercises you do?

● **For Older Children**

Which of the things that Grandma Norris did would you like to do?

The words of 1 Corinthians 6:19 mean that God's Spirit lives in us—the people who love and obey God. Why should we keep our bodies healthy?

What might Grandma Norris have done as she grew up to keep her body healthy? What can you do?

WEEK 2

DAY
4

Ryan Norris did not understand how his eighty-two-year-old grandmother could ever have been young. Ryan thought about how slowly and carefully Grandma Norris walked, and he just could not imagine her riding a pony or jumping into a swimming hole.

Ryan's dad sat on the edge of Ryan's bed and rested his elbows on his knees. "Ryan," Dad said, "when I was your age, Grandma Norris did all the things in our house then that Mom does. Maybe more."

"But how come she can't still be like that?" Ryan asked.

Dad got up off the bed and walked across the room to Ryan's closet. He opened the door. "C'mere, Ryan," he said.

Ryan did as his dad asked. "Look here," Dad said, pointing to some marks on the inside of the closet door. "You know these marks, right?"

"Sure, Dad," Ryan said. "They show how I've grown."

"Right, your body keeps changing," Dad went on. "When you're a child, your body grows. But when you become an adult, change still keeps comin'. Gradually our bodies just plain slow down."

Ryan was listening to every word. Dad kept talking. "Over the years I've watched Grandma change from a young, strong, active woman to the person she is today. Sometimes it's hard to remember what she was like, even a few years ago."

"That seems pretty sad," Ryan said after a moment.

"In a way," Dad agreed. "But we should keep remembering that it's Grandma's body that has changed so much. The real Mary Hatchett Norris is still there."

"You mean her soul," Ryan said.

"Her soul, her spirit, her heart, her mind," Dad added. "She still loves to laugh. She's always been very wise and kind. She still loves her Bible, her church, her family. Grandma's body won't let her do some things she used to do, but she is still very much the same person."

Ryan thought, then he asked, "Do I have a soul or spirit or heart like Grandma?"

"You sure do, Ryan," Dad said. "You sure do."

● *"For in my inner being I delight in God's law." Romans 7:22*

● **For Younger Children**
How had Grandma Norris changed?

What were some of the things Grandma Norris was still good at?

What's one of God's laws or rules you've learned to obey—and will always want to obey?

● **For Older Children**
What made Ryan sad?

What was different about Grandma Norris compared to when she was young? What was the same?

According to Romans 7:22, what's one thing our souls can always enjoy?

DAY
5

"Hey! Ryan!" Grandma's shouting and the bedroom door slamming made enough noise to startle Ryan from his homework. Eighty-two-year-old Grandma burst into the room where Ryan was hunched over his desk.

"Grief, Grandma," Ryan said. "You scared me. What are you doing up here?"

Grandma patted a bundle she was carrying in her arms. "I brought you some things to look at," Grandma said.

She set the bundle on Ryan's desk and carefully unfolded the brown wrapping paper. Inside was a stack of framed photographs. Old framed photographs.

"These are pictures taken when I was young," she said. "I thought you might like to see what I looked like."

"Sure, Grandma," Ryan said, looking at the picture on the top. "What's this?"

"That was my school field hockey team," Grandma said. "Guess which one is me."

Ryan looked at the girls in the picture. Then he looked at Grandma. Then he looked at the picture. "That one," he said, pointing to the girl in the center.

"Right," Grandma said. "I was captain that year."

"Wow!" Ryan said, and began to look at the other pictures. There was a picture of Grandma as a baby. "You look just like Laura when she was a baby," Ryan said, noticing a resemblance to his younger sister. Another picture, taken when Grandma was eight years old, showed her holding two kittens. "They look like the kittens Button had last year," Ryan exclaimed.

Next was a picture of Grandma sitting on the pony she had told Ryan about. There was even a picture of her sitting next to her own grandmother, a woman who looked almost as old as Grandma Norris was now. On Great-Great-Grandma's lap was an open Bible. "Did your grandma tell you Bible stories?" Ryan asked.

"She sure did," Grandma said. "Just like I've done for you and Josh and Laura and Chris. And she prayed for me every day, just like I do for you kids."

"You do, Grandma?" Ryan asked. "What about?"

"Depends on what you kids are up to," Grandma said. "But I always pray that God will help you, the inner part of you, to grow strong and good."

● *"I pray that out of His glorious riches He may strengthen you with power through His Spirit in your inner being." Ephesians 3:16*

● **For Younger Children**
What did Ryan notice about his grandma's pictures?
   What did Ryan learn that his grandma did when she was young?

● **For Older Children**
What surprised Ryan about his grandma's pictures?
   What did Grandma Norris pray for the Norris children?

● ●

Schedule time this week to be together as a family. Select one of these suggested activities to expand your family's understanding of how God wants each person to grow—body, soul, and spirit.

FAMILY TIMES

Interviews
Provide an opportunity for your child to interview an older family member (grandma, grandpa, yourself). Your child will enjoy using a tape recorder. Suggest the child ask questions such as, "What did you like or dislike about your school? When you were growing up, what did you do in your free time? What chores did you do to help your family? Who told you about God?"

For Parents Only
Read Ephesians 3:16-19, Paul's prayer for the believers at Ephesus. Using this prayer as an example, write a prayer for each of your children. Your prayers should include requests for their physical and spiritual growth. Be sure to thank God for specific ways your children have already grown in their faith. Give the prayers to your children. (Hint: Some parents write a prayer each year on their child's birthday.)
   Tip for Younger Children: Read the prayers aloud if children are nonreaders.

The Family Workout
Keep your family healthy and strong. Plan a fun way to exercise together this month. Take a walk every day, skate, ride bikes, swim, or jog together. See if you can gradually increase the distance or time you exercise. Set a goal and establish a reward for your family. During the summer season, classes in a variety of physical activities may be offered in your community.

Key Verse
"A friend loves at all times."
Proverbs 17:17

Key Thought
Good friends make life better, even in hard times.

Making Friends

Everybody wants to have friends. But not everyone is willing to make the effort to build a friendship. Friends are made through caring support and helpful actions, especially when troubles are faced. As you and your child read this week's stories, you will have opportunity to consider some of the basic biblical teaching about building and maintaining healthy, rewarding friendships.

WEEK 3

DAY
1

Aliki was stunned. Her little sister, Midori, was silent. But their mother and father were very excited. Aliki's father had just told the two sisters that they were going to move to a new apartment. "It will be closer to my new job," Father said.

"And it will be easier for me to get to work also," said Mother. "I won't have to change buses."

"It's a nicer building with bigger windows," Father said.

"With new carpet in every room," said Mother.

"Plus," Father said, "it's bigger. The kitchen and living room are bigger."

"It has more closet space," Mother added.

Neither Aliki nor Midori had heard anything they thought was worth getting excited about. They liked their old apartment. They had lived in it all their lives. Carpet and closets and windows and a big kitchen did not hold much interest for Aliki and Midori.

"Best of all," Mother said, "it has three bedrooms."

Three bedrooms. Both girls looked up at the same time.

"That's right," said Father. "One for Mother and me, and one each for. . . ."

Before Father could finish, both girls shrieked at the same time: "I get my own room!"

Mother and Father laughed as both girls danced and hopped around the room, chanting, "My very own room! My very own room!"

Ever since Midori had been born, the two sisters had shared a bedroom. Most of the time they got along fine. But each of them had thought often about someday having a room of her own. This was worth getting excited about.

Suddenly, Aliki stopped dancing. She stopped chanting and smiling. "What about my friends?" she asked. "How will I see my friends?"

"Oh," said Father, "you'll make lots of new friends in the new neighborhood. And at your new school."

"New school?!" Both girls shrieked at the same time. Aliki said, "I don't want to go to a new school."

Midori added, "And I don't want new friends. Kim's my best friend!"

Mother and Father looked at each other. This was going to be an interesting move. A very interesting move.

● *"Be kind and compassionate to one another, forgiving each other, just as in Christ God forgave you." Ephesians 4:32*

● **For Younger Children**
What would you say if your parents said you were moving to a new home?
Why were Aliki and Midori worried about moving to a new apartment?
What would you miss about your best friends?

● **For Older Children**
How would you have felt about moving if you were Aliki or Midori?
Why were Aliki or Midori worried about making new friends?
Why are friends so important?
How does Ephesians 4:32 say people should treat each other? Why?

● ●

WEEK 3

DAY 2

Tomorrow, the Yasuda family was going to move across town to a new, bigger apartment.

Tonight, Aliki and Midori were having a sleep-over party with their best friends. Seven-year-old Aliki had invited Natalie, who lived in an apartment building down the street. Five-year-old Midori had invited Kim, who lived in an apartment down the hall. The four girls were picking at a very large pizza, covered with pepperoni and smothered in extra cheese. No one seemed to be very hungry, or very happy.

"I'm glad you had this party," Natalie said, not looking very glad. "But I'm not glad you're moving away."

"Yeah," Kim said. "Who can I play with now?"

"Lots of kids," Midori answered, then began listing other children in the apartment building. "Ashley, Katie, Rebecca, Barclay. . . ."

"Who wants to play with them?" Kim interrupted. "They're no fun!"

"So?" Aliki whined. "You still have lots of people to play with. We won't have any friends at all."

"That's not our fault," Natalie said. "You're the ones moving away. We'll never see you again."

"Sure you will," Aliki promised. "We'll come back and visit."

"No you won't," said Natalie. "You'll forget."

All four girls kept on complaining to each other about Aliki and Midori moving away. Unfortunately, the complaining quickly turned into arguing. And the arguing turned into name-calling. And the name-calling turned into yelling. And that was when Mrs. Yasuda hurried back into the kitchen from the living room.

"Girls!" she said loud enough to get their attention. "This doesn't sound like four best friends having a pizza party."

"Kim started it!" Midori insisted.

"Did not!" Kim replied.

"Just a minute!" Mom said, a little louder. "When you girls remember each other, do you want to think about all the fun times you've had together, or that you got into a big argument on your last night together?"

The room got very quiet. After a few moments, Midori was the first to speak. "I'm sorry, Natalie," she said. "I shouldn't have called you names."

"That's OK," said Natalie. "I shouldn't have called you names either."

Just as quickly as it had started, the argument was over. Mrs. Yasuda knew it was over when Midori asked, "What's for dessert?"

● *"Love forgets mistakes; nagging about them parts the best of friends."*
Proverbs 17:9, TLB

For Younger Children

What did Midori say to help end the girls' argument?

If you were having a sleep-over, whom would you invite?

What do you like to do with your friends?

For Older Children

What kind of party would you like to have with your friends?

When have you argued with a friend? What happened?

What can friends do to get over their arguments?

200

DAY
3

Aliki and Midori had often watched other families move in and out of their apartment building. They had watched furniture and boxes being carried, stacked in the hallways, and loaded onto the elevator. In all the times they had watched other people move, neither of them had ever thought that one day it would be their family's turn.

Some of the people from their church were helping to carry things out of the apartment and loading them on the elevator. Several more church friends were down on the first floor, carrying things out of the elevator and loading them onto a truck.

Aliki and Midori ran down the stairs whenever an elevator load was sent down. Then they would ride back up after the elevator was unloaded.

It must have been after their fourth or fifth elevator ride that they returned to their apartment and found it almost empty. The rooms seemed so much bigger with no chairs or tables or lamps. And the rooms seemed bare and sad. Suddenly, Aliki really understood that they were leaving this apartment.

"It doesn't feel like home anymore, does it?" Father said, kneeling down next to his daughters. "This was a happy place for us, but it was the people, not the rooms, that made it that way."

"That means," Mother added, "that our new apartment will be just as happy, because the same people will be there."

"Except our friends," Aliki muttered, thinking about the friends she was leaving behind.

"Anybody home?" a voice yelled from the open door to the hallway. It was Aliki's best friend Natalie, holding two small stuffed kittens that looked almost real. "These are for you and you," Natalie said, handing the toy kittens to Aliki and Midori. Then Natalie gave Aliki a hug. "You'll make lots of new friends," Natalie said. "Real soon."

Aliki was sad because she knew she was really going to miss Natalie. But Aliki was also glad that Natalie had come to say good-bye, and that she had said such nice things. And that she had brought those cuddly stuffed kittens.

● *"Friendly suggestions are as pleasant as perfume."* Proverbs 27:9, TLB

● **For Younger Children**
What made Aliki feel sad? What made her feel glad?

201

How did Natalie show she was a good friend to Aliki and Midori?
Who is a friend you can be kind to?

● **For Older Children**
How did the Yasuda's friends help them on moving day?
When did a friend help you or your family?
Tell God thank You for your friends and the ways they help you.

● ●

WEEK 3

DAY 4

For two days after Aliki and Midori and their family moved into their new apartment, the girls had no trouble keeping busy. First, there was the fun and work of unpacking and arranging things in their new rooms.

Almost one whole morning was spent trying to decide which girl's room would be home for Honda, the hamster, and which one would get Gergie, the goldfish. Both girls felt attached to both pets. When they had shared a room, the girls had taken turns feeding the animals and cleaning the cage and the bowl.

Finally, the girls decided that Gergie would do better on top of Aliki's dresser by the big window. And Honda would be happier in the dark corner next to Midori's closet.

They also kept busy exploring their new apartment building, riding the elevator to all eighteen floors, walking down all of the stairs starting up at the top, and visiting the laundry and storage rooms in the basement.

The girls also went for a walk with Father, exploring the neighborhood. They visited a grocery store and looked in the windows of a drug store, a cleaners, two restaurants, a beauty shop, and, best of all, a donut store just around the corner.

But soon the girls ran out of places to explore and things to do. In their old apartment building, Aliki had Natalie to play with. And Midori had been able to walk down the hallway to Kim's apartment. But now the girls did not know anyone in their new apartment building. They had not even seen any other children in their explorations up and down all the hallways.

Mother noticed that Aliki and Midori were both feeling lonely and bored. "Why don't you girls call Natalie and Kim and tell them our new phone number?" Mother suggested.

That was a great idea. It felt so good to hear a friend's voice on the phone. And there was so much to talk about. Best of all, Aliki and Midori both felt like Natalie and Kim were still their friends. Very good friends.

● *"If one falls down, his friend can help him up. But pity the man who falls and has no one to help him up!" Ecclesiastes 4:10*

● **For Younger Children**

What was fun about moving to the new apartment?

Why did the girls start to feel lonely?

What kind of friend does Ecclesiastes 4:10 describe?

● **For Older Children**

What new place have you explored?

What are some of the good things about having friends?

Who is a friend you can write or call?

● ●

WEEK 3

DAY
5

It was Monday morning. The first day at a new school. Aliki was nervous. Midori was nervous. Mother and Father were nervous. Would the girls like their new teachers? Would their new teachers like them? And most important of all, would they meet some new friends?

Mother had visited the school last week and registered the girls. She had seen their classrooms and met their teachers. Mother had also learned that the city bus stopped just a block away from their apartment building and then went straight past the school. Mother was planning to ride with the girls and take them to their classes before she went on to work.

Before Aliki, Midori, and their mother rode the elevator downstairs, they joined hands and prayed. Midori's prayer ended, "And help the kids at this school to be friendly."

Mother softly added, "And please help Midori and Aliki to be friendly also."

Midori looked up at Mother and said, "I AM friendly!"

Mother smiled. "I know you are, dear. But the children at your new school don't know that you are, so you'll need to show them."

Then it was time to go. As Mother and the girls walked outside toward the bus stop, Aliki whispered loudly, "Mom! Look!"

Mother looked. What she saw when she looked was about eight or ten children and several parents waiting at the bus stop. "There ARE kids who live around here," Aliki said.

As they approached the bus stop, Mother smiled at the other children, nodded at the parents, and said cheerfully, "Good morning." The other parents nodded back, then everyone stood quietly and waited. Aliki and Midori tried to look at the other children without staring at them. The other children did the same to Aliki and Midori.

Finally, one boy broke the silence. "Are you girls new?" he asked.

Aliki and Midori both nodded their heads shyly.

One of the girls asked, "Are you going to our school?"

Again, the sisters nodded.

"Do you have any pets?" another girl asked.

"A goldfish," Aliki answered.

"A hamster," Midori added.

Suddenly the children were all telling what pets they had. And just as suddenly, Aliki and Midori started to feel that they really might find some friends in their new neighborhood.

● *"Dear friends, since God so loved us, we also ought to love one another."*
1 John 4:11

● **For Younger Children**
What did Mrs. Yasuda say in her prayer?
How can a person show that he or she is friendly?
Why does 1 John 4:11 say we should show love and friendship to others?

● **For Older Children**
When have you felt nervous like the Yasudas?
What did the Yasudas do when they felt nervous and worried?
How did God help Aliki and Midori?

● ●

FAMILY TIMES   Schedule time this week to be together as a family. Select one of these suggested activities to expand your family's understanding of friendships.

Pass It On!
Choose a family in your neighborhood or from your church. With your family fill a basket or bag with a favorite snack food (cookies, muffins, fruit, etc.). Write a note inviting the recipient to enjoy the contents, fill up the basket again, and share it with another family as a way to show friendship. Sign the note, "From your Secret Friends."

Families Can Be Friends Too!

Plan a fun game to build friendship in your family. Place a small object (key, coin, pencil, etc.) in the center of an open area. Each person writes his or her name on a small piece of paper and puts one end of a piece of tape on the paper. Mark a starting line at one end of the open area. Then each person takes a turn to be blindfolded and turned around a few times. The player holds his or her piece of paper and tries to walk toward the object, taping the paper on the floor next to the object. The player whose paper is taped closest to the object is the winner.

Tip for Younger Children: Mark the starting line closer to the object. After blindfolding the child, do not turn him or her around.

Prayers for Friends

With your family take turns naming friends in each of these categories: neighborhood, church, school, work, older, younger. Write the names on separate index cards. Place the cards in a basket or bowl. Once a day when your family is together (after a meal or before bedtime), choose one of the cards. Pray for that friend. Ask God to help your family show friendship and love to that person.

- -

We Are God's Children

Adoption is a word the Bible uses to help us understand how God brings people into His family. We know that adoption makes a child a full member of the new family. We know that the parents promise always to love and care for their new child.

Key Verse
"This promise is for you. It is also for your children and for all who are far away. It is for everyone the Lord our God calls to Himself."
Acts 2:39, EB

Key Thought
God has adopted us as His children.

The Bible talks about being adopted into God's family. It is good to remember the many promises God has made to love and care for those who become His children. It is also good to recall that we are part of God's family because He has chosen to love us, not because we have done anything to deserve it (Ephesians 1:5).

Sometimes adopted children wonder if they really belong in the family where they live. The parents work very hard to assure the child of their love. God has planned ways to assure His children that we belong to Him. Besides the many promises in the Bible, He also gives His own Spirit to always be with us, helping us to know and to feel His great love for us (Romans 8:15; Galatians 4:6-7).

Knowing that God adopts us into His family is wonderful. It does not mean that we will never have hard times. It does mean that He is always ready to help us, just as a loving, strong mother or father does for a child in need.

WEEK 4

DAY 1

- -

Loud thumps and bumps echoed through the house. Bill and Carol Lacey looked up from the magazines they were reading. They heard voices yelling, then a door slamming against the wall.

"Get out of my room!" they heard Eric shout.

"I don't have to," they heard Jessie yell.

"You do if I say so!" Eric shouted even louder.

"Do not!" Then for a moment, all was quiet. The calm before the storm.

Mr. and Mrs. Lacey waited for the storm to break. They were certain that thirteen-year-old Eric was muttering something to make his eight-year-old sister scream.

Right on time, Jessie shrieked. But it wasn't the usual squeal of brother and sister teasing. There was none of Jessie's typical giggles and laughter to show she was having fun. Instead, Jessie's screeching was filled with pain and sobbing.

"Eric!" Mr. Lacey shouted as he and his wife jumped up and ran toward the back of the house."What are you doing to your sister?"

As they turned the corner, they saw Jessie disappearing into her room and her door slamming shut. They also saw Eric, standing in his doorway, looking shocked and pale.

"Eric! What did you DO to her?" both parents said, bearing down on him.

"Nothing!" Eric protested."Nothing! I never touched her!"

"OK, Eric, but what did you SAY to her?"

"I just told her to get out of my room. Why's that a big deal?"

"Keep going, Eric," Dad said firmly."What else did you say?"

"I, uh . . . I guess I shouldn't have told her I could make her do it 'cause she's adopted."

"Oh, Eric," his Mom said. "No, you shouldn't have said that. Adopting a child is a wonderful thing, not something to tease about."

"Eric, you and I need to talk," Dad interrupted. "And, Carol, I guess you'd better go help Jessie. Grab your jacket, Eric. We're going for a walk."

● " 'I will be a Father to you, and you will be my sons and daughters,' says the Lord Almighty." 2 Corinthians 6:18

● **For Younger Children**

How do you feel when someone teases you?

Why do you think Jessie was so upset about what Eric said?

What do you think her mom will say to Jessie?

What do you think Dad will say to Eric?

● **For Older Children**

Why did Mom say that "adopting a child is a wonderful thing"?

Why do you think the Bible describes our relationship with God as being adopted into His family?

Why is this Bible verse such good news for us to hear?

WEEK 4

DAY
2

Eric jammed his fists deep into his pockets. He tucked his chin tight against his chest. He stared straight down at his feet which scuffed across the sidewalk.

Eric was not enjoying this walk with his dad. Mr. Lacey did not look happy either. He was trying to think of what to say to Eric. Eric was definitely not going to say anything at all unless he had to.

The farther they trudged, the heavier the silence became.

"Well, Eric," Mr. Lacey began.

Eric couldn't keep quiet another second. "What's so wrong with my saying Jessie's adopted? She already knows she's adopted! What's the big deal?"

Breaking the silence seemed to make them both feel better.

"The big deal, Eric, isn't saying that Jessie's adopted. The problem was sounding like being adopted makes Jessie less a part of the family than the rest of us."

"I didn't mean that! I was just teasing." Eric's chin came up a little.

"I know you were teasing." Mr. Lacey took his hand out of his pocket and put it on Eric's shoulder. "But Jessie didn't think it was funny, did she?"

"Boy, she sure didn't," Eric said.

"And she's right. Adopting Jessie was one of the best things that ever happened in our family. Right up there with you being born."

"All the way up there?" Eric asked.

"All the way, Eric. When we adopted Jessie, we made her a full member of the family. We love her and she belongs—and she always will."

Eric grinned at his dad. "I knew that."

"Make sure you don't forget it," Dad said. "I'll race you home!"

"No fair! You've got a head start!" Eric shouted as he began running.

"I need a head start because I'm old!" his dad yelled back.

The race ended in a tie.

● *"The Father has loved us so much that we are called children of God. And we really are His children." 1 John 3:1,* EB

● **For Younger Children**

What is one of the best things about belonging to a family?

How is God like a father to those who love Him?

● **For Older Children**

How would you describe God's love for the people He calls His children?

How does God show His love?

Adopting a child takes a long time and requires that parents do a lot of work. What do you think God has done to adopt people as His children?

● ●

WEEK 4

DAY 3

"Hey, Jessie!" Eric yelled to his younger sister. "Let's play a video game!"

Jessie asked, "Which game?"

"How about 'Macho Driver?'" Eric asked. "We race motorcycles through a maze filled with slime-oozing aliens."

Jessie turned up her nose. "Don't you have anything more civilized?"

"Civilized. She wants civilized. How about 'Time Warp Attack?' It's educational. Sort of."

Jessie looked through the video game stack. "How about this volleyball game? I'm pretty good at volleyball."

"All right," Eric said, sliding the disk into the game machine. "But I warn you. No one's ever beaten me yet."

"Great!" said Jessie, picking up her control lever. "Prepare to lose."

"No way!" laughed Eric as two volleyball teams ran onto the video screen. "But before I crush you, I have one thing to say."

"Too late! It's my serve!" Jessie laughed back. The volleyball on the screen rocketed over the net and landed just out of the reach of Eric's diving players. "Hey! I wasn't ready!" Eric yelled. "I was going to tell you something!"

"One to nothing!" Jessie yelled back. "You can't play volleyball and talk at the same time. SERVICE!" Again the ball shot across the net, scoring another point for Jessie.

"I wanted to apologize!" Eric shouted, loud enough for the neighbors to hear.

"For bragging that you could beat me?" Jessie asked as she pushed the button, firing the ball over the net for a third point.

"No," whispered Eric. "I wanted to apologize for teasing you about being adopted."

"Oh!" said Jessie.

"Yeah," said Eric. "It was a dumb thing to say. I really am glad we're in the same family."

"Thanks for telling me," Jessie smiled. "Will you still be glad after I

209

finish beating you?" And she scored another point.

"Why me?" Eric muttered as he got ready to block Jessie's next shot.

● *"Some people did accept Jesus. They believed in Him. To them God gave the right to become children of God." John 1:12,* EB

● **For Younger Children**

What are some things that make you glad to be in your family?

What do you think are some good things about belonging in God's family?

● **For Older Children**

According to this verse, what must we do to become children of God?

What do you think it means to accept Jesus?

● ●

WEEK 4

DAY

4

Jessie usually jumped off the school bus with her ponytail flying. Then she would skip and run up the sidewalk, happily swinging her lunch box in one hand and her backpack in the other. But today Jessie stepped slowly off the bus. When her feet reached the sidewalk, they plodded instead of skipped. Her lunchbox and backpack looked very heavy, pulling her arms stiffly down at her sides.

"Is that you, Jessie?" her mom asked when the front door opened. Usually her mom didn't need to ask, since most days Jessie cheerfully announced her arrival home.

"Is that you, Jessie?" her mom asked again. Jessie did not answer, but kept plodding down the hall to her room.

Mrs. Lacey came to the door and asked, "Rough day, Jess?"

"Yeah," Jessie answered softly.

"Do you feel OK?" Mom wanted to know.

"Yeah," Jessie answered even more softly.

"Trouble with your friends?"

"No." Mrs. Lacey barely heard Jessie's answer.

"How about your math test?"

Suddenly, Jessie started to cry.

Mrs. Lacey put her arms around her sobbing daughter. "The test was that bad, Jessie?"

"It was awful! I missed so many." Jessie looked up. "But I tried my best. I really did try my best."

"I know you did," Mrs. Lacey said, gently wiping Jessie's eyes.

Jessie sniffed. "I don't want you to be disappointed you adopted me. I'm so sorry I didn't do better."

Mrs. Lacey kept her arms around Jessie. "I'm not disappointed we adopted you. You don't have to be a math whiz to please me. I love you just the way you are."

"But Eric's so good at math," Jessie said. "I want to be as good as he is."

"Jessie," Mrs. Lacey said, "you don't have to be like Eric. You don't have to try to earn my love. You're my daughter. Now and always."

● *"His Holy Spirit speaks to us deep in our hearts, and tells us that we really are God's children." Romans 8:16,* TLB

● **For Younger Children**

Why do you think Jessie was so upset about not doing well on her test?

Why do you think God keeps on loving us even when we make mistakes or do something wrong?

● **For Older Children**

When have you ever wondered if your mom or dad still really loved you? When have you wondered if God really loved you?

Why is it good that God gives His Holy Spirit to tell us we really are God's children?

● ●

WEEK 4

DAY
5

"Watch me, Dad! Watch me float!" Jessie shouted.

"I'm watching, Jessie," Dad said. "Start floating."

Jessie took a deep breath, then she was floating on her back in the calm, lazy waters of the lake. Ten seconds, twenty seconds, thirty seconds . . . Jessie kept floating.

Finally, she rolled over, dove under the water, and came up smiling.

"That's great, Jessie," her dad said. "You sure didn't get that from me. My feet float like a couple of rocks."

"That's right, Jessie," Mom added. "When Dad tries to float, his feet go right to the bottom."

Eric chimed in, "I think he's got rocks in his bottom too. That's why he needs that inner tube to stay up."

Everyone laughed while Eric and Mom teased Dad about not being able to float. Everyone laughed except Jessie. All Jessie could think of were her dad's words, "You sure didn't get that from me."

Remembering that she was adopted, Jessie felt left out.

Jessie heard Eric's voice. "I know one thing Jessie and I got from Dad."

Jessie looked up and saw Eric waving her to come near Dad's inner tube. Quickly, she paddled over. With one big push, she and Eric dumped Dad.

Mom laughed and kept floating on her mattress. "Eric, what did you and Jessie both get from Dad?" she asked.

"Our sense of humor!" Eric laughed, as Dad came up sputtering.

"How can you let them do that to me?" Dad protested.

Mom laughed again. "You can't blame me for that. Everyone knows I'd never tip anyone out of his tube."

Suddenly, Mom noticed Dad, Eric, and Jessie surrounding her floating mattress. Sure enough, they dumped her off.

Fortunately, Mom came up laughing: "I can sure tell who's been raising you two. You're just like Dad, you rascals. And I love it!"

Suddenly, Jessie knew she belonged.

● *"You are God's children whom He loves, so try to be like Him. Live a life of love, just as Christ loved us." Ephesians 5:1-2,* EB

● **For Younger Children**
What are some ways you are like your mom or dad?
What are some ways you can love people as God does?

● **For Older Children**
When is it hard to love people as God does?
What are some things you can do that will help you become better able to love people as God does?

● ●

FAMILY TIMES
Schedule time this week to be together as a family. Select one of these suggested activities to expand your family's understanding of being adopted as one of God's children.

Family Interviews
God's adopted family is special, because God loves each person, and because each person is unique. Similarly, every family is special, because of

the love family members have for each other and because each person in the family is unique.

Assign one family member to tape record each person in the family telling about one or two of their favorite family memories. The interviewer should ask a few questions to raise awareness of the part other family members play in making the memory special: "What did other people in our family do to help make that special? How do you think the rest of the family felt then? Tell one reason you're glad that (name) was with us then?"

After recording each person, gather the family together and listen to the tape. Conclude by leading the family in sentence prayers of thanks for God's love and for a loving family: "Thank You God for. . . ."

"You Are God's Children" Chart

Read aloud Ephesians 5:1-2: "You are God's children whom He loves, so try to be like Him. Live a life of love just as Christ loved us" (EB). Agree as a family to keep track of ways family members show God's love to others during the coming week. Work together as a family to make a chart on a large sheet of paper. Draw seven boxes, one for each day of the week.

Each day, family members write (or dictate) ways they see others in the family showing love. Hang the chart in a central location (i.e., the kitchen) where it will be frequently seen by all family members. Comments may be written the moment the action occurs, or at mealtimes, bedtime, or any other opportunity when the family is all together. Whatever plan is followed for writing comments on the chart, plan a specific time each day for the family to review the day's entries. Conclude with a prayer of thanks for God's love and the love of each family member.

OPTION: If your family finds it difficult to follow through on a project like this, add an incentive by offering a special family treat (ice cream, frozen yogurt, pizza, swimming, etc.) at the end of the week if all seven boxes have been filled in. Guide the children in drawing or cutting from magazines one or more pictures of the promised treat. Mount the picture(s) with the chart as a constant reminder.

Celebrate Our Nation

Key Verse
"Doing what is right makes a nation great, but sin will bring disgrace to any people." Proverbs 14:34, EB

Key Thought
Doing what is right is one of the ways God's people can show His love for each other and for their country.

Patriotism, like religion, has been the motivator of some of history's most noble achievements, as well as some of the most wicked atrocities. Love of country has inspired great acts of loyalty and bravery, as well as acts of treachery and cowardice.

What makes the difference?

The Bible makes it clear that a nation, as well as each individual, must answer to the laws and standards of Almighty God. Love of country by itself is not a reliable guide for living. But when Christians are motivated by love for God and each other, as citizens we can lead others to consider the welfare of all people, not just an intimate circle of friends and family.

As you and your child read this week's stories, discuss the questions, and consider the Bible verses, you will discover some of the qualities that make any nation great.

WEEK 1

DAY 1

The old, dirty truck was starting to look like something completely different. DJ, his twin sister AJ, and their friends from the neighborhood youth club were decorating the old truck as their club's float in the big parade. It was supposed to end up looking like a giant flag. Several of the dads had built a big rectangular frame out of wood. The dads had nailed sheets of plywood onto the frame. Several moms had marked out the flag's design on both sides of the plywood. It was the kids' job to paint the flag's colors.

AJ was painting places that had been marked to be painted blue. She was looking for sections with the letter "B" in them. DJ was on the other side, looking for sections marked "W." He was using white paint. Suddenly, DJ grinned and flicked his brush, painting his friend Cory's nose a brilliant white.

"Watch it!" Cory protested.

"What are you two doing?" AJ asked, poking her head around the end of the big flag.

Again, DJ flicked his brush, this time across AJ's chin. "Clown faces!" DJ crowed, and he put two white circles on both his cheeks. AJ and Cory and

DJ laughed together at how silly they looked.

"DJ!" an adult voice boomed from the other side of the flag. It was DJ's dad, who had been helping AJ with the blue paint. "You're supposed to be working, not fooling around!" Dad came around the end of the flag.

"We're supposed to be celebrating our country," DJ said, holding up his paintbrush as if it were a torch.

Dad took one look at the three children with the shiny white paint on their faces, and he had to laugh. "You guys look really silly," he said. "But that paint could burn your eyes. Besides, if you start slapping paint around, you could mess up the hard work people have been doing." Dad paused for a moment. "So, back to work—all three of you!"

"OK!" DJ said. "But a few clowns really improve a celebration."

● *"Blessed is the nation whose God is the Lord." Psalm 33:12*

● **For Younger Children**
What do you like about parades?

AJ and DJ were getting ready for a parade to celebrate living in their country. What do you like about the country in which we live?

● **For Older Children**
What kind of national holidays can you name?

What does Psalm 33:12 say about a country where the people love and obey God?

How do people in our country show that they love and obey God?

● ●

WEEK 1

DAY
2

The neighborhood youth club cheered as several dads and older boys wrestled the big wooden flag into position on the back of the old truck. After it was securely attached onto the truck, they started fastening bright-colored streamers and signs.

"It's gonna be the best float in the parade," AJ said.

"And the BIGGEST," her twin brother DJ added.

"I hope I get to ride on it."

"Yeah," AJ agreed. "But I don't think we've got a chance."

"Why not?" DJ asked.

"They'll choose older kids," AJ said. "Big kids always get to do the best stuff."

"YO!" a voice shouted. "Listen UP! ALL of you!" It was Mr. Dishman, the club director. He was standing on the back of the truck, trying to get the club members to quiet down.

"Hear the man!" a grownup shouted.

"Sh-h-h-h!" whispered other adults. A lot of people were still talking.

"QUI-ET!" shouted DJ. Suddenly, all the talking stopped.

"Thanks, DJ," laughed Mr. Dishman. Then he began talking to the group. "You're all waiting to hear who gets to ride on this great float," he said.

"Right on!" someone shouted.

Mr. Dishman kept talking. "Every child in the club deserves to ride on the float, but there's not enough room. So we chose eight of you to represent the whole club."

"The Great Eight!" the same someone shouted.

Mr. Dishman kept talking. "We chose eight children who worked hard to decorate the float, and who have shown in many ways that they really care about our club, about other people, and about our country."

Mr. Dishman began to read the eight names. Just as AJ had said, the first six were all older. Then, the last two names Mr. Dishman read were, "AJ and DJ Gorman!"

"Way to go!" someone shouted. It was DJ's friend Cory.

Mr. Dishman kept talking. "The Gorman twins were chosen to show our whole community that even our younger members love their country." He said a lot more about being good citizens and obeying the law. Maybe he said a little too much, because AJ and DJ were both distracted by imagining what it was going to be like riding in the big parade.

● *"Remind the people to be subject to rulers and authorities, to be obedient, to be ready to do whatever is good." Titus 3:1*

● **For Younger Children**
Why were AJ and DJ chosen to ride on the float?
  What does Titus 3:1 say people should do?
  What are some laws you obey?

● **For Older Children**
What kind of people were chosen to ride on the float?
  What kinds of things might AJ and DJ have done to show that they love their country?
  What's something you have done to show that you love your country?

DAY
3

DJ and his twin sister, AJ, were ready to ride on their club's float in the big parade. They knew they were going to sit on opposite sides of the float, with the big wooden flag between them. They knew they were supposed to smile and wave at everyone watching the parade.

"Why can't I wear my black T-shirt?" DJ asked his mom.

Mom groaned and answered. "Two reasons. First, everything on the float is blue, white, and red. A black shirt won't fit in. And second, everyone on the float is supposed to wear a blue club T-shirt."

"But people would notice me more if I wore black," DJ insisted.

"They'd notice, all right," Mom answered. "And they'd all be wondering why you didn't dress to go along with the float."

DJ decided it was worth one more try. He asked, "But what's the point of getting chosen to ride on a float if you have to wear something that makes you blend in with the decorations?"

Just then, the doorbell rang. It was DJ's friend, Cory.

"Hi, Cor!" DJ shouted. "Did you come for my autograph?"

"Your what?" Cory asked.

"My autograph," DJ repeated. "Now that I'm famous, my autograph is going to be valuable."

"Famous?" Cory asked.

"Sure," DJ said. "Only real celebrities like me get chosen to ride in big parades."

"Oh, right," Cory said, a little bothered by DJ's bragging.

"Let's not be jealous," DJ added. "You can't help it that you're a nobody and I'm a somebody."

"Oh, RIGHT!" Cory said, REALLY bothered by DJ's bragging. DJ's mom was also bothered by what she heard DJ saying.

"I thought they chose kids to ride on the float who have shown good citizenship," Mom said.

"That's me!" boasted DJ.

"But, DJ," Mom went on, "bragging about being chosen to ride on a float doesn't sound to me like a good thing to do."

"Bragging?" DJ asked. "Did I sound like I was bragging?" No one said a word. No one had to say a word. DJ suddenly realized how obnoxious he had sounded.

"Oops," was all he said.

● *"Do what is right and good in the Lord's sight, so that it may go well with you." Deuteronomy 6:18*

● **For Younger Children**

What would you choose to wear for the parade if you were AJ or DJ?

What did DJ say that bothered Cory?

How can you obey Deuteronomy 6:18 and show that you are a good citizen?

● **For Older Children**

How would you have felt if you were Cory?

Why did DJ's mom think he wasn't showing good citizenship?

What are some things you can say or do to show good citizenship?

WEEK 1

DAY
4

● ●

DJ looked up at the big wooden flag on the back of the truck his club had decorated. There were bright colored streamers flowing along the sides. A big sign on the back said, "We're proud of our country!" DJ felt very important to be chosen to ride on the float.

As he admired the float, DJ also congratulated himself for being chosen to represent the other members of the club. *DJ,* he thought to himself, *you are an outstanding citizen, a credit to your family, your club, and your country.* Just when he started imagining himself being chosen as the next president of the country, he realized that someone was speaking his name.

"DJ," the voice said. "DJ, I'd like you to meet someone."

DJ turned and saw Mr. Dishman, the club director. Standing next to Mr. Dishman was a tall, athletic-looking man.

"DJ," Mr. Dishman said, "this is Tom Jackson. He's riding on our float with you."

"Oh, hi," DJ answered. His mind was still partly busy imagining that he had become president. He was disappointed to realize that he had just been daydreaming. He was also a little disappointed to learn that some grownup would be riding along on the float.

While DJ shook Tom Jackson's hand, Mr. Dishman kept on talking. "Tom is a real hero. He rescued a child from a burning car that had been in a wreck. He risked his life to get that child out. He's a real hero, all right."

Suddenly, DJ felt a little foolish for thinking he was so special. He had never rescued anyone from anything. He wondered if he would ever risk himself to help someone else. He took another look at Tom Jackson, the hero.

Mr. Dishman kept on talking. "It's people like Tom Jackson who make this country great," he said.

"And," Tom Jackson added, "from what I've been told, kids like DJ help make it great too. I'm proud to ride along with you, DJ."

DJ's smile could be seen from a long way off as Tom Jackson gave him a boost onto the truck as the parade was about to begin.

● *If both you and the king who reigns over you follow the Lord your God—good!"*
1 Samuel 12:14

● **For Younger Children**
Whom do you like to pretend to be?

First Samuel 12:14 says it's good when a king follows God. Why might a king or a president need God's help?

Why might kids your age need God's help?

● **For Older Children**
Who do you imagine you might become when you're a grownup?

First Samuel 12:14 says it's good when the king, or leader of your country, follows God. Why is it good?

Pray for the leader in your country.

● ●

WEEK 1

DAY
5

"How was it?" Cory asked DJ. "Did you like riding on our float? Is it as much fun as watching the parade? Did your arm get tired from waving?"

Cory kept asking questions so rapidly that DJ did not have a chance to answer any of them. Until the last one, that is. Then Cory asked, "And who was that tall dude next to you on the float?"

Whether Cory had run out of questions, or whether he just had to stop to take a breath, DJ jumped right into the opening and said, "Tom Jackson."

"Who?" Cory asked. "Who's Tom Jackson?"

"He's the tall dude who rode next to me on the float," DJ answered.

"Yeah, but who is he?" Cory insisted.

"He's a hero," DJ said.

"A hero?" Cory asked. "What kind of a hero? A war hero? A sports hero? What other kind of heros are there?"

"He's a hero 'cause he saved a kid's life," DJ explained. "There was a car crash and Tom got a kid out of a car."

"Wow," Cory said. DJ expected Cory to say more, but that was all.

"He told me all about it while we rode in the parade," DJ went on. "And he told me he was really scared that the car might explode. But he couldn't just leave that kid trapped inside."

"Wow," Cory said again.

"And he said he was really glad he had done it," DJ added. "He said that's what makes a person or a country really strong."

"What'd he mean?" Cory asked.

"I guess," DJ said, "that doing what God says is right, like helping people when they're in trouble, is what makes people really strong."

"I think he's right," Cory agreed.

● *"Therefore, as we have opportunity, let us do good to all people."*
Galatians 6:10

● **For Younger Children**
Why was Mr. Jackson a hero?

Who is someone you know or have heard about who is a hero?

Mr. Jackson was a good citizen because he helped another person. You may not ever have the chance to rescue someone, but every day you can help others. Ask God's help to obey Galatians 6:10 and do good to others.

● **For Older Children**
How would you have felt if you were Mr. Jackson?

What did Mr. Jackson do when he needed help to rescue the child?

What's one way you can be a good citizen and help a person?

● ●

FAMILY TIMES   Schedule time this week to be together as a family. Select one of these suggested activities to expand your family's understanding of what it means to love God and your country.

Family Field Trip
Look on a map to find a location of historical interest near your home. Plan a time when your family can visit the location. Talk together about the ways people in your nation's past have contributed to your country's history.

Write On!

With your family talk about a topic of concern in your country. Write a letter expressing your concern and your suggestions for action to a governmental leader. Addresses may be found at your local library or in the newspaper.

For Parents Only

Go to your local library or children's bookstore to find a book of historical fiction dealing with events in your country's past. Look for a book in which the main character is a child. Read the book aloud with your family.

"Good Citizen" Project

Plan a "good citizen" project your family can complete to help others in your community. You may donate unwanted items to a local mission, hold a garage sale and give the proceeds to a charitable organization, or clean up the litter at a local park. Your church may be able to offer other project ideas.

Life and Death

Most young children in modern societies have never had a direct experience with death. The most likely contact with death tends to be the loss of a pet or the passing of a grandparent. Even in these cases, the child is often kept at a distance and only knows what grownups are willing to tell.

Thus, it is no surprise that children under five years old tend to view death as temporary, similar to being asleep. They expect the pet or person who died to return, as if he has just gone away for a brief time. Because young children view everything only in terms of how it impacts them personally, their major concern about death focuses on how someone's death may change their daily routines.

Key Thought
The death of a loved one, while causing sadness and separation, is also a reminder to the Christian of God's great love and care.

Seeking to shelter a child from death by hiding our own emotions actually makes it harder for a child to express real feelings and thus begin the healing process. Children need the opportunity to grieve over a loss. They also benefit from opportunity to talk about God's love and care and His gift of eternal life to all who place their trust in Jesus Christ as personal Savior.

WEEK 2

DAY 1

"Let's go for a 'Heads or Tails' walk," Mr. De La Rosa suggested to his family.

"What's that?" asked Hector.

"At every corner, two people flip coins. If both coins come up 'heads,' we turn left. If both come up 'tails,' we turn right. And if one is 'heads' and one is 'tails,' we keep going straight." After quite a few flips, the family ended up at the gate to a cemetery. Hector and Robbie wanted to go inside and explore.

"It looks kinda spooky," Hector said.

Their older sister, Angela, did not want to go in. "It looks very spooky," she said.

Mr. and Mrs. De La Rosa let another flip of the coins decide whether to go through the gate. "Tails!" shouted Hector after flipping his coin.

"Tails here too," said Mrs. De La Rosa.

"Then onward into the graveyard!" Mr. De La Rosa said, leading the way through the tall, open gates.

Slowly and carefully they wandered through the cemetery, looking at the headstones, sometimes calling out names or dates they found interesting.

"Here's someone who died in 1848!" Hector announced.

"Here's a baby who only lived a month," Angela said. "How sad!"

"Here's a poem," Mr. De La Rosa said. "Listen. 'Roses are red; violets are blue. I am dead; how about you?' "

"Why would someone put a poem like that on a tombstone?" asked Mrs. De La Rosa. "Here's a much nicer one. 'Father dear, we love you so. Why, oh why, did you have to go?'"

Meanwhile, four-and-a-half-year-old Robbie wandered among the headstones, looking for ones with pictures or designs. Finally, he stood up straight and looked around. "Hey, Dad," he asked, "are all these people dead?"

"That's right, Robbie," Mr. De La Rosa answered. "All these stones mark where someone is buried. Each stone shows that people cared about that person and missed them after they died."

"But why do people have to die, anyhow?" Robbie asked. "It's too sad!"

Mr. De La Rosa stooped down next to his youngest son. "It IS sad when someone we love dies. But it's also a time when God shows His love by comforting and caring for us."

Robbie liked that answer.

● *"Blessed are those who mourn, for they will be comforted." Matthew 5:4*

● **For Younger Children**

What made Robbie feel sad?

Have you ever felt sad because someone died? Who helped you when you felt sad?

God promises to help us when we are sad. Tell God thank You for His love and care.

● **For Older Children**

Have you ever been to a cemetery? What do you remember about it?

Read Matthew 5:4. What word means the same as feeling sad? What word tells what God will do?

How might God comfort someone who is sad?

WEEK 2

DAY
2

The De La Rosas were walking down a narrow path toward the back end of the old cemetery. As they walked past some tall shrubs, they saw a small group of people walking slowly away from a large mound covered with flowers.

"Sh!" Mrs. De La Rosa whispered. "A funeral just ended."

Robbie asked, "What do they do at funerals?"

"People remember and talk about the person who died," Mr. De La Rosa said. "And they pray. Sometimes they sing. Some people cry."

"Why do people go to funerals if they're so sad?" Angela asked. "It seems so depressing."

"You answer that one, Eva," Mr. De La Rosa said to his wife. "I've never liked funerals."

"Oh, Luis," she said softly, "I don't think anyone LIKES funerals. But a funeral can be very helpful to people who are sad when a loved one dies. It gives them a chance to be with other people who feel the same. And it gives a chance to remember all the good things about that person."

Hector was a little bit ahead of the rest of the family. As he got near the big mound of flowers, he turned and asked, "Why do people give flowers when someone dies?"

"Your turn, dear," Mrs. De La Rosa said to her husband.

Mr. De La Rosa laughed and said, "If I'd known all these hard questions were going to come up, I'd have skipped the cemetery."

"C'mon, Dad," Hector said, grabbing his dad's arm, "answer the question. Why flowers?"

"I'll try," he said. "I don't know how the custom got started, but I've always thought flowers helped people think about life, and God's care. Their color and beauty help to comfort the people who are feeling sad."

"When I'm sad," Robbie announced, "I'd rather have a cookie."

"Hugs," Mrs. De La Rosa said. "Hugs are the best comfort for sad feelings."

"A phone call from my friend," was Angela's idea. "How about you, Hector?"

"I dunno," Hector answered. "Maybe just being with my family."

"Sounds like we might have some interesting funerals in this family," Mr. De La Rosa said laughing.

● *"[God] will swallow up death forever. The Sovereign Lord will wipe away the tears from all faces." Isaiah 25:8*

● **For Younger Children**

What things did the De La Rosa family say helped them when they felt sad?

What helps you feel better when you are sad?

What does Isaiah 25:8 say God will do to comfort sad people?

● **For Older Children**

Do you agree with Angela's statement that funerals seem depressing? Why or why not?

Why did Mrs. De La Rosa say funerals might help someone who is sad about the death of a loved one?

How does Isaiah 25:8 describe God's comforting actions?

● ●

WEEK 2

DAY
3

Mr. and Mrs. De La Rosa sat on a wooden bench in a quiet corner of the old cemetery. Angela, Hector, and Robbie lay on their backs on the grass, enjoying the shade of several tall, leafy trees. Mrs. De La Rosa was telling her children about when her favorite aunt died.

"I was about Angela's age," she said. "I still remember how very sad I was that Tia Rosa Maria had died."

Angela rolled onto her side to look at her mother. "Was Rosa Maria your favorite aunt?" Angela asked.

"I think she was everyone's favorite," Mother answered. "She had a wonderful, big laugh that I loved. And she always gave me a huge, warm hug that took my breath away."

Now Hector rolled over. "Yuck," he said. "I hate it when aunts hug me."

"You'd have loved Rosa Maria's hugs," Mother laughed. "She always had a piece of candy for me after she squeezed me."

Candy caught Robbie's attention. He sat up and asked, "Why did your aunt die?" Robbie sounded like he felt cheated because he had never gotten any candy from his mother's aunt.

"She was pretty old," Mother answered. "She was my mother's oldest sister. And her heart was not very strong."

"Did you cry?" Robbie asked.

"Oh, yes," Mother answered. "Especially when I was by myself and would think about her, and how much I missed her. I used to love to tell her things, and it hurt when I couldn't do that anymore. Even talking about her now makes me feel sad."

"It makes me feel sad too," Angela said. "And I never even knew her."

Mother reached over and gently patted Angela's shoulder. "But remembering Rosa Maria also makes me very happy. I think about her laugh and her hugs and her marvelous big smile, and I know it's going to be wonderful when I see her again."

"See her again?" Hector asked.

"Of course, Hector," Mother said. "I know when I get to heaven, Rosa Maria's going to be there too. What a great hug I'm going to give her then."

● *"For My Father's will is that everyone who looks to the Son and believes in Him shall have eternal life." John 6:40*

● **For Younger Children**

Who is your favorite relative? What do you like about him or her?

Where did Mrs. De La Rosa say she would see her aunt again?

The Bible tells us that the people who are followers of Jesus will live with Him in heaven. What do you think heaven will be like?

● **For Older Children**

What did Mrs. De La Rosa like to remember about her favorite aunt?

What do you know about heaven?

No one knows for sure what heaven is like. But the Bible does tell us that heaven is a wonderful place that Jesus is preparing for the people who love Him. Jesus will always love and care for us, even when we die.

Let's tell Jesus thank You for His love.

● ●

WEEK 2

DAY 4

Hector De La Rosa had found a very old gravestone in the cemetery his family was visiting. The stone had been worn away until the words carved into it were barely visible. "What's it say?" his younger brother, Robbie, asked.

"I think it says, 'Until we meet again,' " Hector read aloud.

"How can you meet a dead person?" Robbie asked. Robbie was very good at asking questions, hard questions.

Hector usually tried to answer his little brother's questions. "I think," Hector began, "I think it means they'll meet in heaven."

"Like Mom and her aunt?" Robbie asked.

"Yeah," Hector answered. "I guess."

Robbie liked learning things from his older brother, but he could always tell when Hector was not very sure about what he was saying. When that happened, Robbie always went to the nearest grownup.

"Mom," Robbie asked, "will you really see your aunt again?"

"Oh, yes, Robbie," she answered. "I'm sure I'll see her, and my grandparents, and many other loved ones who will be in heaven when I get there."

"But how do you know they'll be in heaven?" Robbie insisted.

"That's easy," she answered. "Rosa Maria loved and trusted Jesus. And the Bible tells us over and over again that those who love God will be with Him forever."

"What about your grandparents?" Angela asked.

"I'm sure I'll see them too," Mother answered. "They're the ones who taught my aunts and my mother about Jesus."

Mr. De La Rosa decided it was time he said something. "People don't go to heaven because they were rich or good looking or strong. Even trying to be a good person isn't the answer. We must believe that Jesus is God's Son and trust Him to give us life with God."

"What about the person buried under this old stone?" Hector asked. "Will he be in heaven?"

"If he loved and trusted Jesus," Mother nodded.

Robbie looked like he was about to ask another important question. His mother paused and looked his way. Sure enough, Robbie did have a question. "When do we eat?" he asked.

● *"God has given us eternal life, and this life is in His Son." 1 John 5:11*

● **For Younger Children**
Who were some of the people Mrs. De La Rosa said she would see in heaven?

Why was she so sure these people would be in heaven?

What do you know and believe about Jesus?

● **For Older Children**
How would you have answered Robbie's question, "How can you meet a dead person?"

Why might some people think they are going to heaven?

What does a person need to believe in order to go to heaven?

Have you made the decision to love and trust Jesus?

DAY
5

Robbie was hungry. He felt his family had spent more than enough of the afternoon walking and then exploring the old cemetery. "I want a churro," he announced, planning to lick the sprinkled sugar off his favorite pastry.

"Me too," Hector chimed in. He and Robbie felt that if they both asked for a treat at the same time, their parents would have to go along.

"Sounds good," Mr. De La Rosa added. Everyone knew where Hector and Robbie had gotten their love for sweets. So the whole family set off toward their favorite little snack shop.

While the boys and their father thought about what they were going to eat, Angela was still thinking about their conversation in the old cemetery. As they stood at a corner, waiting for the light to turn green, Angela asked her mother, "How do we know that people who love Jesus really live again in heaven?"

"Well, Angela," her mother said, "because the Bible says we will."

"But how do we know it REALLY happens?" Angela asked. "How can we be sure?"

Just then the light changed, and Hector and Robbie started off to claim their churros. Mr. De La Rosa took his daughter's hand, and they followed the younger boys. He talked as they walked. "I've never met anyone who went to heaven and came back to tell us about it. And I've never gone to heaven to check it out."

"So," Angela interrupted, "how can you be sure you'll go to heaven when you die?"

"I'm sure," Father continued, "because Jesus proved His power over death when He rose from the grave. God's same power that brought Jesus back to life will give God's life to everyone who loves and trusts Jesus."

Angela was silent for a few moments as the family turned the next corner and approached the snack shop. "So," she said finally, "I guess it's pretty important whether or not a person loves Jesus." Her father stopped walking and looked down at her. "It's a matter of life or death," he said.

And the churros were delicious.

● *"Christ has truly been raised from the dead—the first one and proof that those who sleep in death will also be raised." 1 Corinthians 15:20, EB*

● **For Younger Children**
What did Angela want to know?

What did Jesus' dying and coming back to life show us?
What questions do you have about heaven?

● For Older Children

Why did Mr. De La Rosa say that loving Jesus was a matter of life or death?
What proof do we have for God's power over death?
How can you be sure that you will go to heaven with Jesus?

● ●

Schedule time this week to be together as a family. Select one of these suggested activities to expand your family's understanding of God's love and care for us and His gift of eternal life.

FAMILY TIMES

Bible Verse Mix-Up

Letter Psalm 23:4 on a large piece of paper as shown below.

"Zvzn qhough B wxlk qhrough qhz vxllzy of qhz shxdow of dzxqh, B wbll fzxr no zvbl, for you xrz wbqh mz."

Then give your family these instructions: Change every x to a. Change every z to e. Change every b to i. Change every q to t. When all the letters have been changed, read the verse together.

Tip for Younger Children: Simplify the activity by changing only the a and e letters.

Heavenly Plans

Ask each person in your family to find and read one of these Bible passages. John 14:1-3; Revelation 21:1, 4-5, 10-11, 19, 21, 25. Talk about this question: What do you learn about heaven from these verses? Then take turns to finish these sentences: The best part about heaven will be. . . . I'm glad Jesus planned. . . . I wish I knew if heaven. . . . I'm thankful that in heaven. . . .

Tip for Younger Children: Read passages aloud to younger children.

Tombstone Rubbings

A visit to a cemetery may be a valuable experience for your child, and a fine opportunity to talk about issues of life, death, and life everlasting. A child's attitude about a cemetery will largely reflect that of the adults who are there. Collect crayons and/or pencils, masking tape, and several sheets of thin white paper such as tissue paper. Find a cemetery in your community that has old tombstones. Tape a sheet of paper over a section of a tombstone that has an interesting decoration or an unusual epitaph. Color over the paper with crayon or pencil to make a rubbing. After completing the rubbing, talk with your family about the good news that as Christians our lives don't end in a cemetery. Thank God for His gift of eternal life to those who love Him. Be sure to find out if you need permission first.

Tip for Younger Children: Unwrapped crayons will be easier for younger children to use.

When We Do Wrong

Key Verse
"If we confess our sins, He is faithful and just and will forgive us our sins and purify us from all unrighteous-ness."
1 John 1:9

In most people's experience, confession leads to punishment. A person who admits to committing a crime is sentenced by a judge. A student who admits to cheating receives a lower grade. A child who owns up to having broken a parental rule is almost certain to experience unpleasant conse-quences. If the confession is given freely, the severity of the punishment may be reduced, but punishment is imposed, nevertheless.

Is it any wonder most people draw back from confessing sins to God? We expect the Judge of all the earth to visit stern retribution. Instead, God has promised to respond to our confession with mercy and forgiveness. One of the great gifts you can give your child is an awareness of God's great desire to restore all who come to Him. Those who withdraw from Him when they do wrong remove themselves from being able to receive the forgiveness He wants to give.

Key Thought
When we sin, we must admit that we have done wrong (confess) and turn away from our wrongdoing (repent) so that God may forgive us.

WEEK 3

DAY
1

A big red sign on the door clearly said, "Eric's Room: No Girls Allowed." The sign was not intended for Eric's mom, because he liked it when she sat on the edge of his bed and talked to him before he went to sleep. And there were numerous moments throughout any normal day when Eric's mom would go inside his room. No, the sign was not meant for her.

The "No Girls Allowed" message was aimed at just one person: Eric's eight-year-old sister, Jessie. Eric was certain that Jessie lay awake nights plotting attacks on his room. Hardly a day went by that Eric wasn't heard shouting, "Get out of my room, Jessie! And stay out!" Or else he would yell, "Who's been messing with my stuff? Jessie!" Sooner or later, each outburst would end up with Eric stomping into the kitchen or the living room and demanding, "Dad! Mom! You've got to make Jessie stay out of my room!"

Mr. and Mrs. Lacey were convinced that most of Jessie's fascination with getting into Eric's room was because of all the ruckus Eric raised about it. If Eric had put up a big sign that said, "Welcome, Jessie!" and had invited her to come in whenever she wanted, she probably would have been bored with the whole thing. But Eric was so determined to keep her out that she became just as determined to get in whenever she could.

Thus, when Jessie needed a ruler to finish a school assignment, is it any wonder that she crept silently into Eric's room, opened his desk drawer, and borrowed his silver and black ruler? If only Jessie had remembered to put it back when she finished using it. But she didn't.

That's why Eric came storming out of his room later that evening, hollering like he usually did, "Who borrowed my ruler? Jessie!"

Without stopping to think, Jessie quickly answered, "Why do you always blame me when you can't find something?"

"Did you borrow Eric's ruler?" Mom asked.

"No!" Jessie lied. "I haven't seen his dumb ruler."

But Jessie knew she was lying. And the way Eric looked at her, Jessie was sure that he knew the truth.

● *"If you hide your sins, you will not succeed. If you confess and reject them, you will receive mercy." Proverbs 28:13,* EB

● **For Younger Children**
What was the problem between Eric and Jessie?
Why do you think Jessie lied about the ruler?
What do you think will happen next?

● **For Older Children**
If you were Eric, how would you feel about Jessie coming into your room?
If you were Jessie, how would you feel about Eric telling you to stay out of his room?
How did Eric know that Jessie was lying?
What often happens when someone lies?

DAY

2

Jessie sat in her room, with the door closed, looking at Eric's black and silver ruler. It was bad enough that she had taken the ruler from Eric's room without asking him. But it seemed even worse that she had lied about it. She was sure she could slip the ruler back into Eric's desk without being caught. But she was not sure she could get rid of the guilty feeling inside. Jessie did not enjoy feeling like a thief and a liar.

Suddenly, she picked up the ruler, stood up, and walked to the door. She pulled her door open and walked down the hall to Eric's door, which was still covered by the big sign, "No Girls Allowed." She knocked.

"Who is it?" Eric asked from inside.

Very softly Jessie said, "It's me."

For a moment, Jessie thought Eric had not heard her, for there was no sound from inside the room. Then the door opened a few inches, and Eric stood inside staring out at her.

"Here's your ruler," Jessie said, handing it to her brother. Without saying a word, Eric reached out and took it.

"I'm sorry I borrowed it without asking," Jessie said. "And I'm sorry I told you I didn't have it."

Eric looked at his ruler. He looked at his sister. Then he pushed the door open all the way and said, "C'mon in, Jess."

Jessie went in and sat on the edge of Eric's bed. It was the first time she could remember having been invited in.

"Thanks for bringing it back," Eric said. "Why'd you decide to return it?"

"I never meant to keep it," Jessie said. "I just forgot to put it back."

"So," Eric asked again, "why bring it back now?"

"It's yours," was all Jessie said.

"Thanks," Eric replied. "Thanks again. Y'know, you looked pretty nervous when Mom asked if you'd taken it."

"I was," Jessie admitted. "I was afraid I'd get in big trouble. That's why I said I hadn't taken it."

"Well," Eric said, "I'm glad you brought it back. Now I don't have to install locks on my door."

"Locks?" asked Jessie. "You wouldn't put locks on your door!"

Eric just laughed.

● *"Confess your sins to each other and pray for each other so that you may be healed." James 5:16*

● **For Younger Children**

Would you have done what Jessie did? Why or why not?

How did Eric treat Jessie when she brought back the ruler?

Ask God to help you tell the truth and do what's right.

● **For Older Children**

Why did Jessie feel guilty?

When have you felt guilty?

What does James 5:16 say to do when you've done something wrong?

WEEK 3

DAY
3

For a few minutes at least, Eric seemed to have forgotten that girls, especially sisters, were not supposed to be allowed in his room. He and Jessie were sitting in Eric's room, talking about why Jessie had lied about taking Eric's ruler. As they talked, Jessie began looking around the room. This was the first time she could remember being in Eric's room without being in a hurry.

"Take some advice from your big brother," Eric said as Jessie admired his trophies and medals from soccer and baseball. "Y'know," Eric continued, "Dad always says it's better to admit when we've done wrong than to try to hide it."

"But I was afraid," Jessie said. "I thought you'd get REALLY mad. And then Mom and Dad would get mad too."

"I WAS pretty mad," Eric admitted. "I get really ticked when you mess with my stuff."

"I KNOW!" Jessie said. "I thought I saw smoke coming out of your ears when you yelled about your ruler. That's why I said I hadn't taken it."

"But Mom and Dad always find out," Eric added. "I used to try to get away with stuff, but I think they have some kind of radar or something. Besides, they aren't nearly as tough on me if I confess, as they are when they find out some other way."

"Yeah," Jessie replied, "but Mom had that look in her eye."

"Not 'The Look'?" Eric laughed. "If I could learn how to do 'The Look,' nobody'd ever mess with my stuff again."

Jessie laughed too for a moment. Then she got serious again. "I guess I need to tell her what I did," she said.

"Yeah," Eric agreed. "You'd better get it over with. It won't be too bad. She's really on your side."

Jessie got up from the bed. "Well, here goes," she said as she started toward the door.

"And remember one thing, Little Sister," Jessie stopped to hear what Eric had to say. "Stay out of my room, you little twerp!" he laughed and tossed his pillow at her head. It hit the "No Girls Allowed" sign.

● *"Happy is the person whose sins are forgiven." Psalms 32:1,* EB

● **For Younger Children**
Why was Jessie afraid to be honest with Eric?
When have you been afraid to tell the truth?
How does Psalm 32:1 say you'll feel if you tell the truth about something wrong you've done?

● **For Older Children**
What good advice did Eric give Jessie?
When have you been in a situation like Jessie's? What happened?
Why is it better to admit your wrong action instead of trying to hide it?

● ●

WEEK 3

DAY
4

Jessie felt better after she admitted that she had taken her brother Eric's ruler and had lied about it. However, it did bother her that Eric seemed to be enjoying the trouble she had gotten herself into. He seemed especially pleased at the promise she had made to leave his things alone. There must be something she could do to show her big brother that he had not gotten the best of her.

That's when she got her idea. She knew how much Eric valued his trophies. Quickly, she slipped into Eric's room. She picked up the biggest trophy and hid it under the pile of laundry that hadn't made it into the clothes basket! Then she was back in her own room. He might not miss the trophy right away, but he WOULD miss it sometime.

Jessie was already in bed, starting to drift off to sleep, when she heard Eric yell. "Ow! What the. . . ! Oh, no! It broke!"

Jessie sat straight up in bed. Eric kept yelling. Jessie hurried to Eric's room. Eric was holding the trophy in his hands, half of the trophy, that is. The top part, the batter getting ready to swing, was gone.

"Eric, what happened?" Dad asked from the doorway.

"I was reaching into the closet, and I stepped on the pile of clothes.

This," he said, holding up the broken trophy, "was under the pile."

"Eric," Dad said, "if you wouldn't leave your stuff. . . ."

"But I didn't!" Eric interrupted. "I mean, I did leave the clothes out, but not the trophy."

Now Mom entered the conversation. "No one else would touch your trophy," she said.

Suddenly, three pairs of eyes swung slowly to stare directly at Jessie. She looked from one accusing face to another, then looked down at her feet.

"Jessie." That was all Mom said.

Jessie looked up, and said softly, "I hid it there."

Mom took Jessie's hand and led her back to her room. "Jessie," Mom said, "admitting a wrong is good, but you also need to turn away from doing it again. Confessing doesn't fix a broken trophy. Or a broken promise."

Suddenly, Jessie began to sob. She knew she had broken her promise, but she did not know what she could do now to make things right again.

● *"So you must change your hearts and lives! Come back to God, and He will forgive your sins." Acts 3:19,* EB

● **For Younger Children**
What wrong thing did Jessie do?

Was it hard or easy for Jessie to say she hid the trophy?

When might it be hard for you to keep your promise to do something good?

● **For Older Children**
Why did Jessie want to get back at her brother?

If you were Jessie, what would you do now?

How would you say Acts 3:19 in your own words?

●●●

WEEK 3

DAY 5

Jessie sniffed and wiped her nose with her sleeve. Her eyes were red, and her cheeks still showed the marks of the tears that had trickled down. Her mom was sitting on the edge of Jessie's bed with one arm around Jessie's shoulder and the other gently holding Jessie's hand.

"Jessie," Mom said softly. "We've talked about your apology to Eric for going into his room and hiding his trophy. That was good."

Jessie sniffed again and nodded her head.

"And you've told Dad and me," Mom went on, "that you know it was wrong to go against the rule to stay out of Eric's room."

Jessie wiped her nose with her other sleeve.

"And," Mom said, "we've agreed on things you're going to need to do to show you really understand the rule about staying out of Eric's things."

Jessie gulped and nodded again.

"And that's good," her mom added. "But there's someone else who was hurt by your broken promise." Mom paused and waited a moment until Jessie looked up at her. Then she continued. "When we do something we know is wrong, we disobey God. You know what the Bible calls that, don't you?"

Jessie nodded and softly said just one word, "Sin."

"That's right. Do you know what the Bible tells us to do about our sin?" Mom asked.

"Stop it?" Jessie asked.

"You're right," Mom smiled. "And one other important thing. We need to confess to God, admit to Him that we know we have done wrong."

Jessie did not know what to say next. After a moment, Mom asked, "Do you know why it's so important to confess our sins to God?"

Jessie shook her head no.

"Because God wants to forgive us," Mom explained. "But until we admit that we have done wrong, it's like we're keeping ourselves away from God. It's like we're pretending we don't need Him." Mom waited another moment, then she asked, "Do you want to talk to God now?"

Jessie nodded her head, then she bowed it. "Dear God," she began to pray, "I broke a promise. And I broke a rule. I know it was wrong. Please forgive me and help me do right. Amen."

Mom gave Jessie a giant squeeze, and they both smiled.

● *"Everyone who calls on the name of the Lord will be saved." Romans 10:13*

● **For Younger Children**

How would you have felt if you were Jessie? How do you think she felt after she prayed for forgiveness?

What does the Bible call Jessie's actions?

What does God do when we admit our sin to Him?

● **For Older Children**

What were some of the things Jessie and her mom talked about?

Why is it important to confess our sins to God?

Is there a sin you need to ask God's forgiveness for? Do it now. Thank Him for His love and forgiveness and ask His help to do right.

● ●

FAMILY TIMES

Schedule time this week to be together as a family. Select one of these suggested activities to expand your family's understanding of God's loving forgiveness.

Parable Update

Read the Parable of the Lost Son from Luke 15:11-31. Ask, "How is God like the father in this story?" Then with your family rewrite the story in a modern-day setting. Keep a finished copy in your Bible as a reminder of God's forgiveness.

Tip for Younger Children: A younger child may draw pictures to illustrate the story.

Rainbow Writing

Introduce this activity by saying, "Because God loves and forgives us, we know that He wants us to forgive others." Read Ephesians 4:32 together. Talk together about times people in your family have forgiven each other. Ask God's help to continue following His example of forgiveness. Then make a forgiveness reminder using rainbow writing. You'll need paper and three colors of one of these: crayons, felt-tip pens, yarn, ribbon, or glitter pens. Print the word "forgive" with one color of the material you want to use. Outline the letters with the second color, and then the third color. (See sketch.) Display the completed reminder in your kitchen or family room.

Ways to Say "I Forgive"

At the top of a piece of paper, write the words "I forgive you." Ask, "What did God do to show He forgives us?" Then challenge your family to list as many ways as they can which show forgiveness to others. The list may include words and actions. Suggestions of words might be, "That's OK." "It's all right." "I still love you." Suggestions of actions might be hugs, smiles, handshakes. Keep the list and add to it during the coming week.

Made in God's Image

Key Verse
"So God created man in His own image, in the image of God He created him; male and female He created them."
Genesis 1:27

It is tragically easy for a child's natural self-centered view of life to be turned into selfishness and prejudice. Children need the patient guidance of loving, accepting adults to help them grow up respecting people who seem different from them.

This week you can help your child consider the tremendous extent of God's great love for the human race He created. God's love is never the private benefit of a selected few. His love has reached around our globe, seeking people of every nation, race, and language, desiring to bring them to Himself.

Key Thought
All people are made in God's image and deserve love and respect, even when attitudes and actions make this hard to do.

WEEK 4

DAY

1

It happened in the third inning of Arthur's T-Ball game. Two parents got in an argument. No one else knew exactly what started it, but everyone knew the lady in the green sweatshirt did not like something the man in the blue jacket said, so she called him a name.

Then he called her a worse name back. The name-calling got worse, and louder, as the man and the woman got madder and madder, waving their arms at each other and shouting as loudly as they could.

The umpire tried to get them to stop arguing, but they were so mad, they called him names, too.

So the umpire announced the game was over.

Now everybody was mad. Some people yelled at the two parents for arguing. Other people yelled at the umpire for stopping the game. The children on both teams complained loudly because they couldn't finish the game.

Arthur was still grumbling on the way home. "Those kind of people shouldn't be allowed."

His mom asked, "What kind of people?"

"People who start fights," Arthur said. "People who spoil kids' fun. That kind of people."

"And what shouldn't they be allowed?" Mom asked.

"They shouldn't be allowed at games," Arthur said. "They shouldn't be allowed ANYWHERE!"

"Maybe they will have to stay away from the field, at least for a few games," Mom agreed. "But I don't think they shouldn't be allowed ANYWHERE!"

"But they started a fight!" Arthur protested.

"I know, dear," his mom said.

"And they called people terrible names," Arthur continued.

"I know, dear," his mom said.

"And . . . and they ruined the game!" Arthur insisted.

"But, dear," Mom said patiently, "they are still people who are made by God. In fact, the Bible says all people are made to be like God. So everyone is worthwhile, even people who do things they shouldn't."

"Even people who start fights?" Arthur asked.

"Everyone," Mom answered. "You and me and everyone. We're all special to God and should all be treated with love and respect."

The expression on Arthur's face did not look as though he was convinced.

● *"We all have the same Father. The same God made us. So why do people break their promises to each other?" Malachi 2:10, EB*

● **For Younger Children**

What do you think should happen to people who start fights?

Arthur's mom said that everyone is worthwhile or special. Why did she say that? (Read Malachi 2:10.)

How do you think God feels about the people He made?

● **For Older Children**

When have you felt like Arthur about someone who did something wrong?

Why did Arthur have a hard time believing that everyone should be treated with love and respect?

Who is someone you or kids your age might have a hard time treating with respect?

DAY
2

Arthur was giving his friend, Christopher, a vivid description of the big argument at his T-Ball game. First, he sat on a kitchen chair and pretended to be the lady in the green sweatshirt. Then he jumped up and waved his arms like the man in the blue jacket. Christopher was thoroughly enjoying the story, hoping Arthur would tell that the argument turned into a real fight with pushing and hitting and violence. Christopher watched so much TV he thought every argument should end in a fight. When Arthur's story ended, and no one had gotten punched, Christopher was a little disappointed. Then he decided that there may have been a few gory details Arthur had left out.

"What were some of the names they called each other?" Christopher asked.

"I don't remember," Arthur said. "But they were really bad!"

"I bet that lady was a gypsy or a witch," Christopher said, thinking either of those descriptions would explain the woman's actions.

"No way," Arthur retorted. "She's some kid's mom."

"But I bet she was a foreigner," Christopher insisted.

"I don't think so," Arthur said. "But so what?"

"My mom says foreigners cause all the trouble around here," said Christopher. "Foreigners aren't like us."

"They're not?" Arthur asked. Arthur had no idea what a "foreigner" was. He wasn't sure Christopher knew either, but since Christopher was a full year older, Arthur thought he might know what he was talking about.

"My mom says foreigners shouldn't be allowed," Christopher said.

Suddenly Arthur remembered talking with his mother about whether certain people should "not be allowed."

"That's not what my mom says," Arthur replied. "She says all people are worthwhile. She says everybody should be treated with respect."

"Not foreigners," Christopher insisted. "They're not like us."

"But foreigners are people, aren't they?" Arthur asked.

"Yeah," Christopher answered. "I guess so."

"So that means," Arthur said, "they're all special to God."

The expression on Christopher's face did not look as though he was convinced.

● *God said, "I am the Lord, the God of all mankind." Jeremiah 32:27*

● **For Younger Children**

What does the word "foreigner" mean?

Why did Christopher think the lady in the argument must have been a foreigner?

Does God think that only the people from one country are special? Read Jeremiah 32:27 to find out.

● **For Older Children**

Who are some people you know who were born in a country different from yours?

Why might some people not like someone from a different country?

How would you explain to Christopher about the importance of each person, including those from other countries?

● ●

WEEK 3

DAY 3

There was never any doubt about Arthur's mood. When he was happy, he had the biggest smile that could fit on a boy's face. And when he felt gloomy, his face looked like a storm cloud ready to drop buckets of rain. It was the stormy-faced Arthur who greeted his mom after T-Ball practice.

"Practice didn't go too well?" Mom asked.

"I hate baseball!" Arthur answered. His mom had known him long enough, almost six years to be exact, that she could tell when Arthur was bothered by more than whatever he said at first. The trick was helping Arthur talk about the real problem.

"You didn't have fun playing ball?" she asked, hoping Arthur would tell her what was really bothering him. Sure enough, that's just what he did.

"I wasn't playing ball," Arthur declared. "I just stood around in right field. Nobody ever hits the ball to right field. How can I learn to play if I never get to play?"

His mom knew that wasn't the whole problem, but it was a start.

"You know," she said, "some really great players have been right fielders. Roberto Clemente, Henry Aaron, Babe Ruth. . . ."

Arthur interrupted her. "But I bet their managers didn't play favorites."

"Ah," Mom said, finally realizing what was really troubling Arthur, "things are pretty lonely in right field sometimes."

"Nobody pays any attention to right field," Arthur groused. "Coach hit balls to everybody but me. And I never get my ups."

"It feels really crummy when someone seems to play favorites," Mom agreed. "I don't know if the manager did it on purpose, or if he just forgot."

"On purpose," Arthur grumbled.

Mom put her hand on Arthur's shoulder. "I do know that God never treats us like that."

"I hope not," Arthur said, still sounding grumpy.

"Even though people may not be fair with everyone, God always is," Mom said. "I like to think that He's just as loving and caring in how He treats everyone as He was when He first made people back in the beginning."

Arthur looked up. The storm clouds on his face seemed to be lifting.

● *"For God does not show favoritism." Romans 2:11*

● **For Younger Children**

Have you ever felt like Arthur? Why? What happened?

How does Romans 2:11 say God is different than some people?

● **For Older Children**

Has anyone treated you in an unfair way? How did you feel?

Why do you think God always treats people fairly?

What is one way you can show God's love by treating someone fairly?

Ask God's help in treating people fairly.

● ●

WEEK 4

DAY

4

Arthur's mom had taken him to the park to play catch. It was obvious from his difficulties on his T-Ball team that he needed someone to throw a ball back and forth.

"Throw me some grounders, Mom," Arthur yelled.

Mom rolled a ball along the grass. Arthur picked it up and tossed it back to her.

"Harder than that, Mom!" he yelled, sounding insulted that she had just rolled it to him.

The next ball took several good bounces, the last one off the tip of Arthur's glove. As he ran after it, his mom yelled, "Good try, honey!"

Arthur picked up the ball and threw it back. This time he yelled, "Don't call me 'honey' when I'm playing baseball!"

After a few minutes, Mom was able to throw them the way Arthur wanted, and he was able to catch most of them, or at least knock them down with his glove.

Just after trying to catch a ball that his mom had tossed into the air, Arthur looked up and said, "Oh, no!"

"Oh, no, what?" Mom asked.

"It's Sabrina." Arthur answered. "From my class. At school. She's a pest."

Arthur's mom turned to see a girl skipping across the grass toward them. "Hi, Sabrina," Mom said. "How are you?"

"Fine," Sabrina answered. "Can I play catch with you?"

"Sorry!" Arthur answered, trying to sound important. "I have to practice for my game."

"I can help you practice," Sabrina said. "I'm good at baseball."

"Sorry," Arthur said again. "This is just for boys."

"Just a minute, Sabrina," Mom said, walking over to Arthur. "Remember our talk about playing favorites and not including everybody?" she asked him.

Suddenly realizing what his mom was going to suggest, Arthur just nodded his head. "Well, if you don't like other people to play favorites, you shouldn't do it either."

"But, Mom," Arthur started to protest. However, Mom did not give him a chance to complain further.

"Everybody is special. Everybody counts. Everybody deserves a chance."

"I get it," Arthur said softly. Then to Sabrina, he said, "You can borrow my mom's glove so she can rest."

● *"If you really keep the royal law found in Scripture, 'Love your neighbor as yourself,' you are doing right. But if you show favoritism, you sin." James 2:8-9*

● **For Younger Children**

Why didn't Arthur want Sabrina to play catch with him?

How would you feel if you were Sabrina and you knew Arthur didn't want to play with you?

Why is it important not to play favorites?

● **For Older Children**

What would you have done if you were Arthur?

Read James 2:8-9. What does it mean to love your neighbor as yourself?

Your neighbor is anyone, not just the person next door. Who are some of your "neighbors"? How can you show love to those people?

The game was going to start in just a few minutes. Arthur's T-Ball team was gathered around their manager, getting last minute instructions on which positions each one would play. Suddenly, the manager noticed that several of the players were staring at something going on behind him. Then one boy said, "It's her!"

The manager and the rest of the team turned to see who was there.

Coming toward them was the lady in the green sweatshirt, the lady who had gotten so mad at their last game and caused the umpire to stop the game. No one said a word as she walked right up to the team and spoke to the manager.

"Can I say one thing to the team now?" she asked.

The manager did not seem too surprised. He just nodded his head, as though this had all been arranged ahead of time.

The players did not know what to expect. Was she going to start arguing again? Would she start calling people names? Would she yell and wave her arms? Everyone held his breath and waited for her to speak.

"I made a big mistake at the last game," she said. "I lost my temper and said things I should not have said. I'm very sorry that I spoiled your game. I won't ever do that again. I promise."

The manager stood up and shook her hand. "Thanks for coming and talking to us," he said. "Now, team, let's play ball!"

Arthur ran alongside another player on his way to right field. "Wow!" he said. "I thought that lady was bonkers. Maybe she's not so bad."

The other player, on his way to center field, agreed. "Yeah. She's my mom. She's OK most of the time."

All during the game, Arthur kept thinking about the green sweatshirt lady. He remembered how he had thought she was so terrible and should "not be allowed." He thought about his mom saying that everyone was special to God and deserved respect and love. However, the three times that batters hit the ball to right field, Arthur did concentrate on the baseball.

● *"Make every effort to live in peace with all men." Hebrews 12:14*

● **For Younger Children**
What did the green sweatshirt lady say that surprised everyone?
Who is someone you might have a hard time getting along with?
God doesn't expect you to become best friends with someone you don't

like, but God does want you to show respect to the person and care about his or her feelings. Ask God to help you.

● For Older Children

What did the team members think might happen when the green sweatshirt lady came to their game?

Read Hebrews 12:14. What did the lady say that showed she wanted to live in peace?

How can you live in peace with someone you might not like?

• •

FAMILY TIMES

Schedule time this week to be together as a family. Select one of these suggested activities to expand your family's understanding of God's love for all people.

Say Hello!

Help your family become aware of people from different countries by saying "hello" or "good day" in several languages. (If you know someone who speaks a language other than those listed here, ask him or her how to say hello.) Spanish: Hola (OH-lah); Dutch: Goeden dag (KHOO-ten dakh); Swedish: God dag (gud DOG); French: Bonjour (boneJUR); Hawaiian: Aloha (ah-LOH-hah).

Circle Fun

Group your family into pairs. Give each pair a large piece of paper and two pencils. Each pair draws two intersecting circles on the paper and writes their names on the circles as shown in the sketch. In the area that overlaps, the pair writes things that are the same about them. In the separate areas each person writes things that are different. Talk about the fact that God made people alike in some ways and different in others. Ask, "How might a (girl) your age from the country of (name) be the same as you? How might (she) be different?" Thank God for His love for each person.

Tip for Younger Children: A younger child may dictate items to be written on his or her circle.

International Night
Plan a night to experience and appreciate the culture of another country. Choose one or more of these ideas. (1) Invite your family to help you prepare an ethnic dish. Cookbooks often have a section of international recipes. (2) Listen to music. Libraries have a variety of records available to borrow. Or purchase a cassette from a music store. (3) Rent and watch a video featuring a foreign country. (4) Eat at a restaurant which serves food from a different country.

Missions

Key Passage
" 'Everyone who calls on the name of the Lord will be saved.' How, then, can they call on the One they have not believed in? And how can they believe in the One of whom they have not heard? And how can they hear without someone preaching to them? And how can they preach unless they are sent? As it is written, 'How beautiful are the feet of those who bring good news.' " Romans 10:13-15

The world is so huge and the diversity of cultures so numerous that it is very difficult for a young child to begin to understand either distances or differences. However, various actions can be taken to begin arousing a child's interest in missions.

First, before a child can develop a heart for the world, a solid foundation of generosity toward others must be laid. Learning to care for those nearby is crucial to learning to care for those far away.

Then the child should be introduced to missions in meaningful, child-sized steps. This week's story of the Norris family allows a child to learn a little about one needy place in our world and one type of mission work, short-term, vocational mission. Use the interest generated by this story to introduce your child to the work of a specific missionary supported by your church. Help your child begin to enjoy the excitement of being part of the church's great mission of sending people and resources to share God's love throughout our world.

Key Thought
God wants everyone who loves Jesus to help spread the news of God's love to all people in the world.

DAY

1

There was a lot of excitement on the Norris family farm. It was not unusual for things to get exciting there. With three boys and one girl in the family, and horses, cows, sheep, and a few chickens around the barn, there was always something going on. But today's excitement was different.

It all started when the mail carrier tooted her truck's horn. Grandma Norris always enjoyed walking out to the mailbox. She took her time strolling down the long driveway, past where it curved around the big oak tree, then on down to the county road.

She was in no hurry when she reached into the mailbox and pulled out the envelopes. As she started back up the driveway, she began shuffling through the mail. Suddenly, after looking at a long, blue envelope, she tucked the mail under her arm and began walking quickly back up the driveway. By the time she passed the big oak tree, she was starting to breathe heavily, but she did not slow down. As she approached the house, she hollered in between deep breaths, "Evelyn! (puff-puff) Marvin! (puff-puff) It came! (puff-puff-puff) It came!"

Evelyn Norris came rushing out on the porch. Marvin Norris came rushing around the side of the barn. And all four Norris children suddenly appeared from all directions. Everyone in the family knew what Grandma Norris meant when she said, "It came!"

Mrs. Norris was the first to get to Grandma. She took the long, blue envelope from Grandma's hand, took a quick look at where it was from, and said, "This is it!" Then she handed the long, blue envelope to her husband. "I'm too nervous, Marvin. You open it."

Mr. Norris had to take off his heavy work gloves and tuck them under one elbow. Then, without saying a word, he tapped one end of the envelope against his wrist, tore off the envelope's other end, took out a single sheet of paper, and unfolded it.

"What's it say, Dad?" Ryan asked, eagerly.

"Yes!" Mr. Norris exclaimed. "We've been approved! We're going to Africa for the summer!"

● *"Everyone who calls on the name of the Lord will be saved." Romans 10:13*

● **For Younger Children**

What country would you like to go to?

The Norris family was going to Africa to tell others the Good News about

Jesus. What Good News do you know about Jesus that you could tell others?

What Good News does Romans 10:13 tell about?

● For Older Children

Why do you think the Norris family was so excited about going to Africa?

The Norris family planned to go to Africa as missionaries — helping people and telling them God's messages. What message from God's Word do you read in Romans 10:13?

How would you say this verse in your own words?

● ●

WEEK 5

DAY
2

"You're going WHERE for the summer?" Ryan's friend, Alex, was stunned.

"Africa," Ryan answered. "Tanzania, actually. It's on the east coast of Africa."

"I know where Tanzania is," Alex said. "But why on earth are you going there?"

"Dad's going to work with some of the farmers there to help them improve their farming methods. He'll help them with some wells they need to dig to have better water sources. And he and Mom will have lots of chances to talk about Jesus with the people there."

"But why are YOU going?" Alex asked, still sounding like he thought this was the most foolish idea he had ever heard. "And your brothers and sister? And your grandma?"

"Grandma's not going," Ryan answered. "She's gonna stay here and take care of the house."

"But the rest of you are all gonna go?" asked Alex.

"Yeah," Ryan said. "Mom doesn't want Grandma to have to put up with us all summer. Besides, she thinks we'll learn a lot about other people."

"But what about the farm?" Alex asked. Alex could ask more questions than a school teacher. "There's a lot of work to do around here during the summer."

"Dad hired Mr. Ramos to take care of everything while we're gone," Ryan answered. "And people in our church have given money to help pay for us to go." It was obvious Ryan and his family had planned well for this summer adventure.

But Alex still did not sound convinced. "Think of all the good stuff you'll miss. Swimming and baseball and homemade ice cream and the fair and the big picnic. Summer is the best time of year, Ryan, and you're going to waste it?"

"Hey!" Ryan answered. "I don't think we're wasting it. I think we'll be doing stuff that's really important. We'll be helping people."

"I guess so," Alex finally admitted. "But it's gonna be awfully boring without you around."

"How about if I send you lots of postcards?" Ryan asked.

"Neat!" Alex brightened. "I never get any mail."

● *"How, then, can they call on the One they have not believed in?" Romans 10:14*

● **For Younger Children**

What do you like to do in the summer?

Why was the Norris family going to Tanzania?

Why is helping people and talking to them about Jesus important?

● **For Older Children**

Why did Alex think Ryan's summer would be wasted?

Why did Ryan say his summer would NOT be wasted?

If you were Ryan, how would you feel about spending the summer in a foreign country?

● ●

WEEK 5

DAY
3

The airplane was scheduled to land in about an hour. The Norris family felt like they had been traveling for days, although it was only yesterday they had left their family farm. Flying high above the huge continent of Africa, they were getting excited about finally reaching Tanzania. At least seven-year-old Laura was excited. Her younger brother, Chris, was asleep, and her older brother, Ryan, was trying to act as though traveling halfway around the world was no big deal. Eight-year-old Josh would have been excited, except he had just learned that Tanzania was not covered by jungle.

"I thought Africa was ALL jungle!" Josh protested, sounding as though he had made the trip for nothing.

"Central and western Africa have a lot of jungle," Ryan explained. "Jungles need a lot of rain. Tanzania is in the eastern part of Africa, and it's pretty dry there."

"Can we drive to a jungle?" Josh asked hopefully.

"No way!" Ryan answered. "Africa is HUGE! It's got over fifty different countries in it, and Tanzania's big all by itself."

Josh looked like he felt cheated.

"Hey, Josh," Ryan continued, "Tanzania is a neat place even if it doesn't have jungles. It's got the tallest mountain in Africa."

"Yeah," Laura chimed in. "Mount Kill-the-man's-car-o?"

"Mount Kilimanjaro," Ryan corrected.

"That's fun to say," Laura replied. "Kilimanjaro. Kilimanjaro."

"And the biggest lake in Africa is right on the border," Ryan continued showing off what he had learned about Tanzania. "Lake Victoria is part of this huge valley that goes all the way from the top of Africa to the bottom. There are two other huge lakes a little further south in this valley — Tanganyika and Nyassa."

Ryan's lecture was interrupted with an announcement over the plane's loudspeaker. The announcement was made in three different languages, Swahili, French, and English. The Norris children did not understand any of the first two languages, but they did understand the English announcement that they were about to land in Tanzania's largest city, Dar es Salaam.

"It's a big city, Josh," Ryan explained. "Bigger than any towns near home. But we'll be going out in the country."

"I'd rather be going to a jungle," Josh muttered as he checked that his seat belt was securely fastened.

● *"And how can they believe in the One of whom they have not heard?"*
Romans 10:14

● **For Younger Children**
Why was Josh disappointed?

The Norris family was glad to go to Tanzania to talk with people about Jesus. Who first told you about Jesus?

Thank God for people who share the Good News about Jesus.

● **For Older Children**
Have you flown on an airplane? What did you like about it?

The Norris family was going to live in a village in Tanzania. How might the village be different from the place where you live?

Many people throughout the world don't believe in Jesus. Why does Romans 10:14 say these people don't believe?

It was the Norris family's first morning to wake up in Tanzania, Africa. They all felt very out of place in the small house where they were staying. Looking out the windows, they missed the familiar fields of their farm back home. Instead, they saw other small houses and a dusty street which ran through the middle of the village. After they unpacked their suitcases, they spent the rest of their first day exploring the village and visiting the open-air market where everyone bought their groceries.

The people who lived in the village were curious about this new family, and the Norris family was just as curious about the people who lived in the village. Everywhere the Norris family went, they met friendly smiles.

On the second morning in Tanzania, Africa, Ryan went with his father to meet some of the local farmers. Mr. Norris wanted to get started helping the farmers dig a well which would provide water for their crops.

Seven or eight Tanzanian farmers were waiting when Ryan and his dad arrived. One tall, thin man spoke both English and Swahili, so he translated what was being said. When Mr. Norris would say a sentence in English, the tall, thin man would say the same thing in Swahili. When one of the farmers would say something in Swahili, the tall, thin man would say the same thing in English. Quickly, Mr. Norris and the farmers were very busy, talking back and forth.

Off to one side of the group of farmers, Ryan noticed a boy who looked to be about his own age. Ryan walked over to him, smiled, and said, "Hi, I'm Ryan."

The boy smiled back and said, "Hello. I am Kolo." Then Kolo said proudly, "I learn English at school."

Ryan responded, "I don't learn Swahili at school."

Kolo nodded his head, then he asked, "Why do you come to our village?"

Ryan answered, "To talk about farming, and about Jesus."

Kolo smiled and said, "I know Jesus!" Then he added, "Many people here do not know Jesus yet."

"That's why we came," Ryan said.

● *"And how can they hear without someone preaching to them? And how can they preach unless they are sent?" Romans 10:14-15*

● **For Younger Children**
How would you like to have the name Kolo?

What do you know about Jesus that you could tell someone?
Ask God's help in learning about Jesus so you can tell others.

● **For Older Children**

Do you know any words in a foreign language? What are they?

If someone had never heard of Jesus, what would you tell them?

What does Romans 10:14-15 say needs to happen in order for people to hear the Good News of Jesus?

● ●

WEEK 5

DAY
5

While Mr. Norris talked with a group of African farmers, Ryan and his new friend, Kolo, sat in the shade talking about their favorite sports. "I like baseball and basketball," Ryan said. "We have a basketball hoop nailed on our barn, and I'm a pretty good shot. But baseball is my favorite. Someday I hope to play in the World Series."

"World Series?" Kolo asked. "Like World Cup? For baseball?"

"Well," Ryan explained, "it's not really for the whole world. It's just for teams in the United States and Canada. What's the World Cup?"

"Football!" Kolo smiled. "Every four years!"

"Football?" Ryan asked. He did not know of any World Cup in football.

"Yes," Kolo answered. "We kick round ball into goal."

"Oh, you mean soccer," Ryan exclaimed.

"No," Kolo insisted, "I mean football."

"I know," Ryan said. "At home we call it soccer. Do you like soccer . . . I mean, football?"

"Very much," Kolo replied. "Football and running."

"Running?" Ryan asked.

"Yes," said Kolo, laughing. "Many great runners come from Kenya and Tanzania. I will run Olympics."

"Good," said Ryan, laughing also. "You run in the Olympics, and I'll hit a home run in the World Series."

Ryan and Kolo enjoyed talking together, telling each other about their homes, their schools, and their churches. Soon the meeting with the farmers ended, and it was time for Ryan and his dad to return to their house.

Ryan stood up and reached in his pocket. "Thank you for talking with me," Ryan said, "I'd like to give you something." He handed Kolo the New Testament he carried in his pocket. "I'm sorry I don't have one written in Swahili," Ryan explained. "But you speak such good English, I hope you'll like this."

Kolo had seen Bibles at his church, but he had never had one of his own. He held it carefully with both hands. "Thank you," he said with a big smile and one tear that slid down his cheek. "It will help me learn English better," Kolo said. "And learn Jesus better too."

● *"As it is written, 'How beautiful are the feet of those who bring Good News!' "* *Romans 10:15*

● **For Younger Children**
How was Mr. Norris helping the farmers?
  Why was Ryan's gift so special to Kolo?
  How do Bibles help people?

● **For Older Children**
Why was Kolo happy and sad at the same time?
  How many Bibles does your family have?
  How would you feel if your family didn't have even one Bible?

● ●

Schedule time this week to be together as a family. Select one of these suggested activities to expand your family's understanding of ways Christians work together to share God's love throughout the world. In order to complete these activities, ask your church office for a list of missionaries (and their newsletters or prayer requests) supported by your church.

FAMILY TIMES

Map It Out!
On a world map or globe find the location of the countries in which missionaries supported by your church live. Choose one country. On a large piece of paper draw an outline of the country. Write the name of a missionary family who live in that country within the outline. Display the paper on your refrigerator or a wall. Pray for this family.
  Tip for Younger Children: Your younger child will also enjoy coloring the country.

Happy Birthday
Make a list of the birthdays of missionaries and their children. Plan to send birthday cards at the appropriate times. Cards may be purchased or your family may make birthday cards. Cards can easily be made by folding a

sheet of construction paper in half. Decorate the cards with stickers, felt-tip pen drawings, etc. Remember to allow sufficient mailing time.

Picture Exchange
Choose a missionary family who has children close in age to the children in your family. Write the family, sending them your family picture and asking them to send a picture to you. Also ask the missionaries to tell you of several prayer requests they have. When you receive the picture and prayer requests, make a poster with the picture and prayer information.

AUGUST

Take Care of Your Body

Key Verse
"Do you not know that your body is a temple of the Holy Spirit. . . ? Therefore honor God with your body."
1 Corinthians 6:19-20

The human body has long been recognized as one of the marvels of God's creation. Still, vast numbers of people abuse their own bodies by following unhealthy lifestyles. Many people establish unhealthy habits in childhood and carry these into the adult years, increasing their susceptibility to a wide range of disease, and sometimes significantly shortening their lives.

As you and your child read this week's stories, take advantage of this opportunity to evaluate the health patterns you are establishing for your child's life.

Key Thought
Taking good care of our bodies is not only a wise thing to do, it is honoring to God.

WEEK 1

DAY 1

When Aliki's mother told her they were having company for Sunday dinner after church, Aliki was curious. When her father said their guest was speaking for their church service, she was proud. But when her mother told her that this speaker was a former drug addict, Aliki was shocked.

"A drug addict? Here?" she asked.

"A FORMER drug addict," her father said.

"What does 'former' mean?" her little sister, Midori, asked.

"It means he USED to be a drug addict, but he isn't any more," Aliki explained.

"What's a drug addict?" Midori asked.

"Don't you ever watch television?" Aliki asked. "Drug addicts are like . . . gangsters . . . criminals . . . wild people!"

A wild person was what Aliki was expecting for Sunday dinner. Her father explained that if people use drugs too much their bodies need more and more of them. He also explained that many people who become addicts also become criminals to pay for the drugs they need, so Aliki was certain that their guest would be terribly frightening. She could hardly wait!

Aliki was certainly surprised when her father opened the door to their apartment, and she got her first look at Mr. Nobuko Okuni, former drug addict. She was surprised when her father and Mr. Okuni bowed politely to each other. She was surprised that Mr. Okuni appeared so normal and was dressed like her father dressed for church. She was most surprised by the big, friendly smile on Mr. Okuni's face as he came into their apartment.

"Are you a gangster?" Aliki's little sister blurted out. Her parents looked embarrassed, but Mr. Okuni just laughed.

"I used to be," he said to Midori. "I was in very bad trouble all the time because of the drugs and alcohol I craved." The two sisters looked at Mr. Okuni as though he were very dangerous. "But now," he went on, "all that is out of my life. I only think about it when I have a chance to warn parents and children to stay away from alcohol and drugs."

Aliki and Midori were still not sure if it was safe to have Mr. Okuni in their home.

● *"Do not get drunk on wine." Ephesians 5:18*

● **For Younger Children**

Why were Aliki and Midori a little afraid of Mr. Okuni?

How would you have felt if Mr. Okuni came to your house?

What can happen to people who are addicted to drugs or alcohol?

● **For Older Children**

What have you heard about the problem of drug and alcohol addiction?

Why do you think some people use drugs or drink alcohol?

What does Ephesians 5:18 say about drinking alcohol?

● ●

WEEK 1

DAY 2

When the Yasuda family and their guest sat down to dinner, Aliki and Midori both felt nervous about sitting close to Mr Okuni. When their father said that he was going to pray, neither girl wanted to close her eyes while sitting next to a former drug addict. So they each closed one eye and watched their guest with the other eye.

All they saw during the prayer was Mr. Okuni with his head bowed.

After their father said, "Amen," Mr. Okuni raised his head and discovered both girls staring directly at him. He just smiled and nodded his head politely.

As the food was being passed around the table, Mrs. Yasuda asked a question. "Would you mind, Mr. Okuni, telling our girls some of the story of your life?"

"I would be pleased," he said, "although it makes me sad to remember how terrible my life used to be." As Mr. Okuni said this, he smiled again at Aliki and passed her a large bowl of steaming, hot vegetables. Aliki was not sure whether to keep her eyes on Mr. Okuni or to make sure she did not take any vegetables she did not like. She decided to watch Mr. Okuni and take her chances on the vegetables.

"It used to be that I could not go even one day without drugs or alcohol," Mr. Okuni said. "Drugs and alcohol were almost all I could think of. They made me very, very sick in my body and in my mind."

"Why didn't you stop taking them?" Midori asked.

Now Mr. Okuni smiled at the younger sister. "I really wanted to quit," he answered. "Many, many times I said I would stop hurting myself that way. But I could not quit. I was trapped."

Aliki and Midori imagined nice Mr. Okuni caught in a terrible trap. Mr. Okuni kept talking. "Worst of all," he said, "I hurt many other people." Mr. Okuni was not smiling now. He looked first at one girl, then at the other. Then he said softly, "Aliki. Midori. I hope you never, ever, ever let anyone talk you into taking drugs."

Aliki agreed. There was no way she wanted to get caught in a trap like Mr. Okuni.

● *"I pray that you may enjoy good health." 3 John 2*

● **For Younger Children**

What made Mr. Okuni feel sad?

When Mr. Okuni wanted to quit taking drugs but couldn't, what did he say it was like?

How would you feel if someone you knew was caught in the trap of taking drugs?

● **For Older Children**

Why did Mr. Okuni describe drug and alcohol addiction as a trap?

What warning did Mr. Okuni give Aliki and Midori?

Ask God's help in keeping you safe from drug and alcohol addiction.

WEEK 1

DAY
3

While Aliki's mouth was busy chewing her Sunday dinner, her mind was busy thinking about the warning their dinner guest had just given her. Mr. Nobuko Okuni, sitting right next to her at the dinner table, had said to her, "I hope you never, ever, ever let anyone talk you into taking drugs."

While Aliki was thinking, her younger sister, Midori, asked Mr. Okuni a question. "Why did you ever start taking drugs?" she asked.

"I started to use drugs and alcohol," Mr. Okuni said, "because I was lonely and unhappy and afraid."

Aliki looked again at Mr. Okuni's face. He did not look lonely, unhappy, or afraid now. Aliki asked, "Didn't you have friends?"

Now Mr. Okuni did look a little bit lonely and unhappy. "I thought I had friends," he said. "But they were the ones who kept asking me to try drugs. I wanted them to like me, so I did what they did."

"So did they like you?" Midori asked.

"Not really," Mr. Okuni answered. "Their lives were being ruined by drugs already. They kept telling me that drugs would make me happy. They said that drugs would help me forget my problems and unhappiness. They were wrong."

"Wrong?" Aliki asked. The girls were not quite as nervous with Mr. Okuni as they had been at first. They had become very interested in hearing what he had to say. So interested, they weren't even eating.

"For a while, I thought my friends were right about drugs," Mr. Okuni answered. "I thought drugs would be wonderful. But drugs and alcohol only caused me more problems. Worse problems. And they made me miserable."

"How did you change from all that?" Midori asked.

"Jesus helped me break out of the trap I was in," Mr. Okuni said.

"Jesus?" asked Aliki.

"Yes," Mr. Okuni answered. "I found real joy comes in knowing Jesus. I found my first real friends in people who shared God's love with me. Knowing Jesus changed me from being sad and lonely."

● *"A cheerful heart is good medicine." Proverbs 17:22*

● **For Younger Children**
What was wrong with the friends Mr. Okuni used to have?
Who helped Mr. Okuni stop taking drugs and find new friends?
Thank Jesus for His love and for always being your best friend.

● For Older Children
Why did Mr. Okuni start taking drugs?
What kind of drug or medicine does Proverbs 17:22 say is good?
What can you do to have a cheerful heart?

● ●

DAY
4

After Sunday dinner was finished, Mr. Yasuda asked their guest if he would like to join them in walking down to the park.

"I would love to," said Mr. Okuni.

A few minutes later, the Yasudas and their guest were strolling around the large pond in the center of the park. They saw ducks floating on the water. After a few minutes, the ducks began frantically flapping their wings and flew up into the air. A moment later, several joggers ran past, huffing and puffing and sweating.

"Those runners don't look like they're having much fun," Aliki said.

"Yeah," agreed Midori. "They look like they hurt all over."

"I think they're having fun," said Mr. Okuni. "I jog three mornings every week, and it really is fun."

"You jog?" asked Midori, sounding as though she thought jogging couldn't possibly be fun. "Why do you do THAT?"

"I do it to help keep my body healthy," Mr. Okuni answered.

"But do you really like it?" Aliki asked, as she watched two more joggers, two very sweaty joggers, go running past.

"It is hard work, Aliki," he said. "But my body really does feel better when I exercise regularly."

"How can being all out of breath feel good?" Midori asked.

Mr. Okuni paused for a moment before he answered. "I admit, young lady, that being out of breath may not feel much like fun. But it is a very good feeling to know that your body is strong and healthy. And plenty of exercise is needed for that."

"I don't think our girls get nearly enough good exercise," Mrs. Yasuda said. "Our apartment building doesn't allow much room for running around."

"Oh, Mom," Aliki said, "we go up and down the stairs ninety times every day! YOU always take the elevator!"

Mrs. Yasuda laughed. "You're right, dear," she said. "Maybe I should take up jogging."

● *"Training your body helps you in some ways, but serving God helps you in every way." 1 Timothy 4:8, EB*

● **For Younger Children**

How did Aliki say she exercises?

What kind of games or sports do you like to play?

What's a new way of getting exercise you'd like to try?

● **For Older Children**

Why did Mr. Okuni say he liked to exercise?

How does exercise help your body stay strong?

Sometimes it's more fun to exercise or play an active game with a friend. Who is a friend you can exercise with?

WEEK 1

DAY 5

● ●

Mr. Nobuko Okuni stood at the door of the Yasuda family apartment. He was about to leave. He bowed politely and said, "I thank you for the delicious dinner. And I thank you for the very pleasant time I have spent with you."

After Mr. and Mrs. Yasuda told Mr. Okuni how much they had enjoyed his company, Mr. Okuni turned to Midori with a smile. "Little flower, I hope you will remember to exercise to make your body strong."

Midori smiled back at him.

Mr. Okuni then turned to Aliki. "And you, ray of sunlight . . . you should eat your vegetables."

Aliki giggled. She had not noticed that Mr. Okuni saw her leave some vegetables untouched on her dinner plate. "But I don't like them," she said, turning up her nose.

"But they are GOOD for you," Mr. Okuni laughed.

"Then why do they taste BAD?" Aliki asked. "Why aren't they sweet?"

Mr. Okuni laughed even harder. "I do not know," he answered. "I have never thought about why vegetables do not taste sweet." He paused for a moment, then said, "Perhaps it is so we have to make an effort, like exercising."

Aliki looked puzzled. Mr. Okuni tried to explain his idea to her. "Perhaps the taste of vegetables helps us learn to do things that are not easy at first. Perhaps by learning to like them, we keep from getting lazy, and that helps us to be strong."

"Vegetables taste bad," chimed in Midori, "because they're full of icky vitamins and stuff." She paused for a moment and thought about what she had said. "And because there's no way to make icky vitamins and stuff taste good."

Mr. Okuni laughed again. "Whatever the reason, I do know that it's good to thank God even for foods we don't like. We need to trust God in all things, even when we don't always see the good in them."

Aliki did not look very certain about what Mr. Okuni had said.

"I do believe," Mr Okuni said to her as he started out the door, "that when you are thankful even for lima beans, you'll know you're really growing up." And then he winked. And then he left.

● *"So whether you eat or drink or whatever you do, do it all for the glory of God." 1 Corinthians 10:31*

● **For Younger Children**
How do lima beans taste to you?

What's your favorite food to eat?

Thank God for all the foods He has made, and ask His help in staying strong and healthy.

● **For Older Children**
When it comes to eating vegetables, are you more like Mr. Okuni or Aliki?

What are some examples of healthy foods?

First Corinthians 10:31 says that everything you do should show your love for God. How does staying away from drugs, exercising, and eating healthy foods show your love for God?

● ●

Schedule time this week to be together as a family. Select one of these suggested activities to expand your family's understanding of how important it is to develop a healthy lifestyle.

FAMILY TIMES

Family Night Dessert
Try these fun-sounding, but healthy dessert recipes. Invite family members to help you prepare and eat.

LUMBERJACK LOGS
½ cup creamy peanut butter
½ cup honey
½ cup instant nonfat dry milk
½ cup raisins, chopped
½ cup graham cracker crumbs

Blend together peanut butter, honey, and dry milk. Add chopped raisins, mixing thoroughly. Blend in graham cracker crumbs, mixing well. Using teaspoonfuls of mixture, form logs by rolling out on waxed paper. Place logs on cookie sheets and chill for one hour, or longer if desired. Makes about 35 logs.

APPLE CUP AND HONEY
Core an apple and hollow out part of the inside. Fill the center of the apple with honey. Slice another apple and dip the sections into the honey.

Snack Food Alphabet
"What's to eat? I'm hungry?" may be heard frequently around your house. In order to have a quick reference list of healthy snack ideas, work together to write a snack food alphabet. Along the left side of a piece of paper list the letters of the alphabet. For each letter of the alphabet, try to list one or more healthy snack food ideas (apples, bagels, cheese, diced dates, eggs, fruit, granola, etc. Post the list on your refrigerator door.

Tip for Younger Children: Ask a younger child to illustrate your snack food alphabet.

Bible Clues to a Healthy Lifestyle
With your family look for clues to David's healthy lifestyle as a young man. Read aloud: 1 Samuel 17:17-18. After reading the Bible verses, ask: "What do these verses say about the kind of food David ate?" Read aloud, 1 Samuel 17:34-35. "What do these verses say about David's strength and endurance? What are some things our family can do to follow David's example?" How can we be careful to eat food that is healthy?

God Forgives Us

Last month you and your child explored the important concept of confessing sins. Because this issue is so vital, it is good to take another look at it from a slightly different perspective.

Last month the emphasis was on our act of confession. The emphasis this week is on the assurance we have that God truly does forgive. This is brought out by contrasting God's mercy and forgiveness with the attitude of Hector's friend, Mariano, who turns out to be very unforgiving.

WEEK 2

DAY
1

Hector wanted to ride Mariano's new skateboard. His friend had gotten the new board for his birthday, and it was faster and smoother riding than Hector's. That was why, when Mariano had to go inside to help his mother, Hector asked, "Can I borrow your skateboard?" "I don't know, man," Mariano answered.

"I won't hurt it," Hector promised.

"OK," Mariano agreed. "But you'd better not get it chipped or anything."

"I promise!" Hector said. "I'll just ride a little, then I'll bring it right back." So Mariano went inside and Hector took off down the sidewalk. As Hector whizzed around the corner, he saw several friends playing basketball in the playground.

Hector jumped the board off the curb, shot across the street, and popped it onto the sidewalk on the other side. Without slowing down, he spun onto the basketball court and came to a squealing stop right in the middle of his friends.

"Neat board," one of them said.

"Want to play ball?" another one asked.

That sounded good to Hector, so he propped the skateboard up against the basketball pole and joined the game. The team Hector joined was doing well, and Hector made several nice shots. The score was tied, and Hector's team had the ball, when someone yelled Hector's name.

It was his sister, Angela, calling him to come in for dinner. Hector said he'd be right in, but he played for a few more minutes, trying to score the winning basket.

"Hector!" another voice shouted. This time his dad had come to get him.

"Gotta go, guys," Hector told his friends and ran back toward home.

Later that evening, just as he was getting ready for bed, Hector remembered Mariano's skateboard, propped up against the basketball pole. It was too late to go out to get it. Hector sat on the edge of his bed thinking, "Would it still be there in the morning? Why did I ask to borrow it? Why did Mariano let me borrow it? Why didn't I take it back before I started playing basketball? Why didn't I quit playing when Angela called?" Hector did not sleep well that night.

● *"Happy is the person whose sins are forgiven." Psalms 32:1,* EB

● **For Younger Children**
Why didn't Hector sleep well?
  What did Hector do wrong?
  What do you think will happen next?

● **For Older Children**
What made Hector so worried?
  When have you done something like Hector? What happened?
  What would you do if you were Hector?

● ●

WEEK 2

DAY

2

The sun was just barely peeking over the tops of the tall city buildings. Everyone else in Hector's family was still asleep. Hector slipped quietly out of bed and got dressed. He opened the front door of their apartment and tiptoed down the quiet, dark hallway. Once he was downstairs and outside, he broke into a run, all the way to the playground. As he approached the basketball court, Hector saw that the skateboard he had left by the pole was gone.

Could it still be somewhere in the playground? Frantically, Hector began looking behind bushes, inside trash cans, under benches. The skateboard was gone. The skateboard he had borrowed from Mariano, that he had promised to return, it was gone.

Hector's first thought was to call the police or the Army to mount a massive search for the missing skateboard. But his second thought was that he would have to admit where he had left Mariano's skateboard. Then everyone would know what he had done and that it was all his fault Mariano's skateboard was gone.

Hector spent all the rest of that day looking for each of his friends who had been playing basketball with him the day before. "Raul?" he asked. "Did you see that skateboard I had over at the basketball court yesterday?"

"I saw it when you tooled up on it," Raul said.

"Did you see it after I left?" Hector asked.

"I don't think so," Raul answered. "No, I don't remember seeing it."

Hector heard the same answer from each of the other basketball players. No one remembered seeing the skateboard after Hector had left it propped against the basketball pole.

Finding his friends and asking them about the skateboard was one thing Hector did that day. The other thing he did was try to avoid seeing Mariano. And avoid having Mariano see him. But just before dinner, as he was going in the front door of the apartment building, who should be coming out of that same door? Hector gulped. What could he say to Mariano about the missing skateboard?

● *"There is no God like you. You forgive those who are guilty of sin."*
Micah 7:18, EB

● **For Younger Children**
What might Hector say?

Hector did something wrong to Mariano by losing his skateboard. When you do something wrong to God by disobeying Him, what should you do?

What does Micah 7:18 say God does?

● **For Older Children**
How would you describe Hector's feelings?

What was Hector guilty of? When have you felt guilty?

What does Micah 7:8 say God does for guilty people?

DAY
3

"Hey, Hector!" Mariano was not smiling as he came out of the front door of the apartment building. "I've been lookin' all over for you."

"Hi, Mariano," Hector said, not looking his friend in the eye. "I've been real busy today."

"So where's my skateboard?" Mariano demanded. "You said you'd bring it right back."

"Somebody took it," Hector said, still not looking up. "I've spent all day trying to find it and get it back."

"Somebody took it?" Mariano asked. "How? Did they beat you up? Who was it? How many guys?"

Just for a moment Hector was tempted to make up a story for Mariano, so that he would think Hector had bravely fought off a violent gang who had overpowered him with a fierce show of weapons. Just for a moment. "No, not like that," Hector said. "It was my fault. I left it at the basketball court last night, and someone took it before I got back there."

"You left it?" Mariano shouted. "You left my new skateboard?"

"Yeah," Hector admitted. "I'm really sorry."

"You're sorry?" Mariano shouted even louder. Then he called Hector some names, some very unfriendly names. He put his hand on Hector's shoulder and pushed, hard. "I'll make you real sorry. I'm gonna pound you!"

"I said I'm sorry," Hector said, backing away from Mariano. "I'll pay you for the board. I promise."

"Like you promised to bring my board back right away?" Mariano sneered, and he gave Hector another hard push.

Hector had never seen Mariano so angry. He tried to think of something to say that would calm things down. But all Hector could think of was that he deserved everything Mariano was saying about him. He had broken a promise. He had lost his friend's skateboard. The whole mess was his very own fault. But what could he do now?

● *"The Lord our God is merciful and forgiving, even though we have rebelled against Him." Daniel 9:9*

● **For Younger Children**

How did Mariano treat Hector?

What would you have said if you were Mariano?

When we've disobeyed God, if we confess our wrong to Him, He forgives us—no matter what we've done. How does God's love and forgiveness make you feel?

● **For Older Children**

What would you have said to Mariano?

What did Hector admit? Would it have been better if he had lied about what happened?

Do you think Hector deserves mercy? Why or why not?

Does God treat people who have sinned with mercy? How do you know?

● ●

WEEK 2

DAY
4

"I need to earn some money, Mom," Hector said as he walked into the kitchen.

Mom was busy mashing avocados and salsa into a spicy, green sauce. "Good idea," she said. "I'll give you a dime to finish these avocados."

"I mean real money, Mom," Hector said. "Lots of money."

"If you're planning to buy a TV or a video game or a CD player for your room, the answer is no," Mom replied.

"I need to buy a skateboard," Hector explained.

"Is something wrong with your old one?" Mom asked.

"It's not for me," Hector explained further. "I need to buy a skateboard for Mariano."

"I thought he just got a new one for his birthday," Mom said.

"He did," Hector continued explaining. Then he added very softly, "But I lost it."

Suddenly Mom looked up from the bowl of mashed avocados. She did not say a word, but Hector could tell from the look on her face that she expected him to explain every detail about the trouble he was in.

So Hector told her the whole story. He did not skip anything. He made it very clear that the whole problem of the missing skateboard was his own fault.

Mom listened, then she said, "You can't really blame Mariano for being angry."

"I know," Hector replied. "I think that's the worst part. I sure wish I could stop him from being so mad."

"Do you think buying him a new skateboard will fix everything?" she asked.

"I don't know," Hector answered. "But I've got to do it anyway. I owe him." Hector thought for a moment, then he added one more thought. He said, "I didn't just lose a skateboard. I lost a friend."

● *"I will cleanse them from all the sin they have committed against Me and will forgive all their sins of rebellion against Me." Jeremiah 33:8*

● **For Younger Children**
What was Hector's plan?
Do you think Mariano will still be Hector's friend? Why or why not?
Read God's promise of forgiveness and friendship in Jeremiah 33:8.

● **For Older Children**
What made Hector sad?
When you've done something wrong to a friend, how have you tried to fix things?
How does God "fix things" for us when we've sinned against Him?

WEEK 2

DAY 5

Hector walked slowly back to his own apartment. He was not thinking about money. Hector had borrowed money from his mother to pay his friend, Mariano, for the skateboard Hector had lost.

Hector was not thinking about the skateboard, or who might have taken it. Hector was thinking about his friendship with Mariano. Hector had hoped that when he gave Mariano the money, his friend would stop being mad at him. But Mariano had just said, "Don't ever ask to borrow anything of mine again." Hector understood that part of the reason Mariano was still mad at him was that Mariano's father had gotten very angry at Mariano for letting Hector borrow the skateboard.

"Boy," Hector thought to himself, "I make one dumb mistake and it seems like everyone gets mad."

When Hector got home, he found a list of chores his mother had left. Hector was going to have a lot of work to do to pay back his mom for loaning him the money. Hector's first job was sweeping the sidewalk in front of their apartment house. He had never noticed before how much litter there was on that sidewalk. It took much longer than he had thought to finish the job.

Just as he was dumping the last of the litter into a big trash bin, a voice behind him said, "Nice job, Hector." It was Hector's sister, Angela.

"Thanks," Hector muttered.

"How'd Mariano act when you paid him?" she asked.

"He's still mad," Hector said, leaning on the big broom.

"He'll get over it," Angela said. "And you know you did the right thing."

"I guess," Hector said, not sounding very sure about it.

"Aren't you glad," Angela asked, "that God's not like Mariano?"

"What do you mean?" asked Hector.

Angela explained, "Mariano wanted to get even with you, even though you admitted you were wrong and tried to make things right."

"So?" Hector asked.

"So when we confess our sins to God," Angela said, "He wants to forgive us. And He does."

"I never thought of that," Hector said, smiling.

● *"Who will bring any charge against those whom God has chosen? It is God who justifies." Romans 8:33*

● **For Younger Children**

What was the right thing Hector did?

Do you think Mariano will get over being mad?

When we sin against God, do you think God gets mad at us? Why or why not?

● **For Older Children**

Why was Mariano still mad?

How are God and Mariano different? How does God feel when we sin?

Tell God thank You for always keeping His promise to love and forgive you.

● ●

Schedule time this week to be together as a family. Select one of these suggested activities to expand your family's understanding of God's promise of forgiveness.

FAMILY TIMES

Banner in a Sack

Before your family time, collect one or two large pieces of paper, glue, and a variety of items such as felt-tip pens, crayons, cotton balls, ribbon, glitter, stickers, and aluminum foil. When your family gets together, ask, "When you hear the word forgiveness, what do you think of?" Then work together in pairs or trios to make banners. Draw pictures, write words, or make designs to show your feelings about God's forgiveness.

Missing Word

Take turns reading aloud several of this week's verses about forgiveness: Psalm 32:1; Daniel 9:9; Micah 7:18; 1 John 1:9. As each verse is read, however, the person reading the verse leaves out five or six key words. Family members supply the missing words. Pray together, thanking God for His forgiveness.

For Parents Only

Your child's best teacher of God's forgiveness will be you. As you demonstrate love and forgiveness to your child on a regular basis, you will be building an understanding of what God's forgiveness means. The time when your child least deserves your love is probably when he or she needs it the most!

Serving Others

Key Verse
"Serve one another in love."
Galatians 5:13

Key Thought
Learning to serve others is an important way to show God's love.

Everyone likes to have someone else wait on them. Sitting back, relaxing, while someone else fetches, pours, cooks, opens, shuts. Is it any wonder Jesus had to resort to an elaborate object lesson — washing his disciples' feet — to get across the point that serving others is God's way to achieve true greatness.

As you and your child read about Arthur's experience in learning to serve, consider possible ways your family can serve and help someone in need.

WEEK 3

DAY 1

Arthur and his mother had their arms full as they walked into the side door of their church building. Arthur was carrying a big bag full of potato chips. His mom was carrying a large casserole wrapped in a towel. Between holding the chips and smelling the casserole, Arthur was starved!

The church kitchen was full of busy people, working and laughing together. Arthur knew that these busy people were getting ready to serve a meal to homeless people. Arthur's church helped people who had no place to live and who needed a good, healthy dinner.

Arthur kept busy while the grownups set up tables and chairs and brought out dishes and silverware. While he was playing hide and seek with an imaginary friend, Arthur suddenly noticed several people in the back of the large room, people he had never seen before.

Arthur stared at these people. He noticed that their clothes were shabby. Several of the men looked like they had not shaved for a week. Arthur wondered whether any of them had bathed for days. While Arthur inspected these people, several others arrived, and then more. By the time the dinner was ready, forty-three people were in the room. Arthur had counted them.

After one of the men who worked in the kitchen led a prayer, the homeless people got in line to get their dinner. Arthur's job was to hand everyone a paper napkin. His mother had told him to smile at each person and say, "Here you are, sir," or "Here you are, ma'am." Suddenly, Arthur realized he was handing a napkin to a boy his own age. It did not seem right to say "Here you are, sir." So he just handed him a napkin without saying a word.

The boy took the napkin without smiling, and said, "This food sucks."

Arthur pointed down the line to the casserole his mom had made. "That one's really good," he said. "My mom made it."

"Yuck," the boy sneered. "It's all slop."

Arthur did not know what to say.

● *"Whoever wants to become great among you must be your servant."*
Mark 10:43

● **For Younger Children**

How would you have felt if you were Arthur?

Read Mark 10:43. How was Arthur acting like a servant?

When have you helped someone else?

● **For Older Children**

How did Arthur feel about serving food to the homeless people?

What do most people think a great person is like?

What does Mark 10:43 say a person must do to be great?

WEEK 3

DAY 2

Arthur did not want to help serve food to homeless people again. "Those people are dirty, and they smell bad," he said to his mom.

"That's because they don't have a place to live where they can wash their clothes and take regular baths," his mom explained. "Besides," she went on, "I promised to help again this week, and I need to keep my promise."

"Why'd you promise?" Arthur protested. "I hate this stuff."

"I understand," Mom said. "But we are going."

"Besides," Arthur said, "I feel weird carrying a casserole down the street."

Mom handed him a small bag and said, "I'll carry the casserole, Buster. You carry the cookies."

"Cookies?" Arthur asked, his face brightening. "What kind? Who are they for?"

"Yes, cookies," Mom answered, wrapping the casserole dish in a large towel to keep it warm. "Chocolate chip," she said. "They're for any children who come, like that boy who came with his mother last week."

"Oh," Arthur's faced drooped again. "Him."

"Yes," Mom said. "If he comes again, maybe the two of you could play together while we're cleaning up after dinner."

Arthur held the door open while his mom carried the casserole out into the hall. She set it down and locked the door to their apartment. Then she and Arthur started on their three block walk to serve dinner to homeless people at their church. Neither of them said much until they were near the church building. Arthur slowed down when he noticed a group of shabbily dressed people standing outside the front door.

His mom stopped and looked straight at Arthur. "I know you don't feel comfortable doing this," she said. "But when people need help, we need to do whatever we can, even if it's something we don't particularly like to do."

"How come?" Arthur asked.

"Because that's what Jesus would do if He were here," Mom answered. "Because we love Jesus, we try to follow His example."

"OK," Arthur said. "But I hope that kid's not here again."

● *"Carry each other's burdens, and in this way you will fulfill the law of Christ."* Galatians 6:2

● **For Younger Children**
Why didn't Arthur want to see the boy again?
  Why is it important to help other people?
  What might the world be like if no one was willing to help others?

● **For Older Children**
If Jesus lived on earth today, how might He help homeless people?
  Read Galatians 6:2. What is the "law of Christ"? (See Luke 10:27.)
  What's one way you can follow Jesus' example and obey the law of Christ?

● ●

WEEK 3

DAY 3

Once again Arthur and his mom were helping to serve food to homeless people at church. Actually, Arthur's mom was helping to serve the food. Arthur was handing out paper napkins again.

Once again he was smiling and saying, "Here you are, sir," and "Here you are, ma'am" as people came through the line to get their dinners.

And once again Arthur found himself handing a napkin to the same boy as he had last week. "We've got cookies this week!" he said.

The unfriendly expression on the boy's face relaxed just a little. "What kind?" he asked suspiciously, as though he expected them to be full of broccoli chunks or liver strips.

"Chocolate chip," Arthur announced. "My mom brought 'em just for you."

"Let's keep the line movin'," said an older man who was in line right behind the boy.

As the next few people came past, Arthur forgot to say, "Here you are, sir," or "Here you are, ma'am," for he kept watching the boy continue on down the line. Arthur kept watching until the boy got to where Arthur's mother was standing. Arthur watched as she reached into the paper bag and gave the boy several of the chocolate chip cookies.

After dinner, Arthur saw the boy and his mother getting ready to leave. Arthur waved at him and yelled, "How were the cookies?"

"Not bad!" the boy yelled back. "And the other stuff was OK too!"

"My name's Arthur!" Arthur yelled as the boy and his mom started to walk toward the door.

The boy turned and shouted, "I'm Michael!"

While walking home with his mom, Arthur took her hand, the one that wasn't holding the empty casserole dish. "Y'know, Mom?" Arthur said. "What dear?" she replied.

"I decided," Arthur said, "that helping others maybe isn't so bad after all."

● *"We must not become tired of doing good." Galatians 6:9,* EB

● **For Younger Children**

What favorite cookies would you have brought?

What did Arthur and his mom do to make friends with the boy?

What's one way you and your family might help a needy person?

● **For Older Children**

How did Arthur's mom show that she wasn't tired of doing good?

Why did Arthur change his mind about helping people?

If you were Arthur, how would you feel about serving food to homeless people?

DAY
4

Arthur knew this was the day he and his mother would go to church to help serve dinner to homeless people. Arthur found himself wondering if Michael, the homeless boy he had met there two weeks ago, would be back again this week.

Arthur also wondered if there might be some way besides handing out napkins that he could help his new friend. As usual when Arthur wondered about something, he ended up asking his mom about it.

"How come Michael is homeless?" Arthur asked.

"I don't know for sure," Mom answered. "I know his mother was out of work for a long time, and she could not afford the rent for an apartment."

"What's going to happen to them?" Arthur asked.

His mother explained, "I'm working with some people in our church to help Michael and his mom find an apartment. We think we may have one for them in a few weeks."

That was good news, and it helped Arthur decide to ask his mom about his idea. "Would it be OK" he asked, "for me to share some books with Michael?"

"Books?" his mom asked. "What books?"

"I've got so many books in my room I could loan some to him."

"But a lot of your books were gifts from grandparents," Mom reminded him. "And from aunts and uncles. That makes them special."

"But I've looked at all of them dozens of times," Arthur pointed out. "And next year in first grade I won't need so many picture books."

"OK," Mom agreed. "Pick out a few books to share with Michael. Just remember that books are heavy, and you have to carry them all the way to church."

Quickly, Arthur went to his room and began to pack a bag with books he hoped Michael would enjoy. When the bag was almost full, he picked it up and decided that was about all he could carry for three blocks. Just then Mom looked into his room. "You're doing a good thing, Arthur," she said. "I'm proud of you for being willing to help someone else."

● *"Each one should use whatever gift he has received to serve others."*
1 Peter 4:10

● **For Younger Children**
What was Arthur's good idea?

What's something you and your family could share with others?

Ask God's help in sharing with others.

● **For Older Children**

Besides giving them food, what else was Arthur's church doing to help Michael and his mom?

How many ways to help homeless people can you think of?

What's something you could do?

DAY
5

● ●

"Here you are, sir," Arthur said as he handed a paper napkin to a young man wearing a stained sweatshirt. "Here you are, ma'am," he said as he handed a paper napkin to a tall, thin woman who was wearing at least four or five sweaters. Arthur kept repeating his greeting to each homeless person who went through the food line.

Suddenly, Arthur realized he was handing a napkin to a boy his own age. "Hi, Michael," Arthur said. "I've got something for you. After dinner."

"OK," Michael answered. "What are we eating?"

"Casseroles again," Arthur said. "But they smell pretty good."

Right after dinner, Arthur took Michael to a table in the back of the room. He pointed to the bag sitting on one end of the table. "These are for you," he said to Michael.

Quickly, Michael reached into the bag. When he pulled three large, colorful books out of the bag, his eyes and his smile both grew wide. "Wow!" Michael said, reaching back into the bag and pulling out four more big books.

While the grownups visited and then cleaned up after dinner, the two boys had a great time looking at the books Arthur had brought. Each time Michael picked up a book, Arthur said, "That's one of my favorites. I really like this one."

Several of the books were ones that Michael had seen at the school library. "If you like," Arthur said, "I'll bring some more next week," Michael asked, "You've got more?" He thought Arthur was very lucky to have so many books of his own.

Arthur said, "You can borrow these as long as you want."

"Maybe," Michael said, "I could share some with other kids who don't have many books."

"Great idea!" Arthur said. "And if I keep sharing books with you, maybe my room won't be such a mess all the time."

● *"Whatever you do, work at it with all your heart, as working for the Lord, not for men." Colossians 3:23*

● **For Younger Children**

What did Arthur and Michael enjoy doing together?

   Giving, sharing, and helping others is a way to show God's love. Can you think of someone you might be able to show God's love to this week?

● **For Older Children**

Do you think it was hard or easy for Arthur to share his books? Why?

   When has someone shared with you? When have you shared with someone else?

   Thank God for what you have and ask His help in sharing with others.

• •

Schedule time this week to be together as a family. Select one of these suggested activities to expand your family's understanding of ways they may show God's love by serving others in need.

FAMILY TIMES

Volunteers on Call

Contact your church or a local charitable organization to find a way your family can serve or give to someone in need. Consider donating money or usable items, preparing and serving food, purchasing food for a food bank, etc.

Making a Difference Poster

Give each family member a newspaper or magazine to look through to find examples of people who are helping others. See how many different ways you can find. Talk about the variety of ways in which people may use their time, abilities, and possessions to help others. Cut out articles and/or pictures and mount them on a large sheet of paper. Keep the paper up for several weeks and add to it.

Household Hunt

Choose one (or combine several) of these unusual ways to determine a monetary donation to a charitable organization. (1) Count the number of electric lights in your house and give a nickel for each light. (2) How many pencils can you find? Give a penny for each pencil. (3) Count the number of doors and give a dollar for each one. (4) Look for stuffed animals and give a quarter for each.

Telling Others about Jesus

Key Verse
"Christ Jesus came into the world to save sinners."
1 Timothy 1:15

Key Thought
Even a child can share good news about God's love through Jesus Christ.

A witness is someone who was there when something happened. A person cannot witness about an event he or she has only read or heard about. A witness must have been on the scene.

Jesus' first followers were witnesses of all that Jesus did and all that He said. They were on the scene when He spoke to multitudes. Some of them saw Him arrested, and, from a distance, some saw Him die. Several hundred people were with Him after His resurrection and could witness to others that He had truly come back to life.

Today, we can pass on to others what those witnesses have shared with us in the pages of Scripture. In addition, we can be witnesses ourselves of all that God has done in our own lives. We can tell about the ways that God's love has made our lives better. And we can invite them to experience the same new life that we have received.

WEEK 4

DAY 1

AJ came home from Sunday School very excited. This was not totally unusual because AJ always enjoyed her Sunday School class. She always liked being with the other girls in her class. And her teacher, Mrs. Robinson, was one of her most favorite people in the world. This particular Sunday, however, it was obvious that AJ had enjoyed her class even more than usual. It did not take her long to announce the reason for her excitement. "I'm gonna win a video tape!" she exclaimed to her family.

"How you gonna do that?" her twin brother, DJ asked.

"My teacher's gonna give a video to any girl who brings a friend to Sunday School," AJ answered, with perhaps just a touch of bragging.

"Big deal!" DJ grunted. He did not want to admit that he was a little bit jealous that HIS Sunday School teacher had not made the same offer to the boys' class.

"Who are you going to invite?" AJ's dad asked.

"Maybe I'll invite Rhoda," AJ said. "She already knows most of the kids in the class. Or I could invite Kelly . . . or Kate . . . or Rebecca. Rebecca! That's who I'll invite!" AJ seemed pleased that she had so easily resolved that issue.

AJ's Mom had been listening to all this. She asked AJ, "Why do you want Rebecca to come with you?"

AJ thought the answer to Mom's question was obvious. "To win the video tape, Mom."

Mom did not think the answer was quite so obvious, so she asked another question. "Why do you think your teacher is giving a prize for bringing a friend?"

AJ got a pained look on her face that seemed to say, "Parents are SO out of it!" But she answered politely, "So our class will be bigger and more fun." And then she added a question of her own. "Why else?"

"That's a very good question, AJ" Mom replied. "Maybe you should ask Mrs. Robinson."

"OK," AJ said. "I will."

● *"And you will be My witnesses." Acts 1:8*

● **For Younger Children**
What did AJ like about her Sunday School class?
   Why is going to Sunday School a good thing to do?
   Which of your friends would you invite?

● **For Older Children**
What would you give as a prize for bringing a friend to Sunday School?
   Do you agree with AJ's answer about why her teacher was giving prizes? Why or why not?
   How might asking a friend to Sunday School be a way of obeying Acts 1:8?

● ●

WEEK 4

DAY
2

AJ loved talking on the telephone. Ever since she was very small, whenever the phone would ring, she would holler, "I got it!" and rush to grab it before anyone else. She had never been shy about talking to anyone on the phone.

Once she had learned how to push the buttons for her friends' phone numbers, there was no stopping her. She never needed an excuse to call someone on the phone. Thus, when Mother had suggested she ask her Sunday School teacher why she was giving a prize for inviting a friend to class, AJ headed for the phone.

It only took AJ a few moments to find Mrs. Robinson's number. Very carefully, she pushed each button, then waited while the phone rang.

"Hello?" someone said on the other end.

"Hi, Mrs. Robinson," AJ said on her end.

"Hi," said Mrs. Robinson. "Who's this?"

AJ seemed a little surprised that Mrs. Robinson had not recognized her voice immediately. "It's me! AJ! AJ Gorman!" she announced. And without pausing, she added, "My mom wants me to ask you a question."

"Fine, AJ," Mrs. Robinson said. "Fire away."

So AJ did. "My mom wants to know why you want us to bring a friend to Sunday School."

"Two reasons, I suppose," Mrs. Robinson said. "First, I think you'll enjoy the class more if your best friends are there too."

AJ liked that answer, for it sounded just like the one she had already given her mother. She nodded her head, forgetting that Mrs. Robinson could not see her.

"And the second reason," Mrs. Robinson went on, "is even more important. I want your friends to find out how much God loves them so that they can have Jesus as their Friend and Savior."

AJ had not thought of that reason. She was so busy thinking about what Mrs. Robinson had said that she forgot to say anything on the phone.

Finally, Mrs. Robinson said, "Are you still there, AJ?"

"I'm here, Mrs. Robinson," AJ said. "I'm thinking."

● *"How beautiful are the feet of those who bring Good News!" Romans 10:15*

● **For Younger Children**

Whom do you like to call on the phone?

What did Mrs. Robinson say she wanted AJ's friends to find out?

Which friend of yours might not know about God's love?

● **For Older Children**

Why might Mrs. Robinson think it's important for AJ and her friends to learn about God's love?

What is the Good News Romans 10:15 talks about?

How would you say Romans 10:15 in your own words?

282

WEEK 4

DAY

3

As soon as AJ hung up from talking with her Sunday School teacher, she quickly began pushing buttons on the phone. She did not need to look up her friend Rebecca's number, since she called it so often she had it memorized.

After three rings, Rebecca's mom answered. "Is Rebecca home?" AJ asked. "This is AJ." "Just a minute, AJ," Rebecca's mom said. Then Rebecca's mom must have covered the phone with her hand, for AJ heard a muffled shout, " 'Becca! Telephone! It's AJ!"

A few moments later, Rebecca picked up the phone. "Hi, A!" she said.

"Hi Bec," AJ said. "Would you like to come to Sunday School with me this week?"

"Sunday School?" Rebecca asked. "You go to Sunday School?"

"Sure," AJ answered. "You wanna come with?"

"What do you do there?" Rebecca asked. "Do you like it?" she added. "Who else goes?" was her third question.

"Sure I like it," AJ answered. "We have a good time. Angie, Mariannne, Olivia . . . they all come."

There was a pause on the other line for a moment. Then Rebecca asked, "But why do you go? Don't you get enough school during the week?"

"It's different from regular school," AJ said. "Besides, I like learning about Jesus."

"Well, I like learning too," Rebecca said. "But not enough to go to school an extra day."

"Why don't you try it once and see what you think?" AJ asked. She had not expected Rebecca to ask so many questions.

"Maybe," Rebecca said. "I've gotta ask my mom first. Hold on."

While AJ waited, she found herself thinking about the video tape she wanted to win for bringing a friend. But she also found herself thinking about Rebecca, a friend who did not yet know about God's love for her.

When Rebecca came back on the phone and said that she could go one time to see what it was like, AJ knew that she really cared more about Rebecca learning about Jesus than she did about winning a video.

● *"Go into all the world and preach the Good News to all creation." Mark 16:15*

● **For Younger Children**
What might Rebecca learn about Jesus at Sunday School?

What does Mark 16:15 say we are to do?

Ask God's help in telling others the Good News.

● **For Older Children**

What was AJ thinking about on the phone?

AJ was obeying Mark 16:15 by inviting Rebecca to Sunday School. What are other ways someone your age might help a friend hear the Good News?

●●

WEEK 4

DAY 4

AJ's friend, Rebecca, enjoyed her first visit to Sunday School. AJ knew she enjoyed it because she asked, "How'd you like it?"

Rebecca's answer was, "Fine. It was fun drawing these cartoons of that lost sheep." She was holding a booklet she had made with pictures of Jesus' story about a sheep that ran away. The sheep looked a little funny, and the shepherd looked VERY funny, but the cartoons did tell the whole story about the shepherd searching for the runaway sheep.

AJ was never satisfied with one question when she could think of several, so she asked, "How'd you like the kids?"

Rebecca's answer was, "Fine. I already knew half of them."

AJ's next question was, "What about Mrs. Robinson?"

"She's nice," Rebecca answered.

"And what'd you think about the lesson?"

Rebecca paused for a moment, looking down at the cartoons she had drawn. Then she said, "I don't think I liked it."

"Why?" AJ asked.

"I did like making these cartoons," Rebecca said. "But I think that story said I'm lost, like this sheep. And I'm not lost! I know where I am."

AJ decided she should try to answer Rebecca's complaint. She said, "The story didn't mean that you can't find your way home. It means . . . it means . . . well, I think it means that without Jesus, a person is lost from God's love." That was the best explanation AJ could think of.

"No way!" Rebecca said emphatically. But she did not look as certain as she sounded.

"But, 'Becca," AJ replied, pointing to Rebecca's cartoons, "this sheep didn't think it was lost at first."

Rebecca studied her drawings some more. "I never thought of that," she said softly.

"Well," AJ said. "wanna learn some more about this?"

"About sheep?" Rebecca asked.

"No, silly," AJ laughed. "About Jesus."

"Sure," answered Rebecca. "Why not?"

● *"Remember this: Whoever turns a sinner from the error of his way will save him from death." James 5:20*

● **For Younger Children**

Do you like to draw cartoons like Rebecca and AJ?

The cartoon story showed that God loves all people and wants them to know about Him and His love. How was AJ helping Rebecca learn about God's love?

● **For Older Children**

Do you think Rebecca liked Sunday School? Why or why not?

What do you think it means to be lost from God's love?

If you were the lost sheep, how would you feel when the shepherd found you?

● ●

WEEK 4

DAY 5

Rebecca went to Sunday School with her friend, AJ, for several more weeks. Each week AJ asked her how she liked it, and each week Rebecca said she liked the music and the activities. She also said she liked the teacher and the other kids.

AJ decided to ask a new question. "Do you ever pray, 'Becca?"

Rebecca seemed surprised by the question. "In church, sure," she answered.

"Well, I've been praying a lot," AJ said. "For you."

"For me?" Rebecca seemed very surprised. "How come?"

AJ thought very carefully about her answer. Then she said, "That God will help you find how much He loves you."

"How would I find that?" Rebecca wanted to know.

"That's easy," AJ said. "Just ask Him."

Rebecca seemed very interested, but she was not sure she understood. "Ask Him what?" she wanted to know.

"Just ask what I did," AJ said. "I asked God to help me believe that Jesus is God's Son and that He died for the wrongs things I've done."

"OK," Rebecca said. Bowing her head, she prayed the way she had seen

Mrs. Robinson do in Sunday School. "Dear God," she began. "Help me to believe in Jesus." Then she paused.

"Ask Him to forgive you," AJ prompted.

"And please forgive me," Rebecca continued praying.

"Ask Jesus to be with you always," AJ whispered.

"And please have Jesus be with me always," Rebecca prayed, then she looked up. "Anything else?" she asked AJ.

"Why not ask Him to help you love and obey Jesus," AJ suggested.

Rebecca bowed her head again and said, "Please help me love Jesus and obey Him."

"Amen," AJ said.

"Amen," Rebecca echoed. Then she looked up at AJ. "Is that all?"

"I think so," AJ said. "Just ask and then trust Him. That's what Mrs. Robinson keeps telling us."

"I don't feel anything," Rebecca said.

"That's OK," AJ replied. "God loves you no matter how you feel."

"Really?" Rebecca asked. "That's cool."

"It really is," AJ agreed. And then she smiled. Rebecca's prayer had certainly made AJ feel happy. Very happy indeed.

● *"There is rejoicing in the presence of the angels of God over one sinner who repents." Luke 15:10*

● **For Younger Children**
What did Rebecca ask God to do?
  What important thing did AJ say about God's love?
  Who is someone you can tell about God's love?

● **For Older Children**
AJ helped Rebecca become a part of God's family. What does Luke 15:10 say happens when someone prays a prayer like Rebecca did?
  Ask God to help you share the Good News about Jesus with a friend.

● ●

FAMILY TIMES Schedule time this week to be together as a family. Select one of these suggested activities to expand your family's understanding of ways to share the Good News of God's love with others.

Read and Draw

Read Jesus' story of the lost sheep in Luke 15:1-7. Then choose one of these ways to illustrate the parable. (1) Divide a large sheet of paper into four or six sections. Illustrate the story by drawing a different scene in each section. Stick figures are okay! (2) Choose one scene from the story. Draw the scene on a large piece of paper. Glue cotton balls to the sheep.

Verse in Motion

Read Mark 16:15 together. Then work together to think of motions to represent each phrase of the verse. When you've thought of motions for the entire verse, repeat the verse with the motions several times. Then one person does the motions for any phrase in the verse. Other family members say the phrase. Repeat procedure several times until each family member has had a turn to choose a phrase. (Alternate idea: Obtain a sign language book from your local library and learn the verse in sign language.)

Witnesses in Our World

On a large piece of paper draw four concentric circles as shown in the sketch below. Read Acts 1:8, and write the names of the locations in the circles, beginning with Jerusalem in the center. Say, "These are the places where Jesus told His followers to tell the Good News of God's love. If Jesus were speaking to us today, what places might He name? Let's write the name of our city/town in the middle." (Use a pen or pencil of a different color.) Continue to write additional place names representing your state or province, country, and a far-away foreign country.

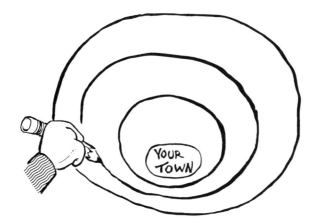

S E P T E M B E R

Key Verse
"Whatever is true, whatever is noble, whatever is right, whatever is pure, whatever is lovely, whatever is admirable — if anything is excellent or praiseworthy — think about such things."
Philippians 4:8

God's Beautiful Gifts

Besides creating a world filled with all that is necessary to sustain life, God also provided marvelous gifts which make life pleasant. Music provides no calories or vitamins, but it certainly does lift our spirits. Visual beauty gives no warmth or shelter to the body, but it greatly enriches our emotions.

Focus your child's attention this week on the evidences he or she can notice of these "bonus" gifts God has given. Affirm your child's unique, God-given attraction to forms of beauty you may not find so appealing. Introduce your child to some of these gifts you enjoy most. And, in all things, give thanks to the Creator.

Key Thought
It is good to praise God for all the beauty He has provided in our world.

WEEK 1

DAY 1

Grandpa Ed helped eight-year-old Jessie up the steps onto the train. Then Grandpa and Eric climbed up after her. The three of them walked down the aisle until they found three seats together. Two were facing forward, the other backward. "Anyone want to ride backward?" Grandpa asked.

"I'll get sick," Jessie groaned.

"I like to ride that way," Eric said, plopping himself down in the empty seat. Jessie and Grandpa took their seats, Jessie getting the one by the window. A few moments later the train's whistle sounded and the train began to move. Grandpa Ed, Jessie, and Eric were on their way into the city. They were going to spend the morning at the art museum and the afternoon at a concert.

For a while, Eric and Jessie said nothing, keeping their eyes focused on the passing scenery outside. Jessie finally broke their silence. "How much longer, Grandpa?" she asked.

Pulling out his pocket watch, Grandpa said, "About thirty-three minutes."

"Can't this train go any faster?" Jessie asked, sounding as though she thought thirty-three minutes was much too long a time. "I just want to get there."

"What time does the museum open, Grandpa?" Eric asked.

"Nine-thirty," Grandpa answered. "Same time it opened last time you asked."

"Oh yeah, huh," Eric said. "I forgot."

Out the windows of the train, they saw the backs of old, dirty industrial buildings, many of them abandoned. All of them looked run down, making the city look very depressing.

"People have made a lot of ugliness in God's world," Grandpa said. "But people have also made a lot of beauty in God's world. That's what we're goin' to see today."

"When was the last time you went to the art museum?" Eric asked.

"Last spring," Grandpa answered. "I go at least two or three times every year."

"Why do you go so often?" Jessie asked. "Don't you get bored seeing the same stuff over and over?"

"It's not all the same," Grandpa explained. "They often change some displays. And I never get tired of the beauty of my favorite paintings and statues." Grandpa paused a moment, then he added, "Sort of like I never get tired of my favorite grandkids."

● *"The inside of the temple was cedar, carved with gourds and open flowers."*
1 Kings 6:18

● **For Younger Children**
What would you like about riding on a train?

What is something beautiful you've seen in our world?

Long ago in Bible times, King Solomon built a beautiful building, called a temple, as a way of showing his love for God. According to 1 Kings 6:18, what things were in the temple?

● **For Older Children**
Have you ever been to an art museum or concert? What did you like about it?

What depressing things did Eric and Jessie see on their train ride?

How might God feel when He sees the ugly things in our world today?

WEEK 1

DAY
2

When the train pulled into the station, Jessie was the first one off. Eric and Grandpa were right behind her. Grandpa looked up at the big clock hanging from the center of the high, arched ceiling. "It's 9:25, kids. We've got a five-minute walk. We should get to the museum just as they're openin' the doors."

Outside the station, Eric and Jessie noticed the noise and speed of city traffic. When a red light turned green, they crossed the street and headed up the block. At the next corner, they saw what looked like a big park with several large buildings set among the trees.

Pointing to the closest building, Grandpa said, "That one's the museum. The one further away is where we'll hear the concert."

Sure enough, just as they climbed the steps to the huge central doors of the museum, one of the doors swung out and a man said, "Mornin' folks. Welcome to the art museum."

Grandpa paid for their admission tickets, then they began to tour the different galleries filled with paintings and sculpture. They saw works of art that were hundreds of years old and some that were almost brand new. They saw some that were huge, filling almost an entire wall, and others that were very, very small. Some of the art amazed the children because the artists had created scenes so accurately. They also saw art where the artists had tried to show feelings or ideas with color and design.

After visiting all the galleries on the first floor, Grandpa, Eric, and Jessie sat on a bench to rest before going up to the second floor.

"What do you like best so far, Grandpa?" Eric asked.

"Tough question, Eric," Grandpa answered. "I think I like best that there are so many different things that I like."

"Huh?" Jessie asked.

"Well, Jessie," Grandpa tried to explain, "God filled the world with different kinds of beauty. And I like the way this museum reflects some of those differences. If we find beauty in only one kind of scenery, or one style of art, or type of music, we'll soon get tired of it all."

● *God said, ". . . I have given skill to all the craftsmen to make everything I have commanded you." Exodus 31:6*

● **For Younger Children**
What were some of the things Eric and Jessie saw in the museum?

Would you rather paint pictures, make sculptures, or write music? Why?

God has given people the ability to make many beautiful things. Think of something you like to see and thank God for it.

● **For Older Children**
Which do you think is harder—painting pictures, making sculptures, or writing music? Why?
Read Exodus 31:6. Who gives people the ability to make beautiful things? What special skill would you like to have?

● ●

DAY
3

Grandpa Ed sat in the shade eating a hot dog. Eric and Jessie had finished theirs in about three bites each and were now chasing each other through the large metal sculptures in the plaza in front of the performing arts center.

Gradually, more people came into the plaza, arriving early for the afternoon concert. As Eric raced near the tree where Grandpa was sitting, he heard a loud finger snap. Eric knew Grandpa wanted his attention, so he slowed down and jogged back to Grandpa's tree.

"You snapped, sir?" Eric asked.

"You betcha," Grandpa laughed. "The plaza's gettin' a little too crowded for you and Jessie to keep runnin' around. Besides, it's time for ice cream."

"All right!" Eric exclaimed, as Jessie arrived on the scene. The three of them walked over to a colorful cart under a more colorful umbrella. It took awhile for Eric and Jessie to decide what they wanted, but they still had almost an hour before the concert would begin.

Suddenly, they heard the clear, high sound of a violin. Turning around, they saw a man playing a very loud and fast tune on his violin. "Let's go over and listen," Grandpa suggested.

Soon, several other musicians had begun playing instruments at various places around the large plaza. Grandpa Ed and the two kids strolled around the plaza, finishing their ice cream and enjoying the outdoor music.

When Grandpa Ed finished the last bite of his cone, he reached into his pocket and took out two dollar bills. "Here's a dollar for each of you. Put it in the instrument case of the musician you like best."

While Eric and Jessie tried to decide whom to give their dollar to, Grandpa ambled over to a man and a woman playing flutes. He dropped a dollar in each of their cases.

When Jessie and Eric had given away their dollars, Jessie asked Grandpa, "Why'd we do that?"

"Mostly," Grandpa explained, "to encourage these people to keep doin' somethin' worthwhile. Even if they may not know their talent is a gift God gave them, they're doin' a good thing."

● *"I will sing to the Lord, I will sing; I will make music to the Lord, the God of Israel." Judges 5:3*

● **For Younger Children**
What kind of musical instruments do you like to listen to?
Why did Grandpa say he gave money to the musicians?
What's something you can do to show a talent or ability God has given you?

● **For Older Children**
What other kinds of instruments do you think Eric and Jessie might have heard?
Playing music is one talent or ability God gives people. What are some other talents He gives?
What talent or ability do you have?

● ●

WEEK 1

DAY
4

Eric and Jessie loved listening to the orchestra warm up. "It sounds like they're fighting," Jessie laughed. Sitting just about in the middle of the auditorium, Jessie, Eric, and Grandpa Ed had a perfect view of the orchestra on stage.
"Which instrument would you like to play?" Grandpa asked Eric.
Eric answered instantly, "The kettledrums," he said. "They're awesome."
"Not me," Jessie said. "I like flutes."
"Flutes?" Eric asked as if a flute were the last instrument he would ever want to play.
"Sure," Jessie said, not caring at all about Eric's opinion. "They sound neat, and they're real small and easy to carry."
Grandpa laughed. "She's got you there, Eric. I can see you trying to lug a couple of kettledrums around."
Just then the lights dimmed, and the orchestra and the audience both became silent. A man in a tuxedo walked across the front of the stage and stepped up onto a small stand.
"That's the conductor," Grandpa whispered to Jessie.

"I know, Grandpa," Jessie whispered back.

The conductor raised both hands in the air, held them there for a moment, then brought them down together, and the music began. It was magnificent. The violinists stroked their bows across the strings. The trombonists moved their long slides in and out. The other horn players filled the air with rich, brassy sounds.

"I can hear the flutes," Jessie whispered to Grandpa.

Just then there was a dramatic roll on the kettledrums, and Eric whispered, "All right!"

As the concert continued, Grandpa, Eric, and Jessie thoroughly enjoyed all the music. Well, almost all the music. There were some parts that Eric and Jessie found a little boring. Well, very boring. But those parts did not last long and were quickly followed by more interesting music. Near the end of the concert, Grandpa noticed Jessie yawn once or twice. A few moments later, she was asleep, with her head on Grandpa's shoulder.

"Look here, Eric," Grandpa whispered over the music of the orchestra. He pointed at Jessie. "Here's something God made that's even more beautiful than music."

● *"Sing to the Lord with thanksgiving; make music to our God on the harp."*
Psalm 147:7

● **For Younger Children**

What instrument would you like to learn to play?

What instrument does Psalm 147:7 talk about?

Think of something you want to thank God for. If you wrote music to say thank You to God, would the music be loud, soft, fast, or slow? Why?

● **For Older Children**

Which instrument do you think is the hardest to play?

Read Psalm 147:7. What do you think it means to make music to God? Since God is the One who gives people their abilities, playing an instrument or painting a picture the best you can shows honor to God.

Think of something you're good at doing. How can you do your best at it in order to honor God?

WEEK 1

DAY
5

Grandpa Ed, Jessie, and Eric were on their way back home on the train. What a day it had been! A train ride! The museum of art! Hot dogs! Ice cream! A concert! And pepperoni pizza in a little restaurant near the train station while they waited to catch the train home.

Jessie's short little nap near the end of the concert had left her wide awake and full of energy. "Can we walk through the train, Grandpa?" she asked.

"I suppose you two can walk up to the front and back," Grandpa said. "I'll just sit here and figure out how much I spent on you today."

The best part of walking up to the front of the train was going from one car to the next. As the door at the front of the car would open, the noise of the tracks became louder. Somehow, that made the movement of the train seem greater, and it was always necessary to touch the sides of the passageway to keep balanced.

When Eric and Jessie made it back to their seats, they saw that Grandpa Ed was now taking a nap. Eric motioned for Jessie to stay behind him, then he slipped quietly next to where Grandpa was sitting. In his best imitation of a symphony orchestra, Eric went, "Da da da dum! Da da da dum!"

Grandpa opened one eye. "Not bad," he chuckled. "But do you remember the next part?" Grandpa began to hum some of the music they had heard at the concert. Eric did remember the music and began to hum along with Grandpa Ed. Jessie decided to join in.

Suddenly, Jessie noticed that other people on the train were looking at them a little oddly. She stopped humming. Grandpa Ed saw why she had stopped and reached over to pat her hand. "It's OK, Jessie," he said. "Don't be embarrassed. All these other people had to spend the day workin'. We spent the day enjoyin' great art and great music—some of God's best gifts to people."

● *"Speak to one another with psalms, hymns and spiritual songs. Sing and make music in your heart to the Lord." Ephesians 5:19*

● **For Younger Children**
If you were Eric and Jessie, what would you have liked the best about their day?

Why does God give us wonderful things like great art and music?

Thank God for loving you and ask His help in learning to use the abilities He's given you.

● **For Older Children**
What made Eric and Jessie's day so special?
  If you could plan a day to enjoy God's gifts, what would you plan to do?
  Tell God thank You for His gifts of art and music.

● ●

Schedule time this week to be together as a family. Select one of these suggested activities to expand your family's understanding of the wonderful gifts God has given you.

FAMILY TIMES

Listen Up!
Play a musical game together. The first player thinks of a song. He or she hums the first three notes of the melody. Other family members try to guess the song. If they cannot identify the song, the first player hums the first four notes of the melody. He or she continues adding notes until the song is guessed. Repeat the game until each person has had a turn.
  Tip for Younger Children: Pair a younger child with an older family member. The younger child may suggest the name of a song for the older person to hum.

Family Night Out
Plan a time for your family to enjoy a special arts event. Consider these options: museum, concert, art gallery, mural display, sculpture garden. Many communities offer low-cost arts events which are for children. After the event, take turns answering questions such as, "What did you like best? What would you like to (see or hear) again? If you were the owner, how would you make it better? What surprised you?"
  Tip for Younger Children: Too much of a good thing is liable to make your family night unpleasant for younger children. Unless the event or exhibit is planned specifically for young children, plan to limit your time.

Finger Paint Fun
Experience the fun of art! For each family member put a small amount of thick paint, shaving cream, or chocolate pudding on a separate sheet of damp white paper. Experiment with a variety of painting motions. Use one or two fingers, the palm of your hand, and the side of your hand to finger paint. Then read one or more of these Bible verses aloud: Psalms 107:33; 135:6-7; 139:14; 148:3. Each person chooses a verse to illustrate by finger painting.

Key Verse
"The fear of the Lord is the beginning of knowledge, but fools despise wisdom and discipline."
Proverbs 1:7

Key Thought
God encourages us to learn facts but also to learn to make wise judgments.

School Days

In a society where many people brag about their inabilities to do math or to spell, there are diverse factors which discourage people from pursuing learning. In contrast, the Bible places a high premium on learning, the right kind of learning.

Encourage your child this week to value the attainment of knowledge. Affirm your child's efforts and achievements in learning. And stress the need to learn the difference between right and wrong in all areas of life.

WEEK 2

DAY 1

Tomorrow was the first day of school. Tonight, the Norris family farm was a very hectic place. Some of the confusion was because the Norris family had just returned two days ago after spending the summer in Africa. The rest of the confusion was just the normal excitement of trying to get four children ready for a new school year.

"I don't know what to wear!" Laura lamented, looking at the piles of clothes spread all over her bed. "Should I wear a dress? Jeans? A jumper? A skirt? I just know that whatever I choose, everyone else will be wearing something different."

"How about if I choose your outfit?" Grandma Norris asked helpfully.

"That's OK, Grandma!" Laura replied. "I'll figure it out."

Down the hall, Chris was sitting on the edge of his bed swinging his feet back and forth, banging his heels against the side of the bed. The worried expression on his face showed his concern that first grade would be too hard.

His oldest brother, Ryan, was trying to encourage him. "Just think, Chris. If Josh could make it, you'll have no trouble."

"Very funny!" Josh said, throwing his pillow at Ryan.

Just before the pillow made a return trip, Mom stuck her head in the boys' room. "What Ryan means, Chris, is that you're good at learning. You did very well in kindergarten last year. You'll do very well in first grade this year."

Just before Mom pulled her head out of the boys' room, she added, "And Ryan, hand that pillow back to Josh. And Josh, leave it on the bed where it belongs."

Deciding that the noise in the boys' room was more interesting than the TV news, Dad appeared. He was not sure what all had been going on, but he had heard Mom's last comment. So he added a comment of his own. "Besides, Chris," he said. "You probably learned more this summer in Africa than you'll need to learn all year in first grade."

That made Chris feel better. For a while.

● *"Apply your heart to instruction and your ears to words of knowledge." Proverbs 23:12*

● **For Younger Children**
What was Chris worried about?
   How would you feel if you were starting school tomorrow?
   What kinds of things do you learn in school?

● **For Older Children**
What do you look forward to on the first day of school?
   What is something you learned last year in school? Was it easy or hard?
   Thank God for being with you in your school and for helping you learn.

● ●

WEEK 2

DAY
2

It was the morning of the first day of school. Everybody in the Norris house was rushing to get ready. Everybody except Grandma Norris who had turned her hearing aid down and was enjoying a quiet cup of coffee.

Grandma Norris did not hear Josh yelling that he could not find his other shoe. She did not hear Chris complaining that his lunchbox was "for sissies." Neither did she hear Laura bewailing her lack of anything decent to wear to school.

However, even with her hearing aid turned down, Grandma Norris did hear Ryan bellowing that he could not find his pencils.

"I spent all afternoon sharpening them!" Ryan yelled. "Now someone has ripped me off! Where are my pencils?"

Mom showed remarkable patience by answering Ryan calmly. This was remarkable because she had just gotten through finding Josh's other shoe, assuring Chris that his lunchbox was fine, and helping Laura pick out an outfit. Mom said, "You spent less than five minutes sharpening your pencils, and you will find them on the dining room table where I put them so they wouldn't get stepped on."

"Oh, thanks, Mom," Ryan said quickly, a little embarrassed that he had made such a fuss.

At last the four children were ready to go. Ryan opened the front door and started out to walk down the long driveway to the school bus stop. "Just a minute, Ryan," Dad called. Then he had the whole family, including Grandma, join hands and bow their heads. "Dear God," he prayed. "Give the kids a good day and and a good year of learning what You want them to know. Amen."

"Amen!" Mom added. Then she said, "And make sure you learn something good!"

Chris and Laura got quick hugs, but Josh and Ryan were out the door and on their way. The two younger ones started after them, and Dad caught the door just before it slammed behind Chris. Suddenly the house seemed very quiet, even though Grandma Norris had turned her hearing aid back up.

● *"Let the wise listen and add to their learning." Proverbs 1:5*

● **For Younger Children**
What did Mr. Norris pray for his children?

What does Proverbs 1:5 say wise people do in order to keep learning?

Who is someone you can listen to who will help you learn?

● **For Older Children**
How do you think the Norris children felt about going to school?

What's something you like about your school? What's something you don't like?

Thank God for what you like and ask His help in getting through the part you don't like.

DAY
3

The first bell had rung, and the children at Elm Creek School started to gather outside their classroom doors. "Hey, Josh!" Henry Kolchek teased. "Is your sister gonna be in our class?"

Josh made a face. It was true that he and Laura were both going to be in Mrs. Poindexter's third and fourth grade class. Josh was going into fourth grade, and Laura was just starting third. Josh thought that having his younger sister in his class was a terrible insult to him.

"They'll put her back in second grade when they find out how dumb she is," Josh said. All the kids laughed, so Josh decided to poke some more fun at Laura.

"She's so dumb," Josh said, "that . . . that. . . ." He was having a hard time thinking of something really clever to say. But since all the kids were looking at him, he felt he had to say something. So he blurted out, "She's so dumb, we make her sleep in the barn."

This time no one laughed. Oh, two or three boys snickered a little, but that was all. Perhaps no one laughed because Josh's comment really was not funny. Or perhaps it was because Mrs. Poindexter had just opened the classroom door and was standing directly behind Josh.

"Welcome to the first day of school," Mrs. Poindexter said.

"Everyone come in and find your name on your desk. Except you, Josh. We need to talk." All the other children hurried into the room.

Mrs. Poindexter waited till they had all gone by, then she said, "Josh, I'm sure you haven't forgotten our rules of good behavior."

"No, ma'am," Josh mumbled.

"Well," Mrs. Poindexter continued, "the rules you learned last year, Josh, the ones about being considerate to other students, definitely include students who also happen to be sisters."

"Yes, ma'am," Josh mumbled.

Mrs. Poindexter was not finished yet. She said, "I thought you had learned that everyone in our class, everyone in our school, deserves to be treated with respect."

"Yes, ma'am," Josh mumbled again.

"Now let's go inside, and you can start showing me you haven't forgotten everything I taught you last year."

● *"Every wise person acts with good sense, but fools show how foolish they are."* *Proverbs 13:16,* EB

● **For Younger Children**

What mistake did Josh make?

Josh acted in a foolish way because he forgot to obey the wise rules of his teacher. What rules have you learned? Who taught them to you? How can you obey these rules?

● **For Older Children**

What does Proverbs 13:16 say about wise and foolish people?

Would you describe Josh's actions as wise or foolish?

When have you acted in a foolish way? When have you shown wisdom in your actions or words?

● ●

WEEK 2

DAY
4

During morning recess on the first day of school, Chris Norris yelled to his brother, Josh. Josh was playing with his friends and did not want to be interrupted by his little brother. Even though Chris yelled again, Josh pretended that he did not hear him or see him.

"Hey, Josh!" Henry Kolchek teased. "Is that your little brother yelling at you?"

"You know it is, Henry," Josh grumbled. "He's sure a pest."

"Hey, guys!" Henry yelled. "Josh's little brother is a pest!"

"Get out of here, Pest!" several of Josh's friends yelled at Chris.

Just then Josh heard his name being called. His full name. "Joshua Norris!" It was Mrs. Poindexter. "You too Henry Kolchek!" she called. The two boys walked slowly over to their teacher.

"Josh," she said. "Do you remember our little talk about Laura?"

"Yes, ma'am," Josh said. He seemed to be saying that a lot today.

"Do we need to have the same talk about being considerate of Chris?" Mrs. Poindexter asked.

"No, ma'am," Josh said.

Turning to Henry, Mrs. Poindexter said, "And you also should have learned our rules about treating people with respect."

"Yes, ma'am," Henry said. He sounded just like Josh.

"Both of you need to start showing me that you really do understand our rules," Mrs. Poindexter said, and then she walked away.

"Yes, ma'am," both boys said in unison.

Josh went over to where Chris was climbing on the monkey bars. "I'm sorry I ignored you, Chris," Josh said. "I'm really glad you're my brother."

"What about me?" Laura asked, coming up behind the boys.

Before he could stop himself, Josh said, "I'm glad he's your brother too." Then all three of them laughed.

- *"I will praise You with an upright heart as I learn Your righteous laws."* Psalms 119:7

For Younger Children

Josh was having a hard time remembering his teacher's rules. What's a rule you have a hard time remembering?

For Older Children

What would you have done if you were Josh?

Who was helping Josh learn to do good things? Who can help you?

Ask God's help as you keep learning to do good things.

• •

WEEK 2

DAY
5

The first school day of the year was over. The four Norris children got off the school bus and walked slowly up the driveway, comparing stories about their first day back at Elm Creek School.

"First grade is tough," Chris complained and bragged all in one sentence.

"I've got so much homework," Ryan bragged and complained in one sentence also. Then he added for impact, "I've got math and science and reading AND social studies. I'll NEVER get to watch TV this year."

"Mrs. Poindexter is really mean!" Josh lamented, trying to sound like his fate was worse than his brothers'.

"She is not! She's very nice!" Laura countered.

"To girls!" Josh retorted.

"To anyone who follows the rules!" Laura shot back.

The four children kept walking up the long driveway. They almost did not notice when they passed the big oak tree, they were so intent on swapping school stories. However, they did notice their mom coming down the driveway toward them, tucking her work gloves into the back pockets of her jeans.

"Hi, guys!" Mom greeted them. "Anybody learn anything today?"

The four children all looked at one another, hoping someone would volunteer an answer. When all three boys decided to look to Laura to say something, she volunteered one comment: "Josh did."

"Yeah!" Chris volunteered. "Josh did!"

Josh shot a hard look at Laura and then Chris, seeming to say, "You were supposed to tell her something YOU learned!"

Mom noticed the look on Josh's faced and asked, "Really, Josh? What was it?"

Josh knew he was trapped, but he decided it was worth a try. "We didn't really start anything new yet, Mom. Mostly just review."

Looking back and forth between Laura and Chris and Josh, Mom was certain there was more to this story. "And what else, Josh?" she asked.

"Well," Josh answered. "I learned I need to do right . . . even . . . even if my friends think I'm a dork." Before Mom could say anything, Josh corrected his story. "Not really, Mom. I learned to do what's right, period."

Ryan put his hand on Josh's shoulder. "That, little brother, may be harder to learn than math and science."

● *"Stop doing wrong, learn to do right! Seek justice, encourage the oppressed."* *Isaiah 1:16-17*

● **For Younger Children**

What did Josh say he had learned?

What's something right you're learning to do?

Ask God to help you learn to do good and right things.

● **For Older Children**

If you were Josh, would you think Mrs. Poindexter was mean? Why or why not?

Why do you think it is so hard to learn to do right?

How would you say Isaiah 1:17 in order to help kids know wise ways to act at school?

● ●

FAMILY TIMES

Schedule time this week to be together as a family. Select one of these suggested activities to expand your family's understanding of the value of learning.

First Day Traditions

If you have not already done so, start one or two "first day of school" traditions. Choose from these ideas. (1) Let your child choose his or her favorite breakfast to eat. (2) Buy something new for your child to wear. (3) Take your child's picture in the same place each year. (4) Choose a key Bible verse to remember throughout the year. Write the verse on an index card and keep it posted in your child's room. Talk about specific ways your child may put the verse into practice. Suggested verses: Matthew 5:9; John 14:27; Romans 1:16; Ephesians 4:32; Philippians 4:6-7; James 1:5.

Handprint Learning

Ask each person to trace around both his or her hands on a large sheet of paper. On each finger of the right hand, each person writes a skill he or she has learned to do (read, play piano, make cookies, play soccer, drive a car, etc.). On each finger of the left hand, each person writes a positive character trait he or she exhibits (friendly, cheerful, loves God, helps others). If someone has difficulty thinking of items to write, family members may suggest ideas. (Just for fun, compare the size of these handprints with any made by your children when they were younger.)

Tip for Younger Children: Suggest a younger child draw pictures on the palms of his or her handprints.

For Parents Only

"How was school today?" "Good." If this limited conversation regularly takes place in your home, consider asking one or more of these questions in order to encourage your child to share his or her school experiences. "What was the best thing that happened at school today? The worst thing? What's something you did today at school that you've never done before? What were you doing at (specify a time)? What's something you did inside your classroom today? Outside your classroom? What's your favorite game at recess? Would you rather be a teacher, a student, or the principal at your school? Why? If you could change one thing about your school, what would it be? Why? What advice would you give to a new student at your school?"

Problems at School

Key Verse
"Therefore do not worry about tomorrow, for tomorrow will worry about itself. Each day has enough troubles of its own."
Matthew 6:34

Key Thought
The way we respond to problems in life has a great impact on the kind of person we become in the future.

School days are not always "dear old Golden Rule days." In many places, schools struggle with lack of adequate resources due to continuing financial crises. At the same time, drugs, gangs, and violence are no longer limited to overcrowded, big city high schools. They have infected suburban, small town, and rural school districts, and the damage they cause is felt even in the youngest grades.

Whether your child attends a school beset by the problems of modern society, or enjoys a safe haven for children, there are still pressures and problems that growing children will face. This week you have an opportunity to support your child as he or she seeks to cope with the challenges a child encounters. It is good for your child to be able to talk with you about situations about which he or she is concerned. You may not be able to remove all the problems your child will face, but your encouragement and support are vital in helping to equip your child to deal with the diverse problems life presents.

WEEK 3

DAY 1

Schoolwork had always been easy for Angela. She enjoyed reading and writing. She was very good at spelling, science, history, and geography. And she was even better in math.

Angela could add and subtract, multiply and divide quickly and with almost no mistakes. She liked the challenge of solving hard problems.

However, Angela did have one problem with math that she had not been able to solve. This problem was that the other children in her class teased her because she was so smart. They called her names, names like "The Brain," "School Girl," "Teacher's Pet," and "Math Nerd."

"I don't mind a little teasing," she told her Aunt Carmela. Tia Carmela came to their apartment each afternoon to take care of Angela's younger brothers, Hector and four-and-a-half-year-old Robbie.

"So what's bothering you?" Carmela asked.

"Some of the kids treat me like I'm odd because I get good grades," Angela explained. "They're not just teasing for fun. I think they really don't like me to do better than them."

"That sounds like it's their problem, not yours," Tia Carmela said.

"But I want them to like me," Angela replied. "I want them to like me, but I want to do well in school also. What should I do? Should I pretend I'm dumb?"

Tia Carmela asked, "What does your mother say?"

"I haven't talked to her," Angela admitted. "But I know what she'd tell me to do. She'd say, 'Forget those friends and keep studying.'"

Tia Carmela laughed. "You do a great imitation of your mother. I guess what I'd say first is, 'Why don't you tell God what you just told me?'"

"Pray?" Angela asked.

"Sure," Tia Carmela said. "I always find it helps to pray when I don't know what to do about a problem."

"What do I say?" Angela asked.

"Just talk to God about the problem the same way you talk to me. And ask Him to help you know the best thing to do."

"That's what you do about your problems?" Angela asked. When Tia Carmela nodded "Yes," Angela decided it was a good idea.

● *"I sought the Lord and He answered me; He delivered me from all my fears."*
Psalm 34:4

● **For Younger Children**
How did Angela feel about the kids who teased her?
   Why is it a good thing to talk to God about your problems?
   What does Psalm 34:4 say God will do when we ask Him for help?

● **For Older Children**
What is your favorite subject in school?
   When has someone teased you? How did you feel?
   What other problems might someone have at school?

● ●

WEEK 3

DAY
2

"Hey, Brain Lady!" one of the boys in Angela's class called as she walked home from school. "How come you're always ruining it for the rest of us?"

"Yeah, Genius," another boy said. "Did you have to get ALL those problems right?"

"Give us a break sometime!" Angela's friend Melissa added as she walked alongside Angela. "You make the rest of us look bad."

Angela stopped walking and silently said a quick prayer. "Dear God, help me do the right thing," was all she said. She even forgot to say, "Amen." Her prayer had been so quick, Melissa did not even notice that Angela had done it. Angela smiled at Melissa and asked, "How about if we do a swap?"

"Huh?" asked Melissa. "Whatd'ya mean?"

"A swap," Angela repeated. "My math for your basketball."

"Huh?" asked Melissa again. "I don't get it."

"You're good at basketball, right?" Angela asked.

"Right." Melissa said. "So?"

"And I'm good at math," Angela continued. "So how about if we swap what we're good at. You can be good at math, and I'll be good at basketball."

"We can't do that!" Melissa protested.

"I know," Angela admitted. "But wouldn't it be neat if we could?"

"It would?" Melissa asked, still puzzled by Angela's idea.

"Sure," Angela said. "You don't like getting beat on a math test, and I absolutely HATE the way you always beat me in basketball."

"You do?" Melissa asked, just starting to catch on to what Angela was talking about.

"I really do," Angela added. "But you're so much better than me, I really never have a chance against you."

"Oh, yeah," Melissa agreed.

"And, Melissa," Angela said with a little touch of sarcasm in her voice, "when we play basketball, I never notice you missing shots on purpose so I won't look bad."

"I see what you mean," Melissa said finally. "OK. You win. I won't bug you anymore about being a math whiz."

"Thanks," Angela laughed. "And I won't call you a hotshot ball hog anymore either."

● *"So we say with confidence, 'The Lord is my helper; I will not be afraid.' "*
Hebrews 13:6

● **For Younger Children**
What problem did Angela have on the way home from school?
    What did Angela remember to do when she needed help?

● **For Older Children**
What would you have said to Melissa?

Is doing less than your best ever a good idea? Why or why not?
How did God answer Angela's prayer and help her?

● ●

WEEK 3

DAY
3

"Anybody hassle you about your math today?" Angela's Aunt Carmela asked when Angela got home from school.

"Yeah," Angela answered. "It was neat!"

"Neat?" Tia Carmela asked.

Angela then told her aunt about her conversation with Melissa. "I didn't know what to say when she complained that I was making the rest of the class look bad. So I prayed."

"Right there on the sidewalk?" Tia Carmela asked.

"Well, I didn't kneel down or bow my head," Angela explained. "I just real quick asked God to help—and I think He did."

"So what happened?" asked Tia Carmela.

Angela went on with her story. "I don't know if what I said was all that great, but I think praying helped me talk to her in a friendly way so we still like each other."

"That's great!" Tia Carmela said. "Praying has always helped me too."

"But now I've got a new problem," Angela said. "My teacher wants me to take a test to qualify for a special math program."

"That's a problem?" asked Tia Carmela.

"Yes," answered Angela. "If I get in this program, I won't be in the regular class with my friends. And if I don't get in the program, I think I'll be real disappointed."

"I see," was all Carmela said.

"Can you help me with this problem?" Angela asked.

"I'd suggest the same thing as before," Tia Carmela answered.

"Pray? Tell God what I just told you?" Angela asked. "But how do I know God really cares about my school problems?"

"You believe He helped you today, don't you?" Tia Carmela replied. Before Angela could answer, her aunt went on. "And you believe God made you?"

This time Angela had time to answer. "Sure," she said.

"Well, those sound like two big reasons to believe that He cares about you—and everything that happens to you."

"Gracias, Tia," Angela replied. "Thanks a lot for listening."

● *"Our help is in the name of the Lord, the Maker of heaven and earth."*
Psalm 124:8

● **For Younger Children**

Why might some people think that God doesn't care about their problems?

Because God made us, we know He loves us and cares about what happens to us. What's something good that happened to you today? Tell God about it.

What's one way you need God's help at school? Ask Him and thank Him for His love.

● **For Older Children**

What choice did Angela have to make?

What would you choose to do if you were Angela?

Why do you think God cares about what happens to you?

● ●

WEEK 3

DAY 4

Tomorrow was the day Angela was to take the special math test. If she did well, she would be placed into a program for advanced students. Angela's teacher had encouraged her to take the test, and she had decided to do it to find out how good she really was.

While making a sandwich for an after-school snack, Angela told Aunt Carmela about the test. "I'm really nervous" Angela said. "The smartest kids in school are taking the test. I don't know if I can do as well as the others."

"Aren't you one of the smartest kids too?" Tia Carmela asked.

"I guess," Angela said as she opened the mayonnaise jar. "But there'll be kids from other schools too."

Tia Carmela watched Angela spread the mayonnaise on her bread, then said, "Sounds like you'll have to do your best tomorrow."

Angela placed two bologna slices and a lettuce leaf on the bread. "That's the whole problem," she said. "I just know I won't do well. I'll be so nervous. Maybe I'm not as good as I think." Angela stopped talking to take a bite.

Tia Carmela said, "I think you're going to discover that you really are good."

Angela swallowed. "But no one in our family is really good at math. No one else has ever been in an advanced program."

"Do you know what else I think?" asked Tia Carmela. Without waiting for Angela to answer, she said, "You're worried you have too much against you. You should start thinking about what's FOR you."

"What do you mean?" Angela asked, finishing her sandwich.

"Think about how much you like math, how you enjoy solving problems, how you're good at taking tests . . . things like that," said Tia Carmela.

"Oh," Angela said with her mouth full.

"And best of all," said her aunt, "think about who you can talk to about the test."

"Who's that?" Angela asked, wiping a crumb from her lower lip.

"You can talk to God," said Tia Carmela. "Even during the test. And if God's with you, how important can any of those problems really be? Just trust Him to help you do your best."

"OK," Angela agreed. Then she asked, "Is there anything else for snack?"

● *"If God is for us, who can be against us?" Romans 8:31*

● **For Younger Children**

What do you like to eat for snack?

When you're worried about a problem, what should you remember about God?

Why is it important to remember that God is always with you?

● **For Older Children**

What was making Angela nervous?

When have you felt nervous?

How can the promise in Romans 8:31 help you when you feel nervous?

● ●

WEEK 3

DAY
5

Angela walked nervously into the classroom and slid into one of the desks. It was time to take the big math test to find out if she could be in a special program. Angela reached into her book bag, took out three newly sharpened pencils, and arranged them neatly at the top of the desk. Next, Angela folded her hands on the desk and waited for the test to begin.

As she waited, Angela worried. "I just know it's going to be too hard for me," she thought to herself. "What if I don't know how to do any of the problems? What am I even doing here? I wish I were home." That was when Angela noticed that her palms were sweating. Her heart was beating so loud she was sure it must be bothering the other kids who were finding their places in the room. Her stomach felt like it was twisted into a knot and someone kept pulling it tighter and tighter.

A teacher gave some instructions, then began to hand out the test booklets. Angela swallowed, bowed her head for a moment, and prayed silently. "Dear God," she began. "Please help me do my best." Just then the test booklet was placed on her desk. "Amen," she said softly, opened her eyes and picked up one of her pencils.

When everyone had his or her test booklet, the teacher announced that they could now begin. Angela took a deep breath and wrote her name at the top of the test booklet. Somehow she always felt a little better after she wrote something down, even if it was just her name. Another deep breath and it was time to look at the first question. She read it over once, then she read it again. Suddenly, Angela realized she knew the answer. "Thank You God," she mumbled as she wrote her answer down.

"Sh-h-h," the boy in front of her whispered.

"Sorry," Angela said silently, a big smile spreading across her face. She was beginning to believe she really could do well on this test.

● *"Trust in the Lord with all your heart and lean not on your own understanding." Proverbs 3:5*

● **For Younger Children**
What did Angela pray?
　When is a time you need to ask God to help you do your best?
　What do you think it means to trust in the Lord?
　When we trust in God it means we believe He will keep His promises and always love us.

● **For Older Children**
How do you feel when you take important tests at school?
　How did Angela show that she trusted in the Lord?
　What can you do to show you trust in God?

Schedule time this week to be together as a family. Select one of these suggested activities to expand your family's understanding of the ways God will help them know what to do when facing difficult problems.

FAMILY TIMES

Words of Help

On separate small pieces of paper write these words: God, pray, help, me, you, school, neighborhood, problem, trust, choice, decision, ask, believe, love, nervous, worry. Put the slips of paper in a bag or hat. Each person takes a turn to choose three slips. Then he or she makes up a sentence which includes the three words. The sentence should tell something about how God can help us when we have a problem or hard choice to make.

Tip for Younger Children: Allow a younger child to make up a sentence which includes any one of the three words.

Mixed-Up Cards

Letter each word of Proverbs 3:5 on an index card. Make several sets. Read the verse aloud. Ask, "What are the benefits of trusting in the Lord? What do you know about God that would cause you to trust Him?" Then play a game to help your family memorize the verse. Mix up the cards and give each player an equal number, putting any extras facedown on the table or floor. The first player places one card face up on floor or table (for example—"the"). The second player tries to put a card before or after this word (for example—"in" or "Lord"). If a player cannot play a card, he or she may exchange one card with the extras pile, or player may pass. Play continues until one player has played all of his or her cards.

Tip for Younger Children: Numbering the cards in order (Trust = 1; in = 2, etc.) will make it easier for a younger child to play this game.

Shape Drawings

Ask each family member to tell a place where he or she might face a problem or difficult choice. Then each person draws a picture of that place using only circles, triangles, rectangles, or squares. To make it more difficult, add other shapes such as parallelograms, trapezoids, or octagons. When the pictures are completed, take time to pray for each person, asking God's help in handling problems in good ways.

Tip for Younger Children: Suggest that a younger child choose which, if any, shapes to use in his or her drawing.

Differences among Christians

Key Verse
"It is good and pleasant when God's people live together in peace!" Psalm 133:1, EB

Key Thought
Christians are called by God to unity and tolerance in dealing with the many ways we are different from each other.

Jesus prayed that His followers would be united, but for 2,000 years the church has been marked by divisions. A wide variety of differences among Christians have been factors causing one group to separate from another group. At times the differences have caused deep and bitter divisions. Still, those who follow Jesus, in spite of factors which tend to divide, have far more in common with each other than with those outside the church. In spite of the differences, all Christians share a strong, common bond which truly does unite us as the body of Christ.

WEEK 4

DAY 1

Midori looked up from the colorful scraps of paper she was busily gluing together. She noticed a tall, dark-skinned man standing in the doorway to her Sunday School room. Then she noticed the small dark-skinned boy standing next to the tall man. Midori stared as Mrs. Tokita stooped down next to the small boy. Midori could see Mrs. Tokita's big smile, but she could not hear what her teacher was saying.

Midori saw Mrs. Tokita stand up and take the boy's hand. She saw the teacher and the boy coming straight toward the table where Midori sat.

Quickly, Midori reached out to the pile of colorful paper scraps and pulled them toward her. Then she grabbed tightly onto the glue bottle she had been using.

"Midori," Mrs. Tokita said. "this is Keshav. He is new to our Sunday School. Keshav and his family moved here from India."

Midori just stared at Keshav. Keshav just stared back at Midori.

"Keshav," Mrs. Tokita said, "Midori has been gluing designs with this paper. There's plenty of paper and glue for everyone, so you can glue a design too."

Midori still stared at Keshav. She thought he looked odd. She did not want him to use any of her paper and glue. Keshav sat down. He reached across the table and pulled a sheet of green paper to himself. Midori glared at him.

Keshav picked up the other glue bottle and squeezed a large blob into the middle. "He's using too much glue!" Midori complained.

Keshav picked up some scraps of green paper and began gluing them to his larger green sheet. "He's gluing green on green," Midori announced. "That looks yucky!"

"I kind of like green on green," Mrs. Tokita said. "And I like all the different colors Midori has glued together. I'm glad that God made us all to be different from each other in many ways."

Midori looked up at her teacher. Mrs. Tokita looked back at Midori.

Then Mrs. Tokita said, "I'm even more glad that God made us alike in many ways too. One way that Midori and Keshav and Mrs. Tokita are the same is that we all love Jesus."

Midori was not sure she wanted to be like Keshav in any way.

● *"There is neither Jew nor Greek, slave nor free, male nor female, for you are all one in Christ Jesus." Galatians 3:28*

● **For Younger Children**
How did Midori feel about Keshav?
    When have you felt like Midori?
    How do you think God wants you to treat the people He made?

● **For Older Children**
Why do you think Midori felt unfriendly toward Keshav?
    What things were the same about Midori and Keshav? What things made them different?
    What does Galatians 3:28 say about people who are different from each other?

● ●

WEEK 4

After Sunday School, Midori told her older sister, Aliki, about the boy from India who had come to her class. "I don't like him," Midori announced.
    "Why not?" Aliki asked.
    "He talks funny," Midori said. "I don't like that."
    "Is that all?" Aliki asked.
    "He has dark skin," Midori said. "I don't like that either."

DAY

2

"But lots of people have dark skin," Aliki said. "Nice people."

"He wears big glasses," Midori said. "I don't like that."

"It's not his fault he needs glasses," Aliki said. "Father wears glasses. Mrs. Tokita wears glasses."

Before Aliki could name more people who wore glasses, Midori jumped in with what she thought would clinch her argument. "He uses too much glue," Midori said. "I don't like that."

"Sometimes the glue comes out of the bottle too fast," Aliki said.

"And he glues green paper onto more green paper," Midori said. "I don't like that."

"Maybe he likes green," Aliki said. "I like green."

"He has a strange name," Midori said. "I don't like that."

"His sister has kind of a strange name too," Aliki said. "But I like her."

"His sister?" Midori asked. She had not imagined that Keshav had a family. Especially not a sister.

"She was in my class," Aliki said. "Her name is Ranjit. She's very nice."

Midori was not going to be talked out of her decision not to like Keshav. She told Aliki, "I don't think I'd like her." After a moment's thought she added, "And I sure don't like her brother."

"But they're nice—like us," Aliki said. Midori did not answer.

"And they're Christians—like us," Aliki said. Midori still did not answer. "Besides," Aliki added, "what if they start to come to our church all the time?"

"I wish they'd go to another church," Midori said. And she stomped out of the room.

● *"For there is no difference between Jew and Gentile—the same Lord is Lord of all and richly blesses all who call on Him." Romans 10:12*

● **For Younger Children**

What were some of Midori's reasons for not liking Keshav?

What were some of Aliki's reasons for liking Keshav and his sister?

What reason does Romans 10:12 give for treating all people the same?

● **For Older Children**

Are you more like Midori or Aliki? Why?

When two people are both Christians, they are both part of God's family. How do family members help each other?

How can you help someone who is part of God's family?

314

DAY
3

"I don't see why we have to like people who are strange," Midori complained to her sister, Aliki. The two girls balanced on the teeter-totter at their neighborhood park. Mother sat on a nearby bench, reading a magazine.

"Do you think God should have made everybody the same?" Aliki asked as she pushed herself up. "That would be boring," she added quickly, just in case her little sister did not come up with the right answer to the question.

Midori tried to keep her feet on the ground and hold Aliki up in the air. Just as the teeter-totter began to lift her feet off the ground, Midori began to realize that what Aliki said made sense. But she was not ready to give in.

"Anyhow," Midori declared as her feet dangled from the top of the teeter-totter. She sounded as though she had just come up with an argument no one could answer. "I don't see why God made boys," she said.

"You wish God had made just girls?" Aliki asked pushing off again. As the teeter-totter lifted her upward again, for just a moment or two, Aliki found herself agreeing with her little sister. Perhaps a world with no boys wouldn't be such a bad place. But then Aliki thought of a problem. "If there were no boys," she said as she began to drop toward the ground again, "we couldn't have a father! 'Cause fathers are boys. At least they used to be."

Midori was not finished yet. "And I don't see why He made people from India," she declared. "Or China. Or Africa. Or anywhere else."

Now Aliki thought she knew just what to say to change Midori's mind. "But, Midori," Aliki said, "Mrs. Lee next door is Chinese. And Mrs. Kinta at church is from Africa."

"I don't like that they're not like us," Midori pouted, sliding off the side of the teeter-totter, holding on to her end so that it did not fly straight up in the air.

"You wish God made everyone Japanese?" Aliki asked, jumping off the teeter-totter.

"Yeah," Midori sighed. "All like us."

"Wait'll I tell Mrs. Lee," Aliki replied. "And Mrs. Kinta. And Ranjit."

● *"It is good and pleasant when God's people live together in peace!" Psalm 133:1,* EB

● **For Younger Children**
Imagine you were Keshav coming to a new Sunday School class. How might you feel? What could you do to be friendly to someone who is new?

Why is it important to be friendly to others—especially people who are new or different?

● **For Older Children**
How many people from different countries do you know?

When might kids your age have a tough time being friendly to someone who is different?

Ask God's help in being friendly to people different from you.

WEEK 4

DAY
4

● ●

For several days that week, Midori kept thinking about why she did not like Keshav, the boy from India who had visited her Sunday School class. She did not like him because he looked, talked, acted, and dressed differently from Midori and her friends. By the end of the week, though, she had gotten busy doing other things and had forgotten about Keshav.

The next Sunday morning, Midori was surprised to see Keshav was in Sunday School again. She did not like it that he was playing in the Home Living corner, using "her" dishes, "her" dolls, and "her" table and chairs. She decided to do puzzles instead and stay away from Keshav.

Later when the class gathered for singing, Midori made sure she was on the opposite side of the circle from Keshav. She noticed that he did not join in the singing.

When all the children said the Bible verse together, Midori was certain that Keshav had not said it right. And he did not act like he had ever heard the Bible story before.

Then, Mrs. Tokita led the children to the table to do their worksheets. Midori noticed that Keshav did not know how to letter his name on his paper. She decided to point out Keshav's failings to the class. "That boy," Midori said loudly, "can't write his name."

Mrs. Tokita smiled at Midori. "I'm glad you know how to write your name, Midori. And I'm glad I can help Keshav learn to write his name." Mrs. Tokita drew a dot pattern that Keshav could trace to letter his name. She said, "Different people learn different things and are good at different things. I know that Keshav is good at music."

Midori remembered that Keshav hadn't sung any of their songs. How could he be good at music? Mrs. Tokita explained, "Keshav is learning to play the sitar. It's a beautiful stringed instrument." Midori had never heard of a sitar.

"And," Mrs. Tokita added, "he is learning to speak English as well as he already speaks Hindi and Bengali. Imagine! Keshav can speak three different languages. And he can pray in all three. Let's all thank God for the different things He helps us learn to do."

● *"God has given each of us the ability to do certain things well."*
Romans 12:6, TLB

● **For Younger Children**
What did Midori learn about Keshav that surprised her?

How many ways can you think of in which people are different from each other?

God made people different, but He also made people a lot alike. What does Romans 12:6 say God gives to each person?

● **For Older Children**
What would the world be like if God made everyone the same?

Why do you think God planned for so many different kinds of people?

How can people use their abilities to help each other?

● ●

WEEK 4

DAY
5

It was two weeks after Keshav, the boy from India, had first come to Midori's Sunday School class. Midori had met Keshav's older sister, Ranjit. Ranjit and Midori's sister, Aliki, were becoming good friends. Because Aliki liked Ranjit, Midori had finally decided that there were probably some people in India who were nice.

But she still did not like Keshav. He still seemed like a strange little boy who was much too different from Midori and her friends. She had decided the best thing to do was just ignore him. That was why all during Sunday School she had managed not to sit near him even once. Until it was time for snack. Suddenly she realized that Keshav was sitting down in the chair right next to her.

When the napkins were passed around, she had to hand them on to Keshav. When the cups were passed around the other way, Keshav handed them to Midori. She did not like that at all. But she decided to just eat her crackers and drink her juice quietly and pretend he wasn't even there.

"Do you eat raw fish?" Keshav asked. Midori was startled. She had not expected Keshav to actually talk to her. Besides, why should she talk to him about what she and her family ate. Especially since she was the only one in her family who did not like raw fish.

So she asked Keshav, "Do you eat curling rice?" She thought she had heard about that somewhere.

"It's curry, not curling," Keshav said. "It's a spice for cooking. And it's OK. But I like ice cream better."

Midori laughed. "Me too. I like chocolate best."

"I like chocolate with chunks of chocolate in the ice cream," Keshav said.

"Do you like Sunday School?" Midori asked.

"Oh, yes," Keshav answered. "Especially the singing."

"But you don't sing," Midori said.

"When I know the words, I will," Keshav said. "We sing different songs at my church in India."

"Are the Bible stories different in India too?" Midori asked.

Keshav laughed. "No, the Bible is the same."

Midori decided she she just might like Keshav after all.

● *"Make every effort to keep the unity of the Spirit through the bond of peace."* *Ephesians 4:3*

● **For Younger Children**

What would you rather eat — raw fish, curry rice, or ice cream?

What was the most important thing Midori learned about Keshav?

God wants us to show that we accept the people He made and loves. What are some ways you can show that you accept someone?

● **For Older Children**

When has something happened which caused you to change your opinion about something?

Why did Midori change her mind about Keshav?

In your school, church, or neighborhood, how can you obey Ephesians 4:3?

● ●

FAMILY TIMES

Schedule time this week to be together as a family. Select one of these suggested activities to expand your family's understanding of what it means for Christians to love and accept each other as part of the body of Christ.

Read All about It!

Read Acts 2:42-47 together with your family. Ask, "How would you describe the first Christians? How did they show they loved and accepted each other, despite their differences?" Then work together to write about the first Christians in the form of a newspaper article. Look at the news section of your newspaper to get ideas for your article. Be sure your article answers the questions "Who? What? When? Where? Why?"

Tip for Younger Children: A younger child may draw a picture illustrating the article.

Guess My Country Game

Play this game as a reminder that members of God's family live in countries all over the world. The first player thinks of a country. Other players attempt to guess the country by asking questions that can be answered with "yes" or "no." The player who guesses the country correctly takes the next turn.

Tip for Younger Children: Pair a younger child with an adult or older child who can help as needed in responding correctly to questions.

God's Family Drawing

On a large piece of paper draw a stick figure person. Then, as a family, list the many abilities God has given people and the ways they may use them to help others. Write each ability near the appropriate body part. (See sketch.) For example, by the mouth, write "Mouth good for singing praise to God and praying for others." By the ear, write "Ears needed to be a good listener." After completing your list, each person tells one or two abilities God has given him or her.

October

Peer Pressure

Key Verse
"Blessed is the man who does not walk in the counsel of the wicked or stand in the way of sinners or sit in the seat of mockers."
Psalm 1:1

Key Thought
A wise person chooses friends carefully, seeking to avoid being influenced in the wrong direction.

During the first few years of life, a child's values are formed primarily by parental influence. Gradually, however, they come to be influenced more and more by others. This can be very positive when the child is spending time with other adults and children whose values are positive and healthy. It can be very destructive, however, when a child associates with those who lack godly character and thus demonstrate selfishness and other negative qualities.

Equipping a child to withstand negative peer pressure requires more than just lecturing the child on a list of do's and don'ts. Even warning a child about the dangers of associating with the wrong crowd is not enough. Parents need to actively seek to provide other positive relationships for their child. Sunday School teachers, club leaders, and other Christian adults can become significant role models in a child's life. And consistent participation in a church's children's ministry enables a child to build a network of friends who are being guided in the same, positive direction.

WEEK 1

DAY 1

Every afternoon when Arthur's mother picked him up from day care, he had a story to tell of something that happened that day. One day he told about Rebecca laughing while trying to drink milk through a straw.

Another day he told about Raul scraping his knee on the asphalt. Anytime there was a little blood, the result was a dramatic story from Arthur. Even when nothing much happened, Arthur could make it sound like the World Series, the Super Bowl, and a giant birthday party all rolled into one.

Since he made every little thing sound like it had been very exciting, his mother did not always listen closely to his stories. It was not always easy for her to sound interested in the latest happenings on the monkey bars or who spilled what during snack. Thus, she was not exactly filled with curiosity when Arthur bounded out the front door of day care and enthusiastically asked, "Guess what happened today, Mom?"

"I don't know, dear," she answered without much interest.

"Christopher got sent to the principal's office!" Arthur announced.

"Oh, he did?" Mother asked automatically. As well as she knew their first-grade neighbor, she imagined that Christopher regularly got sent to the principal. "What for?" she asked.

Arthur was ready for the question. "He used some bad words. And he called a teacher a name."

Suddenly, Arthur's mother was paying full attention. It sounded like Christopher had done something worse than just talk when he should have been listening, or get up when he should have been sitting. "Arthur," she said. "I hope you never do anything like that. I would feel so bad if I ever heard of you causing that kind of trouble at school."

"Don't worry, Mom," Arthur assured her.

"But you spend so much time with Christopher, I worry that you'll pick up some of his bad attitudes. You know he's not a very good example."

"Oh, Mom," Arthur moaned, sounding as though he thought his mother was making a fuss over nothing. "I won't get in trouble."

● *"Do not follow the crowd in doing wrong." Exodus 23:2*

● **For Younger Children**
Why might kids you know get in trouble?
　What was Arthur's mom worried about?
　What's a good way for you to stay out of trouble?

● **For Older Children**
What does being sent to the principal's office usually mean?
　Why do you think Arthur sounded so sure he wouldn't get in trouble?
　What advice would you give Arthur?

● ●

Arthur was almost always glad when his afternoon at day care was over. When his mother picked him up, he usually ran to greet her. Occasionally he would be deeply involved in a game or other activity and would ask to stay "just a few more minutes, please." But that did not happen often.

Going home with his mother always gave Arthur a chance to tell about something interesting from that day. Every time he asked, "Guess what happened?" his mother never knew. But that never mattered, because it was more fun to tell her something she had not heard before.

Yesterday he had told his mom about his friend Christopher being sent to the principal's office. Today he had another story ready to tell. As soon as he spotted his mom, he could hardly contain himself until he could begin telling his important news.

"Guess what, Mom?" he blurted out the moment they walked outside the day care center. Before his mother could say anything, he gleefully announced, "After school yesterday, Christopher was with some big boys. They spray painted their names on an empty building. I wish I could do that."

"Did someone give them permission to do that?" his mother asked.

"I dunno," Arthur said. All he knew was that it sounded very exciting to paint your name where everyone in the neighborhood would see it.

"Arthur, it's against the law to mark up someone else's property," Mom explained.

"It is?" Arthur asked. "How come?"

"Would you like it if someone marked up your bike, or your books, or anything else?" Mom asked.

"No," Arthur said. "I guess not."

"So it's wrong to mark up things that belong to someone else," Mom said. "Kids who do that are hurting other people."

"Oh," Arthur responded. Suddenly, spray painting his name did not seem quite so exciting.

"And that's a reason why I don't like you spending time with those boys. They do wrong things when they're in a group, things that probably none of them would do by themselves."

Suddenly, Arthur wished he had thought of a different story to tell his mom.

● *"Do not set foot on the path of the wicked or walk in the way of evil men."* *Proverbs 4:14*

● **For Younger Children**

How would you feel if someone spray painted on your house?

How does doing wrong things hurt others?

Ask God's help in doing good to others.

● **For Older Children**

Why might people do things when they're in a group that they wouldn't do by themselves?

What is the main idea of Proverbs 4:14?

How can you show that you obey Proverbs 4:14?

DAY
3

"I got an invitation, Mom!" Arthur announced when she picked him up after day care. Arthur's mom took the envelope from his hand and turned it over. It said, "To Arthur, a party." She opened the envelope and slid out the card from inside. Before she could read what it said, Arthur declared, "I get to go to a sleep-over party at Christopher's."

Mom read aloud, "You're invited to a sleep-over party at Christopher's. Friday night. Pizza, games, videos, and a whole night of fun."

"I can't wait," Arthur bubbled. "I've slept over before, but not with a bunch of guys."

"A bunch of what guys?" Mom asked. "Who else is coming?"

"Trevor and Ian and Jake and Conrad. And a few other guys," Arthur said.

"But they're all older than you," Mom said. "And they're older than Christopher."

"That's 'cause there aren't any kids our age in our whole apartment building," Arthur explained. "Except girls."

"I know that, dear," Mom answered. "But I don't like you staying over-night with a bunch of older boys. Especially ones who always seem to be getting into trouble."

"But, Mom," Arthur tried to interrupt.

"No buts, Arthur," Mom said, interrupting his interruption. "Do you know what videos Christopher is going to show?"

"They're all good ones, Mom," Arthur declared. "They're all rated PG–13."

"Arthur, honey," Mom said. "PG–13 means they have things in them that are not good for children younger than thirteen to watch. And you're only five! And none of those other boys are over ten!"

"But, Mom," Arthur tried to interrupt again.

"I'm going to talk to Christopher's mother," Mom said before Arthur could get any further. "I'll tell her you can come for the pizza and games, but that you'll need to come back to our apartment before the videos start."

"Aw, Mom," Arthur groaned, "that won't be any fun."

"I'm sorry, Arthur," she explained, "but I'm really concerned about those other boys being a bad influence on you. They do too many things they shouldn't do, and I don't want you to start acting the same way."

"Aw, Mom," Arthur groaned again, "you treat me like a baby."

● *"Do not be yoked together with unbelievers." 2 Corinthians 6:14*

● **For Younger Children**

Why did Arthur think his mom was treating him like a baby?

How was Arthur's mom trying to help him?

What rules do your parents have to try to help you do good things?

● **For Older Children**

Have you ever been in a situation like Arthur's? What happened?

What would you do if you were Arthur's mom?

The Bible tells us how important it is to have friends who want to love and obey God. Who are some of your friends who love God?

WEEK 1

DAY 4

It was Saturday morning and Arthur was still sulking about not being able to spend the night at Christopher's party. Arthur's mom had promised to take him out to get a donut as a way to make up for the fun he might have missed. Since donuts were Arthur's favorite food, that promise had brightened him up a little. While his mom was getting ready, Arthur went down the hall to Christopher's apartment to see how the party had ended.

It seemed that he was gone only a few minutes when their apartment door flew open and Arthur shouted, "Guess what happened, Mom?"

Mom was just slipping on her jacket. Obviously, she had no idea what Arthur's story would be this time.

Since Arthur did not wait for her to answer, it did not matter. "The guys had a food fight in Christopher's kitchen!" Arthur announced. "They made so much noise a neighbor called the police."

"The police?" Mom asked. "Oh, Arthur! I'm so glad you weren't there."

As she and Arthur walked toward the donut shop, Arthur told the rest of the story, almost without taking a breath.

"The guys told Christopher they wanted a snack, but he said it was too late and they were supposed to be sleeping, but they kept bugging him and he finally said OK and they got some grapes out of the refrigerator and Trevor threw one at Conrad and . . . and no one remembers all that happened until the police came." Finally Arthur took a breath.

"Where was Christopher's mom?" Mom asked.

"Sleeping," Arthur said. "I guess she sleeps hard."

"Why did Christopher let his friends do that?" Mom asked.

"He had to," Arthur said. "They're older, and they're his friends, and he wants them to like him, and . . ." Arthur stopped. He had run out of reasons.

Mom held open the door of the donut shop. "Christopher didn't have to. He let his friends push him into a bad situation. That's why it's so important to be careful about choosing friends, Arthur."

"How about choosing donuts?" Arthur asked.

"I never met a donut I didn't like," his mom laughed.

● *"A righteous man is cautious in friendship." Proverbs 12:26*

● **For Younger Children**

Why is it important to choose friends carefully?

What do you think makes a good friend?

How can your friends help you do good things? How can you help your friends?

● **For Older Children**

Why did Christopher let his friends push him into a bad situation?

What could Christopher have done instead?

Ask God to help you and your friends do good things.

● ●

WEEK 1

DAY
5

It was still Saturday morning. Arthur and his mom had returned from the donut store. Mom went inside the apartment building to start doing the week's laundry. Arthur came back outside to ride his bike up and down the sidewalk, pretending he was a helicopter pilot flying low between the city's tall buildings.

Just as he finished a breathtaking dive up the narrow alley behind the apartment building, a group of neighborhood boys swung through the back door into the alley. It was the same boys who had been at Christopher's party the night before.

"Hey!" yelled the tallest one. That was Trevor. "Here's the little mama's boy who's afraid to sleep without his own blanky."

"Mama's boy!" teased the heaviest of the boys. That was Jake. "I'll bet you're the one who called the cops on us."

"We don't let mama's boys play in our alley," sneered the shortest of the group. That was Conrad.

"Go home, mama's boy!" they all shouted at Arthur.

"Unless!" shouted Trevor. "Unless you do something to prove you're not a mama's boy." Trevor pulled a can of spray paint out of his jacket pocket. "Spray your name in big letters on the wall there. Then we'll let you stay."

Arthur gulped. He wanted the kids to stop calling him names. He wanted the older boys to like him. But he remembered what his mother had said about hurting things that belonged to someone else.

Just then, another voice yelled out. "Leave him alone, guys," the voice shouted. Arthur turned around. It was Kevin, a boy who lived on the top floor of their building. Kevin was even older and taller than Trevor.

Kevin walked up next to Arthur's side. "These guys got themselves in trouble last night. Now they just want to get someone else in trouble too."

After the other boys left, Arthur thanked Kevin for sticking up for him. Kevin said, "Anytime. Just make sure you don't let those guys drag you down."

Arthur decided that Kevin would make a much better friend than Trevor or Jake or Conrad.

● *"If one falls down, his friend can help him up." Ecclesiastes 4:10*

● **For Younger Children**
How would you have felt if you were Arthur?
Who would you choose to be your friend in this story? Why?
Ask God to help you choose friends who will help you.

● **For Older Children**
If Kevin hadn't come by, what do you think Arthur would have said and done?
Why do you think the older boys were bothering Arthur?
What can you do that is like Kevin's actions?

● ●

FAMILY TIMES
Schedule time this week to be together as a family. Select one of these suggested activities to expand your family's understanding of the importance of choosing friends who love and obey God.

Backward Quiz
On separate index cards or pieces of paper write each of these sentences. "Friends can help us make good choices." "A friend can help you remember a way to obey God." "A good friend will defend you." "Ask for

God's help to choose good friends." "Find another friend to spend time with." "Look for ways to encourage your friend to do what is right." Put all the cards or papers in a bowl or hat. Then tell your family that you are going to take a backward quiz. "Instead of thinking of answers to questions, we're going to think of questions for answers." Each person chooses a card or piece of paper, reads the answer aloud, and suggests an appropriate question.

Tip for Younger Children: Read the answer to a younger child and talk together about possible questions. Your child may also enjoy drawing a picture of a favorite friend.

Words of Friendship

On a large piece of paper letter the word "FRIEND" in large block letters. With your family take turns writing verbs inside the block letters that tell actions of a good friend (help, care, share, take turns, love, etc.). As you write the words, take turns naming people who have been good friends and describe their actions.

Tip for Younger Children: It may be easier for a younger child to write or dictate answers to the question, "What is a good friend like?"

Time Out for Friends

Think of another family with whom you would like to become better acquainted. Perhaps there is a family who has recently moved to your neighborhood or visited your church. Think of a single-parent family, or a family who has experienced difficult times. Plan a fun time together—barbeque, picnic, make ice cream sundaes, bike ride, game night, video night, etc. The invitation can be as simple as a phone call or make your own invitation to mail. Thank God for good friends and ask His help in showing friendship to others.

Trusting God

This week you will be helping your child to again think about God's care and protection in difficult situations. While fear is often a very valuable protection when faced with danger, it is important to help a child learn to trust God's help in such times. Thus, the verses which are used this week are the same ones used in September, "Problems at School." Applying these timeless words of Scripture to a new set of anxiety producing troubles will strengthen your child's sense of trust in God's loving care and protection.

Key Verse
"Trust in the Lord with all your heart." Proverbs 3:5

Key Thought
People who love and obey God can put their trust in His protection and care, rather than being fearful and worried.

It is interesting in reading the four Gospels to notice the frequency with which Jesus' closest followers needed to be reminded of something they had supposedly already learned. Having seen Him miraculously feed 5,000 people, they still were doubtful of what to do when 4,000 people people were hungry (Matthew 14:13-21; 15:32-38). In spite of having explained that the greatest in the kingdom of heaven is the humble, childlike person (18:1-4), Jesus still had to wash their feet to teach them that same lesson (John 13:3-17). It is rarely adequate to tell something once. Most of us need repeated hearings of important truths. Learning to trust God instead of giving in to fear and anxiety is certainly a truth of great importance.

WEEK 2

DAY 1

Laura was very quiet at dinner time. It was not unusual for Laura to be quiet, because she rarely made much noise, unless one of her three brothers was teasing her. But she usually had something to say at dinner. Not a lot, but something.

Since Mom was already serving dessert (hot apple pie with big chunks of cheese) and Laura had not said even one word since she sat down, the rest of the Norris family knew that something was bothering her.

"Are you feeling OK, dear?" Grandma Norris asked.

Laura mumbled something that Grandma did not hear. "What's that dear?" Grandma asked rather loudly. Laura mumbled something again, but again Grandma did not hear her. To avoid having Grandma start shouting, Josh decided to explain Laura's mumble to Grandma.

"She says she's worried about her soccer game tomorrow," Josh said.

Ryan, the oldest of the four Norris children, was sitting next to Laura and he had heard something Josh had missed. "She's mostly worried about playing goalie," Ryan said to Grandma.

"Goalie?" Grandma asked. "You're playing goalie? Isn't that dangerous?"

"That's why she's nervous," said Chris, the youngest of the four and the only one not playing on a soccer team the next day. "She's scared," Chris went on, "she'll get hit in the face."

"There's nothing to be scared of," Josh assured his sister.

"Well, boys don't care if their noses get smashed," Laura said plainly.

"Your nose won't get smashed," Ryan assured her. "Just keep your hands ready."

"Then I'll probably break a finger," Laura protested.

"But you're good at catching balls, Laura." Now it was Mom trying to assure her.

Laura still had doubts. "I can catch easy balls," she said, "but not hard ones."

"So duck," Chris suggested.

"Oh, right," Laura shot back, "and let a goal score and have all my teammates mad at me. I'm so nervous I won't be able to sleep tonight."

And no one could think of anything else to say to help Laura not be worried and afraid.

● *"Therefore do not worry about tomorrow, for tomorrow will worry about itself. Each day has enough trouble of its own." Matthew 6:34*

● **For Younger Children**

When have you felt like Laura?

It's normal to feel afraid or nervous about some things. What are some things you have felt afraid of?

How can someone help you when you feel afraid?

● **For Older Children**

What would you have said to help Laura feel better?

What are some things you worry about?

What do you usually do when you're worried or afraid?

WEEK 2

DAY 2

The Norris family sat around the breakfast table on Saturday morning. Ryan and Josh were excited about going to the soccer field for their games later in the morning. Ryan's team was called Pink Under Protest because the league had given them bright pink shirts. Josh's team was called the Bulldozers, although no one knew why they had chosen it.

"What's your team called, Laura?" Chris asked. He was one year away from playing soccer, but was very interested in what his sister and older brothers were doing. "Golden Butterflies," Laura mumbled. She was still worried about playing goalie.

"Laura," Dad said, "will you thank God for our food this morning?"

Laura bowed her head and prayed softly. "Dear God, thank You for food. Amen. . . . Oh, and help me not be afraid to be goalie. Amen. . . . And please don't let me get hit in the face by a hard shot. Amen again."

"Pretty nervous, eh, Laura?" Dad asked.

"I'm not nervous," she said. "I'm scared to death."

"I know what will help," Ryan suggested. "Before we leave, I'll shoot some practice shots at you on the front lawn."

Laura agreed, although she was still so worried, she just sat through breakfast letting her corn flakes get soggy. When Ryan finished eating, the four kids went out on the lawn. The three boys took turns kicking the ball to Laura, and she tried to catch them or block them.

"Don't let that ball go in my flowers!" Mom yelled out the window.

"Don't worry, Mom!" all four kids yelled back.

Laura did quite well catching and blocking shots. And the ball only went in Mom's flowers four or five times. When Mom and Dad came outside to drive the family to the soccer field, Laura seemed to be feeling much better.

As they climbed into their minivan, Ryan said to Laura, "If you can stop my shots, you can stop anything the girls in your division will shoot."

"I hope so," Laura answered. "I sure hope so."

"So," Dad said as he started the van, "practice really helps, eh?"

"Probably," Laura said. "And I think praying helped too."

● *"I sought the Lord and He answered me; He delivered me from all my fears."* *Psalm 34:4*

● **For Younger Children**
If you were on a soccer team, what would you name it?

What does Psalm 34:4 say God will do?

Thank God for His promise to help us when we feel afraid.

● **For Older Children**

Why did practicing help Laura feel better?

Why did praying help Laura feel better?

What can you do when you feel afraid?

● ●

WEEK 2

DAY
3

At half time in the soccer game between the Golden Butterflies and the Flamingos, the score was tied 2-2. Laura Norris had played forward during the first half, but now the coach was going to put her in goal.

As Laura drank from her water bottle and sucked on an orange slice, she remembered the team warmups before the game.

Amber, the other goalie, had stopped a lot of practice shots. As good as Amber was, the Flamingos had scored two goals against her. All Laura could think was, *If they scored two goals against Amber, who's better than I am, how many will they score when I'm goalie?*

Then Laura remembered that during team warmups before the game, she had ducked out of the way of some of the hard shots that came at her. "Don't be afraid of it!" the other girls had yelled at her. That was easy for them to say. They didn't have to be goalie.

"Laura," her coach said, putting her hand on Laura's shoulder, "I know you're nervous about playing goal."

Laura thought, *You just don't know HOW nervous!* She almost said to the coach, "Please don't make me play goalie! Please !" But she just stood there.

The coach smiled and kept talking. "Just do your best, Laura. Remember, it's just a game."

Laura took the goalie shirt from Amber and ran toward the goal. As she stood in front of the goal, getting ready to pull on the shirt, she noticed two of the girls on the other team pointing at her. Laura was sure they could tell how frightened she was. And they both looked like they could kick the ball hard. Very hard.

Laura took a deep breath and pulled the goalie shirt on over her head. At the same moment, she whispered a very quick prayer. She opened her eyes and waved to the referee that she was ready. The referee's whistle blew. The second half was starting.

● *"So we say with confidence, 'The Lord is my helper; I will not be afraid.' "*
Hebrews 13:6

● **For Younger Children**

How would you feel if you were Laura?

What do you think Laura said when she prayed?

When is a time that you prayed to God for His help?

● **For Older Children**

What do you think will happen during the second half?

What do you learn about God from Hebrews 13:6?

Tell God about something that worries you and thank Him for His help.

WEEK 2

DAY

4

Laura's soccer game was over. She was sitting on the grass with her older brother, Ryan, watching their brother, Josh, play his game.

"Those were tough goals the Flamingos scored on you," Ryan said, trying to cheer up his sister.

"Amber would have stopped them both," Laura declared, looking at the ground.

"I don't think I could have stopped those shots," Ryan said. He was looking out at the field, watching Josh's game. "Once they got past your fullbacks, they had you."

"At least," Laura said, still looking down, "I didn't get hit in the face."

"Maybe all that worrying was for nothing," Ryan suggested. Then he yelled, "Nice pass, Josh!"

Laura looked up just in time to see the goalie on the Thunderbolts catch a shot from one of Josh's teammates. "I wonder if that kid's as scared as I was," Laura said.

"I doubt it," Ryan laughed. "You were probably more scared about playing goalie than any kid in the history of soccer." Ryan noticed that Laura was not laughing at his joke. He apologized. "Sorry, Laura, I was just kidding."

"Have you ever been afraid?" Laura asked Ryan.

"Oh, yeah," Ryan admitted, "I used to really be afraid of the horses. Mom says I just screamed the first time they tried to get me to sit on one."

"Even Old Blue?" Laura asked, mentioning the oldest, gentlest horse on their farm. Laura had never been afraid of a horse in her life.

"He wasn't all that old, then," Ryan said. "And I was scared to death about going in a swimming pool. I was sure I'd drown, even though the water only came to my waist."

Ryan also admitted to being frightened out in the barn after dark. "The noises were so creepy, I imagined someone was going to get me."

"What did you do to stop being afraid?" Laura asked.

"I still get frightened sometimes," Ryan answered. "But it always helps to have Dad or Mom around. And they taught me to pray if I get scared. That really helps."

Laura knew just what Ryan meant.

● *"Our help is in the name of the Lord, the Maker of heaven and earth."*
Psalm 124:8

● **For Younger Children**

What did Laura find out about her brother Ryan?

When you are afraid or worried, what do you feel like doing?

Tell the main idea of Psalm 124:8.

● **For Older Children**

Do you think God helped Laura when she felt afraid? Why or why not?

Think of a time when you might feel afraid. What does God want you to do?

● ●

WEEK 2

DAY
5

The Norris family had enjoyed their morning at the soccer field. Although Laura's team had lost, Josh's team had tied and Ryan's team had won. Even more important, the games had all been fun.

As they drove back to their farm, Laura described each of the times the other team had shot at her goal. "I thought that tall girl was going to kick it right at my head," Laura said. "I've never been so scared in my life."

"I think your mother was more scared then than you were," Dad said.

"Have you ever been scared, Dad?" Laura asked.

"Scared?" Dad asked with a laugh. "You'd better believe it!"

"Tell us!" all four kids said at once.

"The most frightening thing I can remember was a night when Ryan was a baby," Dad said. "A big storm hit that night, with pouring rain and howling winds. Two trees blew down and all the electricity went off. The animals were going wild in the barn, and Mom was trying to take care of Ryan in the house."

"What happened?" Chris asked.

Dad continued. "I tried going back and forth between the barn and the house. I didn't feel I could leave either place. I thought the house and the barn would both blow away."

"What did you do?" Laura asked.

"The best I could. When I was in the barn, I prayed for Mom and Ryan. When I was in the house, I prayed for the animals. And when the wind finally died down, I prayed again."

"How come?" Josh asked.

Dad smiled. "To thank God for keeping us safe and for helping me trust Him during the storm."

"What do you mean?" Ryan asked.

"Well," Dad answered, "early in the storm, I was really afraid. I was sure we were doomed. But after I prayed, I realized that I could trust God. I could depend on Him to be with us, even in the middle of the storm."

"Sort of like He was with me in the goal?" Laura said.

"Exactly," Dad said.

There was a pause, then Laura had one more thing to say. "But I still don't want to play goalie next week." And the whole family laughed with her.

● *"If God is for us, who can be against us?" Romans 8:31*

● **For Younger Children**
Why might a grownup be afraid?
   What can you depend on God to do?
   How can you show that you depend on God, even when you're afraid?

● **For Older Children**
What do you think it means to trust God?
   How did Mr. Norris show that he trusted God?
   How can remembering Romans 8:31 help you?

Schedule time this week to be together as a family. Select one of these suggested activities to expand your family's understanding of how to trust God when they feel afraid or worried.

FAMILY TIMES

Spin a Word

Using a sheet of paper, a pencil, and a paper clip, make a spinner as shown in the sketch. Letter each of these words in a separate section of the spinner: afraid, worried, nervous, pray, God, help. Each person takes a turn to spin the paper clip and use the word the clip points to in a sentence. The sentence should tell something about this week's topic of trusting God when we're afraid. Variations: Use the word in a sentence to tell about a past experience when God helped you. Or use the word in a question asking another family member about a way to trust God.

Obstacle Course

Work together as a family to build a short indoor or outdoor obstacle course. Use chairs, tables, large pillows, wastebaskets, cardboard boxes, etc. Explain that each person will be blindfolded and go through the course as another person gives verbal directions. After each person has had a turn to complete the course, talk about how important it was to have someone's help to make it through the course. Emphasize that when we are in difficult or fearful situations in our lives, we need to ask God's help to make it through.

Tip for Younger Children: Before putting on a blindfold, a younger child may want to go through the course without the blindfold. Or while wearing the blindfold, a younger child may wish to hold onto someone's hand.

Scrambled Verse Game

Choose one of the Bible verses listed for this week. Write four or five key words from the verse at the top of a piece of paper. As each word is written, ask, "Why is this word so important? What does this word remind you of?" While other family members close their eyes, choose one word and write it with the letters scrambled. At your signal, family members open their eyes and see how fast they can identify the scrambled word. Continue process until each person has had a turn to scramble a word. (Use additional verses if needed.)

Tip for Younger Children: If you are playing this game with a younger child, eliminate the competitive aspect of the game. Each child takes a turn to identify a scrambled word by matching the letters.

Growing to Be Like Jesus

Sanctification is a big word. It is also an important word. In simplest terms, it is the process which goes on in every Christian's life, helping him or her become more like Jesus.

The Bible frequently describes this process in terms of growing. Everyone has had experience with physical growth, seeing the changes that occur in plants, animals, and people. Similarly, God's Spirit works within a Christian, bringing changes in attitudes and actions. Whether a child or an adult, each of us is capable of this wondrous process of growth.

Key Verse
"We will grow up in every way into Christ."
Ephesians 4:15, EB

Key Thought
God wants us to grow to be more like Jesus.

WEEK 3

DAY
1

AJ and her twin brother DJ were sprawled on the living room floor reading. Their mom tried to step between their legs and make her way to the couch. "You two are sure getting long," she said.

"Why don't we see how tall you both are now," Dad suggested.

AJ and DJ jumped up and headed toward the hall closet. DJ got there first and opened the door. On the back of the door were pencil marks and numbers showing how tall the twins were when they were younger.

"Ladies first," AJ announced, moving in front of the closet door.

"Stand straight," Dad said, as he held a long pencil above her head. "Look straight ahead," he instructed, and he made a mark on the door. Then it was DJ's turn and Dad marked how tall DJ was. Finally, holding a tape measure, Dad measured from the floor up to both new marks.

"AJ," Dad announced, "you've grown almost half an inch since the last time I measured you. And, DJ, you've grown almost five eighths of an inch."

DJ looked closely at the marks and the measuring tape. "Am I growing faster than AJ?" he asked.

"That's what it looks like," Dad answered. "You've grown one eighth of an inch more than AJ."

DJ started to chant, "Boys are bigger! Boys are better! Boys are bigger! Boys are. . . ."

AJ could chant just as loudly as DJ. "Girls are smaller! Girls are smarter!"

Dad interrupted the chanting. "That's enough, you two. I wish I could measure the most important way you two need to grow."

Both twins asked the same question at the same time "What's that?"

Dad closed the closet door and smiled at the twins. "The most important way for anyone to grow is to be more and more like Christ."

● *"As newborn babies want milk, you should want the pure and simple teaching. By it you can grow up and be saved." 1 Peter 2:2,* EB

● **For Younger Children**

What does your family do to keep track of your growth?

Why is it important to grow more and more like Christ—to follow His example in loving God and others?

What's one way you've grown to be like Jesus?

● **For Older Children**

How have you grown and changed in the past few months?

How might someone grow to be more like Christ?

First Peter 2:2 talks about what causes both physical and spiritual growth. What do you need to grow spiritually?

● ●

WEEK 3

DAY 2

DJ and his dad were shooting baskets. DJ bounced the ball and shot. It hit the rim and bounced away. DJ's dad jumped up, caught it, and shot it again. This time it went in.

"Can you slam it, Dad?" DJ asked.

"Not quite," Dad answered, taking another shot. Again, it went in.

"Can you touch the rim?" DJ asked. He seemed more interested in asking questions than in playing basketball.

"Almost," Dad said.

DJ asked, "Can you touch the net?"

"That I can touch," Dad said. "Watch." He ran a few steps toward the basket, jumped high, and touched the few strands of net hanging from the rim.

"Will I be able to slam it when I'm grown up?" DJ asked.

"If you keep exercising and growing," Dad said, taking another shot and making it.

"When will I be full grown?" DJ wanted to know next.

Dad decided to rest for a minute. "Probably when you're about seventeen or eighteen," he puffed.

"When did you stop growing?" DJ asked.

"I don't remember," Dad said. "In many ways I'm still growing."

DJ took a good look at his dad. "How?" DJ asked, curious about his dad still growing somehow.

Dad explained, "I know I'm still growing as a dad. There's a lot more I need to learn."

DJ scratched his head. "You're already a good dad."

"Thanks," Dad said. "I want to get better. And as a husband too."

DJ seemed surprised. "Really?" he asked. "Does Mom know?"

"You better believe it," Dad laughed. Then he added, "And I want to get better at my job."

DJ was really puzzled now. "But aren't you the boss?" he asked.

Dad nodded his head. "I'm one of them. But we all want to keep improving."

"I thought," DJ said, "once you were a grownup, you didn't have to keep learning."

Dad laughed again. "Why do you think Mom and I go to church and Sunday School every week? 'Cause we want to keep growing as Christians, to become better people in every way we can."

"I never thought about that," DJ said. Then he bounced the ball twice and took a shot. This time it went in.

● *"But grow in the grace and knowledge of our Lord and Savior Jesus Christ."*
2 Peter 3:18

● **For Younger Children**

What's something you'd like to be able to do when you're a grownup?
    What's something you'd like to do better right now?
    Ask God's help in growing and learning.

● **For Older Children**

Why might DJ have thought that grownups didn't need to keep learning?
    In what ways did DJ's dad say he was still growing?
    What are some ways you are growing and learning?

WEEK 3

DAY
3

While DJ and Dad were shooting baskets, DJ's twin sister, AJ, was around the corner bouncing a ball against a wall with her friend, Rebecca. AJ would throw the ball, and Rebecca would catch it on the rebound. Then Rebecca would throw it, and AJ would catch it. AJ decided to throw it hard and low against the wall, so it would be hard for Rebecca to catch it.

AJ threw the ball as hard as she could. It was low, all right. It was so low it bounced high and to the side, breaking a window with a loud crash.

"Run for it!" Rebecca yelled, starting to dash around the corner.

AJ started to run after her, but then she stopped. "Go tell my dad," she shouted after Rebecca. "Tell him to come here," she yelled.

Rebecca stopped running and turned around. "Why?" she asked. "You don't want him to find out."

"Just do it," AJ said. "I'd better wait here."

A moment later, AJ's dad came running around the corner, and AJ explained what happened. Together they knocked on the door of the building and told the person inside about the broken window. AJ's dad agreed to pay to get it fixed.

Afterward, Rebecca asked AJ, "Why'd you do that? If you'd run, nobody'd know you broke it. You could have got away easy!"

AJ answered softly, "Not from my conscience."

Rebecca looked at her friend. "What?" she asked, sounding very surprised.

AJ explained, "I'd have known I did wrong. I'd have felt crummy."

"Not me," Rebecca said. "I'd have been glad I got away with it."

"Maybe," AJ said, "but, if anyone broke something of mine, I'd want them to admit it."

Rebecca was still puzzled. "But what about the money to fix the window?" she asked.

"I know," AJ admitted. "Dad's gonna take it out of my allowance. But if I'm gonna grow up, it's still better not to do something wrong."

● *"Dear friends, let us turn away from everything wrong."*
2 Corinthians 7:1, TLB

● **For Younger Children**
What was the wrong thing Rebecca wanted AJ to do?
   Why did AJ say no?

AJ showed she was growing to be more like Jesus when she made a right choice. When have you decided to do something right instead of wrong?

● **For Older Children**

What would you have done if you were AJ?

Have you ever tried to run away from your conscience? How did you feel?

What is one way you can grow to be more like Jesus and obey 2 Corinthians 7:1?

● ●

WEEK 3

DAY
4

AJ and DJ sat in the second row at church. Their dad was an usher and sat in the back. Mom sat with the choir. Sitting close to the front usually kept the twins from misbehaving during the church service.

AJ found the place in her Bible where Rev. Jamison was reading out loud. She followed along with her finger under the words as the pastor read, "You will live the kind of life that honors and pleases the Lord in every way. You will produce fruit in every good work and grow in the knowledge of God." AJ listened carefully as Rev. Jamison began to preach about growing to be like Jesus. At least, she listened for a few minutes. Then she wrote a note on the back of her Sunday School paper. Very quietly, she handed it to DJ.

DJ read the note. It said, "How can we grow like Jesus?"

DJ borrowed AJ's pencil and wrote, "I don't know." Then he handed the note to AJ.

AJ took back the pencil and wrote, "Does God give a test like at school?"

DJ read what AJ wrote, then he wrote, "I don't think so."

AJ turned the Sunday School paper over to find space to write some more. This time she wrote, "What if we get a report card from God?"

DJ read her question, then wrote, "Be seerius."

AJ wrote back, "That's serious. Not seerius."

DJ wrote back, "If yur so smart, how com you ask me the qestuns."

AJ wrote back, "Can't you spell anything?"

DJ wrote back, "Anything."

AJ wrote back, "I still want to know how to grow like Jesus."

DJ wrote back, "I still don't know." Then, before he handed the note back to AJ, he crossed out his answer and wrote, "We coud listen to Reverund Jamisun preech."

AJ wrote back along the top edge of the paper, "It's could, not coud. It's Jamison, not Jamisun. And it's preach, not preech."

DJ wrote back along the bottom edge of the paper, "I know that. When is church over?"

Just then AJ noticed that everyone else was standing up getting ready to sing. "Right now," she said.

● *"You will live the kind of life that honors and pleases the Lord in every way. You will produce fruit in every good work and grow in the knowledge of God." Colossians 1:10, EB*

● **For Younger Children**
What was AJ's question?

How would you have answered her question?

How does Colossians 1:10 answer AJ's question? How can you do what this verse says?

● **For Older Children**
It's easy to see the ways people grow physically. What does Colossians 1:10 say is the result of growing to be more like Jesus?

What are some ways kids your age can show that they honor and please the Lord in their lives?

What can you do?

● ●

WEEK 3

DAY 5

The church service was over. As people walked outside, Rev. Jamison stood by the door, shaking hands with everyone. This slowed the crowd down and made it hard for the Gorman twins to make their way outside quickly.

As the twins finally reached the front door, Rev. Jamison winked at them and stooped down. "Those must have been interesting notes you two were passing," he said.

The twins were embarrassed. They did not think anyone had seen them passing notes. They especially did not think Rev. Jamison had seen them. He did not look like he was going to get them in trouble, but the twins still did not know what to say to him.

Just then, AJ got a brilliant idea. She said, "Well, the notes were kind of about the sermon."

Rev. Jamison smiled. The twins had always liked his smile. Even though they were shy around him, they knew he was a kind, friendly man who liked children. "Good," Rev. Jamison said. "Did the sermon give you any ideas on how to get to grow more like Jesus?"

Now the twins were trapped. They had been so busy passing notes, they had missed the whole sermon. All the twins could think of to say was, "Uh . . . uh . . . uh. . . ."

Rev. Jamison was still smiling. "Let me suggest one thing," he said. "I'll give you this idea as an extra bonus just for you two."

What could the twins say? Even though they really wanted to get outside, the pastor was being so nice, they just had to listen.

"Ready?" Rev. Jamison asked. The twins nodded. "Ask God to give you a heart that's clean," the pastor said. "Ask Him to forgive you whenever you do something you shouldn't. That will help you grow more than anything else I know. Got it?"

The twins both said, "OK" at exactly the same time.

Rev. Jamison stood up and started to hold out his hand to a woman standing right behind the twins. Then he looked again at DJ and AJ. "And," he announced with a wink, "it never hurts to listen during the sermon either." Then he laughed.

● *"Create in me a pure heart, O God." Psalm 51:10*

● **For Younger Children**

Why were AJ and DJ embarrassed?

What did Rev. Jamison say the twins should ask God for?

When a person has a clean heart, it means that he or she loves God more than anything in the world and wants to obey God's commands. Read Psalm 51:10 as your prayer.

● **For Older Children**

What did AJ and DJ learn about how to grow more like Jesus?

Read Psalm 51:10. What is the main idea of this prayer? How would you describe a pure heart?

Rewrite this verse in your own words to make your own special prayer to God.

● ●

FAMILY TIMES

Schedule time this week to be together as a family. Select one of these suggested activities to expand your family's understanding of what it means to grow more like Jesus.

Watch Me Grow!

To reinforce this week's topic of growth, plant a carrot or sweet potato with your family. Check your plant every day for signs of growth and add water as needed. Comment, "How has the (carrot) grown? What changed? As we grow more like Jesus, we change too. What are some ways our attitudes and actions might change?"

Carrot: Cut off about 2-inches of the top of a carrot. Place cut end down in a shallow bowl. Fill bowl with water. Watch for leaves to grow within a few days. Sweet Potato: Fill a large jar or glass with water. Use toothpicks to hold sweet potato in water. (See sketch.)

Milestones

Choose one or more of these ways to enjoy your children's milestones of growth. Use these visual reminders as ways to build your child's understanding of spiritual growth. Talk about specific ways you have observed your child grow to be more like Jesus. Share a way you want to grow and improve. Ask your child how he or she is learning to be more like Jesus. (1) Look at your child's baby books. Tell what you remember about your child at that young age. (2) Look through several family photo albums—one from your child's early years and a more recent album. (3) Choose one or more home videos showing some of your child's growing up experiences. (4) If your family has a place where you record your child's height, look at the records together. For each height, describe a skill your child had learned at that age or another way he or she had grown.

Sunburst Writing

Each person draws a sunburst diagram on a large piece of paper. (See sketch.) Say: "Write your name on the sun. On each line write a way you are growing." Suggest family members include areas of physical and spiritual growth. For ideas, read Colossians 1:10-12 together. "What kinds of actions and attitudes are pleasing to the Lord? When are you learning to show those actions and attitudes?"

Tip for Younger Children: Younger children will find it easier to understand and identify areas of physical growth. Instead of writing, suggest they draw pictures on the lines showing ways they have grown.

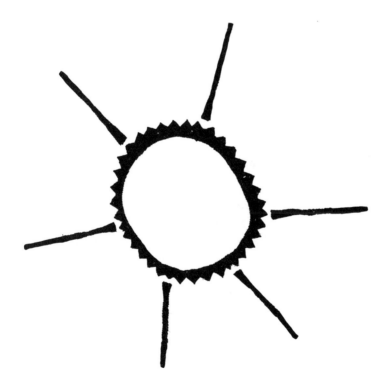

Key Verses
"For I am convinced that neither death nor life, neither angels nor demons . . . will be able to separate us from the love of God that is in Christ Jesus our Lord."
Romans 8:38-39

Key Thought
While the presence of evil is very real in our world, the power of Jesus Christ is greater.

Evil in Our World

"The devil made me do it," has long been a popular line that is good for a laugh whenever someone wants to excuse himself for having done something he knew all along was wrong. Behind the humor is the grim reality of evil at work in human life.

Children learn very young that our world is not all sweetness and light, but often it is grim, unfair, and dangerous. Talking about the presence of evil is not a scare tactic, but rather a very necessary means to prepare the child to withstand the pressures and enticements of the evil one. At the same time, they also need the assurance that the power and goodness of God is always greater than the forces of evil. Scripture assures us that, with God's help, we can overcome the threat which evil presents.

WEEK 4

DAY 1

"What are you gonna be?" Eric asked his younger sister Jessie.

"I dunno yet," she said. "What are you gonna be?"

Eric and Jessie were planning their costumes for a big kids' party their church was going to have on Halloween. There were going to be games and food and, the most fun of all, a costume contest.

"I thought about being a zombie, but they won't let us do that at church." Eric did not sound at all happy with this restriction. He quoted the sing-song verse from the party announcement sheet: "Come for the fun, but follow the rules: no Ghosts, no Goblins, and no ghastly Ghouls."

"Sounds like a costume discussion," Dad said, walking into the room. "Any decisions yet?"

"I had a great idea for a devil costume," Eric said. "I'd rig up a tail so it would swing when I walk."

"I want to be a witch," Jessie added. "I could wear a black robe and a tall black hat."

"A devil and a witch, huh?" Dad asked.

"But the church has a dumb rule about wearing that kind of stuff to the party," Eric complained.

"Dumb rule?" Dad asked.

"I don't see why we can't wear whatever we want," Jessie stated firmly.

"Could it be that dressing up like the devil or a witch doesn't fit with anything that our church stands for?" Dad asked.

"Huh?" Eric and Jessie both asked in unison.

"Well, the devil and demons and witches all use evil powers. And doesn't the world have more than enough evil going on without our church encouraging kids to dress up like the enemies of goodness."

"But it's just pretend!" Eric insisted. "What's the harm in that?"

"Maybe pretending leads to the real thing." Dad said. "Think about it."

● *"Surely wickedness burns like a fire." Isaiah 9:18*

● **For Younger Children**

What would you wear to a costume party?

What costumes might remind people of the good things in our world?

Why is it important to think about good and not evil?

● **For Older Children**

Do you think pretending leads to the real thing? Why or why not?

What does it mean to be an enemy of goodness?

Why does the Bible compare wickedness or wrong things to a fire?

● ●

WEEK 4

"What are you gonna be?" Eric's friend, Jason, wanted to know what Eric was going to be for Halloween.

"I don't know yet," Eric said. "I'm still thinking about it."

"I'm gonna be a vampire," Jason said. "With a black cloak and fangs and blood and everything."

"Sounds cool," Eric replied, "but I can't wear anything neat like that."

"How come?" Jason wanted to know.

"I'm goin' to a party where they don't allow it," Eric explained.

"What kind of Halloween party doesn't allow vampires?" Jason asked.

"It's not really a Halloween party" Eric explained. "Our church is havin' a big kids' party that night, and I guess they think there's enough bad

DAY

2

things in the world without kids pretending to be evil."

"But it's just pretending! There's no such thing as demons and devils!" Jason insisted.

"Are you sure?" Eric asked.

"Everyone says. . . ." Jason started to say. But Eric interrupted him.

"I know what 'everyone' says, but do you know what the Bible says?"

"The Bible?" Jason sounded puzzled. "What does the Bible have to do with this?"

"A lot! The party's at our church," Eric explained, "and our church believes the Bible."

"So?" Jason challenged.

"So," Eric answered, "the Bible says there's a real devil, Satan. And he's the main reason there's so much bad stuff in the world."

Jason thought for a minute. "So what are you gonna be? A clown? Or the world's ugliest ballerina?"

"Could be," Eric laughed. "You wanta come?"

"If you're gonna be a ballerina," Jason said, joining in the laughter, "I wouldn't miss it for anything."

"I can't promise that," Eric said. "But it will be lots of fun. And the snacks are incredible."

"Sounds good," Jason said, still laughing. "Want me to help look for ballet slippers in your size?"

● *"And lead us not into temptation, but deliver us from the evil one."*
Matthew 6:13

● **For Younger Children**

What does Matthew 6:13 call Satan?

What are some of the bad things Satan has caused to happen in our world?

Instead of being afraid of Satan, what does Matthew 6:13 say we should pray?

● **For Older Children**

The Bible says that Satan is real and that he is God's enemy. Do you think Satan is a strong or weak enemy? Why?

What wrong things might God's enemy try to tempt you to do?

Ask God's help in resisting Satan's efforts to tempt you.

DAY
3

"Did you give up on the devil costume?" Jessie asked her brother Eric.

"Yeah," Eric sighed. "There's no way. Besides, I could never figure out how to make the tail move like I want."

"No tail, no devil," Jessie laughed. Then she stopped. "Does the devil really have a tail?" she asked.

"How should I know?" Eric answered. "But I have been thinking about the devil. Some kids at school say they're into Satan worship."

"Who's Satan?" asked Jessie.

"He's the devil, oh dumb and ugly one," Eric answered.

"Mom!" Jessie shouted. "Eric called me dumb and ugly!"

"I'm sorry," Eric laughed. "I meant to say ugly and dumb."

"Mo-om!" Jessie shouted louder. "Now he says I'm ugly and dumb."

"I'm really sorry this time," Eric said, trying to look serious and sympathetic. "I'm really sorry you're ugly and dumb."

Just at that moment, Mom walked in the door.

"Eric," she said sternly, "why'd you call your sister those names?"

"I was just teasing!" Eric said, trying to sound innocent. "I was just having fun."

Mom was not accepting Eric's innocent expression. "Why do you think it's fun to hurt someone's feelings?" she asked.

"I dunno," Eric answered. He realized that almost any answer he gave could get him in worse trouble.

"Could it be," Mom asked, "that we live in a world where so many things have been twisted and spoiled that it's easy for people to get pleasure from hurting others? Where do you think that kind of attitude comes from, Eric?"

"Satan?" Eric suggested, knowing it was the right answer, but not wanting to admit that calling his sister names had anything to do with anything REALLY evil.

"You said it," Mom replied. "Do you know what we can do to keep from letting Satan be in control?"

"No," Eric said, even though he had a very good idea of what his mom was going to suggest.

"We can do what Jesus did," she said. "Did you know that Jesus prayed that God would protect us from the evil one, from Satan?"

"No," Eric said.

"God will help us stand up against Satan," she said. "No matter what evil

Satan might try to get us to do, God's power makes it possible for us to not give in."

● *"My prayer is not that you take them out of the world but that you protect them from the evil one." John 17:15*

● **For Younger Children**

Why is calling someone names a wrong thing to do?

What is a wrong thing you are tempted to do?

Thank God for His power over Satan and ask His help for the times you are tempted to do wrong.

● **For Older Children**

When you hear the word, "Satan," what do you think of?

How might someone your age stand up against Satan?

When can you stand up against Satan?

● ●

WEEK 4

DAY 4

Eric's friend, Jason, had decided to go with Eric to the big party for kids at Eric's church. Eric was dressed as a Martian, all in green, including his hair. His mom had said the food coloring would wash right out. Jason was dressed as a television set, wearing a cardboard box with a TV screen cutout opening. The boys had decided to Trick or Treat a few neighborhood houses before leaving for the party. Eric's sister, Jessie, and her friend, Monica, agreed to go one way while Eric and Jason went the other way up the street.

At the third house the boys visited, the lights were all off. "They're not home," Eric said. "Let's skip this house."

"Let's try the doorbell," Jason said. "They might be in a back room." Jason rang the doorbell seven times before conceding that no one was home. "Hey Eric," Jason said after the seventh ring, "let's do something to their house."

"Do something?" Eric questioned.

"Yeah, some kind of trick," Jason said. "After all, this IS called 'Trick or Treat!' If they don't give us a treat, we get to trick them."

"I don't think we should do anything," Eric said. "Besides, we've got time to hit a few more houses."

"Forget those houses," Jason urged. "This'll be a lot more fun. Let's turn on their sprinklers or dump over their garbage or. . . ."

"Let's not, Jason," Eric said. "That sounds more like vandalism than a trick."

"Are you scared?" Jason demanded.

"No," Eric answered, "I just don't think it's good to cause trouble for people. That's the main reason we're going to this party tonight, so we won't get in any trouble. Let's get out of here."

"OK, you're probably right," Jason gave in. "But wouldn't it be a kick to hide their welcome mat up in the tree?"

"You're weird, Jason," Eric laughed. "Let's get going. I hear a candy bar next door calling my name."

"I'm weird?" Jason laughed. "A guy with green hair says I'm weird?"

● *"But the Lord is faithful, and He will strengthen and protect you from the evil one." 2 Thessalonians 3:3*

● **For Younger Children**
What was wrong with Jason's idea?

Has anyone ever tried to talk you into doing wrong? What happened?

When you're tempted to do wrong, how does 2 Thessalonians 3:3 say God will help you?

● **For Older Children**
Why do you think Jason wanted to play a trick?

How was Eric being tempted?

Do you think it was hard or easy for Eric to resist temptation? Why?

Is it hard or easy for you to resist temptation? Whom can you depend on to help you?

● ●

WEEK 4

DAY

5

Mr. Lacey did not usually read the newspaper at breakfast. He usually saved it to read on the bus on the way to work. However, on the morning after Halloween, he spotted an article about several young teenagers being arrested. They had been caught on Halloween night shooting out car windows with a BB gun. The car windows that had been hit were just one street away from where the Lacey family lived.

Mr. Lacey thought it would be a good idea to read the article to Eric and Jessie. So he did, ending with the last sentence of the story: "One of the youths said they had just thought it would be a fun Halloween prank."

Mr. Lacey looked up from the paper. "A Halloween prank?" he snorted. "Shooting out car windows is a prank? Eric, I'm sure glad you and Jason wouldn't get involved in anything like that."

"Me too, Dad," Eric said, remembering how close he and Jason had come to getting involved in a different kind of prank. Eric took a deep breath and thought about how glad he was that he and Jason had not done anything wrong the night before. "What's going to happen to those kids?" he asked his dad.

"They'll probably have to pay to have all those car windows fixed. That'll cost a lot of money."

"Yeah," Eric agreed. "Is that all?"

"No," Dad said, "they might have to spend some time in jail. And their parents are probably not going to trust them for quite a while."

"Maybe they've learned a good lesson," Eric suggested.

"Maybe," Dad agreed. "But learning from doing something bad is never easy. Even though God forgives us when we confess and turn away from doing wrong, there's still all the damage that we caused."

"Sort of like all the broken glass from those car windows?" Eric asked.

"Exactly," Dad agreed.

● *"For I will forgive their wickedness and will remember their sins no more." Jeremiah 31:34*

● **For Younger Children**
What's the difference between a prank or a trick and doing something wrong?

How do you usually feel when you've done something wrong?

How does God promise to help when we've sinned?

● **For Older Children**
Why do you think Mr. Lacey thought it would be a good idea to read the newspaper article to Eric and Jessie?

How might giving in to temptation and doing wrong things affect a person's life?

The Bible tells us that God is more powerful than anyone, even Satan. What else do you learn about God in Jeremiah 31:34?

● ●

Schedule time this week to be together as a family. Select one of these suggested activities to expand your family's understanding of God's goodness and His power to help us resist Satan's temptations.

FAMILY TIMES

Choose Your Number!

Letter these questions on index cards. "What words would you use to describe Satan in this story? What words would best describe Jesus? What would you have done if you were Jesus? How did Jesus use the Bible to resist temptation? Which part of this story would you have liked to have seen? What might have happened if Jesus had given in to Satan's temptation? What can we do to follow Jesus' example and resist temptation?" Number each card from 1–7. Then, with your family, read the story of Jesus' temptation in Matthew 4:1-11. To discuss the story, each person chooses a number between 1 and 7, then reads and answers the question with that number.

Tip for Younger Children: Ask a younger child to choose a scene to illustrate. While the child is drawing, talk with him or her about the story.

Fall Surprise

Collect a variety of nature items (colorful leaves, Indian corn, acorns, gourds, small pumpkins, etc.) and arrange them on a tray or in a basket for a table centerpiece. Talk together about ways these items remind you of God's goodness to you. Ask, "What do you see in our world that shows God's power? What do you see in our world that reminds you of God's love to you? How can knowing about God's love and power help you when you are tempted to do wrong?"

Bible Character Masks

Each person secretly chooses a Bible character and makes a mask to wear representing that person. Simple masks may be made by drawing faces on large paper bags or white paper plates. As each person wears his or her mask, others ask *yes* or *no* questions to determine who the character is. When the character has been identified, talk about temptations that character may have faced and how God helped him or her.

Tip for Younger Children: Suggest several well-known Bible characters from which your younger child may choose. Pair the child with an older family member for help in answering the *yes* or *no* questions.

Key Verses
"But the fruit of the Spirit is love, joy, peace, patience, kindness, goodness, faithfulness, gentleness and self-control." Galatians 5:22-23

Key Thought
Success in life and in the Christian walk requires self-control. God helps His people learn to discipline themselves.

Self-Discipline

Self-discipline is a lot like patience. It is a virtue that everyone commends, especially in others. However, no one wants to go through the problems and challenges that produce those good results.

Children, because they are children, are not highly disciplined. No group of youngsters will automatically arrange themselves in an orderly, single-file line. Children are not likely to eat all their vegetables, pick up their toys, brush their teeth, do their homework, or tackle their chores without some continuing adult guidance. Nor are they likely, or even able, to practice regularly any spiritual disciplines: prayer, Bible reading, church attendance, giving to others, sharing their faith, without adult encouragement.

The challenge in guiding a child's development, is to properly balance the necessary imposition of adult discipline with the need to let the child begin to make choices and take responsibility for his or her own decisions. This week's stories about Hector's aversion to practicing his piano will be a useful aid in encouraging your child to think about the importance of developing self-control.

WEEK 1

DAY 1

Hector did not want to practice the piano. There were times when he wanted to practice, but those were mostly when there was work to be done. Then he would say, "I can't do the dishes, Mama. I have to practice the piano." Or "I can't fold the laundry, Mama. I have to practice the piano."

However, whenever there was something interesting to do, Hector was full of excuses about why he could not practice the piano right now. His favorite was, "I'm too tired, Papa. I can't play good when I'm tired." If that didn't work, he would say, "I hurt my finger playing basketball." If none of his excuses got him any sympathy, he would finally try, "Can't I PLEASE practice later? I promise I'll do it."

Tuesday, Wednesday, and Thursday were always the hardest days to get Hector to practice. That was because he had his lesson Tuesdays and would usually be given some new pieces to learn. Getting started with new music was often slow and difficult. Hector wanted to be able to play new songs instantly. Instead, he had to play each one slowly and carefully, over and over, before he could play them very well. As far as Hector was concerned, that was boring.

Everyone was used to hearing Hector moaning, "It's too hard. I'll never get this one." So no one paid much attention one afternoon when he interrupted his practice to announce, "I hate the piano! I'll never learn to play it. I quit!"

"Try the next piece, dear," Mama said.

"Use the soft pedal," his sister, Angela said. "I'm trying to study."

"Play the one that sounds like a jungle," his dad said. "I really like the way you play that one."

"But I don't want to practice anymore!" Hector whined. "I'm tired of practicing! I want to do something fun!"

Hector knew exactly what his dad's next comment would be. Dad said, "If you had spent the time practicing instead of griping, you'd be done by now."

With a sigh, Hector turned the page of his piano book and began to struggle through the next piece.

● *"Like a city whose walls are broken down is a man who lacks self-control."*
Proverbs 25:28

● **For Younger Children**

If you were Hector, how would you feel about practicing the piano every day?

How can practicing the piano every day help Hector?

What's something you've learned to do because you practiced it a lot?

● **For Older Children**

When have you felt tired of practicing something?

When Hector kept on practicing even when he didn't want to, it showed he had self-control. How does Proverbs 25:28 describe a person without self-control?

What's something you do that shows you have self-control?

DAY
2

Hector's piano teacher was going to have a family piano duet evening at her house. "If your mother or father play the piano, you can work up a parent/child duet. I'll help you choose a piece you will have fun playing together."

"But my parents don't play the piano," Hector said, "and I don't want to do a duet with Angela." Angela was Hector's older sister, and the few times they had tried playing duets together had not been wonderfully successful. "The only other relative who plays piano at all is my Uncle Manuel," Hector added.

Hector's teacher suggested, "Perhaps your uncle would play a duet with you."

Hector thought that was a great idea. He really liked his Uncle Manuel. He had heard him play the piano a few times at family gatherings and thought it would be great fun to play a duet with him. Hector borrowed several books of piano duets that his teacher thought would be good for him and Uncle Manuel to play together. As soon as Hector got home, he picked up the telephone and dialed Uncle Manuel's number.

"Buenas tardes, Tio Manuel," Hector said when his uncle picked up the phone. He explained about the evening of piano duets and asked Uncle Manuel if he would play a duet with him that night. Uncle Manuel agreed to do it and told Hector he would come over on the weekend so they could practice together.

"You pick out two or three pieces you like and start practicing them," Uncle Manuel said. "When I come over, we can try them together and decide which one we'll really work on."

Hector thought that sounded great, and he told his parents all about his chance to play with Uncle Manuel.

"That sounds great, Hector," his dad said.

"When are you going to start practicing for it?" his mom asked.

"Oh, I've got lots of time," Hector assured her. "The songs in these books are easy. I'll start in a day or so."

But when Uncle Manuel came over, Hector hadn't practiced his part. He had gotten busy doing other things and had forgotten to practice.

"Hector," Uncle Manuel said. "If we're going to do this, let's do it right. That means we've both got to practice—a lot!"

Hector promised to practice, but everyone in his family wondered if that was a promise Hector would keep.

● *"Make every effort to add to your faith goodness; and to goodness, knowledge; and to knowledge, self-control; and to self-control, perseverance."*
2 Peter 1:5-6

● **For Younger Children**
How do you think Uncle Manuel felt when he found out Hector hadn't practiced the duets?
　What kept Hector from practicing the duets?
　What keeps you from doing something you've said you would do?
　Ask God's help in keeping your promises.

● **For Older Children**
Do you think Hector will keep his promise? Why or why not?
　What are some things it's easy for you to put off doing? Why?
　Make a plan to do something you've been putting off.

● ●

WEEK 1

DAY
3

Hector and his Uncle Manuel sat down together at the piano to work on a duet. "Do you want to play the top part or the bottom part?" Uncle Manuel asked.

"I dunno," Hector answered. "Whichever's easier."

"Why don't you try the bottom?" Uncle Manuel suggested, as he looked at the music. "It's got lots of loud, low notes that are fun to hit."

So, they switched places on the piano bench. Uncle Manuel began to tap his foot. "Let's take it slow to start," he said. Then the music began. At least it was supposed to be music. Since Hector had not been practicing his part and Uncle Manuel had never seen the music before, neither of them played their parts very well. And since they had never practiced together before, they did not stay together very well. What it sounded like was two totally different songs being played at the same time instead of two parts of the same song.

"Are you guys playing on the same song?" Mama asked.

"Are you guys even playing on the same team?" Papa asked. "Or is that song supposed to sound like a dog and cat fight?"

"It's called 'Valley of the Giants,' " Uncle Manuel said. "And it's going to sound a lot better."

"I hope that will be soon," Papa laughed.

"Never mind him," Uncle Manuel said. "Let's try it again." And they did.

And it did sound a little better. At least everyone wanted to think it sounded a little better. The third time there was a definite improvement. They only had to stop five or six times so that Manuel or Hector could play a hard part again.

"It's starting to come together, Hector," Manuel said. "A few more times and we'll be off to a good start."

"Do we have to play more now?" Hector asked. "I'm getting bored. Do you wanta come outside and shoot some baskets?"

"I'd love to play basketball, but I really need more practice on this song. If you're gonna get good, Hector," Manuel said, "you have to stick to it. And I can't do it for you. You have to do it yourself."

"I know," Hector said, "but I'm tired. I'm gonna get a snack." And Hector went into the kitchen.

● *"Perseverance must finish its work so that you may be mature and complete, not lacking anything." James 1:4*

● **For Younger Children**

Are you more like Hector or Uncle Manuel? Why?

What does it mean to "stick to" something?

What's something you need to "stick to"?

● **For Older Children**

What kinds of choices did Hector make in this story?

Do you think his choices will help him become a better person? Why or why not?

What are some choices you'll be making in the next few days? Which choices will show your self-control and perseverance?

● ●

WEEK 1

DAY 4

"Hey, Mom!" Hector yelled as he started out the door of the apartment with a basketball under his arm. "I'm gonna shoot baskets with some friends."

"What about your piano?" Mama asked. "Have you practiced your duet today?"

"I'm good enough, Mama," Hector said. "I know the song."

"Then," Mama said, "let's hear it."

"Now?" Hector asked.

"Now," Mama answered.

"But the guys are waitin'," Hector said.

"It won't hurt them to wait a few more minutes," Mama insisted. "Let's hear your part of the duet."

Hector knew he had no choice. He shuffled over to the piano and opened the music for the duet he was going to play with his Uncle Manuel. He took a deep breath and began to play. The first few notes sounded fine, but then Hector began to make mistakes, one after another. It was obvious that Hector had not been practicing, but he decided to try telling his mother that everything was fine.

"See," he said boldly, "I've almost got it. It just needs a little more polishing."

"Then start polishing, Son," Mama said.

"But I can do that later," said Hector. "There's lots of time. Can't I play basketball now?"

"You know the rules, Hector," she said. "Homework and piano first, then you can play."

"Why can't I play first and then practice?" Hector asked. "I usually play better after I've had a little time for fun and. . . ."

"Hector!" Mama interrupted. "Start practicing! Now!"

Hector could tell that Mama meant business. It was not likely that she would change her mind and allow him to shoot baskets now. Perhaps he could practice for a little while. Then, when Mama wasn't looking, he could slip out to play basketball.

"Practice," Hector muttered. "Practice, practice, practice. I don't see why I have to practice all the time."

The sounds that Hector produced from the piano that day were not very happy ones. They were not even very musical. Even so, Mama brought her sewing box into the living room where she could listen. That ended Hector's hope of slipping out quickly to shoot baskets.

● *"Let us not become weary in doing good, for at the proper time we will reap a harvest if we do not give up." Galatians 6:9*

● **For Younger Children**

What rules does your family have about work and play?

Do you spend more time doing jobs or playing?

What's something you have to work at? What's something you like to do when you have free time?

● **For Older Children**

When have you felt like Hector and wished you didn't have to do something?

Everyone gets tired of practicing or working sometimes. How can Galatians 6:9 help you when you're tired of doing your chores?

What are some of the good things you need to keep doing?

WEEK 1

DAY 5

Hector had not been looking forward to the family duet night at his piano teacher's house. He didn't mind having to play a duet with Uncle Manuel. Once he had started to practice, he enjoyed the song, and he really liked playing alongside his favorite uncle. The problem with the family duet night was mainly that his mother made him wear nice clothes.

"Hector," she said sternly, "I'm not going to take you over there looking like you've been rolling around in the dirt."

The discussion went on for a while. Hector insisted that he looked fine as he was and that if he dressed like Mama said, all the other kids would think he was a sissy. Mama insisted that a special evening deserved special effort. Finally, they compromised. Hector did not have to wear a tie, but he did have to wear a nice shirt and his one pair of slacks.

When they arrived at the piano teacher's house, Hector quickly saw that all the other piano students must have had the same discussion with their parents. They were all wearing nice clothes too.

When the duets began, Hector enjoyed listening to the music. Some of the students and their parents were very good. Several of the duets sounded very interesting, and Hector wondered if he and Uncle Manuel could try to learn those songs next. Then it was Hector and Manuel's turn.

"Just like we practiced," Uncle Manuel whispered as they sat down on the piano bench. All the way through the song, they stayed together, and only one time did one of Hector's fingers hit a wrong note. When they finished, everybody clapped. "Way to go!" Uncle Manuel whispered as they got up and took a bow.

Later, while enjoying refreshments that the teacher had fixed, an older boy walked over to Hector. His name was David, and he was one of the best students in the group. "I really liked your duet, Hector," David said. "I played that piece two years ago, so I know you did a good job. Keep practicing. It really pays."

"Thanks," Hector said. "I will."

● *"No discipline seems pleasant at the time, but painful. Later on, however, it produces a harvest of righteousness and peace for those who have been trained by it." Hebrews 12:11*

● For Younger Children

How do you think Hector felt before the piano duet? How do you think he felt after the piano duet?

Do you think Hector was glad he had practiced? Why or why not?

What's something you're glad you've practiced and learned to do?

● For Older Children

What good advice did David give Hector?

How might David's advice help Hector when he gets tired of practicing the piano?

Think of something that's hard for you to work at (homework, music lessons, sports practice, etc). Ask God to help you stick with it.

● ●

Schedule time this week to be together as a family. Select one of these suggested activities to expand your family's understanding of self-control and perseverance.

FAMILY TIMES

Who Am I?

One person in your family chooses a famous person in history (Thomas Edison, Alexander Graham Bell, Florence Nightingale, Albert Einstein, Marie Curie, Helen Keller, Benjamin Franklin, Eli Whitney, etc.). He or she may wish to read about the person in an encyclopedia. Then play a game of twenty questions. Family members take turns asking no more than twenty *yes* or *no* questions to determine the person's identity. After the person has been identified, talk about the ways in which this person must have learned self-control. Ask questions such as, "What skills did (he) have to learn? How hard do you think it was to learn and practice those skills? What if (she) had given up at the first sign of difficulty? What benefit did (he) gain from (his) practice and work?"

String Pictures

Cut string in varying lengths, giving each person 8–10 pieces. Each person thinks of something he or she practices or works at and draws a string picture showing his or her actions. (See sketch for sample string picture.) The string picture may be saved by gluing the string to a piece of paper. Variation: Use toothpicks instead of string.

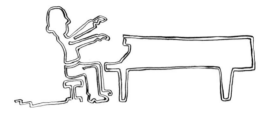

Just for Fun
Plan a fun game to play with your family: play catch using baseball hats as gloves; toss Ping-Pong balls into coffee cans; toss a Frisbee into a box; see who can walk across the room the quickest with an orange between his or her knees. Comment, "The first time you tried (catching a ball with a baseball hat), it probably was a little hard. The first time you try any new skill or task, it will probably be a little hard. Learning to do anything well takes time and effort."

Prayer

Key Verse
"Pray continually."
1 Thessalonians 5:17

Key Thought
Talking with God is not just asking for things; it builds our relationship with Him.

Many young children view prayer as something like magical incantations. They believe that if they say the right words in the right way, God will answer their prayers. Most children enjoy repeating memorized prayers, perhaps feeling confident that the words are "approved."

This week your child will explore the part that prayer plays in building a personal relationship with God. Prayer is not just a means of asking God to do things. It is primarily the way we build a loving, trusting relationship with God.

WEEK 2

DAY 1

Midori never liked having to go to bed earlier than her older sister Aliki. Midori was certain she was missing something exciting that only happened once she went to sleep.

"I know you want to stay up, honey," her mother said, "but it is time for you to be in bed."

"But . . ." Midori tried to think of something to say that would convince her mother to let her stay up later.

"No buts," Mother said firmly. "You're not going to miss anything wonderful by going to bed now."

Midori realized that arguing was not going to help. She noticed that Mother had that look in her eye that said she was tired and was not about to give in to any foolishness about staying up late.

Midori climbed into bed and started to lay her head back on the pillow. Mother asked, "Do you want to pray first or last tonight?" They usually took turns. One night Midori would pray first. The next night, whichever parent was putting her to bed would start off.

"I don't want to pray," Midori said. Her mother was surprised. Midori had never said that before. "Why not, Midori?" her mother asked.

"I don't know what to pray about," Midori explained.

"What about your little bedtime prayer?" Mother asked.

"I think God's tired of it," Midori said. "I'm tired of it too."

"Then," Mother said, "just tell God about your problems, your hopes, and thank Him for something. You could even tell God you're tired of always saying your bedtime prayer."

"Really?" Midori asked. "He wouldn't get mad?"

"He won't get mad," Mother answered. "God's interested in everything about you. He wants you to tell Him whatever you're thinking or feeling."

"OK," Midori said. "Here goes." And she told God all about her day.

● *"Be joyful in hope, patient in affliction, faithful in prayer." Romans 12:12*

● **For Younger Children**
How do you feel when it's time for you to go to bed?
What's something you do every night before you go to sleep?
Why is it a good thing to pray every night before you go to sleep?

● **For Older Children**
What would you tell God about your day?
Why do you think God is interested in what you think and feel?
What do you think it means to be "faithful in prayer?"

●●●●●●●●●●●●●●●●●●●●●●●●●●●●●●●●●●●●●●

WEEK 2

DAY
2

The very last thing Midori said in her prayer that night was, "And please help Uncle Tomoko get better. In Jesus' name, Amen." Tomoko was her father's brother, and he had been very sick for several days with the flu.

Just as her Mother was about to begin her prayer, Midori rolled over onto one elbow and asked, "Why do we pray for other people?"

"What do you mean, dear?" Mother asked, surprised by another one of Midori's questions.

"Doesn't God already know Uncle Tomoko is sick?" Midori asked.

"Of course," Mother said.

Midori thought for a moment, then she asked, "Does God wait till we pray before He decides to help Uncle Tomoko?"

"No, dear," Mother replied. "God doesn't need to be talked into doing what's best for Uncle Tomoko."

"So why pray for him?" Midori wanted to know.

"That's a good question for a little girl so late at night," Mother answered. "Remember, I don't understand everything about God or about prayer. God is so much greater than I am."

"I know, I know," Midori said. "So why should we pray for Uncle Tomoko?"

"Let me ask you something," Mother said. "Something that might help you understand why praying for people is so important."

"OK," Midori said.

Mother asked, "Do you remember the other night when Aliki's friend Natalie spent the night with us?"

"Sure," Midori said.

"Do you remember that you and Aliki talked with Natalie about your pets and your friends and your teachers?"

"Sure," Midori said.

"Why did you and Aliki talk with Natalie about those things?"

"Because . . . uh . . . because . . ." Midori mumbled. She did not know what to say. So Mother answered her own question.

"You did it, Midori, because talking with a friend about things that are important to you helps to make you into better friends." Mother paused for a moment, then she went on. "In the same way, talking to God about people and things we care about, helps us to become better friends with God. It helps us know He really cares."

Midori rolled onto her back and smiled. "OK, Mother," she said. "Your turn to pray now."

● *"And pray in the Spirit on all occasions with all kinds of prayers and requests. With this in mind, be alert and always keep on praying for all the saints." Ephesians 6:18*

● **For Younger Children**

What do you like to talk about with your friends?

Why is God like a good friend?

What's something you'd like to tell God about?

● **For Older Children**

How would you have answered Midori's question about praying for others?

Read Ephesians 6:18. Why might someone need to be alert when praying for others?

Whom would you like to pray for?

WEEK 2

DAY
3

"Would you thank God for our breakfast?" Mother asked Aliki. Aliki bowed her head and quickly said, "God is great, God is good, and we thank Him for our food, Amen."

"That was supposed to be a prayer, Aliki," Mother commented, "not a race." Before Aliki could say anything, Midori announced, "I talked to God last night."

Aliki looked up from pouring her cereal. "You did not," she said.

Midori came back with, "Did so!"

"Did not!"

"Did so!"

"Girls!" Mother interrupted their argument. "Aliki, Midori is talking about her prayer last night. That's when she talked with God."

Aliki replied, "Well, I talked to God this morning."

Midori was not impressed. "Did not," Midori said.

Aliki insisted, "Did so."

"Did not."

"Did so," Aliki repeated. "I just said, 'God is great, God is good.' "

Midori disagreed. "That's not a real prayer," she said.

Aliki disagreed right back. "Is so," she said.

Midori was certain she knew what she was talking about. "You were just repeating," she said. "You weren't really talking to God."

Mother decided there had been enough disagreeing. "You're both right," she said. "The important thing in our prayers is our attitude, not the specific words we use."

Midori was not about to admit her sister might have been even partially right. "Even if she just says something she memorized?" Midori asked.

Mother answered, "If we just say words and don't think about what our words mean, we're not really praying. But if a memorized prayer or poem really says what we think or feel, that's fine."

Aliki remembered how she had rattled off her prayer a few moments before. "I guess I should be more careful about how I pray."

"And," Midori added, "you can just talk to God."

"I get it," Aliki said. "We can tell God how we really feel about something. We can tell Him if we're happy or sad or afraid."

Midori agreed. "That helps us know God really cares for us."

Mother relaxed for the first time since breakfast started. "You two catch on so quickly."

● *"Is any one of you in trouble? He should pray. Is anyone happy? Let him sing songs of praise." James 5:13*

● **For Younger Children**
What do you think it means to pray?
    What reasons does James 5:13 give for praying?
    When is a time you can remember to pray?

● **For Older Children**
How would you define prayer to someone?
    Which do you think are better—memorized prayers or praying with your own words? Why?
    What did Aliki and Midori's mom say was most important about prayer?

● ●

WEEK 2

DAY
4

Midori came home from after school Bible club. Even before she asked what was for dinner, she asked her mother, "Who's Father Witchheart?"

"Father Witchheart?" Mother asked. She was slicing vegetables for dinner and was not really thinking about Midori's question.

"Yes," Midori said. "At Bible club we prayed for him. But he's in heaven, and I don't know why he doesn't just talk to God himself."

"Oh," Mother said, sliding the vegetables into a big bowl, "I know what you mean. You're talking about 'Our Father, which art in heaven.' "

"That's what I said," Midori replied.

"Let me say that line slowly," Mother said, wiping her hands on her apron. "It's from a famous prayer Jesus taught. It starts out, 'Our Father.' "

"Father Witchheart?" Midori asked.

"God," Mother said. "God is our Father in heaven.' "

"Oh," Midori said, looking puzzled.

"Now listen carefully. 'Our Father, (pause) which (pause) art in heaven.' Another way to say that is 'Our Father (pause) who (pause) is in heaven.' "

"Oh," Midori said, looking like she was beginning to understand. "But what's the Halloween part?" she asked.

"Jesus taught us to tell God, 'Hallowed be Your name.' Hallowed means holy, special, wonderful."

"Why do we say that?" Midori asked.

"It's important when we pray to remember how great God is. We are not talking to just anybody, we're praying to God."

"Oh," Midori said.

"And while you're setting the table, Midori," Mother said, "why don't you think about some of the great things you know about God. You can tell us about them at dinner."

"OK," Midori agreed. "Can we pray that prayer then too?"

Mother smiled. "What a great idea."

● *Jesus said, "This, then, is how you should pray: 'Our Father in heaven, hallowed be Your name, Your kingdom come, Your will be done on earth as it is in heaven.' " Matthew 6:9-10*

● **For Younger Children**

What did Midori learn the word "hallowed" means?

One important part of prayer is praising God—thanking Him for the wonderful things He's done.

What's something great you know about God?

Tell God thank You for His greatness.

● **For Older Children**

What was Midori confused about?

How is talking to God different than talking to just anybody?

Why might Jesus have taught His followers to begin their prayers by talking about how great God is?

● ●

WEEK 2

DAY 5

Midori still did not like going to bed earlier than her older sister Aliki. Midori was still certain she was missing something exciting that only happened once she went to sleep. She crawled into bed, pulled the covers up under chin, and glared up at her father who was putting her to bed.

Her father folded his arms across his chest and smiled down at his youngest daughter. "Just think of it like this," he suggested. "You get a head start on some happy dreams."

Midori liked that idea. "You mean, while Aliki's still brushing her teeth and stuff, I can be dreaming already?"

"Right," Father agreed.

"And," Midori added, "I can get my prayers in before her?"

"What does that mean?" Father asked.

" 'Cause," Midori said, getting excited about her idea, "if we both ask for the same stuff, I'll get it 'cause I asked first.''

"Wait," Father laughed. "Didn't you and Mother talk last night that prayer is not just asking God for things?"

"Oh, yeah. I forgot," Midori answered. She could never understand how Father and Mother always knew whatever she had said to the other parent.

"So," Father asked, "what's the real reason we pray?"

Midori had to think about that question for a moment. She sat up in bed and then she guessed, "To know God better?"

"Precisely," Father said. "So what are some important things you want to talk to God about tonight?"

Midori thought for a moment, then she said, "Nothing really important."

"Nothing?" Father asked. "Are you sure?"

"Except," Midori wondered, "could I thank Him for listening to me even when I don't have much to say?"

"You sure can," Father laughed. "I really think He'd love to hear you say 'thank You.' "

● *"Hear my prayer, O God; listen to the words of my mouth." Psalm 54:2*

● **For Younger Children**
What did Midori say was the real reason we should pray?

Do you think God only listens to our prayers when we pray about important things? Why or why not?

What's something you want to tell God?

● **For Older Children**
Why do you think God likes to hear our prayers?

When is a time you like to talk to God?

Thank God for listening to your prayers.

● ●

Schedule time this week to be together as a family. Select one of these suggested activities to expand your family's understanding of what it means to pray to God.

FAMILY TIMES

Psalm of Prayer
Choose one of these Scripture passages to read: Psalms 136:1-5; 146:1-3; 150:1-5. Discuss the Scripture by asking, "What do these verses tell you

about God? What was the writer of these verses praising God for?'' Letter the words of the passage on a large piece of paper. With your family decide who will read each sentence or phrase (solo, duet, trio, all). Then decide the expression for each sentence or phrase (loudly, quietly, whispering, slowly, quickly). Mark your decisions on the paper. (Optional: You may also decide to clap, snap fingers, or stamp feet to provide emphasis for certain words.) Read the psalm together as a family prayer.

Prayer Booklet

Talk about these different kinds of prayers—praising God for His greatness, thanking God for what He's given us, asking God's help for others, asking God's help for ourselves. Each person chooses one or more of these categories and on separate pieces of paper writes a sentence prayer in the category. When the prayers are complete, staple them together to make a family prayer booklet. Read the booklet together.

Tip for Younger Children: A younger child may draw a picture to represent his or her prayers. He or she may also enjoy decorating a cover for the booklet.

Mealtime Prayers

Choose one or more of these ways to encourage family members to participate in mealtime (or bedtime) prayers. (1) Begin by saying, "Thank You, God, for. . . ." Each person completes the sentence with a word or phrase. (2) Sing a familiar praise song together such as "The Doxology," "God Is So Good," or another song with which your family is familiar. (3) Each person tells something for which he or she is thankful that starts with the same letter as his or her first (or middle) name. One person includes these items in a prayer of thanks. (4) One person gives these directions, one at a time, for a short time of silent prayer. "Tell God thank You for something great He's made. Thank God for something good He's given you. Ask God to help a friend in need. Ask God to help you in a special way."

The Ten Commandments

Many people view laws, at least certain laws, as restrictions on their rights and freedoms. Often the Ten Commandments are described as being negative regulations, focusing on what people cannot do.

A better balanced view of the Ten Commandments is to recognize the protection they provide by calling attention to actions and attitudes which are destructive. Only when we understand potential dangers are we able to live safely in true freedom.

Key Verse
"You shall have no other gods before Me."
Exodus 20:3

Key Thought
God gave the Ten Commandments to teach all people the right way to live.

WEEK 3

DAY 1

Josh and Laura's Sunday School teacher finished the story of God giving the Ten Commandments to Moses. "To help us remember this story and the commandments," Mr. Welsh announced, "we're going to do two projects. You can create pictures of Moses receiving the Ten Commandments. Or you can make a plaster model of the stone tablets on which God wrote the commands."

It took a few minutes for everyone to decide which project they preferred. Laura ended up in the group making pictures. Josh chose to make the tablets.

"Before we start," Mr. Welsh said, "there is one important question we all need to answer."

The third- and fourth-graders were anxious to get started on their projects. But when Mr. Welsh had a question to ask, they knew they were going to have to answer the question.

"The question is," Mr. Welsh continued, "why are the Ten Commandments important?"

Emily Potter raised her hand. "Because God gave them," she announced.

"That's a big part of why they're important," Mr. Welsh said. "But why did God give them?"

When Mr. Welsh called on him, Josh said, "To help us know how to live?"

Mr. Welsh smiled and said, "That's another big part of why they're important. But why does God care how we live?"

"Because He loves us," Laura blurted out.

"Right, Laura," he said. "Because God loves us and does not want us to be hurt, He gave us these commands as warnings. As you work on your projects, we'll talk about how obeying these commandments makes our lives better."

The children hoped they could get started on their projects now. But Mr. Welsh had one more question. "For example," he said, "the first two commands say, 'You shall have no other gods before Me,' and 'You shall not make for yourself an idol.' How do those commands make our lives better?"

No one raised a hand.

"We need God's help to live the best lives possible," Mr. Welsh said. "But God can only help us if we recognize that He is the only, true God." Mr. Welsh paused for a moment, then he asked, "Are you ready to start work?"

Everyone said, "Yes."

● *"You shall not make for yourself an idol in the form of anything in heaven above or on the earth beneath or in the waters below." Exodus 20:4*

● **For Younger Children**

When you hear the word "rules," what do you think of?

When you're playing a game, how do rules help you?

Why are God's rules important?

● **For Older Children**

What do you know about the Ten Commandments?

What were some of the reasons Mr. Welsh said God gave the Ten Commandments?

Which reason do you think is the most important? Why?

● ●

DAY 2

Josh and Laura's Sunday School class was hard at work on projects about the Ten Commandments. Laura's group was making pencil sketches of scenes at Mt. Sinai. Josh's group was measuring plaster and water to mix together and pour into a mold of the tablets of stone. As they worked, Mr. Welsh asked the class, "What do you think the third command means about misusing God's name?"

A large boy with plaster dust on the front of his shirt said, "That's swearing when you get angry. Sayin' stuff like, uh, like. . . ."

Mr. Welsh interrupted him. "You don't need to say it. We've all heard swearing. What's wrong with swearing?"

A girl who had spilled water on her blouse said, "Swearing's against the commandment."

Mr. Welsh was not satisfied. "Why is it against the commandment? Did God just think up a list of things and decide to say they were wrong?"

All together, the class said, "No."

Mr. Welsh nodded his head. "You're right. God had a reason for warning about how we used His name. Think for a minute. What's another time when people use the word 'swearing'?"

Emily Potter knew this one. "In court, with a judge, when you're a witness."

Josh chimed in, "When someone swears to tell the truth."

"Right," said Mr. Welsh. "Can you tell me another word we could use in that sentence instead of 'swear' to tell the truth?"

Laura answered. "Promise? I promise to tell the truth?"

"Right again," said Mr. Welsh. "Someone who promises or swears to tell the truth, and who uses God's name to make that promise sound stronger, is misusing God's name. Especially if the promise is not true."

The boy with the plaster on his shirt asked, "But what if someone just says God's name and doesn't mean anything by it?"

Mr. Welsh answered, "God's name is so wonderful and so important that it shows lack of respect to use His name without thinking what it means. And," he went on, "if we don't really respect God for His power and greatness, we won't be able to trust Him to help us when we need Him."

● *"You shall not misuse the name of the Lord your God." Exodus 20:7*

● **For Younger Children**

Why is God's name so special?

God wants us to show respect or honor to Him when we talk about Him. What can you say about God to show that you honor Him?

Ask God's help in respecting Him in your words and actions.

● **For Older Children**

Why do you think some people swear?

How do some kids show disrespect for God? How might someone your age show respect for God?

What can you do to show respect for God?

WEEK 3

DAY 3

Josh and Laura's Sunday School class was still hard at work on projects about the Ten Commandments. Laura's group was finishing pencil sketches of scenes at Mt. Sinai. Josh's group had just poured a wet plaster mixture into a mold of the tablets of stone.

Mr. Welsh was pleased with everyone's work. He asked the class a question about the fourth and fifth commandments. "Why do you think God wants us to keep the Sabbath Day holy and to honor our parents?"

A girl who had a plaster smudge on her left cheek asked, "What's the Sabbath?"

Mr. Welsh explained. "In Bible times, the Sabbath was Saturday, the seventh day of the week."

The same girl asked, "So why was Saturday supposed to be special?"

Mr. Welsh laughed. "Isn't that what I asked you?"

Several of the children answered all at once, "It's good," "It's holy," and "It's like Sunday now."

Mr. Welsh gestured that he wanted more of an answer. He asked, "What was good or holy about Saturday?"

Emily Potter answered that one. "God rested on the seventh day after making the world."

"Right, Emily," Mr. Welsh said. "Now, what happens to people who don't keep one day a week as special?"

The children looked at one another. "I dunno," Josh admitted.

Mr. Welsh explained. "The Sabbath was to be a day of rest so that people and animals would not be forced to work every day of their lives. No one would be very healthy or happy if they had to work all the time. The

Sabbath was also a day for honoring God. Every week, one day was to be set aside to help people remember God's love and goodness."

Laura spoke up and said, "Otherwise, we'd forget God."

"Right," Mr. Welsh said. "And don't forget the next command. Why do you suppose God wants us to honor our parents?"

The children looked at one another again. "I dunno," Josh claimed.

"Oh, right!" Mr. Welsh laughed. "You guys just don't want to admit it. During the week, think about the reasons to honor parents. Next Sunday we'll add color to the pictures and carve the commands into the plaster."

● *"Remember the Sabbath day by keeping it holy. . . . Honor your father and your mother." Exodus 20:8, 12*

● **For Younger Children**

What do you think it means to honor your parents?

What does your family usually do on Sundays?

What can a family do to show they remember God's love and goodness?

● **For Older Children**

What reasons can you think of for honoring your father and your mother?

Why is it good for people to have a day of rest?

God wants us to remember Him all the days of the week. But what is something you can do one day a week as a special reminder of who God is?

● ●

WEEK 3

DAY
4

Riding home from church, Laura and Josh told their family about their Ten Commandments projects.

"I'm drawing a picture of Moses climbing up the mountain to meet God," Laura said.

"And I'm making a big plaster block for writing the Ten Command-ments," Josh said.

Their younger brother, Chris, asked, "What are ten commands?"

"Command-ments, Chris," Laura said.

"So what are they?" Chris asked.

Their older brother, Ryan, decided to show what he knew. "They're ten laws God gave to Moses," he said.

"God wrote them on stone tablets," Josh added.

Chris looked puzzled. "Tablets?" he asked.

Ryan explained. "They were like big, flat, smooth stones that words could be carved on."

Mom decided to join the conversation. Dad was busy driving and just listened without saying anything. Mom said, "You three seem to know a lot about the commandments. How many do you remember?"

Josh answered with the first one, "Worship no other god."

Laura named the second, "Don't make any idols."

Mom nodded and said, "That's two."

Laura named the third commandment, "Don't use God's name in a wrong way."

Josh added the fourth, "Keep the Sabbath special."

Ryan asked, "Isn't there one about honoring your parents?."

Mom laughed and said, "There sure is. And you kids had better not forget it."

Josh was counting on his fingers and knew they had named five commandments so far.

"And we're not supposed to murder, or steal."

Laura added, "Or commit adulthood."

Mom and Dad both laughed. "The word is adultery, Laura," Mom said.

"I knew that," Laura said. "What does it mean?"

Mom looked over at Dad, hoping he would answer this one. He just kept driving, so she said, "Adultery would be if I broke my promise to your dad and started acting like I was married to some other man."

"Dad, you wouldn't let her do that, would you?" Josh said.

"No way!" Dad laughed.

Mom added one more thing as Dad turned their minivan into their long driveway. "Adultery would hurt our whole family. That's why God gave us these commands, to warn us against doing things that hurt ourselves and other people."

"Good answer," Dad said as he turned off the engine.

● *"You shall not murder. You shall not commit adultery. You shall not steal."*
Exodus 20:13-15

● **For Younger Children**
How many of the Ten Commandments can you remember?
What is something the commandments say to do?
What is something the commandments say NOT to do?
If you disobey a commandment, how might it hurt you?

● **For Older Children**

How would you summarize what the Ten Commandments say about how we should treat God?

How would you summarize what the commandments say about how we should treat others?

Thank God for giving us the Ten Commandments and ask His help in obeying them.

● ●

WEEK 3

DAY
5

Josh and Laura's Sunday School class was finishing the Ten Commandments projects they had started a week earlier. Laura's group was adding color to their scenes of Mt. Sinai. Josh's group was using nails to carve each command into the plaster tablets they had made.

Josh looked up from writing the ninth commandment. "What is 'give false testimony'?" he asked Mr. Welsh.

"False testimony," Mr. Welsh answered, "means to accuse a person of something he didn't do. It means to lie about someone."

Josh looked over at the table where Laura was working and asked loudly, "Like when my sister said I ate the last piece of cake this week?"

Laura retorted. "You did so eat the last piece. You had cake on your face!"

Josh spread out his hands to show his innocence. "No way!" he said. "The last piece was already gone. I just finished off some crumbs."

Laura looked surprised, "Really?" she asked.

Mr. Welsh decided to use Josh and Laura's situation to explain a little more about the commandments. "It doesn't sound like Laura lied," he said. "But the accusation she made was wrong. What do you need to do to fix the problem, Laura?"

Josh answered before Laura had a chance. "She needs to give me her dessert after dinner," he claimed. " 'Cause I got cheated out of mine because of what she said."

Laura did not like that suggestion. She said, "But Mom made apple pie for today. It's my favorite!"

Josh looked smug. "Too bad," he said. "I get your piece."

Suddenly, Mr. Welsh thought that it wasn't such a good idea to use Josh and Laura's situation. He said, "Maybe you two should think about the last commandment God gave."

Laura looked at a chart on the wall and read aloud, " 'You shall not covet?' What's covet?" she asked.

Mr. Welsh said, "Covet means to want something that belongs to some-one else, and to be jealous or envious of that person."

Laura looked at her brother and warned, "So don't covet my pie, Josh!"

Josh looked right back at her. "It's not yours anymore. It's mine. All mine!"

Mr. Welsh felt he had to say something. He said, "I think I detect a little greed in the air. Maybe we need to talk a little more about God's commands."

Josh leaned back in his chair and said, "I was joking! I was joking! Laura can have her pie!" And the whole class laughed together.

And by the way, the pictures and the plaster tablets turned out just fine.

● *"You shall not give false testimony against your neighbor. You shall not covet . . . anything that belongs to your neighbor." Exodus 20:16-17*

● **For Younger Children**

What had Laura said about her brother that wasn't true?

If you were Laura, how would you have fixed the problem her untrue words caused?

When might it be tempting to lie about someone else? Ask God to help you always tell the truth.

● **For Older Children**

How might a person who is covetous act?

When have you wanted something that belonged to someone else? What did you say or do?

Instead of letting envy cause you to act in unkind ways, what should you do to obey Exodus 20:16-17?

● ●

FAMILY TIMES
Schedule time this week to be together as a family. Select one of these suggested activities to expand your family's understanding of the ways God's rules, the Ten Commandments, can help us.

Mystery Shape Puzzles

Cut two large pieces of construction paper into the shapes of stone tablets (see sketch).

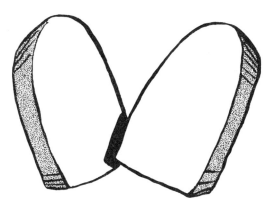

On one tablet use a felt-tip pen to letter the words of Exodus 20:3. On the other tablet letter (in a different color) the words of Exodus 20:16-17. Cut apart each tablet to make two puzzles of 8–12 pieces each. You may wish to add a design or decoration to each piece of puzzle so it's obvious which side is face up. Mix up the puzzle pieces. Without identifying the shape of the completed puzzles, invite family members to sort the pieces and put together the puzzles. After the puzzles are complete, read the verses together. Ask, "How would you say these verses in your own words—using six words or less?"

Tip for Younger Children: Cut the puzzles into fewer pieces.

Penny Flip

On a large piece of paper in random fashion write these key words for each of the Ten Commandments: lie, adultery, Sabbath, gods, covet, parents, idol, murder, steal, name. Put the paper on a table or the floor. Each person takes a turn to flip a penny onto the paper and reads the word on which the penny lands (or the word closest to where the penny lands). Then he or she tells the commandment from which that word is taken. Players may refer to Exodus 20:3-8, 12-17 for help.

The Greatest Commandment

Here's a way to enrich your studies of the Ten Commandments this week. Ask, "Which of God's commandments do you think is the greatest? Why?" After each family member has had a chance to respond say, "Let's find out how Jesus answered this question." Read Matthew 22:34-40 aloud. Then each person tells a way he or she will obey these commandments.

Giving Thanks

Key Verse
"Give thanks to the Lord, for He is good; His love endures forever."
1 Chronicles 16:34

Key Thought
God's goodness and love deserve our thanks and praise.

When King David brought the ark of the covenant back to Jerusalem, he led a great celebration of all the people (1 Chronicles 15–16 and Psalm 105). There was dancing and music and food. But it was more than just a time of great enjoyment. It was a time of expressing gratitude to God for "all of His wonderful acts" (1 Chronicles 16:9). David wrote a psalm of thanks to the Lord, a psalm which recounts many of God's "wonders," "miracles," and "judgments" (v. 12). David describes numerous reasons why the Lord is "most worthy of praise" (v. 25) and challenges all people and all of creation to "ascribe to the Lord the glory due His name" (v. 29). The final stanza of the psalm begins with a declaration which is repeated numerous times throughout the Psalms and other parts of Scripture: "Give thanks to the Lord, for He is good; His love endures forever" (1 Chronicles 16:34). Of all the heritage parents can pass on to children, perhaps none is greater than the sense of gratitude and appreciation for all that God has done.

WEEK 4

DAY 1

"Where we goin' for Thanksgiving, Dad?" DJ asked as his dad was stretched out on the couch reading the paper. Dad looked over the top of the newspaper at his son and said, "We're stayin' home this year. Mom and I both have to work the next day, so there's not time to go very far." He lifted the newspaper and started to read again.

"Then who's comin' here with us?" DJ's sister, AJ, asked.

Dad lowered the paper and explained, "Grandma's going up north to Aunt Claire's, and Uncle Cedric's family is going to be with his in-laws. None of our relatives can come this year."

"Bummer!" DJ snorted. "It's gonna be an awful Thanksgiving."

"No," Dad replied, "I think it's going to be our best Thanksgiving ever."

"How can that be?" AJ wanted to know.

"First," Dad said, "the night before, we're all going to work together to make a huge batch of Mom's famous whipped gelatin salad. It'll be a Gorman family extravaganza!"

DJ thought his dad was trying to make something boring sound exciting. "Why do all that?" DJ asked. "Is Mom gonna let me eat all I want this year?"

"There's a reason, DJ," Dad declared. "On Thanksgiving morning, you two will help me take most of that whipped salad down to the City Mission. It'll be part of the big Thanksgiving dinner they're serving for homeless people."

DJ thought that was an intriguing idea. But AJ wasn't so sure. "Is Mom coming?" she asked.

"No," Dad said. "Mom's going to stay right here and cook a big Thanksgiving dinner for us and our company."

"Company?" the twins asked in unison.

"We've invited two other families to have dinner with us," Dad answered.

"Who?" the twins asked in unison.

"People who wouldn't have much Thanksgiving if we didn't invite them," Dad answered.

"Oh," the twins said in unison.

"We won't have a boring Thanksgiving," Dad added. "We get to help some other people have more to be thankful for. That might turn out to be even more fun than what we usually do."

Dad lifted the paper and started reading again. The twins just looked at each other.

● *"Do not worry about anything. But pray and ask God for everything you need. And when you pray, always give thanks." Philippians 4:6,* EB

● **For Younger Children**
What do you like about Thanksgiving?

What was the Gorman family going to share with others at Thanksgiving?

What's something your family might share with another family at Thanksgiving?

● **For Older Children**
If you were AJ or DJ, how would you feel about their family's plans for Thanksgiving?

How does your family usually celebrate Thanksgiving?

How might your family help others at Thanksgiving?

WEEK 4

DAY
2

AJ and her twin brother DJ were not excited about having Thanksgiving dinner with strangers. They wanted to have cousins and uncles and aunts around for a holiday. AJ sat on the floor by the couch where her dad was still reading the newspaper. She waited until he started to turn a page before she asked the question she had been thinking of for several minutes.

"Dad, can't we have a normal Thanksgiving?" AJ asked.

"What's normal?" Dad asked from behind the newspaper. "Especially with this family!"

AJ ignored Dad's attempt to make a joke. She said, "A big dinner, cousins to play with, funny stories by Uncle Cedric, great desserts. THAT'S normal!"

"Yeah," DJ added, "we ALWAYS play with our cousins and stuff!"

Dad lowered the newspaper, looked first at AJ and then at DJ. Then he asked, "How come I didn't hear anything in there about thanksgiving?"

"That WAS Thanksgiving!" AJ insisted.

"REAL Thanksgiving!" DJ added.

"But where's the giving thanks part?" Dad asked.

"Uh . . . uh . . . uh . . ." the twins stammered in unison.

Dad sat up on the couch and put the newspaper aside. "How about if this year we really try to focus on the reasons why we're thankful?" Dad asked.

"I'm always thankful for all the food," DJ replied.

"And I'm thankful when our cousins come to play," AJ added.

"Especially the great pies and whipped cream," DJ continued.

"Except maybe for Cousin Eddie," AJ said, "he's kind of a brat sometimes."

"And last year we played hide-'n-seek in the dark down in Uncle Cedric's basement," DJ remembered.

"I was thankful I got to play with Chantel and Jessica," AJ declared, hoping she sounded thankful enough to impress her dad.

"Wait a minute, you two," Dad interrupted. "I'm not talking about just being thankful for what we do to celebrate a holiday. We need to think about ALL the ways God has been good to us."

"Oh," the twins said in unison.

"I have an assignment for you two," Dad said. "I want each of you to make a list of reasons why you're thankful."

DJ looked at his sister. This sounded like homework.

● *"I will give thanks to the Lord because of His righteousness and will sing praise to the name of the Lord Most High." Psalm 7:17*

● **For Younger Children**

What were some of the things that AJ and DJ were thankful for?
Why does Psalm 7:17 say we should thank God?
What are some reasons you're thankful?
Tell God thank You.

● **For Older Children**

Why might AJ and DJ not be excited about sharing Thanksgiving with strangers?
What did Mr. Gorman say we should be thankful for at Thanksgiving?
What are you thankful for?

● ●

WEEK 4

DAY
3

The kitchen in the Gorman home was a very busy place the night before Thanksgiving. Mom, Dad, and the twins were all wearing aprons as the family finished what seemed like dozens of whipped gelatin salads. The next morning the twins were going with their dad to take the salads to the City Mission for their big Thanksgiving dinner for homeless people. There were really only twelve salads, but the kitchen was full of clutter.

"Can I pour the last one?" AJ asked.

"Is there enough gelatin left?" Mom asked.

"Just barely," DJ answered.

"The real question," Dad asked, "is can we fit one more container in the refrigerator?"

"We could set it outside," DJ suggested. "It's cold enough."

"Oh, sure," AJ replied as filled the last container. "Happy Thanksgiving for all the cats out there."

Mom opened the refrigerator door, looking for an empty space for that last dish. "I think I can balance it on top of the green dish in the back," she said. "Then we're done."

"Except for cleanup," Dad said.

"I'll lick the beaters and spoons!" DJ announced.

"I'll lick the bowl with the whipped cream," AJ added.

"You two are so helpful!" Dad laughed as he started stacking pots and pans in the sink.

Mom wedged the last dish into the refrigerator and checked to be sure nothing would spill. "I'm sure glad our neighbors left town this afternoon. I've got their refrigerator full of everything for our dinner tomorrow." Then she gently closed the refrigerator door.

As the door closed, a magnet holding a large sheet of paper on the front of the door slid down to the floor. "Even the outside of the refrigerator is full," Mom said, picking up the sheet of paper. "What is this big thing, anyway?"

"That's my list of things I'm thankful for," AJ answered.

"And my list is underneath," DJ added.

"Wow!" Mom said, holding up the two lists. "You two sure have a lot of reasons to be thankful. God must be very, very good to you."

"He is, Mom," the twins said in unison.

● *"The Lord is my strength and my shield; my heart trusts in Him, and I am helped. My heart leaps for joy and I will give thanks to Him in song." Psalm 28:7*

● **For Younger Children**

What are some examples of ways God is good to people?

How is God good to you?

How can you show your thankfulness to God?

● **For Older Children**

What do you think were some of the items on DJ and AJ's lists?

How did the writer of Psalm 28:7 feel about God? Why?

How has God helped you? Thank Him for His loving care.

● ●

WEEK 4

DAY 4

DJ and his twin sister AJ got out of the car. "Each of you carry one salad at a time," their dad said. They were delivering twelve whipped gelatin salads to the City Mission as part of Thanksgiving dinner for homeless people.

Dad balanced a salad in each hand and led the twins toward the side door of the mission. "One of you will have to hold the door open," Dad said. "I will!" DJ shouted and pulled on the door handle. "It's locked!" he said.

"Well, knock on it," AJ said. DJ knocked twice, but not very loudly.

"Knock louder," AJ said. Just as DJ was getting ready to pound on the door, it opened from the inside. "Great looking salads!" the man at the door said. "Come on in!"

It took three trips to bring in all twelve salads. The big kitchen was full of people working. Next to the kitchen was a large room with many long tables set up.

"How many people are going to eat here?" DJ asked.

"Hundreds," the man said. "You're helping a lot of people today, kids. A lot of lonely people."

In the car on the way home, the twins were very quiet. For a few minutes, that is. Then AJ said, "It's not a very cheery place for a holiday dinner, is it?"

DJ added, "I bet those people don't have much to be thankful for."

AJ agreed, then she said, "Well, they can be thankful for our salads."

DJ disagreed. He said, "I mean, besides the dinner. What can they be glad about if they have to go there for Thanksgiving?"

"Good question, Deej," Dad said. He decided to ask another question. "Do you think only people who have a nice house and family can be thankful?"

The twins thought about that. Then AJ asked, "What's the main thing you're thankful for, Dad?"

"That's easy," Dad said. "I'm thankful for Jesus, for showing me God's love. Everything good that happens grows out of God's great love."

The twins thought about that the rest of the way home.

● *"Thanks be to God—through Jesus Christ our Lord!" Romans 7:25*

● **For Younger Children**

If you were celebrating Thanksgiving at a mission, how would you feel?

How would you answer the question, "What's the main thing you're thankful for?"

Why does knowing about Jesus' love help a person to be thankful?

● **For Older Children**

What did the twins notice about the City Mission?

What do you think causes someone to be thankful?

How does knowing about Jesus' love make you feel?

Tell God about your thankful feelings.

WEEK 4

DAY 5

The doorbell rang. "I'll get it!" AJ announced. She opened the front door and saw a man and a woman and two girls, both a little younger than AJ.

"Hi," the woman said. "We're the Robinsons."

"Happy Thanksgiving!" AJ's dad said, coming to the door behind her. "Come on in."

AJ stepped back as the Robinsons came inside. Everyone shook hands and AJ learned that the girls' names were Tricia and Alexa. DJ was given the job of taking everyone's coats and putting them away.

Just then, the doorbell rang again. AJ decided to let her dad open the door this time. She suddenly felt shy about meeting more new people.

This time a lady was at the door with an older boy and a younger girl. These were the Jensons. The children's names were Mark and Tracy. Again, DJ took the coats.

"AJ," Mom said, "why don't you show the kids your room and find some things everyone can play with?"

AJ led Tricia and Alexa, Mark and Tracy back to her room. They met DJ coming back from putting the coats away. DJ invited Mark into his room, while the girls went with AJ. At first, everyone seemed shy. But after a short time of getting acquainted, the twins quickly discovered that just because these children were poor, they were not different.

Just then, Mom called them for dinner. Everyone gathered around the dining room table. Dad invited everyone to join hands, and then he thanked God for all the good gifts He has given.

As everyone was being seated, Mr. Robinson said to Dad, "You have a lot to be thankful for, Mr. Gorman."

"I know," Dad answered.

"So do I," Mr. Robinson said.

AJ whispered to Tricia, "How can your dad be thankful when you have to live all jammed in a motel room you don't even like?"

Tricia whispered back, "Dad says God's still good to us. Even when things go wrong, He still loves us."

"That sounds like what my dad says," AJ said out loud and began to help herself to some of Mom's famous whipped gelatin salad.

● *"Give thanks in all circumstances, for this is God's will for you in Christ Jesus." 1 Thessalonians 5:18*

386

● **For Younger Children**

What did AJ learn that surprised her?

How did God show His love to Tricia and her family?

How has God shown His love to you?

● **For Older Children**

Why do you think AJ was feeling shy at first?

What difficult circumstances might kids your age be in?

Why might God want us to always be thankful—no matter what situation we're in?

Being thankful in a difficult situation means we recognize that God is always with us and will keep loving and helping us no matter what happens to us. Thank God for His love.

● ●

Schedule time this week to be together as a family. Select one of these suggested activities to expand your family's understanding of being thankful for all God's gifts.

FAMILY TIMES

Thanksgiving Cornucopia

Roll a 10-inch square of brown, yellow, or orange construction paper into a cone and staple to make a cornucopia (see sketch). With your family collect nuts, autumn leaves, fruit, dried stalks of grain, etc., and arrange in your cornucopia to make a Thanksgiving decoration.

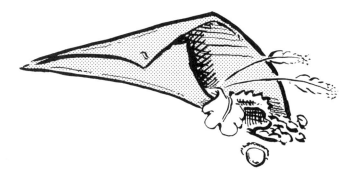

Number Art

Use a pencil or crayon to write a number from 0–9 on a blank piece of paper. Give your paper to someone in your family. He or she draws a picture of something for which he or she is thankful, incorporating the number into the picture. Repeat the process until each person has had a turn to write a number and draw a picture. Then, thank God for His goodness, mentioning the items in the pictures.

Tip for Younger Children: Instead of writing a number, a younger child may draw a doodle, squiggly line, etc.

Thankful Dinner

Plan and prepare a special dinner together as a reminder of God's gifts of food. On separate pieces of paper letter these parts of a meal: beverage, salad, vegetable, meat, bread, dessert. Put the pieces of paper in a bowl. To receive his or her meal assignment each person chooses one of the pieces of paper. Then, each family member thinks of his or her favorite food to have for that part of the meal, lists ingredients for a shopping list, and prepares the item for the dinner.

Tip for Younger Children: A younger child will need extra help or may be paired with an older child.

• •

The Church

A child's concept of the church is formed mainly by the church experiences the child has had. The idea that people all over the world form one great body, the church, is very difficult for a child to grasp. Equally difficult is for a child to understand the purpose and meaning behind many of the familiar things that go on in the life of the local church. Typically, the child views the church in very self-centered terms. That which affects them personally is to them the most important feature of the church. This week you have the opportunity to encourage your child to look beyond the shape of the building and the form of the programs. Help your child think about what the church really is: people committed to following Jesus Christ and to encouraging each other.

Key Verse
"He is the Head of the body made up of His people — that is, His church."
Colossians 1:18,
TLB

Key Thought
The church is people — not a building or an organization — who love Jesus and trust Him to forgive their sins.

• •

WEEK 5

DAY
1

It was a sad day at church. Pastor Daniels had resigned, and this was his last day at the church. He had been at the church for almost fifteen years and was the only pastor that Eric and Jessie Lacey had known. Now he was going to be pastor of a church in another city, and Eric and Jessie were not the only ones who were sad that he was leaving.

During the church service, people were invited to come to the front and tell a good memory they had about Pastor Daniels. Eric's dad was one of the first to talk. He told about a time a group of men went fishing, and he and Pastor Daniels both caught cold, but neither of them caught any fish.

"These were supposed to be GOOD memories," Pastor Daniels laughed.

"I'm getting to the good part. Instead of grumbling and complaining, Pastor Daniels stayed cheerful and friendly. He showed me that a Christian can show God's love even when things aren't going so well."

Another man thanked Pastor Daniels for teaching God's Word clearly so that it was easy to understand. A woman thanked Pastor Daniels and his wife for being good examples of the things they taught.

Some people told funny stories. Some people told sad stories. Suddenly,

Eric decided he had a story to tell. He walked up to the microphone, feeling very nervous. "I have a good memory about Pastor Daniels," he said. "He plays basketball with us kids out in the parking lot. I beat him once."

"He made a lucky shot!" Pastor Daniels laughed.

Jessie decided that if Eric could tell a story, she could too. She walked to the microphone. She said, "I remember when our Sunday School class went to Pastor Daniels' house. Mrs. Daniels made the best brownies."

After the service, there were refreshments and a chance to say good-bye. Even though people had brought many kinds of desserts, including Mrs. Daniels' fudge brownies, everyone felt sad that the Daniels were leaving.

Afterward, as the Lacey family drove home, Jessie said what they were all thinking, "Our church'll never be the same again."

● *"Now you are the body of Christ, and each one of you is a part of it."*
1 Corinthians 12:27

● **For Younger Children**
What made the Lacey family sad?

People who love and obey God are like members of a family. What does 1 Corinthians 12:27 call this family?

Who are some people you know who are part of God's family?

● **For Older Children**
What did the Lacey family like about Pastor and Mrs. Daniels?

Why are the people who love and obey God like a family?

Who in God's family has helped you? How?

WEEK 5

DAY 2

Sunday morning usually meant a special breakfast at the Lacey house. Dad either fixed pancakes or waffles. Or sometimes Mom fixed scrambled eggs or French toast. Today it was cold cereal.

"Sorry, kids," Dad said, "we've got a lot to do at church this morning to get ready to welcome our new pastor."

"I liked our old pastor," Jessie muttered.

"Do you mean our old pastor who was young or our new pastor who is old?" Eric asked, trying to make a joke.

"Pastor Murray is not old," Mom corrected. "He's old-er. At least he's older than Pastor Daniels."

"He probably won't play basketball with us like Pastor Daniels did," Eric said. "If he's too old to play ball, he's old."

"Well," Dad said, "his children are all grown."

"With no kids around," Eric said, "he probably won't care much about what's goin' on for our age."

Mom decided to change the subject slightly. "I understand," she said, "that his wife works for a bank."

"She probably won't have time to invite our Sunday School class to their house," Jessie grumbled.

"Yeah," Eric agreed, "no more fudge brownies like Mrs. Daniels made."

"Wait a minute," Dad interrupted. "Those things may or may not be different about our new pastor. But they really don't have much to do with what's most important for a church."

"Whaddya mean?" Eric asked. "How can you have a church without fudge brownies?"

"Brownies and basketball are not what makes a church," Dad said. "A church is people who are drawn together because of faith in Jesus."

"Dad's right, kids," Mom said.

"Thank you, Dear," Dad said.

"There are a lot of things," Mom went on, "things we enjoy as part of our church life that are nice, but aren't the reason we go to church."

"Mom's right, kids," Dad said.

"Thank you, Dear," Mom said.

"We can have a church without brownies and basketball," Dad continued, "but we can't have a church without Jesus."

"I'm still gonna miss the brownies," Jessie said.

● *"Now we are all children of God through faith in Jesus Christ."*
Galatians 3:26, TLB

● **For Younger Children**
What special breakfast does your family like to eat?
What are some things you think a church needs?
Why did Mr. Lacey say you can't have a church without Jesus?

● **For Older Children**
What were some of the things Jessie and Eric liked about their church?
What do you like best about being a part of God's family?
Why is believing in Jesus so important for a church?

●●●●●●●●●●●●●●●●●●●●●●●●●●●●●●●●●●●●●●

WEEK 5

DAY
3

Driving home after their new pastor's first Sunday morning, the Lacey family talked about all the things he did things differently from their former pastor. "He sure prayed different," Eric commented. "It wasn't at all like one of Pastor Daniels' prayers."

"The kids' sermon was sure unusual," Jessie added. "I like the way Pastor Daniels did it better."

"And he read the Bible from a different translation," Mom noted.

"And the Communion service was changed around," Dad said. "I don't think I've ever seen Communion served like that."

"And he didn't know my name either," Jessie said.

Thinking maybe they were being too critical, Mom decided to try a different approach. "Well," she began, "do you think God heard his prayer, even if it was different from how Pastor Daniels prays?"

"I guess so," Eric said.

"Did you learn something from the children's sermon, Jessie," Mom asked, "even if it was different from how Pastor Daniels used to do it?"

"Uh, yeah," Jessie answered.

Mom went on. "And I guess the Bible reading was very easy to follow and understand."

"And I have to admit," Dad said, "the Communion service did help us remember that Jesus died for us."

"Maybe," Mom suggested, "it's good for us to be learning that the church is really a lot bigger with a lot more variety than we thought."

Dad picked up Mom's thought and said, "Since the church is people, and all people grow and change, we've got to expect the church to change and grow also."

"But he still didn't know my name," Jessie muttered.

"I guess next time you see him," Mom said, "you'll just have to tell him who you are."

"Oh," Jessie said. She had never thought about doing that.

● *"Consequently, you are . . . fellow citizens with God's people and members of God's household." Ephesians 2:19*

● **For Younger Children**
Would you feel like Jessie and Eric about a new pastor coming to your church? Why or why not?

How do you think Pastor Murray felt about coming to a new church?
How could you help someone who was new to a church?

● **For Older Children**
How was Pastor Murray different from Pastor Daniels?
What are some ways people grow and change?
How might a church grow and change?

● ●

WEEK 5

DAY
4

On Mondays after school, Jessie had children's choir practice at church. When practice was over, she usually walked with her friends to the parking lot. Today as she came out of practice, she happened to look the other way down the hall. She saw the new pastor getting a drink from the drinking fountain.

Jessie remembered that her mom had suggested that the next time she saw the new pastor, she should introduce herself to him. She decided this was as good a time as any.

Pastor Murray looked up as Jessie walked toward him. "How was choir today?" he asked.

"Fine," Jessie said.

"I shook hands with you on Sunday, didn't I?" the pastor asked.

"Yeah," Jessie answered.

"But I haven't learned your name yet, have I?" the pastor asked.

"Nope," Jessie answered.

"It's pretty important to learn people's names, isn't it?" the pastor asked.

"Yeah," Jessie answered.

"And isn't it especially important in a church where God wants us to be kind and gentle and patient with each other?" the pastor asked.

"Yeah," Jessie commented, still not able to think of more than one word at a time.

"Do you have any ideas on how I can learn everybody's name really fast?" the pastor asked.

"Uh, ask 'em?" Jessie suggested, getting out two words and an "uh."

"Not a bad idea," the pastor agreed. "Can I start with you?"

"Sure," Jessie said, back to one word at a time.

"What's your name?" the pastor asked.

"Jessie. Jessie Lacey." That was three words, although two of them were the same.

"Jessie Lacey," the pastor said. Then he asked, "How many chances will you give me if I forget?"

"Uh, how many do you need?" Jessie asked. She was starting to not be so nervous talking to the pastor.

"Sometimes lots," the pastor said. "But if you'll be patient with me, I'm sure it shouldn't take me too long."

"OK," Jessie said. "I'll remind you if you need it."

"Thank you, Jessie Lacey," the pastor said. "I'm glad we're both part of God's family—and this church."

"Me too," Jessie said with a smile.

● *"Therefore, as God's chosen people, holy and dearly loved, clothe yourselves with compassion, kindness, humility, gentleness and patience."*
Colossians 3:12

● **For Younger Children**
At the end of her conversation with Pastor Murray, how do you think Jessie felt about him?

Who is someone you're glad is part of God's family?

Thank God for that person and ask God's help in showing kindness to him or her.

● **For Older Children**
How do you feel when talking to a grownup for the first time?

How were Jessie and Pastor Murray showing kindness to each other?

Who is someone in God's family you can show kindness to? How?

● ●

WEEK 5

DAY 5

The Lacey family was relaxing in the living room. Jessie was telling about meeting the new pastor by the drinking fountain at church. "And I told him my name," she said. "And that I'll be patient if he forgets it sometimes."

Eric decided that if Jessie was going to tell about meeting the new pastor, he would too. "He came by our middler group yesterday and we challenged him to play basketball with us," Eric said. "He said he has a bad knee, but he'll come out and cheer for us. And he said his oldest son's name is Eric."

"How'd he know your name was Eric?" Dad asked.

"I told him," Eric said, sounding as though the answer was so obvious, his dad should have known it.

Dad ignored the tone of Eric's answer and told a story of his own. "Pastor Murray was at our men's prayer breakfast this morning. He had some really helpful things to say about some problems I've been struggling with at work."

Now it was Mom's turn. "Am I the only one in the family," she asked, "who hasn't met the new pastor yet?"

"You shook his hand after church on Sunday," Dad reminded her.

"That doesn't count," Mom said. "It was in the middle of a crowd. He'd never remember me."

"But you talked with his wife for quite a while," Dad reminded her again.

"And I really like her," Mom said, "but I found out some bad news, guys."

"What's that?" Jessie asked.

"She doesn't make fudge brownies," Mom said with a laugh.

Jessie did not see anything funny in Mom's little joke. Jessie was worried about something else. "If we start to like the new pastor," she asked, "does it mean we can't like Pastor Daniels anymore?"

"Not at all," Dad said. "If you can love more than one parent, you can love more than one pastor."

"Who says we love more than one parent?" Eric snickered. "We really only like Mom."

The pillow Dad tossed at Eric just missed his head. It's hard to throw straight when you're laughing.

● *"Therefore encourage one another and build each other up, just as in fact you are doing." 1 Thessalonians 5:11*

● **For Younger Children**

How did the Lacey family help and encourage Pastor Murray and his wife?

What would God's family be like if people did not obey 1 Thessalonians 5:11?

What's one way you can obey this verse?

● **For Older Children**

What is the main idea of 1 Thessalonians 5:11?

How has someone in God's family encouraged and helped you?

How can you encourage and help others in God's family?

Ask God's help in obeying 1 Thessalonians 5:11.

FAMILY TIMES

Schedule time this week to be together as a family. Select one of these suggested activities to expand your family's understanding of how God's family, the church, can show love for God and each other.

Then and Now

Ask, "What do you think the very first church was like?" Then take some time to compare the early church with the church today. Read Acts 2:42-47. Ask these questions, "What did the Christians in the early church do that was the same as the church today? What was different? How has the church grown and changed? Are the changes good or bad? Why?"

Tip for Younger Children: A younger child may enjoy drawing a picture of favorite church activities.

Designer Drawings

Give each person a blank sheet of paper and crayons, pencils, and/or felt-tip pens. "Draw a symbol or design on your paper that reminds you of God's family, the church." To help family members think of ideas, ask questions such as, "What are the main characteristics of God's family? How can you show one of these characteristics in a drawing?" Symbols and/or designs may incorporate traditional Christian symbols such as crosses, hearts, or doves. After each person has drawn and explained his or her symbol, display symbols on a bulletin board or wall in your house.

Helping Hands

Find a way your family can lend a helping hand at your church. Ask a member of your church staff for project ideas. Gardening, cleaning, working in the office (folding, filing, mailing), preparing curriculum materials, or helping in the nursery may be some of the ways your family can show God's love to others in a practical way.

DECEMBER

Worshiping Together

Church services are rarely designed with children in mind. Some churches deal with that fact by providing separate children's programs. Some churches include a children's feature during the worship service. Some assume that by just being in the same room with parents and other adults, children will somehow begin to absorb the meaning of what is going on. Still others virtually ignore the presence of children unless a child creates a disturbance.

Few churches and parents plan for ways children can be helped to benefit from their experiences in a worship service planned for adults. Wrapped up in this week's story of Arthur are many of the most common problems children encounter in an adult worship service. Also included are a few simple examples of actions parents and children can take to make worship more meaningful for a child.

Key Verse
"I rejoiced with those who said to me, 'Let us go to the house of the Lord.' "
Psalm 122:1

Key Thought
God's people need to meet together regularly for worship, learning from and encouraging each other.

WEEK 1

DAY

1

"Do we have to stay for church today?" Arthur asked his mom. He had just come out of Sunday School and hoped he could talk his mom into going home.

"Of course, we're staying for church," his mom said. "We always stay."

"Huh uh," Arthur insisted. "I remember times we went home after Sunday School."

"Those were when one of us wasn't feeling well," his mom answered, "or when we had to go somewhere."

"Well," Arthur whined, "I'm not feeling very good today."

"Arthur," his mom said sternly, "there's nothing wrong with you. We are going to church, and that's final."

Arthur knew he had lost, but he couldn't resist one parting shot. He frowned, stuck his hands in his pockets, and complained, "But it's so boring."

Together they walked into the foyer where Arthur's mom greeted several people and received a church bulletin. As they entered the back of the auditorium, an usher said hello to Arthur's mom and led them to two seats near the back.

Arthur slumped down in his seat and looked miserable. When everyone stood to sing, Arthur stayed in his chair and carefully studied the cracks in the floor. When everyone bowed their heads to pray, Arthur stared up at the ceiling. When everyone listened to the choir sing, Arthur started to conduct a search of his mom's purse. She stopped him when he loudly dropped her keys on the floor.

When the offering plates were passed along each row, Arthur tried to hold the plate long enough to count how much money was in it. When the Bible was being read, Arthur whispered loudly that he had to go to the bathroom.

During the sermon, he repeated the bathroom request three more times and twice asked if he could get a drink. Those questions were not a big problem, but his mom was certain everyone in the building heard the two times he asked how much longer the sermon was going to go. The worst moment for her came when the pastor finished preaching and Arthur sighed, "Finally!"

All in all, it was a fairly typical morning at church for Arthur and his mom.

● *"They joined with the other believers in regular attendance at the apostles' teaching sessions and at the Communion services and prayer meetings."* Acts 2:42, TLB

● **For Younger Children**
If you were Arthur, how would you have felt about going to church?
Why do you think Arthur's mom wanted him to go to church with her?
What do the kids usually do during the worship services at your church?

● **For Older Children**
Have you ever felt like Arthur? When? What did you do when you were bored at church?
What usually happens in the worship service at your church?
What would make church more interesting for you?

●●●

DAY
2

After church, Mom decided to tell Arthur about her childhood in a family that did not go to church. "There was nothing special about Sunday. I didn't know it then, but I missed a lot not being part of a church."

"When did you start going to church?" Arthur asked.

"I was in college when I became a Christian," Mom said. "A friend invited me to church."

Then Arthur asked, "If you didn't have to go to church when you were a kid, how come I have to?"

"Because I don't want you to miss out like I did," Mom answered.

Arthur didn't say anything. He was thinking it might not be too bad to stay home on Sunday mornings.

"I never got to go to Sunday School," Mom went on. "I never heard any of the Bible stories you know."

"How about Noah and the bulrushes?" Arthur asked.

"That was MOSES and the bulrushes," Mom said.

"Oh yeah," Arthur said.

"And I didn't know anything about Jesus," Mom continued. "The only time I heard His name was when people swore."

"Like Christopher's mom?" Arthur asked.

"Worse," Mom answered. "I never got to be in a Sunday School class with other kids who were learning about God. And I never had a Sunday School teacher who loved me like Mrs. Donohue loves you."

Arthur liked Sunday School, so it was easy for him to be glad that his mom took him to Sunday School every week. While he was thinking about that, his mom kept talking.

"I can't tell you how many times going to church has helped me. Sometimes a song or the sermon or a Bible verse has been just what I needed to hear. Sometimes a person has encouraged me with a kind word. You don't know how lucky you are having a church to go to."

Arthur had not heard everything his mom said. He had heard the part about being lucky he could go to church. That reminded him of how bored he had been during the service this morning. That was why he said, "You're the one who had it made. You didn't have sit through boring old church when you were my age."

● *"Let us not give up meeting together . . . but let us encourage one another."*
Hebrews 10:25

● **For Younger Children**

Why did Arthur's mom say she liked to go to church?

What good things did Arthur's mom not want Arthur to miss out on?

What does Hebrews 10:25 say Christians can do when they are together at church?

● **For Older Children**

How was Arthur's childhood different from his mom's?

What good things have happened to you at Sunday School or church?

How can going to church help people?

WEEK 1

DAY
3

●●●

Arthur and his Mom were sitting at the kitchen table. Mom had a pencil and several sheets of writing paper. "Arthur," she said. "You and I need to work on some ideas to help you not be so bored at church."

"I know," Arthur volunteered. "We could come home right after Sunday School."

"That is not an option," she said, reaching over and tickling Arthur. "You can do better than that!"

"OK," Arthur said. "Get them to make the meetings shorter."

Mom tickled Arthur again. "Get serious, Arthur! We're trying to think of what we could do to help you enjoy the services more."

That seemed to stump Arthur. For once, he had nothing to say.

"How about if we make a list of the things you find most interesting at church?" Mom suggested. "That might give us some ideas."

"I don't like any of it," Arthur said.

"That's not true, Arthur," Mom said. "You know you enjoy your Sunday School class."

"That's different from church," Arthur explained. "In Sunday School we do activities, we sing, we hear stories, we see friends. Sunday School's OK."

"What about the church service?" Mom asked as she wrote down the things Arthur had mentioned.

Arthur thought for a moment. "The music is nice, usually," he said. And that was all.

"So," Mom said after a few moments, "let's list the things you find most boring."

"In Sunday School?" Arthur asked. Mom nodded. "Well," Arthur said, "sometimes the stories are boring, and I don't like having to sit still when I feel like doin' stuff."

"How about in church?" Mom asked.

"When people stand up front and talk," Arthur said, "I don't know what they're talking about. That's boring."

"Did I ever tell you that sometimes I get bored too?" Mom asked.

"So, then," Arthur replied, "let's both go home during the offering."

"Just because I'm bored sometimes," Mom said, "doesn't mean it's all boring. When I feel bored, I find it always helps me to remember why I'm there. I think about God's love for me, and that helps me pay better attention and then I'm not bored anymore."

Arthur thought that sounded like something a grownup would say.

● *"Worship the Lord with gladness; come before Him with joyful songs." Psalm 100:2*

● **For Younger Children**

What do you like about going to your church?

What don't you like about your church?

What words does Psalm 100:2 use to describe the attitude of someone who is worshiping God?

● **For Older Children**

What do you think is the most interesting about going to your church? Least interesting?

Why might thinking about God's love help someone be interested in a worship service?

● ●

WEEK 1

DAY 4

When Arthur's Mom picked him up at day care, she was whistling a tune that sounded familiar to Arthur. But he could not remember where he had heard it before. When they reached home and got out of the car, Mom, now humming that same tune, reached into the backseat and picked up a shopping bag. When they got inside their apartment, mom opened the bag and took out a hymnal and songbook she had bought that day.

"We're going to start learning some of the hymns and choruses we sing at church," she explained to Arthur. "I'm not very good at music, but I think these books will help."

While Arthur thumbed through page after page of notes and words that made absolutely no sense to him, Mom opened last Sunday's church bulletin. "Look at hymn number 541," she said. "It's a song we sang last week in church."

It only took a minute and Arthur had found Sunday's opening hymn.

It's called "Come Christians, Join to Sing." Mom began to sing the first line, "Come Christians join to sing, Alleluia, Amen." It was the tune she had been whistling and humming.

"I remember that one," Arthur said. "It was loud."

"Do you remember any of the words?" Mom asked.

"No," Arthur said, "I just remember it was full of Halley-lulus."

"That's Al-le-lu-ia," Mom corrected.

"It's a funny word," Arthur laughed.

"It sounds funny to us because it's a Hebrew word," Mom explained. "It means 'praise the Lord.' "

"Oh," Arthur said. "What else does the song say?"

Mom looked at the page, then said, "It talks about Jesus being our King, and we're rejoicing before His throne."

"What's rejoicing?" Arthur asked.

Mom answered, "Rejoicing means being joyful, glad."

Arthur was quiet for a moment. Then he said, "Goin' to church doesn't make me very glad."

"I know, dear," Mom said, "but it will help if you try thinking about God's love for you."

Arthur was quiet again, this time for several moments. Finally he said, "OK. I'll try."

● *"Talk with each other much about the Lord, quoting psalms and hymns and singing sacred songs, making music in your hearts to the Lord."*
Ephesians 5:19, TLB

● **For Younger Children**
What songs do you like to sing?

Ephesians 5:19 says to make music in our heart to the Lord. That means to show how much we love God by the songs we sing. How can a song show love to God?

● **For Older Children**
What songs do you remember singing at your church?

Read Ephesians 5:19. What do you think it means to make music in your heart to the Lord?

What's something God has done for you that makes you so glad you feel like singing?

● ●

DAY
5

"Do we have to stay for church today?" Arthur asked his mom after Sunday School.

"Of course," his mom said. "And remember, today we're going to do a few things to help you enjoy the service more."

"OK," Arthur said, curious about the experiment he and his mom were trying.

Together Arthur and his mom walked into the lobby where Arthur's mom said hello to a woman handing out bulletins. Then Mom said, "This is my son, Arthur. Arthur, do you remember Mrs. Halliday?"

Arthur nodded and Mrs. Halliday said something about how tall Arthur was as she handed him a bulletin.

Arthur and his mom entered the auditorium, and Arthur's mom said hello to an usher. Then she said, "And this is my son, Arthur. Arthur, do you remember Mr. Miller?" Mr. Miller started to show them to seats near the back, but Arthur's mom asked if they could sit near the front where Arthur could see better.

Arthur slid into in his seat and looked around. Arthur's mom opened the bulletin and explained to him some things that were going to happen during the service. When everyone stood to sing, Arthur found the right page in the hymnal and held one side of the book while his mom held the other. By the time they got to the fourth verse, Arthur had figured out the melody and was humming along. Since he couldn't read yet, the words in the book did not help, but he liked helping his mom hold the book steady.

When everyone bowed their heads to pray, Arthur closed his eyes and thought about God's love for him. When everyone listened to the choir sing, Arthur drew a picture about the song the choir sang.

When the offering plates were passed along each row, Arthur still tried to count the money. But when the Bible was being read, Arthur looked in his mom's Bible and pointed out each of the words he could read.

During the sermon, Arthur went back to drawing. In the middle of the sixth picture, the pastor finished preaching. Arthur looked up and sighed, "Already?"

All in all, it was a most enjoyable morning at church for Arthur and his mom.

● *"One thing I ask of the Lord, this is what I seek: that I may dwell in the house of the Lord all the days of my life, to gaze upon the beauty of the Lord and to seek Him in His temple." Psalm 27:4*

● **For Younger Children**

What did Arthur like about going to church this week?

How did Arthur's mom help him enjoy church more?

If you were Arthur, which do you think you would like the most: learning the song tunes, reading words in the Bible, or drawing pictures about the words in the songs?

● **For Older Children**

What was different about Arthur's experience in church this week?

To enjoy your church's worship service more, what can you do that is like what Arthur did?

Going to church is important because it is a good way to show your love for God and to learn about Him. Ask God's help in remembering to pay attention to Him at church.

● ●

FAMILY TIMES

Schedule time this week to be together as a family. Select one of these suggested activities to expand your family's understanding of ways to make worship more meaningful for a child.

Making Music

Follow the example of Arthur's mom and purchase a book of hymns and/or choruses. (Or you may be able to borrow a songbook from your church.) Read the words of several songs your family sings at church, paying special attention to unfamiliar words. Clarify their meaning as needed. Discuss the songs by asking questions such as, "What do you think is the main idea of this song? How does this song show love and praise for God?" Choose one song to sing, hum, or whistle together.

Tip for Younger Children: Ask a younger child to draw a picture of one or two words in the song. Or, if the song is short, letter it on a large piece of paper, leaving space for your child to illustrate several words in the song.

Slogans

Ask your family to work together to think of several slogans encouraging people to worship God together at church. For ideas, read Psalms 100:2; 122:1, or rewrite a popular commercial or song. Letter the slogans in some form of decorative writing (using a variety of colored felt-tip pens, in block letters, etc.) on a strip of paper. Display the slogans on a bulletin board or wall.

For Parents Only

In order to help your children enjoy positive experiences at your church, here are some guidelines to follow. (1) Sit toward the front of your church sanctuary. Children need to see in order to fully participate. (2) Take time to look through the printed order of worship with your child. Explain unfamiliar parts of the service. (3) Ask your child to find and read the words to one or more of the songs that will be sung. Define unfamiliar words. (4) Before or after the worship service or during a greeting time, be sure to introduce your child to at least one other adult. (5) After the service, tell one thing you liked about the service or something you learned and ask your child to do the same. (6) If your child expresses negative feelings about attending church, accept your child's feelings by saying, "I know some parts of the service may not be interesting to you, but it's a good thing for our family to show our love for God and learn more about Him by going to church together."

The Future

Jesus said, "Do not let your hearts be troubled. Trust in God; trust also in Me. In My Father's house are many rooms; if it were not so, I would have told you. I am going there to prepare a place for you. And if I go and prepare a place for you, I will come back and take you to be with Me that you also may be where I am."
John 14:1-3

Key Thought

God has provided clear assurance that the future is in His control and that He will reward those who love and obey Him.

Children are much more interested in the present than the past or the future. Having been alive only a few short years, it is hard for them to be very concerned about events that happened before they were born or that will occur "someday."

However, it is still very reassuring to a child to know that the God of the universe, who loves and cares for the child now, is in control of the future as well as the past and present.

DAY

1

Ryan Norris came home from Alex's birthday party all excited about the future. Alex had shown two science-fiction videos about space travel. "It'd be so cool to live on a space station," Ryan told his younger brother Josh. "Especially with all the robots and gadgets and aliens from other galaxies."

"Aliens?" Josh exclaimed. "Green slimy creatures with their eyes bulging out?"

"Yeah," Ryan enthused. "In one of the videos, the aliens were little tiny creatures that could fit in your hand."

"I like the ones where people get beamed from one place to another," Josh said. "I wish we could do that going to school. We wouldn't have to wait for the bus anymore."

"And they had cars that you just get in and say where you want to go, and they take you there," Ryan added.

"Beaming is faster," Josh insisted.

"But you don't get to see where you're going," Ryan countered.

"Is all that stuff really going to happen?" Josh asked.

"Nobody knows what's gonna happen in the future," Ryan explained. "But it's fun to imagine weird stuff that might come true."

"Hey, Dad," Josh asked, "when you were a kid, did you ever imagine there'd be stuff like TV and VCRs and space shuttles and all that?"

Dad looked over the top of his glasses at Josh, and in a very old, quavery voice, said, "No, sonny. Back in the cave where I grew up we never even dreamed of electricity or telephones or horseless carriages. We did have one feller who experimented with making fire, but he could never get it out once it was lit."

"Oh, Dad," Ryan said, "quit joking. We're really interested in what's going to happen in the future."

"Do you guys know what the Bible says about the future?" Dad asked in his normal voice.

"I thought the Bible was an old book about stuff that happened a long time ago," Josh said.

"It is a very old book," Dad agreed, "but it tells a lot about things that haven't happened yet."

"Really?" Ryan asked. "Like what?"

"The main thing it says is that God is in charge of the future, and He plans good things for all His people."

● " 'For I know the plans I have for you,' declares the Lord, 'plans to prosper you and not to harm you, plans to give you hope and a future.' " Jeremiah 29:11

● **For Younger Children**

Would you like to live on a space station? Why or why not?

What do you think it means to say that God is in charge of the future?

How does Jeremiah 29:11 describe God's plans for you?

● **For Older Children**

What do you think the world will be like in the future?

Why might people be interested in knowing what the future will be like?

In Jeremiah 29:11 what does God say about your future?

● ●

WEEK 2

DAY
2

"Hey, Alex!" Ryan yelled to his best friend who was getting on the school bus. "Guess what?"

Alex swung into the seat next to Ryan and said, "What am I supposed to guess?"

"Did you know," Ryan went on, "that I know what's going to happen in the future?"

"G'wan," Alex laughed. "Nobody knows the future. No one knows stuff that hasn't happened yet."

"God does," Ryan said.

"Well, sure," Alex admitted. "And I suppose He told you all about it."

"In a way," Ryan said.

"Whaddya mean?" Alex asked. "What way?"

"In the Bible," Ryan answered. "He's told lots of things about the future. And I read some of it. So now I know too."

"Name one," Alex demanded.

"I'll name two," Ryan said. "One, Jesus is going to rule everything, and two, He's going to come back to earth just like He left."

"Prove it," Alex insisted, still suspicious that Ryan was making all this up. Alex remembered other times when his good friend Ryan had invented stranger stories than this.

"Easy," Ryan said, opening his backpack and taking out a small New Testament. "Look right here. Matthew 26:64. Read it."

Alex took the small book from Ryan and read out loud. " 'Jesus said . . .' Jesus really said this?" he asked.

Ryan pointed at the verse. "That's what it says, right there in black and white. Keep reading."

"OK," Alex said and began reading again. " 'In the future you will see the Son of man. . . .' Who's that?" he asked.

"That's a title Jesus used for Himself," Ryan said. "It meant He was both human and God's Son."

"OK," Alex said and read some more. " '. . . the Son of man sitting at the right hand of the Mighty One' . . . I guess that must be God. '. . . and coming on the clouds of heaven.' " Alex handed the New Testament back to Ryan. "OK," Alex said. "I admit it. You were right. For once."

Ryan tapped his New Testament. "If you want to know the future," he said as he slid it into his backpack, "it's all right here."

● *Jesus said, "In the future you will see the Son of man sitting at the right hand of the Mighty One and coming on the clouds of heaven." Matthew 26:64*

● **For Younger Children**
If you saw Jesus returning, how would you feel?

What kind of ruler do you think Jesus will be when He returns?

● **For Older Children**
What do you think will happen when Jesus returns?

If Jesus were ruling over everything in our world right now, what do you think He would do?

● ●

WEEK 2

DAY

3

Ryan was doing one of his regular jobs, taking out the trash. He had to separate the garbage from the recyclables. As he was loading up the kitchen trash, his mom heard him grumble, "I don't see why we have to worry about all this ecology and environment stuff."

Mom asked, "Why's that, Ryan?"

Ryan set the trash bag on the counter and said, "The Bible says God's in charge of the future, and He's promised that He's gonna make everything turn out good. So why worry about recycling and all that stuff?"

Mom replied, "Not everything will turn out good."

"Sure it will," Ryan insisted. "The Bible says."

"No, the Bible doesn't say that," Mom answered. "The Bible is very clear that there will be many bad things that will happen in the future."

"Really?" Ryan asked. "Like what?"

"Can you find the Book of Isaiah in the Bible?" Mom asked.

"Piece of cake," Ryan answered, walking over to the kitchen table and picking up the Bible that Mom and Dad often read. "What chapter?"

"Chapter 13, verse 11," Mom said.

Ryan thumbed through the pages, then said, "Got it." It says, " 'I will punish the world for its evil, the wicked for their sins.' Wow, that's heavy."

Mom agreed. "It sure is. Especially if you realize that one of the ways God punishes is just to let people experience the results of their wrong actions."

Ryan wrinkled his forehead in thought and asked, "What does that mean?"

"For example," Mom said, "if we keep polluting the world God gave us, the pollution poisons our air, and water, and food, and that damages our health. When people ruin something God created to be good, the result is always bad."

"So what can we do about it?" Ryan asked.

Mom thought a moment, then said, "Keep learning about how God wants us to live. Obey His rules, and you'll enjoy the good results He promises."

"Anything else?" Ryan asked.

"Yes," Mom answered, "take this garbage out of the kitchen and separate the recyclables."

● *"I will punish the world for its evil, the wicked for their sins." Isaiah 13:11*

● **For Younger Children**

What's something your family does to help take care of the good world God created?

Why is it important to show our love for God and obey Him?

Ask God's help in following His rules.

● **For Older Children**

What is one way people often disobey God? What happens as a result of their wrong actions?

What are some of God's rules you already obey?

How can you keep learning about God's rules?

DAY

4

●●

"Hey, we got a new calendar for next year!" Laura announced, as she and Mom came home from shopping. "It's got a different kind of puppy for every month."

"Let's see," Chris said. Laura handed the calendar to him.

"Look at the little cockers," Laura said. "I can't believe how cute they are."

"February has St. Bernards," Chris announced as he turned the page. "Aren't they adorable!" Laura enthused.

"Collies!" Chris announced, turning another page.

"Look how fluffy they are," Laura said.

Older brother Ryan looked over their shoulders and noticed the Doberman puppy in May. "He sure doesn't look very fierce, does he?"

Josh was intrigued by the picture of three Labrador puppies trying to decide whether to jump into a pond.

"Which puppy do you like best?" Chris asked.

"December," Laura answered. "Take a look."

Chris flipped to the back of the calendar. "What kind of dog is that?" he asked.

"It's just a mutt!" Ryan said.

"But who could resist those big brown eyes?" Laura asked.

"New calendars are cool," Josh announced.

"If they have pictures like these," Laura said.

"Even without pictures," said Ryan. "I think it's neat looking ahead to a new year. All those months and weeks and days that haven't happened yet."

"I always look to see what day my birthday will be," Laura said.

Josh said, "I wanta know when summer vacation will start."

"Some year," Ryan said, "there's gonna be part of everybody's calendars that won't get used."

"How come?" Laura asked.

"Dad told me," Ryan said, "that the Bible says Jesus is gonna come back and end all the things that are wrong in the world and make everything new and good."

"Really?" Laura asked.

"Sounds great!" Josh added.

Chris wanted to know, "Do you think He'll do it next year?"

"Nobody knows," Ryan said, "but we could sure use a brand new world."

"No more pollution!" Josh declared.

"No more fighting and war!" Laura added.

Chris thought for a moment about a world where everything was new and good. "No more hoeing weeds!" he cheered.

● *"Behold, I will create new heavens and a new earth." Isaiah 65:17*

● **For Younger Children**

What kind of puppy do you like best?

Do you agree with Ryan that we need a brand new world? Why or why not?

What would a perfect, new earth be like?

● **For Older Children**

What part of a new year do you like thinking about?

What good things do you think will be part of a new earth?

Why should we believe God's promise in Isaiah 65:17?

WEEK 2

DAY 5

● ●

"Ryan says God's going to make us a new world," five-year-old Chris said to his dad.

"That's what the Bible says," Dad agreed.

"What's it gonna be like?" eight-year-old Josh wanted to know. "Will there be ice cream?"

"I hope there's pizza!" Chris said.

"And chocolate candy!" Josh added.

Chris thought of something even better. "And all the soda you can drink!" he shouted.

"Hold it! Hold it!" Dad said. "I think you two may have a little bit of a wrong idea."

"How?" Josh asked.

"Well, the Bible doesn't promise any of those things," Dad said, "but it does tell us a few other things God's going to do."

"Like what?" Chris asked.

Dad thought a moment. "Well," he said, "the last couple chapters in the Bible describe some things about the new heaven and new earth. It says that God's glory and goodness will shine everywhere. There will be no night, and the streets will be pure gold. Nothing that is dishonest or evil will ever be there, 'cause it will be the home of all that is right and fair."

"Wow!" Chris exclaimed.

"Sounds great!" Josh agreed.

"When's it gonna happen?" Chris wanted to know. He was hoping the answer would be "soon," because Chris hated to wait for anything good.

"No one knows," Dad answered. "Only God knows. But we don't need to know when. All we need to do is live the way God wants us to. Then we'll be ready whenever God decides it's time for Jesus to come again."

"Oh," Josh said.

"And do you know what that means, Josh?" Dad asked.

"No," Josh answered.

"It means you still have to do your spelling homework tonight. And Chris, you have a room to clean."

As the two brothers headed off together, Dad overheard Chris say, "Rats! If Jesus came back tonight, we wouldn't have to do this stuff."

Just before they headed upstairs together, Josh replied, "Yeah, but then we might not get a snack before bedtime."

● *"But in keeping with His promise we are looking forward to a new heaven and a new earth, the home of righteousness." 2 Peter 3:13*

● **For Younger Children**

Why was Chris hoping Jesus would come back that night?

What do you do to get ready for a friend to visit you? Being ready for Jesus' return means we show our love for Him and obey Him as best we can.

What's something you can do today to show your love for Jesus?

● **For Older Children**

Why do you think the Bible doesn't say exactly when Jesus will return?

What do you know about how God wants you to live?

Ask God's help showing your love for Him and others.

● ●

Schedule time this week to be together as a family. Select one of these suggested activities to expand your family's understanding of God's plans for the future.

FAMILY TIMES

Heavenly Plans
(Note: If your family did this activity in July, you may prefer to choose one of the other suggestions.) Ask each person in your family to find and read one of these Bible passages: John 14:1-3; Revelation 21:1, 4-5, 10, 19, 21, 25. Talk about your answer to this question: What do you learn about heaven from these verses? Then take turns to finish these sentences: The best part about heaven will be. . . . I'm glad Jesus planned. . . . I wish I knew if heaven. . . . I'm thankful that in heaven. . . .

Tip for Younger Children: Read passages aloud to younger children.

Picture That!
Read God's promise of a new earth in Isaiah 65:17. Then give each person felt pens or crayons and a sheet of paper. Say, "Draw a line to divide your paper in half. On the left side of your paper write the word 'BEFORE' at the top and draw a picture or write a description of something wrong in our world today." After family members complete their pictures, they trade papers. Then say, "On the right side of the paper you just received, write the word 'AFTER' and draw a picture or write a description of how the wrong action might be corrected in God's new earth."

Puzzle in a Bag
Letter the words to John 14:1-3 on a large piece of paper. Cut apart the paper into 8–10 puzzle pieces. (Note: If a piece does not have any lettering on it, draw a heart shape on the piece to indicate which side is faceup.) Place all the puzzle pieces in a paper bag. Shake the bag. The first player reaches into the bag, removes a puzzle piece, and places it on the table or floor. Then other family members take turns removing puzzle pieces and trying to add them to the first piece. Continue until the puzzle is complete. Read the verse aloud. Discuss the verse by asking, "When we feel afraid or worried about what might happen in the future, what does this verse tell us to do? What does it mean to trust in God? Why is God a good person to trust?"

Tip for Younger Children: Cut paper into 4–6 puzzle pieces.

• •

God Sent Jesus

Most of the predictions about the coming of Jesus are buried deep in the prophetic books at the end of the Old Testament. These books are rarely used in teaching children. Even adult Christians read these Scripture portions infrequently, if at all.

This week your child has the opportunity to consider several of the most prominent prophecies about Jesus. Two of these prophecies (Isaiah 7:14 and Micah 5:2) are quoted by Matthew (1:23 and 2:6), showing how the birth of Jesus fulfilled the ancient promises. And the third prophecy (Isaiah 9:6) is one of the Bible's most memorable descriptions of who Jesus is and what He came to do. Your exploration of these verses this week will provide a solid preparation for your family's celebration of the Savior's birth.

Key Verse
"This is how God showed His love among us: He sent His one and only Son into the world that we might live through Him."
1 John 4:9

Key Thought
God carefully planned and promised to send a Savior who would bring His love and forgiveness to the world.

• •

WEEK 3

DAY 1

Hector, Robbie, and Angela had each been assigned a Bible verse to memorize for the Christmas program at church. Since Robbie could not read yet, Angela read his verse to him so he could start learning it. "Can you repeat the first part?" Angela asked.

Instead of trying to say the verse Robbie demanded to know, "What does this verse have to do with Christmas? There's nothing in here about shepherds or wise men or Santa Claus!"

Hector decided to complain about his verse also. "You should see my verse. It has all these big words. Even if I didn't have dyslexia, I couldn't read them."

Angela said, "You two make such a big deal out of nothing. What big words, Hector?"

"How can I tell you what they are?" Hector asked. "They're so big I can't read them."

"Let me look at it," Angela offered. "Show me the words you don't know."

Hector pointed at a word.

"That's 'virgin,' " Angela said.

"What's it mean?" Hector asked.

Angela thought for a moment. Then she yelled toward the next room, "Mama, will you explain 'virgin' to Hector?" Mother came into the room and looked at Hector's verse.

"In this case," she said, "it means a young woman who's not married yet." Mother pointed to the next part of the verse. "See, it says she's going to have a child."

"An unwed mother?" Angela asked.

"What does this have to do with Christmas?" Hector asked.

"Who do you think this child is?" Mother asked in reply.

Hector looked down at the verse. "Somebody named Im ... Imman. . . ."

"That's Immanuel," Angela said.

"Immanuel." Hector repeated. "Who was he?"

"Immanuel means 'God with us.' " Mother explained. "Who does that sound like to you?"

"Jesus?" Hector asked.

"Right," Mama said. "This verse is about Jesus being born to Mary."

"Why doesn't it just say that?" Hector asked.

"Because Isaiah wrote this maybe six or seven hundred years before Mary got pregnant," Mother went on. "It's just one of many, many verses in the Bible that told hundreds of years in advance about Jesus coming to earth."

● *"The Lord Himself will give you a sign: The virgin will be with child and will give birth to a son, and will call Him Immanuel." Isaiah 7:14*

● **For Younger Children**

What do you think of when you hear the word "Christmas"?

Because God wanted us to know what He was like, He sent Jesus to be with us on earth. What was Jesus like when He lived on earth?

How would you describe His actions?

How did He help people learn about God?

● **For Older Children**

When have you had to memorize something for a church or school program?

Read Isaiah 7:14. How would you answer Hector's question, "What does this verse have to do with Christmas?"

What other names for Jesus have you heard?

● ●

WEEK 3

DAY
2

Four-and-a-half year-old Robbie complained to his sister Angela. "You helped Hector with his verse," Robbie said. "How about mine?"

"Let me see your verse again," Angela said. "What do you remember about it?"

"It's about some girl named Beth or something with a long last name," Robbie said.

"Oh, Robbie!" Angela laughed. "That's Beth-lehem! It's not a girl! It's a town!"

"Oh," Robbie said. "Well, what's that next big word?"

Angela looked at the verse. "Ephrathah? That's the rest of the town's name. Mostly people just called it Bethlehem."

Robbie looked down at the verse as if he could read it. "Why am I memorizing a verse about a town?" he asked.

"Actually," Angela said, ignoring Robbie's question, "it was just a small village."

"So why am I memorizing a verse about a small village?" Robbie persisted.

"It's where Jesus was born," Angela explained.

"Oh, yeah," Robbie said. "I knew that."

Angela wanted to explain some more. "This is the verse someone showed to the wise men so they would know where to go to find the new king they were looking for."

"Oh, yeah," Robbie said, "I remember."

"So start memorizing," Angela said, sounding like a big sister.

"I can't do it by myself," Robbie claimed. "I can't read yet."

"Oh, yeah," Angela said. "I knew that." She looked at the verse. "Here's how it goes: 'O Bethlehem Ephrathah, you are but a small Judean village, yet you will be the birthplace of My King who is alive from everlasting ages past.' Micah 5:2."

"Who was Micah?" Robbie asked.

"He must have been the prophet who wrote this," Angela said. "Hey

Dad!" she yelled toward the next room. "Do you know when Micah lived?"

"Micah?" Dad yelled back. "About the same time as Isaiah, I think."

"Wow, Robbie," Angela said. "This verse was written maybe 700 years before Jesus was born, and it told the exact little village where it would all happen."

"OK, I've got it." Robbie said.

"Got what?" Angela asked.

"The verse memorized." And he did.

● *"O you, Bethlehem Ephrathah, you are but a small Judean village, yet you will be the birthplace of My King who is alive from everlasting ages past."* Micah 5:2, TLB

● **For Younger Children**
What word does Micah 5:2 use to describe Jesus?

Where are kings usually born? What kind of place was Bethlehem according to Micah 5:2?

If you had lived in Bethlehem, would you have believed that a baby born in a stable was a king?

● **For Older Children**
What do you know about why Jesus was born in Bethlehem? (Hint: Read Luke 2:1-5.)

Why might people in Bible times have been surprised that Jesus, God's Son, was born in Bethlehem?

Why is it important for people today to know about the birth of Jesus so many years ago?

● ●

WEEK 3

DAY

3

"What's your verse, Angela?" Hector asked his sister.

"Isaiah 9:6," Angela answered.

"Is that all?" Hector asked. "I memorized that already."

Angela realized Hector was teasing her. "I don't have to say 'Isaiah 9:6,' Hector. I have to say the verse in Isaiah 9:6."

"Oh," Hector said innocently. "I knew that. What's it say?"

"It tells what Jesus will be like," Angela said.

"What do you mean, 'will' be like?" Hector asked. "We already know what Jesus is like."

"Remember, little brother," Angela answered, "Isaiah wrote this about 700 years BEFORE Jesus was born."

"Oh, yeah," Hector said. "I knew that. Do you have it learned yet?"

"I would if I hadn't spent so much time helping you and Robbie learn your verses," Angela said.

"OK. I'll help you," Hector offered. "Let's hear it."

Angela began to recite. " 'For to us a child is born, to us a son is given. . . .' "

Hector interrupted her. "Is that the same child as in my verse about Immanuel?" he asked.

"Sure," Angela said. "Both verses talk about Jesus. Seven hundred years before He was born."

"I know that," Hector said. "Keep going."

Angela recited, "And the government will be on His shoulders. . . ."

"What does THAT mean?" Hector asked.

"It's an expression," Angela explained. "It means Jesus'll be the Ruler, the King."

"Like in Robbie's verse about Jesus being born in Bethlehem?" Hector asked.

"Sure," Angela answered. "These verses are all about Jesus. Now where was I?"

Hector tried to remember what she had recited last. "The government is on His back?"

"Shoulders," Angela said. " 'The government will be on His shoulders. And He will be called. . . .' That's as far as I've learned."

Hector looked down at the verse. "It says He'll be called. . . . You'd better read this. These are BIG words."

Angela read aloud: "And He will be called Wonderful Counselor, Mighty God, Everlasting Father, Prince of Peace."

"You can learn those," Hector assured her.

"I know. Just give me a little time," Angela said.

"It's easy," Robbie said as he walked through the room. " 'Wonderful Counselor, Mighty God, Everlasting Father, Prince of Peace.' "

"How'd you learn those so fast?" Angela asked.

Robbie answered, "Just 'cause I can't read doesn't mean I'm stupid!"

● *"For to us a Child is born, to us a Son is given, and the government will be on His shoulders. And He will be called Wonderful Counselor, Mighty God, Everlasting Father, Prince of Peace." Isaiah 9:6*

● **For Younger Children**

Is it easy or hard for you to memorize things?

How many names for Jesus do you read in Isaiah 9:6?

The word "counselor" means someone who will help you know right things to do. What do you think the words "Prince of Peace" mean?

How might Jesus help you know what to do? How might He give you peace?

● **For Older Children**

Read Isaiah 9:6. Which of the names for Jesus is your favorite? Why?

Which of these names would be the most helpful for someone your age to know about? Why?

Thank God for His wonderful gift of Jesus.

● ●

WEEK 3

DAY 4

"Does everybody know his or her verse for the program?" Mother asked her three children. Angela, Hector, and Robbie were all freshly scrubbed and wearing their best clothes. It was almost time to leave for the Christmas program at church.

"Except that I keep messing up on Beth-le-hem Eph-ra-tath," Robbie said.

"That's Eph-ra-thah," Angela corrected her little brother.

"That's what I mean," Robbie said. "It's hard to say."

Angela asked, "Are there more verses like these that told about Jesus before He was born?"

"Lots," Mother said. "But the ones you've learned are some of the most famous."

As the family started out the door of their apartment, Angela had another question. "Why did God tell all this stuff about Jesus so long before it all happened?"

"Yeah," Hector said. "It didn't do any good for those people. They all died without ever seeing Jesus."

Mother answered, "Oh, I think it did those people a lot of good."

"How?" Angela asked. "They lived all their lives, and the promise never happened."

"But they knew about the promise," Mother said. "It gave them hope. And that hope made it easier for them to put up with the bad things that happened in their lives."

Father finished locking the door and caught up with the rest of the family. "The people who lived back then trusted that God would do what He said at just the right time. It didn't hurt them to wait."

"Is that what God did?" Angela asked. "Wait for just the right time to send Jesus?"

"It sure was," Father answered. "The Bible says, 'When the time had fully come, God sent His Son.' Many hundreds of years had passed, but God kept His promise."

"So let's hear these verses one more time while we walk to church," Mother insisted. "The De La Rosa children are going to know their verses perfectly!"

And they did. Robbie even pronounced Bethlehem Ephrathah correctly.

● *"But when the time had fully come, God sent His Son." Galatians 4:4*

● **For Younger Children**
When have you waited a long, long time for something to happen?

What were you waiting for? How did you feel while you were waiting?

What would be different about our world today if God had not kept His promise to send Jesus?

Tell God thank You for keeping His promise and sending Jesus.

● **For Older Children**
If you had lived when Isaiah and Micah did, would you have found it hard or easy to believe God would keep His promise?

Why do you think God waited so long to send Jesus to be born?

Jesus' birth was special to the people in Bible times because it showed that God was keeping His promise. Why is Jesus' birth special to you?

● ●

WEEK 3

After the church Christmas program, the De La Rosa family walked home together.

DAY

5

"What part did you like best?" Angela asked her brother Hector.

"Everything after I said my verse," Hector said. "Then I wasn't nervous."

"I liked the little kids dressed like angels," Angela said.

"I liked the big kids dressed like shepherds," Robbie added.

Mother said, "The songs. I really liked the music."

Hector agreed. "I even remembered some of the words from last year."

"How about you, Papa?" Angela asked.

Dad thought for a moment as he walked along with his hands stuffed into his coat pockets. "I liked very much when we all stood and read that verse together at the end."

Robbie, who was skipping on ahead, stopped and turned around. "I can say that verse, and it wasn't even one I was supposed to learn."

"Let's hear it, Señor Memory," Father said.

"I might miss a few words," Robbie admitted.

"That's OK," Father said. "It's just us out here tonight."

Robbie began: " 'God so loved the world and gave His Son, that anybody who believes in Him shall not die but live forever.' John 3:16. How'd I do?"

"Great," Father said, taking his hands out of his pockets to applaud. "Do you know what I like to do with that verse?" he asked.

"What?" asked Robbie.

"I put my own name in it," Father explained. "Where it says 'God so loved the world,' I like to say 'God so loved Luis De La Rosa.' "

Mother added her comment: "And where it says 'whoever believes in Him shall not perish,' I can say, 'and Eva De La Rosa believes in Him and shall not perish.' "

"Could I put my name in there?" Hector asked.

"Sure," Father answered. "Everyone who believes that Jesus is God's Son and who trusts Him to forgive their sins has already started to enjoy that eternal life God promises."

When the family got back to their apartment, Hector was still thinking about God's wonderful plan to send Jesus. "Immanuel really is a good name for Jesus," Hector told his father. "Because of Jesus, God really is with us."

● *"For God so loved the world that He gave His one and only Son, that whoever believes in Him shall not perish but have eternal life." John 3:16*

● **For Younger Children**

Would you rather be dressed as an angel or a shepherd for a Christmas program?

Why does John 3:16 say God sent Jesus into the world?

What's the good news about Jesus that all people need to know?

● **For Older Children**

Read John 3:16. What was God's plan in sending Jesus into the world?

The De La Rosa family participated in a special Christmas program as a way to celebrate the good news of Jesus' birth. How can you show your happiness that Jesus came to be born on earth?

● ●

Schedule time this week to be together as a family. Select one of these suggested activities to expand your family's understanding of God's plan in sending Jesus to be born on earth.

FAMILY TIMES

Christmas Card Game
Collect a variety of Christmas cards showing pictures from the story of Jesus' birth. Put the cards in a bag or bowl. Each person takes a turn to choose a card and tell what happened either before or after the event pictured on the card. Optional: Family members arrange the cards in sequential order.

"Who Am I?" Riddles
Take turns thinking of "Who Am I?" riddles about characters in the Christmas story. As each person says a riddle aloud, other family members try to identify the person being described. For example: "I was working late at night on a hillside when I heard some surprising news. Who am I?" (Shepherd.) "I felt sorry for a man and woman and gave them a place to sleep. Who am I?" (Innkeeper.)

Tip for Younger Children: To help younger children identify the characters, you may need to give more than one clue.

What's Wrong Here?
Divide this week's key verse, 1 John 4:9, into 8–10 sections, one or two phrases in each section. Letter each section on an index card. Letter three or four incorrect phrases on other index cards. Place cards face up in random order. Family members place the cards in the correct order, identifying and removing incorrect cards as they work. Read the verse aloud and thank God for His love.

Christmas

Key Verses
"But the angel said to her, 'Do not be afraid, Mary, you have found favor with God. You will be with child and give birth to a Son, and you are to give Him the name Jesus. He will be great and will be called the Son of the Most High. The Lord God will give Him the throne of His father David, and He will reign over the house of Jacob forever; His kingdom will never end.' "
Luke 1:30-33

Key Thought
Christians everywhere celebrate the birth of Jesus in many different ways.

Every family has its own traditions, and Christmas is a time when many of these are observed. For most children, and a great many adults, the way their family celebrates Christmas is the "official" way to do it. Different customs followed by other families may be interesting, but changing a child's expectations of Christmas is no easy task.

However, most Christian families struggle with keeping the focus on celebrating the coming of Jesus, rather than on gifts, food, and family reunions. Even though life gets hectic for most families, it is well worth it to take time each day this week to consider the Bible's great message of Christmas joy.

DAY
1

Arthur was setting out the wooden figures for the nativity scene when he heard Christopher knock at the door. Three quick knocks and one loud knock. Arthur got up and opened the door.

"Whatcha doin', Arthur?" Christopher asked.

"Puttin' out Christmas decorations," Arthur answered.

"We did ours last week," Christopher said.

"I know," said Arthur. "I saw that big Santa on your door."

"Where's your Santa?" Christopher asked.

"We don't have one," Arthur answered, "but we've got this neat nativity scene."

"No Santa?" Christopher seemed shocked. "What's a nativity?"

"It's a manger scene," Arthur explained. "It's got Mary and Joseph and Baby Jesus. And some animals, and shepherds. It's got wise men too, even though Mom says they didn't get to Bethlehem 'til a long time later."

"That's weird," Christopher said. "We've got Rudolph and Frosty and sleigh bells and candy canes . . . you know, REAL Christmas stuff."

"That's OK," Arthur said, shifting one of the sheep in the manger scene.

Christopher looked insulted. "OK? It's better than OK! It's . . . it's Christmas!"

Arthur moved one of the shepherds closer to the manger. Christopher knelt down beside him. "What's so great about this native scene anyway?" Christopher asked.

"Nativity scene," Arthur corrected. "It shows where Jesus was born. It's what Christmas is really about."

"No way," Christopher said. "Christmas is about Santa and presents and candy and stuff."

"Well," Arthur said thoughtfully, "that stuff is fun. But it's really Jesus' birthday."

"Are you sure?" Christopher asked.

From the kitchen doorway, Arthur's mom answered Christopher's question. "That's the truth, Christopher. Christmas really is to celebrate Jesus' birthday and there's something else we do to remember that."

"Oh," Christopher said.

"Every day Arthur and I each pick a Christmas card that came in the mail that day. We set the card on the table and at dinner we pray for the people who sent it."

"Oh," Christopher said again.

"Do you know whose card Arthur chose today?" Mom asked.

"No," Christopher said.

"Yours!" Arthur shouted.

"At dinner," Mom went on, "we'll pray that you and your mom will have a wonderful Christmas and that you'll learn just how much Jesus really loves each of you."

Christopher did not know what to say.

● *"Do not be afraid, Mary, you have found favor with God. You will be with child and give birth to a son, and you are to give Him the name Jesus. He will be great and will be called the Son of the Most High. The Lord God will give Him the throne of His father David, and He will reign over the house of Jacob forever; His kingdom will never end." Luke 1:30-33*

● **For Younger Children**

What Christmas decorations does your family usually put up?

What was Christopher surprised to learn about Christmas?

What's something you can do to celebrate Jesus' birthday?

● **For Older Children**

Which Christmas decorations are your favorites?

What's something fun you like to do at Christmas?

What's something your family does to remember that Christmas is Jesus' birthday?

WEEK 4

DAY 2

Aliki's father was excited. "Mr. Ling finally agreed," Mr. Yasuda said. "Tomorrow we will take him downtown to see the Christmas decorations."

"How?" Aliki asked. "He can barely walk."

Mr. Yasuda laughed. "He has a wheelchair. We will push him."

"All the way downtown?" asked Midori, Aliki's younger sister.

Mr. Yasuda laughed again. "We can take his wheelchair on the subway."

The next morning the four Yasudas and Mr. Ling headed downtown. On the subway Mr. Ling loudly told everyone nearby that "my neighbors are taking me downtown to see the Christmas decorations."

When they came out of the subway downtown, a lady was ringing a bell. Next to her was a box for money to help the poor. Mr. Ling pulled out a small, blue coin purse.

"Mr. Ling," Mrs. Yasuda said, "you don't need to put money in the box. You need your money."

"What fun is Christmas," Mr. Ling asked loudly, "if I cannot give?" Very carefully he took three fresh dollar bills and dropped them in the box.

The sidewalk ahead was crowded with people looking in the windows of a large department store. "Mr. Ling and the girls will never see through this crowd," Mrs. Yasuda said.

Mr. Yasuda said. "I'm sure people will let us in."

And they did. People made room for the wheelchair, and Mr. Ling and the girls laughed and pointed at each window.

Inside the store was a large Christmas tree decorated with angels, each attached to a card. "What are those cards?" Mr. Ling asked.

"Each card has the first name and age of a needy child," Mr. Yasuda explained. "People choose a card. Then they go buy a present for that child and bring it back to the lady at that desk to give to the right child."

Of course, Mr. Ling, with help from Aliki and Midori, had to buy a present for a child. When he handed it to the lady at the desk, he said, "Christmas always means giving. Because of Jesus." Then he turned to Mr. Yasuda, "Thank you for giving me this very happy day."

● *"Joseph, son of David, do not be afraid to take Mary home as your wife, because what is conceived in her is from the Holy Spirit. She will give birth to a son, and you are to give Him the name Jesus, because He will save His people from their sins." Matthew 1:20-21*

● For Younger Children

What did the Yasuda family give to Mr. Ling?

Because God gave us Jesus at the first Christmas, we show God's love by giving to others. Who gives to you at Christmas? Whom can you give to?

● For Older Children

Why do you think Mr. Ling thought it was fun to give?

How many different gifts were given in this story?

What is a way you can give to help others this Christmas?

● ●

WEEK 4

DAY
3

Eric and his sister, Jessie, were helping their mom bake Christmas cookies. There were moments when Mom wanted to tell them to go outside and play so that she could finish baking in time to wrap the cookies and give them to their neighbors.

"Eric!" Mom said, almost in a shout. "Quit eating the cookies!"

"We ARE doing this for our neighbors," Jessie reminded.

"I know," Eric said, "but I only eat broken ones. Besides, deduct the ones I've eaten from Mr. Warren's package. He needs to lose weight and shouldn't eat cookies anyway."

"That's SO thoughtful, Eric," Mom laughed. "Eating cookies to protect Mr. Warren."

Just then the timer rang. Eric shoved his hands into oven mitts and lifted out two trays of great smelling cookies.

"Here's the last batch going in!" Jessie announced, sliding two more trays of cookie dough into the oven.

As she closed the oven door, Jessie asked, "Why do we always make cookies for the neighbors?"

"It's a family tradition!" Eric proclaimed. "The Lacey family ALWAYS makes Christmas cookies for the neighbors! If we didn't give cookies, our neighbors would never know if it was Christmas or not!"

"Be serious, Eric," Jessie giggled. "Really! Why do we do it?"

"Eric's partly right," Mom admitted. "Grandma Lacey got me started doing it years ago, and I've just kept it up. People seem to like the cookies, so it's been a good way to share our joy with others."

"And don't forget my poems," Dad hollered from the living room.

"Is Dad sticking one of his poems in with the cookies again?" Eric asked.

"Sure," Mom said, "we get more comments about Dad's poems than we do about the cookies."

"Do you want to hear this year's?" Dad hollered again.

"Do we have a choice?" Eric hollered back.

"Very funny," Dad said, this time from the doorway. "Tell me what you think." Then he read the poem he had written.

> "This time of year,
> Is filled, I fear,
> With surface joy
> And empty cheer.

428

We trust you feel
The love that's real.
Christ came to earth
To save and heal.
Merry Christmas from the Lacey Family."

"Not bad, Dad," Eric said. "That's pretty rad."
"I guess Eric likes it," Mom laughed.

● *"But the angel said to them, 'Do not be afraid. I bring you good news of great joy that will be for all the people. Today in the town of David a Savior has been born to you; He is Christ the Lord.' " Luke 2:10-11*

● **For Younger Children**
What's something fun you like to do with your family at Christmas?
Mrs. Lacey said giving cookies to their neighbors was a way of sharing joy with them. What does Luke 2:10-11 say gives us joy at Christmas?
How can you show your joy about Jesus' birth?

● **For Older Children**
What is one of your family's Christmas traditions?
What is the good news Luke 2:10-11 talks about? How was the Lacey family helping others to hear the good news?
What can your family do to tell others the good news about Jesus?

● ●

WEEK 4

DAY
4

Ryan Norris and his best friend, Alex Kolchek, were looking out the front window of the Norris farmhouse. It was the afternoon of Christmas Eve and both boys were excited.
"When does your family open presents?" Ryan asked.
"Christmas morning," Alex answered.
"We do ours Christmas Eve," Ryan said. "I'd die if I had to wait till morning."
"What do you look forward to, then?" Alex asked. "All the fun's over too soon if you do it tonight."
"No way!" Ryan insisted. "We open our stockings in the morning. And we get all day to play with our new stuff. And we still get to open any presents our relatives bring with them."

"Yeah," Alex admitted, "But getting up Christmas morning and seeing the presents under the tree is the best part of Christmas."

"Maybe," Ryan admitted, "but what do you do on Christmas Eve?"

"We go to church," Alex said.

"So do we," said Ryan.

"And we sing some carols and eat Christmas treats," Alex said.

"So do we," said Ryan.

"And somebody reads the Christmas story," Alex said.

"So do we," said Ryan. "But no presents? I'd DIE if I had to wait till morning. How do you get to sleep knowing there are presents to open?"

"That's the hard part," Alex said. "But the sooner you get to sleep, the sooner it seems that morning comes."

Just then Ryan's dad came in the front door. "Hi, guys! Merry Christmas, Alex," he said. "You too, Mr. Norris," Alex answered.

"Hey, Dad!" Ryan said. "Did you know Alex's family doesn't open their presents until Christmas morning?"

"Really?" Mr. Norris asked. "Maybe we should try it this year."

"No way!" Ryan yelled. "We do it tonight!"

"How can you two be such good friends and not agree on the best time to open presents?" Mr. Norris laughed.

The two boys looked at each other and laughed too.

"Just make sure," Mr. Norris said, "that you don't get so interested in presents that you forget the truly best thing about Christmas."

The two boys looked at each other again. They HAD forgotten.

● *"Glory to God in the highest, and on earth peace to men on whom His favor rests." Luke 2:14*

● **For Younger Children**

When does our family open Christmas presents?

It's fun to get and give presents. And Christmas presents are a good reminder of the best present of all. What do you think is the best present of all? Who gave this present?

Tell God thank You for His gift of Jesus.

● **For Older Children**

What does your family do on Christmas Eve? Christmas morning?

Why is it so easy to forget the real reason we celebrate Christmas?

What would you tell someone was the best thing about Christmas?

DAY
5

AJ and DJ Gorman did not usually look like twins. Some people were not even sure they were brother and sister. DJ tended to look like an accident going somewhere to happen, while AJ usually looked liked she was on her way to the library. Anyone who knew them both learned that DJ loved to read just as much as his sister did, and AJ could run just as fast and play just as hard as her brother. In spite of their similar interests, however, they usually did not look like twins.

Christmas Eve was different. Their mom made sure they were both scrubbed clean. Their dad oversaw the selection of their very best clothes. DJ hated to get dressed up, but he was not about to complain on Christmas Eve. If there was any night of the year when DJ was on his best behavior, this was it. As the family walked into their church building before the Christmas Eve service, AJ and DJ actually looked like twins. Well-behaved, freshly scrubbed, nicely dressed twins.

The people who sat behind the Gorman family noticed that the twins enjoyed singing Christmas carols. Had they peeked during the prayer, they would have seen both AJ and DJ with heads bowed and eyes closed. They even said "Amen!" along with the rest of the congregation. They listened intently as the pastor read the Christmas story from the Bible and talked about God sending Jesus to earth as a baby.

But when the service was over, all this good behavior was starting to wear a little thin for the twins. "Dad!" DJ whispered loudly as they made their way back up the center aisle. "Don't stay around and talk to people tonight! Let's get home!" AJ whispered the same message to her mom.

Mr. and Mrs. Gorman felt that they rushed away from church that night, but the twins thought their parents would never leave.

When they reached home, their dad put a hand on each twin's shoulder. "I want you to know how much Mom and I are enjoying celebrating Jesus' birthday with you two. Let's play some Christmas music, have hot chocolate and dessert, then I'll read the Christmas story."

"Can we change clothes first?" DJ asked.

● *"This is how God showed His love among us: He sent His one and only Son into the world that we might live through Him." 1 John 4:9*

● **For Younger Children**
What do you think AJ and DJ enjoyed the most about their Christmas Eve?

Singing Christmas carols, reading the story of Jesus' birth, and thanking God for Jesus are all good ways to celebrate Jesus' birthday. Which of these have you already done this Christmas season? Which can you do now?

● **For Older Children**
How would you describe the feelings of AJ and DJ in this story?
How do you feel when you think of celebrating Jesus' birthday?
What can you do to help you remember how important Jesus' birthday is?
Ask God's help in reminding you of the real reason for Christmas.

● ●

FAMILY TIMES Schedule time this week to be together as a family. Select one of these suggested activities to expand your family's understanding of ways to celebrate the coming of Jesus.

God's Gifts at Christmas
Place a large sheet of paper and a variety of felt-tip pens on a table. Letter "God's Gifts at Christmas" at the top of the paper. Ask each person to name something God has given us (Jesus, love, joy, peace, forgiveness, kindness, hope, etc.) Talk about how Jesus makes it possible for us to receive these gifts. Then each person draws a wrapped Christmas present labeled with one of God's gifts (see sketch). Display this poster of God's gifts on a bulletin board or wall in your house.
    Tip for Younger Children: A younger child may enjoy gluing small pieces of holiday wrapping paper onto the drawings.

Christmas Ornament

Make Christmas tree ornaments with your family. Follow these directions or find an ornament idea in a Christmas craft book. Collect several Christmas cards, scissors, red or green construction paper, hole punch, glue, and red or green ribbon. To make each ornament, cut around a large picture on the front of a Christmas card (angel, bell, star, wreath, etc.). Glue the picture onto a piece of construction paper. Cut the construction paper in the shape of the picture leaving a ¼-inch margin of paper. Punch a hole at the top of the picture and thread it with ribbon, making a loop as an ornament hanger. Optional: Spread glue on a portion of the picture and sprinkle glitter on the glued area as an added decoration.

Share the Joy!

Choose one or more of the ideas from this week's stories for showing God's love to others this Christmas: (1) With your family choose a way to give a gift to a needy family. Contact your church or a charitable organization for ideas. (2) Each day choose a Christmas card you received. Put it in a central location such as your dining room table. Pray for the people who sent the card. (3) Make a favorite Christmas recipe to share with your neighbors. Include a card which pictures or tells about Jesus' birth. (4) Invite an elderly or disabled friend or relative to come with your family to see Christmas decorations and shop.

Living in Heaven

Key Verses
Jesus said, "Do not let your hearts be troubled. Trust in God; trust also in Me. In My Father's house are many rooms; if it were not so, I would have told you. I am going there to prepare a place for you. And if I go and prepare a place for you, I will come back and take you to be with Me that you also may be where I am."
John 14:1-3

Heaven is a fascinating subject for people of all ages. However, considering that heaven is mentioned over 400 times in the Bible, we know very little about it. Something within us would like to know more details, but Scripture is very sparse in that department.

What is that we really can know about heaven? We know that God is there. We know that it is ultimately indescribable, even beyond our human ability to imagine. And we know that all who love and trust Jesus are assured of being welcome there. What other details do we need?

Key Thought
God has planned that those who love Jesus and trust Him to forgive their sins will live with God in heaven forever.

DAY

1

● ●

Midori was lying on her bed looking up at the ceiling. Her big sister, Aliki, was lying on the floor, also looking at the ceiling. They were both trying to imagine what they would be when they grew up.

"I'm going to be a famous ballerina," Midori announced.

"I'm going to be mayor or governor. That's better than a ballerina," Aliki said.

"No, it's not," Midori protested, sitting up on her bed. "People will pay money to see me dance. I'll be famous and have my picture in magazines."

"But governors get to to tell everybody what to do," Aliki said. "They get to be on the news every night. Governors are more important than ballerinas."

"Mother!" Midori shouted, hoping to get support for her side. When Mother looked in the door of Midori's room, Midori asked, "Ballerinas are better than governors, aren't they?"

Mother laughed. "Are you two arguing about ballerinas and governors?" she asked. "Do you two ALWAYS have to try to outdo each other?"

The sisters looked at each other innocently as if they had never argued with each other in their lives. Mother said, "At least when I get to heaven I won't have to listen to arguments like this."

"Why not?" Midori asked. She could not see what heaven had to do with arguing over governors and ballerinas.

Mother walked into the room and sat on the edge of Midori's bed. "The reason I know there won't be this kind of arguing in heaven," she said, "is because of what Jesus said would make someone really great in heaven."

Midori had never thought about the possibility of ballerinas in heaven. But maybe the best dancers would be the most important people there. She was certain governors would not be considered very great in heaven, especially since she had no real idea of what it was governors actually did.

Suddenly, Midori realized she had been daydreaming, and her mother had been explaining who would be greatest in heaven. "Imagine," Mother said, "the greatest person in heaven is anyone who is humble or modest, like a child. Not someone who tries to be more important than everyone else."

● *Jesus said: "I tell you the truth, unless you change and become like little children, you will never enter the kingdom of heaven. Therefore, whoever humbles himself like this child is the greatest in the kingdom of heaven."*
Matthew 18:3-4

● **For Younger Children**

What would you like to be when you grow up?

What were Midori and Aliki arguing about?

What do you think it means to be humble or modest?

● **For Older Children**

When you're humble, it means you don't think you're better than others. Why do you think God says being humble or modest makes a person great in the kingdom of heaven?

What might a person your age do to show that he or she is humble?

How can you show that you are humble?

WEEK 5

DAY 2

● ●

Midori and her father were riding the elevator up to their apartment. Midori must have been thinking, because she abruptly asked, "Are you the boss at your work?"

Her father looked a little surprised at the question. He answered, "I'm in charge of several people in my department, but I'm not the main boss." The elevator stopped at their floor and the doors opened.

"When do you get to be boss?" Midori asked as they stepped out into the hallway.

"I might become head of my department in a few years," Father said, reaching in his pocket for his keys. "But I'll never be boss of the whole company."

"That's not fair!" Midori declared. "You should get a turn."

"I'm glad you think I'd be a good boss," Father said with a smile. He put the key in the lock and began to open the door. "However," he said, "there are more important things in life than being boss."

"What things?" Midori asked as she walked into the living room.

Father closed the door behind them and asked, "Do you remember that Bible verse Mother quoted? The one about how to be great in the kingdom of heaven?"

"Yes," Midori answered.

"Good," Father said, sitting down in the big living room chair. "Since greatness in heaven is measured by how we love and help others, it seems we should be loving and helpful to others now."

"Oh," was all Midori said. She climbed up on the arm of the chair, something she did when she wanted to keep talking with her father.

He decided to explain a little more. "Did you know, Midori, that how we live now will make a difference in heaven?"

"No," Midori answered

"It's true," Father said. "Jesus taught that doing good for others, even forgiving those who do things we don't like, is like storing up treasure in heaven. The more good things we do now, the more God will reward us, the better heaven will be."

Midori thought for a moment, then she leaned over and whispered in her father's ear, "I don't think Aliki is doing enough to make heaven a better place."

● *"But store up for yourselves treasures in heaven, where moth and rust do not destroy, and where thieves do not break in and steal." Matthew 6:20*

● **For Younger Children**

Where do you like to keep valuable things you want to save?

Has something you were saving ever gotten lost or damaged?

What are some ways we can store up treasure in heaven?

● **For Older Children**

Why do you think doing good things for other people will earn rewards in heaven?

Who are some people who have done good things for you?

Whom can you do something good for?

● ●

WEEK 5

DAY

3

It was dinnertime in the Yasuda family apartment. Aliki and Midori were both showing unhappiness about eating their vegetables. Father dipped the serving spoon into the bowl again and asked, "Do you girls want more vegetables?"

"No!" they both gasped, holding their hands over their plates. They thought that Father was teasing, but he was not smiling, so they were not sure.

Father moved the vegetable bowl closer to Aliki's plate. He said, "Such unhappy faces make me think you have not been getting enough vegetables to make you strong and healthy."

Mother decided to join the conversation. She asked, "How do you girls expect to grow up if you don't eat right?"

437

"I don't want to grow up," Aliki answered quickly. She did not like the way this conversation was going.

"Me neither," Midori said.

"Why not?" Mother asked. "I thought ALL children wanted to grow up."

Aliki thought fast. After a moment she gave the only answer she could think of: "Grownups have to work too much."

Midori thought of another reason not to grow up. She said, "Grownups don't get toys for birthdays."

"Or Christmas," Aliki added.

"Grownups don't like cartoon shows," Midori said.

"Grownups get old," Aliki declared.

"Besides, heaven is for kids," Midori claimed.

"Heaven is for kids?" Mother interrupted. "What gave you that idea?"

"That's what Jesus said," Midori maintained.

"That's right!" Aliki agreed, even though she had no idea where her younger sister had gotten such a notion.

"When grownups tried to send children away from Jesus," Midori explained, "Jesus said that heaven belongs to children."

Mother and Father looked at each other. Finally, Father said, "That's what He said, all right. God certainly loves children. But He loves grownups too."

"But He likes kids best," Midori insisted.

"Maybe," Father said, "Jesus meant that heaven is for everyone who loves and trusts Him as a child does."

The girls looked puzzled.

Mother reminded the girls of their talk about who would be greatest in heaven. "A lot of people," she said, "both grownups and children, forget that the only things that really count in heaven are loving, trusting, and obeying Jesus."

"Then eating vegetables doesn't matter?" asked Midori.

● *"Jesus said, 'Let the little children come to Me, and do not hinder them, for the kingdom of heaven belongs to such as these.'" Matthew 19:14*

● **For Younger Children**

Do you think it's better to be a child or a grownup? Why?

How do you know that God loves children?

How can a child show that he or she loves and obeys God?

● **For Older Children**

Do you think it's easier for children or grownups to love and trust Jesus? Why?

How might a grownup show that he or she loves Jesus?

How can you show that you love Jesus?

● ●

WEEK 5

DAY
4

Aliki was lying on the floor in Midori's room, looking up at the ceiling. Midori was lying on her bed, also looking up at the ceiling. They were imagining what life in heaven will be like.

"I think we'll sit on fluffy, white clouds and play harps," Aliki said.

"I can't play the harp," Midori protested.

"That's OK," Aliki said. "They probably have angels who give lessons."

"I'd rather play drums," Midori muttered.

"Whoever can't play a harp will be in a huge choir and sing all day," Aliki said.

"All day?" Midori asked. "When do I get to use my wings?"

"Wings?" Aliki asked.

"Sure," Midori stated. "Everyone in heaven has wings. But will we have to wear long robes?"

"That would be neat," Aliki thought. "Imagine, floating on the clouds with a long robe blowing in the wind."

"But," Midori wanted to know, "how can I run or climb or jump in a robe?"

"I guess we won't have to worry about that if we have wings," Aliki said.

"But," Midori wanted to know, "how can we get the robe on over the wings?"

"Maybe we won't have wings," Aliki suggested.

Midori did not like that suggestion. "Mother!" she shouted. "Will we have wings in heaven?"

Mother looked in the door of Midori's room. "I've wondered that too," she said. "Cartoons about heaven usually show everyone with wings and halos and long, white robes."

"But is that right?" Midori asked.

"I don't know," Mother said. "I've never been to heaven. The Bible does tell us that Jesus will change our bodies."

"How?" Aliki asked, examining her hands and arms.

"Right now our bodies can get tired and sick and injured," Mother said.

439

"That won't happen in heaven. The Bible tells that Jesus will make our bodies like His own wonderful body after He rose from the dead. We will be like Him."

"Wow!" Aliki said.

"And something else," Mother added.

"What's that?" Midori asked.

Mother answered, "Heaven will be far better than anything we can possibly imagine. The Bible says we can't even begin to think about the wonderful things God has prepared for everyone who loves Him."

"Wow!" Alike said.

"Me too!" Midori added.

● *"It is written . . . 'No one has ever seen this, and no one has ever heard about it. No one has ever imagined what God has prepared for those who love Him.' " 1 Corinthians 2:9, EB*

● **For Younger Children**

Who does 1 Corinthians 2:9 say will go to heaven?

What are some things you have heard about what heaven will be like?

What is the best thing you can imagine about heaven?

● **For Older Children**

What things have ever gone wrong with your body?

What do you think it will be like to have a perfect body in heaven?

Why has God made heaven such a perfect, wonderful place? (Hint: Read 1 Corinthians 2:9.)

WEEK 5

DAY 5

On New Year's Eve, Aliki and Midori announced to their parents that they wanted to stay up until midnight.

"That is very late," Father said. "That's four hours past your bedtime."

"Last year I fell asleep too early," Aliki said. "This year I'm going to stay awake."

"I don't remember last year," said Midori. "Is a new year any different from an old year?"

"Not really," Aliki answered. "Except people make revolutions."

"Res-o-lutions," Father corrected. "Not rev-o-lutions."

Mother decided to explain a little more. "New Year's resolutions," she said, "are promises people make to change or improve. My New Year's resolution is to lose five pounds in January."

"What if you don't?" Midori asked. "Will you get in trouble?"

"No," Father laughed, "but she won't get into her best clothes either."

"Very funny," Mother said.

"Will it keep you from going to heaven?" Aliki asked.

Mother looked at her oldest daughter and asked, "What do YOU think would keep someone from going to heaven?"

"Not doing good enough stuff?" Aliki guessed.

"How many good things?" Mother asked. "How could you know if you had done enough?"

Aliki thought. Then she asked, "Maybe not doing bad things is more important?"

Father asked, "Have you ever done anything bad?"

"Not very bad," Aliki said.

"How could you know if the bad things you have done would keep you out of heaven?" Father asked.

"I don't know," Aliki answered.

"That's why Jesus died for us," Father said. "Jesus took the punishment for all the bad things we've ever done."

"And," Mother added, "He rose from the dead to show that His power, not ours, will bring us to heaven."

"Oh," Aliki said.

"Our part is to believe," Father said, "and to trust Jesus to forgive us for the bad things we do."

"OK," Aliki said.

"Midori," Father said, turning toward his youngest daughter, "Do you understand?"

"Sh-h-h," Mother whispered. "She's asleep already."

● *"Set your hearts on things above, where Christ is seated at the right hand of God. Set your minds on things above, not on earthly things." Colossians 3:1-2*

● **For Younger Children**

What does your family do to welcome the new year?

What did Aliki's father say Jesus did to make it possible for us to go to heaven?

What must we do to go to heaven?

● **For Older Children**

Have you ever tried to stay up until midnight? What happened?

At the end of a year, people often think about what they want to do in the new year. What's something you'd like to do in the new year?

Colossians 3:1-2 reminds us to think about ways we can grow to be more like Jesus. What is one way you'd like to become more like Jesus?

● ●

FAMILY TIMES

Schedule time this week to be together as a family. Select one of these suggested activities to expand your family's understanding of how they can grow to be more like Jesus in the new year.

Finish the Sentence

Letter each of these sentence starters on separate index cards: "I'm glad God has helped me. . . ." "In the new year I'd like to. . . ." "I need God's help to. . . ." "The best thing about starting a new year is that. . . ." "By the time this year has ended I'd like to. . . ." "One thing that worries me about the new year is. . . ." "One way I can grow to be more like Jesus is. . . ." "This year I hope. . . ." Put the index cards in a bowl or hat. Each person takes a turn to choose a card and complete the sentence.

Tip for Younger Children: Read the sentence starter for a younger child.

Thanks for the Memories

Spend some time as a family looking back at memories of the past year. You may look at one or more home videos or photo albums. Or, ask each family member to find an object that represents a highlight of the past year. As you talk about the events of the year, focus on the ways in which God has helped your family—in happy and sad times. Thank Him for His love this year and ask Him for guidance as you look ahead to the new year.

For Parents Only

Write a New Year letter to your child, expressing appreciation for specific ways in which the child has grown and matured in the past year. Assure your child of your love and confidence in him or her. Ask your child's help as your family begins a new year together. This confidence-building technique will go a long way in encouraging your child's positive outlook for the future. Close your letter by suggesting a Bible verse for your child to read as your prayer for his or her new year.